ACCA

Applied Skills

Financial Reporting (FR)

Practice & Revision Kit

For exams in September 2023, December 2023, March 2024 and June 2024

BPP

First edition 2008

Seventeenth edition 2023

ISBN 9781 0355 0110 6

Previous ISBN 9781 5097 4757 3

eISBN 9781 0355 0114 4

British Library Cataloguing-in-Publication Data

A catalogue record for this book is available from the British Library

Published by

BPP Learning Media Ltd

BPP House, Aldine Place

142-144 Uxbridge Road

London W12 8AA

learningmedia.bpp.com

Printed in the United Kingdom

Your learning materials, published by BPP Learning Media Ltd, are printed on paper obtained from traceable, sustainable sources.

The contents of this book are intended as a guide and not professional advice. Although every effort has been made to ensure that the contents of this book are correct at the time of going to press, BPP Learning Media makes no warranty that the information in this book is accurate or complete and accept no liability for any loss or damage suffered by any person acting or refraining from acting as a result of the material in this book.

We are grateful to the Association of Chartered Certified Accountants for permission to reproduce past examination questions. The suggested solutions in the practice answer bank have been prepared by BPP Learning Media Ltd, unless otherwise stated.

A note about copyright

Dear Customer

What does the little © mean and why does it matter?

Your market-leading BPP books, course materials and e-learning materials do not write and update themselves. People write them on their own behalf or as employees of an organisation that invests in this activity. Copyright law protects their livelihoods. It does so by creating rights over the use of the content.

Breach of copyright is a form of theft – as well as being a criminal offence in some jurisdictions, it is potentially a serious breach of professional ethics.

With current technology, things might seem a bit hazy but, basically, without the express permission of BPP Learning Media:

- Photocopying our materials is a breach of copyright
- Printing our digital materials in order to share them with or forward them to a third party or use them in any way other than in connection with your BPP studies is a breach of copyright

You can, of course, sell your books, in the form in which you have bought them – once you have finished with them. (Is this fair to your fellow students? We update for a reason.) Please note the e-products are sold on a single user licence basis: we do not supply 'unlock' codes to people who have bought them second-hand.

And what about outside the UK? BPP Learning Media strives to make our materials available at prices students can afford by local printing arrangements, pricing policies and partnerships which are clearly listed on our website. A tiny minority ignore this and indulge in criminal activity by illegally photocopying our material or supporting organisations that do. If they act illegally and unethically in one area, can you really trust them?

IFRS

Contents

Question index

Question index

The headings in this checklist/index indicate the main topics of questions, but many questions cover several different topics.

Past exam questions are designated with the date of the exam in which they featured, although some have been amended to reflect subsequent changes to the syllabus or in the format of the exam. There are four exam sittings per year, but ACCA only publish two exams' worth of questions per year. These releases are compiled from questions selected from the preceding sessions. These compilation exams are denoted as 'Mar/Jun' and 'Sept/Dec' in the index below.

Topic index

Listed below are the key Financial Reporting (FR) syllabus areas and the numbers of the questions in this Kit which cover those areas. If you need to concentrate your practice and revision on certain topics or if you want to attempt all available questions that refer to a particular subject, you will find this index useful.

Syllabus topic	Question number(s)	Workbook chapter
Agricultural assets	134–136	15
Associates	96, 280–287, 314, 316, 317, 329, 334, 335	11
Conceptual Framework	1–8, 20–24	1
Consolidated statement of financial position	94, 97–100, 253–266, 298–305, 307, 308, 310, 313–317, 328, 330, 333–337	7, 8
Consolidated statement of profit or loss	95, 247, 249, 267–274, 306, 309, 311, 312, 329, 331–333	9
Disposal of subsidiaries	244, 245, 249–251, 276–279, 332	10
Earnings per share	198–205, 215, 343	19
Events after the reporting period	130, 131, 183	14
Financial instruments	101–109, 164–168, 339, 341, 344, 345	12
Foreign currency transactions	190–192, 211	18
Government grants	80, 81, 83, 84, 89, 149, 150, 327	6
Impairment of assets	40–48, 51–53, 57, 58, 67–71	5
Intangible non-current assets	35–39, 74–78, 342	4
Interpretation of financial statements	216, 217, 239–252, 325, 347	20
Inventories	132–140, 340, 342, 345	15
Leasing	110–121, 169–173	13
Limitations of financial statements	222–229	21

Syllabus topic	Question number(s)	Workbook chapter
Not for profit and public sector entities	230–237	23
Preparation of financial statements	246, 288–292, 338–345	17
Provisions	122–129, 179–182, 339, 340, 342, 344	14
Ratios	218–221, 238, 243–251	19, 20
Regulatory framework	9–19	2
Reporting financial performance	184–189, 193–197, 206–210, 212–214, 246	18
Revenue	79, 82, 85–88, 90–93, 152–158, 341, 344, 345	6
Statement of cash flows	293–297, 318–324, 326, 342, 346, 347	22
Tangible non-current assets	25–34, 49–51, 54–56, 59–66, 72, 73, 159–163, 338–344	3
Taxation	141–148, 174–178, 338–341, 343–345	16

The Financial Reporting (FR) exam

Approach to examining the syllabus

The technical articles section on ACCA's website include one called 'Financial Reporting – examiner approach'. This article outlines the key features of the syllabus, and the qualities candidates should demonstrate when answering FR questions. We reproduce some of the main points here:

- Candidates will be expected to understand the main principles and objectives of IFRS Accounting Standards and be able to apply these when required.
- The concept of business combinations and the preparation of consolidated financial statements are important elements of the FR exam.
- Where an IFRS Accounting Standard appears in both FA and FR, any examination of that topic in FR will be at a more advanced level, requiring greater understanding and appropriately higher-level skills.
- FR places emphasis on the interpretation of what particular ratios are intended to measure and the impact that consolidation adjustments may have on any comparisons of consolidated financial statements.

To be successful in the FR exam, candidates need to:

- understand the concepts underlying the preparation of an entity's financial reports;
- apply their knowledge of IFRS Accounting Standards to prepare financial statements of both single and group entities; and
- demonstrate their analytical skills in the assessment of the financial statements of a single entity or a group and the accounting ratios that are derived from them

Format of the exam

Applied Skills exams are all computer-based exams (CBE).

The examination lasts three hours and all questions are compulsory.

The exam will comprise three exam sections:

Section	Style of question type	Description	Proportion of the exam %
A	Objective test (OT) question	15 questions × 2 marks	30
B	Objective test (OT) case question	3 questions × 10 marks Each question will contain 5 subparts, each worth 2 marks	30
C	Constructed response (long questions)	2 questions × marks	40
Total			100

All questions are compulsory.

Sections A and B account for 60% of the total marks available in the exam. The use of OT questions in Sections A and B give the examining team scope to examine the whole of the syllabus and bring in topics that do not feature in the longer questions. It is really not possible to pass this exam by only revising certain topics.

Section C will contain one accounts preparation question and one interpretation question. The accounts preparation question could be a group accounting question which may require the preparation of a consolidated statement of financial position or consolidated statement of profit or loss and other comprehensive income or extracts thereof. The syllabus states that a simple group could contain a parent, up to two subsidiaries controlled by the parent and one associate of the parent. The question may also include the disposal of a subsidiary. You must revise all the consolidation workings and you must know how to apply equity accounting for an associate.

A single company accounts preparation question allows the examining team to bring in more complex IFRS Accounting Standards. You could be asked to prepare a statement of financial position, a statement of profit or loss and other comprehensive income, a statement of changes in equity or extracts from a statement of cash flows using the indirect method. Make sure you can deal with the more complex areas of leases, revenue recognition, deferred tax, calculating finance costs using the effective interest rate, prior period adjustments and discontinued operations.

The interpretation question may be based on a single company or group scenario. You may be asked to calculate specific ratios and provide reasons for their movement based on information within the scenario. You may also be asked to critically analyse the information you have been provided with by management by considering the validity of the information in the context of the ratios calculated. You must ensure that you use the scenario provided when discussing the movement in ratios and do not provide generic statements.

Syllabus and Study Guide

The complete FR syllabus and study guide can be found by visiting the exam resource finder on the ACCA website

Helping you with your revision

BPP Learning Media – ACCA Approved Content Provider

As an ACCA Approved Content Partner, BPP Learning Media gives you the opportunity to use revision materials reviewed by the ACCA examining team. By incorporating the examining team comments and suggestions regarding the depth and breadth of syllabus coverage, the BPP Learning Media Practice & Revision Kit provides excellent, ACCA-approved support for your revision.

These materials are reviewed by the ACCA examining team. The objective of the review is to ensure that the material properly covers the syllabus and study guide outcomes, used by the examining team in setting the exams, in the appropriate breadth and depth. The review does not ensure that every eventuality, combination or application of examinable topics is addressed by the ACCA Approved Content. Nor does the review comprise a detailed technical check of the content as the Approved Content Provider has its own quality assurance processes in place in this respect.

BPP Learning Media do everything possible to ensure the material is accurate and up to date when sending to print. In the event that any errors are found after the print date, they are uploaded to the following website: www.bpp.com/learningmedia/Errata.

The structure of this Practice and Revision Kit

Using feedback obtained from ACCA examining team review:

- We look at the dos and don'ts of revising for, and taking, ACCA exams
- We focus on Financial Reporting (FR); we discuss revising the syllabus, what to do (and what not to do) in the exam, how to approach different types of question and ways of obtaining easy marks
- There are also four mock exams which provide you the opportunity to refine your knowledge and skills as part of your final exam preparations.

Question practice

This is the most important thing to do if you want to get through. Many of the most up-to-date exam questions are in this Kit. Practise doing them under timed conditions, then go through the answers and go back to the Workbook for any topics you are having trouble with. Come back to a question a week later and try it again – you will be surprised at how much better you are getting. Be very ruthless with yourself at this stage – you have to do the question in the time, without looking at the answer. This will really sharpen your wits and make the exam experience less worrying. Just keep doing this and you will get better at doing questions and you will really find out what you know and what you don't know.

Selecting questions

We provide a full question index to help you plan your revision.

Making the most of question practice

At BPP Learning Media we realise that you need more than just questions and model answers to get the most from your question practice.

- Our top tips included for certain questions provide essential advice on tackling questions, presenting answers and the key points that answers need to include.
- We show you how you can pick up easy marks on some questions, as we know that picking up all readily available marks often can make the difference between passing and failing.
- We include marking guides to show you what the examining team rewards.
- We include comments from the examining team to show you where students struggled or performed well in the actual exam.
- We refer to the 2023 BPP Workbook (for exams in September 2023, December 2023, March 2024 and June 2024) for detailed coverage of the topics covered in questions.

Attempting mock exams

There are four mock exams that provide practice at coping with the pressures of the exam day. We strongly recommend that you attempt them under exam conditions. Mock exam 1 is the ACCA CBE Practice Exam 1. Mock exam 2 is the ACCA CBE Specimen. Mock exam 3 is the ACCA CBE

Practice Exam 2. Mock exam 4 has been formed from a mixture of exam standard questions. Sections A and B contain questions which come from various recent past exams. Section C is from the Sep/Dec 2021 CBE.

Gaining marks in the FR exam

Section A Objective test (OT) questions

Introduction Content

Some OT questions are easier than others. Answer those that you feel confident about as quickly as you can. Come back later to those you find more difficult. This could be a way of making use of the time in the examination most efficiently and effectively. Some questions are more time-consuming than others.

The first more time-consuming OT question will involve doing a computation. You will probably need to jot down a quick proforma to answer a computational question. If the OT question is a multiple-choice question, remember that the wrong answers will usually involve common errors, so don't assume that because you have the same answer as one of the options that your answer is necessarily correct! Double check to make sure you haven't made any silly mistakes. If you haven't got the same answer as any of the options, rework your computation, thinking carefully about what errors you could have made. If you still haven't got one of the options, choose the one which is nearest to your answer.

The second more time-consuming OT question is one in which you are asked to consider a number of statements and identify which one (or more) of them is correct. Make sure that you read each statement at least twice before making your selection. Be careful to follow the requirements of the OT question exactly – for example, if you are asked to identify two correct statements. Make sure that you understand the wording of narrative OT questions before selecting your answer.

Section B Case OT questions

Introduction Content

The general advice for Section A OT questions stands for the OT case question in Section B. Additional advice is to make sure that you read the whole case scenario. Make a note of any specific instructions or assumptions, such as 'Ignore the calculation of depreciation' for a non-current asset question. The questions are independent of each other and can be answered in any order, so if you find one requirement particularly difficult, move on to the next.

Discussions in Section C questions

Introduction Content

Your answer to the interpretation question should be focused on the specific organisation and events described in the question and you should analyse the information provided to determine what is relevant in explaining the ratios calculated. This will gain more marks than regurgitation of knowledge. Read the question carefully and more than once to ensure you are actually answering the specific requirements.

Pick out key words such as 'describe', 'evaluate' and 'discuss'. These all mean something specific.

- 'Describe' means to communicate the key features of
- 'Evaluate' means to assess the value of
- 'Discuss' means to examine in detail by argument

Clearly label the points you make in discussions so that the marker can identify them all rather than getting lost in the detail.

Provide answers in the format requested. Many interpretation questions now include a pre-formatted response area that you should use to give your answer structure.

Remote invigilated exams

In certain geographical areas it may be possible for you to take your exam remotely. This option, which is subject to strict conditions, can offer increased flexibility and convenience under certain circumstances. Further guidance, including the detailed requirements and conditions for taking the exam by this method, is contained on ACCA's website at https://www.accaglobal.com/an/en/student/exam-entry-and-administration/about-our-exams/remote-exams/remote-session-exams.html.

Essential skills areas to be successful in Financial Reporting

We think there are three areas you should develop in order to achieve exam success in Financial Reporting (FR).

(a) Knowledge application

(b) Specific FR skills

(c) Exam success skills

These are shown in the diagram below:

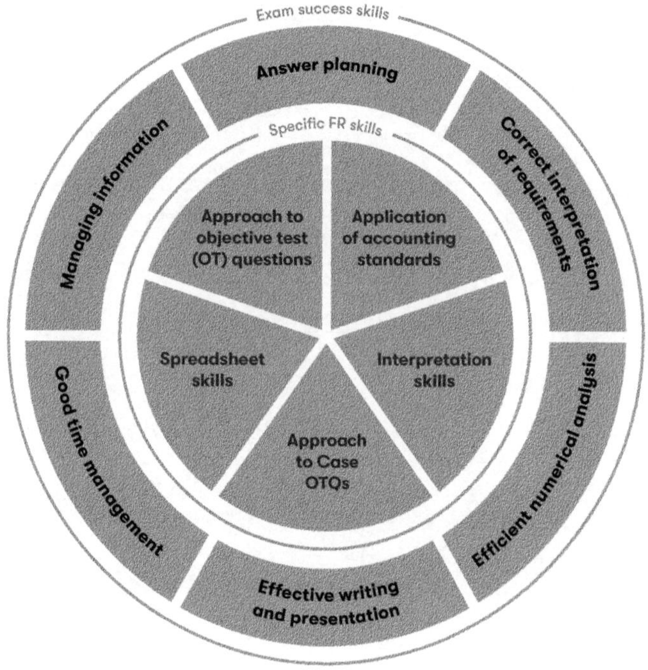

Specific FR skills

These are the skills specific to FR that we think you need to develop in order to pass the exam.

In the BPP Workbook for FR there are five Skills Checkpoints which define each skill and show how it is applied in answering a question. A brief summary of each skill is given below.

Skill 1: Approach to OT questions

As 60% of your marks will be gained by correctly answering OT questions, you need to ensure that you are familiar with the different types of OT question and the best approach to tackling them in the exam.

A step-by-step technique for ensuring that you approach the OT questions in the most efficient and effective way is outlined below:

Skills Checkpoint 1 covers this technique in detail through application to a series of exam-standard questions.

Skill 2: Approach to objective test (OT) case style questions

In the exam, you will have three OT Case style questions, each worth 10 marks each. They are OT style questions, however, they will be linked along a common theme, such as recognising revenue (including government grants) or accounting for non-current asset acquisitions and resulting deferred tax adjustments. This allows the Examining Team to ask questions on specific areas in greater detail than what a single Section A OT question will permit.

Therefore, it is imperative that you are familiar with the OT style of question and recognise the style of a case question.

A case question will be scenario based, so there will be a short description together with some financial information, and five questions will be asked about the information. There will be a combination of narrative and numerical questions.

Key steps in developing and applying this skill are outlined below:

STEP 1: Read the scenario

Read the scenario to understand the context and key technical content. You will need to revisit the scenario in detail when you are answering each question so don't worry about doing any calculations or thinking about the relevant IFRS Accounting Standard in too much detail at this point.

↓

STEP 2: Work through questions methodically

Apply your technical knowledge to the data presented in the question.

Work through calculations taking your time and read through each answer option with care. OT questions are designed so that each answer option is plausible. Work through each response option and eliminate those you know are incorrect. If there are any questions you don't feel confident in answering, flag them for review and move on.

↓

STEP 3: Be aware of time

Stick to your time carefully, as each question is worth two marks, so spending more than the allocated time of 18 minutes on each case question is an inefficient use of your time. If you are running out of time, or you cannot answer any of the questions, guess the answer from the options provided. You do not lose marks for incorrect answers.

↓

STEP 4: Revisit any flagged questions

If you have flagged any questions for review because you didn't feel confident in answering them, it is essential that you make time to go back to these and provide an answer. Remember you are not penalised for incorrect answers so it is always worthwhile to provide an answer.

Skills Checkpoint 2 covers this technique in detail through application to an exam-standard question.

Skill 3: Using spreadsheets effectively

Section C of the exam will require the use of the spreadsheet functionality, so you need to be familiar with the software and what the FR examining team is expecting to see in terms of presentation.

The Section C question, which requires you to prepare primary financial statements or extracts thereof (this may be for a single entity or for a group), should be attempted using the spreadsheet software.

A step-by-step technique for using spreadsheets in the exam is outlined below.

STEP 1: Understanding the data in the question

Where a question includes a significant amount of data, read the requirements carefully to make sure that you **understand clearly what the question is asking you to do.** You can use the highlighting function to pull out important data from the question. Use the data provided to think about what formula you will need to use. For example, if the company calculates the allowance for receivables as a percentage of the balance, use the percentage function.

↓

STEP 2: Use a standard proforma working.

You will be asked to prepare an extract or a set of financial statements. This could involve a statement of profit or loss, statement of financial position, statement of cash flows or statement of changes in equity. Before you start to work through the question set out the relevant pro forma statements. This will give you the basis structure from where you can enter the data in the question.

Format your cells to ensure the workings look consistent, for example, using the comma function to mark the thousands in numerical answers.

↓

STEP 3: Use spreadsheet formulae to perform basic calculations.

Ensure you are showing your workings by using the spreadsheet formula for simple calculations, for example, the cost of sale figure will be made up of different balances, so add them together using the formula. Cross refer any more detailed workings, and link workings into your main answer.

↓

Step 4: Include the results of workings in the proforma

You must ensure that you include your workings form in the proforma and complete your final answer. Remember to show how you have included your workings by cross referencing to the relevant working and by using the formula within the cell to add/subtract the balance.

Skills Checkpoint 3 covers this technique in detail through application to an exam-standard question.

Skill 4: Application of IFRS standards

Knowledge of the IFRS standards will be required in all sections of the FR exam. You are unlikely to be asked to explain the requirements of an IFRS Standard in a narrative question, but may be asked questions about the application or impact of accounting standards in an OT question, or it may be relevant in the interpretation of an entity's performance and position in Section C.

A step-by-step technique for applying your knowledge of accounting standards is outlined below.

STEP 1: Overview of key standards

Ensure you have a high-level overview of the key standards covered in the FR exam. Use the summary diagrams at the end of the chapters in the Workbook to act as your summaries. These are a useful way of remembering the key points.

↓

STEP 2: Numerical question practice

Practice the numerical questions in the Workbook and in the Practice & Revision Kit. These will test your knowledge of the mechanics of the accounting standards. Often there can be a difference between understanding what the standard does and how it applies to a specific scenario. Practice OTQs as well as longer, Section C questions to consolidate your knowledge.

↓

STEP 3: Narrative question practice

Practice the narrative questions which test your understanding of how the standard can affect the financial statements. This will help you to revise your understanding of why the accounting standard is important in a scenario. For example, what are the key tests for impairment of assets and why would this be important for the financial statements?

Skills Checkpoint 4 covers this technique in detail through application to an exam-standard question.

Skill 5: Interpretation skills

One of the Section C exam questions will require you to interpret the financial statements of a single entity or group. The question is likely to require the calculation of ratios, but the majority of marks will come from the interpretation of those ratios to explain the performance and position of the single entity or group you are presented with.

Given that the interpretation of financial statements will feature in Section C of every exam, it is essential that you master the appropriate technique for analysing and interpreting information and drawing relevant conclusions in order to maximise your chance of passing the FR exam.

STEP 1: Read and analyse the requirement.

Read the requirement carefully to see what calculations are required and how many marks are set for the calculation and how many for the commentary.

Work out how many minutes you have to answer each sub-requirement.

↓

STEP 2: Read and analyse the scenario.

Identify the type of company you are dealing with and how the financial topics in the requirement relate to that type of company. As you go through the scenario, you should be highlighting key information which you think will play a key role in answering the specific requirements.

↓

STEP 3: Plan your answer.

You will have calculated the ratios and understand the performance and position of the company. You must now plan the points you will make in interpreting the ratios. Read through the information in the scenario and identify the points that help you to explain the movement in ratios. Using each ratio as a heading, create a bullet point list of the relevant points.

↓

STEP 4: Type your answer.

You should now take the bullet point list created at the planning stage and expand the points, remembering to use information given in the scenario and to avoid generic explanations.

As you write your answer, explain what you mean – in one (or two) sentence(s) – and then explain **why this matters in the given scenario**. This should result in a series of short paragraphs that address the specific context of the scenario.

Skills Checkpoint 5 covers this technique in detail through application to an exam-standard question.

Exam success skills

Passing the FR exam requires more than applying syllabus knowledge and demonstrating the specific FR skills; it also requires the development of excellent exam technique through question practice.

We consider the following six skills to be vital for exam success. The Skills Checkpoints show how each of these skills can be applied in the exam.

Exam success skill 1

Managing information

Questions in the exam will present you with a lot of information. The skill is how you handle this information to make the best use of your time. The key is determining how you will approach the exam and then actively reading the questions.

Advice on developing Managing information

Approach

The exam is three hours long. There is no designated 'reading' time at the start of the exam.

You should consider the order in which you will attempt the questions; some candidates will prefer to attempt the OT questions first and others will prefer the Section C questions. Always attempt questions in the order of your preference but remember to adjust the time available for each question appropriately – see Exam success skill 6: Good time management.

If you find that this approach doesn't work for you, don't worry – you can develop your own technique.

Active reading

You must take an active approach to reading each question. Focus on the requirement first, highlighting the key verbs such as 'evaluate', 'analyse', 'explain', 'discuss', to ensure you answer the question properly. Then read the rest of the question, highlighting important and relevant information, using the scratch pad (or response option in Section C questions) to make notes of any relevant technical information you think you will need.

Exam success skill 2

Correct interpretation of the requirements

The active verb used often dictates the approach that written answers should take (eg 'explain', 'discuss', 'evaluate'). It is important you identify and use the verb to define your approach. The correct interpretation of the requirements skill means correctly producing only what is being asked for by a requirement. Anything not required will not earn marks.

Advice on developing the Correct interpretation of the requirements

This skill can be developed by analysing question requirements and applying this process:

Step 1 **Read the requirement**

Firstly, read the requirement slowly and carefully and highlight the active verbs. Use the active verbs to determine what you need to do. In the Section C questions, make sure you identify any sub-requirements.

Step 2 **Read the rest of the question**

By reading the requirement first, you will have an idea of what you are looking out for as you read through the scenario. This is a great time saver and means you don't end up having to read the whole question in full twice. You should do this in an active way – see Exam success skill 1: Managing Information.

Step 3 **Read the requirement again**

Read the requirement again to remind yourself of exactly what you are being asked to do. Pay attention to negative wording such as NOT or WILL NOT in requirements as these sometimes need you to apply a different thought process. In the Section C questions, you should consider forming an answer plan based on the requirements to ensure that you address each requirement and sub-requirement.

Exam success skill 3

Answer planning: Priorities, structure and logic

This skill requires the planning of the key aspects of your Section C answers which accurately and completely responds to the requirement.

Advice on developing Answer planning: Priorities, structure and logic

Everyone will have a preferred style for an answer plan. For example, it may be creating a list in the word processing answer space, creating short notes using the scratch pad within the CBE software or creating the proforma for key workings in the spreadsheet answer space. Remember that the markers can't see what you type in the scratch pad and therefore you must copy it into the answer space.

It is recommended for Section C that you copy the requirements, and potentially keywords or relevant headings from the question, into the response area to ensure you stay focused on the requirements, to help give your answer structure and encourage logical writing.

Exam success skill 4

Efficient numerical analysis

This skill aims to maximise the marks awarded by making clear to the marker the process of arriving at your answer in Section C. This is achieved by laying out an answer such that, even if you make a few errors, you can still score subsequent marks for follow-on calculations. It is vital that you do not lose marks purely because the marker cannot follow what you have done.

Advice on developing Efficient numerical analysis

This skill can be developed by applying the following process:

Step 1 **Use a standard proforma working where relevant**

If answers can be laid out in a standard proforma then always plan to do so. This will help the marker to understand your working and allocate the marks easily. It will also help you to work through the figures in a methodical and time-efficient way.

Step 2 **Show your working**

Keep your workings as clear and simple as possible and ensure they are cross-referenced to the main part of your answer. You can use the formula within the spreadsheet software to, for example, perform calculations or you can write out the workings. When preparing the financial statements in the Section C question, you can insert your final figures for, for example, goodwill by cross-referencing to the goodwill working. Where it helps, provide brief narrative explanations to help the marker understand the steps in the calculation. This means that if a mistake is made you do not lose any subsequent marks for follow-on calculations.

Step 3 **Keep moving!**

It is important to remember that, in an exam situation, it can sometimes be difficult to get every number 100% correct. The key is therefore ensuring you do not spend too long on any single calculation. If you are struggling with a solution then make a sensible assumption, state it and move on.

Exam success skill 5

Effective writing and presentation

Written answers should be presented so that the marker can clearly see the points you are making, presented in the format specified in the question. The skill is to provide efficient written answers with sufficient breadth of points that answer the question, in the right depth, in the time available.

Advice on developing Effective writing and presentation

Step 1 **Use headings**

Using the headings and sub-headings from your answer plan will give your answer structure, order and logic. This will ensure your answer links back to the requirement and is clearly signposted, making it easier for the marker to understand the different points you are making. Underlining headings or making them bold will also help the marker.

Step 2 **Write your answer in short, but full, sentences**

Use short, punchy sentences with the aim that every sentence should say something different and generate marks. Write in full sentences, ensuring your style is professional.

Step 3 **Do your calculations first and explanation second**

Questions often ask for an explanation with suitable calculations. The best approach is to prepare the calculation first but present it on the bottom half of the page of your answer, or on the next page. Then add the explanation before the calculation. Performing the calculation first should enable you to explain what you have done.

Exam success skill 6

Good time management

This skill means planning your time across all the requirements so that all requirements have been attempted at the end of the 3 hours available and actively checking on time during your exam. This is so that you can flex your approach and prioritise requirements which, in your judgement, will generate the maximum marks in the available time remaining.

Advice on developing Good time management

The exam is 3 hours long, which translates to 1.8 minutes per mark. Therefore a 10-mark requirement should be allocated a maximum of 18 minutes to complete your answer before you move on to the next task. At the beginning of a question, work out the amount of time you should be spending on each question and the total time you should spend on each section.

Keep an eye on the clock

Aim to attempt all requirements, but be ready to be ruthless and move on if your answer is not going as planned. The challenge for many is sticking to planned timings. Be aware this is difficult to achieve in the early stages of your studies and be ready to let this skill develop over time.

If you find yourself running short on time, have an educated guess at the OT questions in Sections A and B. In Section C, if you know that a full answer is not possible in the time you have, consider providing your plan in overview form and then add key terms and details as time allows. Remember, some marks may be available, for example, simply stating a conclusion which you don't have time to justify in full.

Questions

PART A: THE CONCEPTUAL AND REGULATORY FRAMEWORK FOR FINANCIAL REPORTING

Questions 1–8 cover the *Conceptual Framework*. Questions 9–19 cover the regulatory framework, including the impact of the measurement basis applied to assets on the financial performance of the company. Questions 1–19 are objective test (OT) questions in the style of Section A of the exam.

The Section B Questions 20–24 cover the *Conceptual Framework* and the regulatory framework.

Section A

Conceptual Framework (29 mins)

1 How does the *Conceptual Framework* define an asset?

- O A present economic resource, which is a right that has the potential to produce economic benefits, owned by an entity as a result of past events
- O A present economic resource over which an entity has legal rights. An economic resource is a right that has the potential to produce economic benefits
- O A present economic resource controlled by an entity as a result of past events. An economic resource is a right that has the potential to produce economic benefits
- O A present economic resource to which an entity has a future commitment as a result of past events. An economic resource is a right that has the potential to produce economic benefits

(2 marks)

---

2 Which of the following would meet the *Conceptual Framework* definition of a liability?

- O Dexter's business manufactures a product under licence. In 12 months' time the licence expires and Dexter will have to pay $50,000 for it to be renewed
- O Reckless purchased an investment 9 months ago for $120,000. The market for these investments has now fallen and Reckless's investment is valued at $90,000
- O Carter has estimated the tax charge on its profits for the year just ended as $165,000
- O Expansion is planning to invest in new machinery and has been quoted a price of $570,000

(2 marks)

---

3 Which of the following would correctly describe the value in use of a two-year old asset?

- O The original cost of the asset less two years' depreciation
- O The amount that could be obtained from selling the asset, less any costs of disposal
- O The cost of an equivalent new asset less two years' depreciation
- O The present value of the future cash flows obtainable from the continued use of the asset and its ultimate disposal

(2 marks)

---

4 Which **TWO** of the following statements are true regarding the Conceptual Framework for Financial Reporting (*Conceptual Framework*) of the International Accounting Standards Board (the Board)?
(Mar/Jun 2022)

- ☐ It is principles-based rather than rules-based but it is not an IFRS Accounting Standard

- ☐ The principles contained in the *Conceptual Framework* override any IFRS Standard that exists
- ☐ It requires accountants to evaluate and address threats to compliance with fundamental ethical principles
- ☐ If it is revised it will not automatically lead to changes to the IFRS Accounting Standard

(2 marks)

---

5 The *Conceptual Framework* identifies four enhancing qualitative characteristics of financial information.

Which ONE of the following is NOT an enhancing qualitative characteristic?

- O Verifiability
- O Timeliness
- O Consistency
- O Understandability

(2 marks)

---

6 Which **TWO** of the following are purposes of the *Conceptual Framework*?

- ☐ To assist preparers to develop consistent accounting policies when no IFRS Accounting Standard applies to a particular event
- ☐ To issue rules regarding the accounting treatment of elements in the financial statements
- ☐ To assist in determining the treatment of items not covered by an existing IFRS Accounting Standard
- ☐ To be authoritative where a specific IFRS Accounting Standard conflicts with the *Conceptual Framework*

(2 marks)

---

7 Recognition is the process of including within the financial statements items which meet the definition of an element according to the *Conceptual Framework.*

Which of the following items should be recognised as an asset in the statement of financial position of a company?

(1) A secret formula for the manufacture of a best-selling sauce. The recipe is kept secure at the company premises and known only by the company directors

(2) A highly lucrative contract signed during the year which is due to commence shortly after the year end

(3) Items that are to be sold via a third-party agent which the company can no longer control and cannot be returned to the company of they are unsold

(4) A receivable from a customer which has been sold (factored) to a finance company. The finance company has full recourse to the company for any losses

- O (1) and (3)
- O (3) and (4)
- O (1) and (4)
- O (2), (3) and (4)

(2 marks)

---

8 In accordance with the *Conceptual Framework* which of the following is/are true in relation to the enhancing characteristic of comparability?

(1) Permitting alternative accounting treatments for the same economic phenomenon enhances comparability

(2) Comparability requires uniformity

(ACCA, Examiners Report 2017)

- O Both 1 and 2
- O Neither 1 nor 2
- O 1 only
- O 2 only

(2 marks)

(Total = 16 marks)

Regulatory framework **(40 mins)**

9 The process for developing an IFRS Accounting Standard involves a number of stages. Following receipt and review of comments on a Discussion Paper, what will be the next step undertaken by the International Accounting Standards Board (the Board)?

- O Publication of an Exposure Draft
- O Establishment of an Advisory Committee
- O Consultation with the Advisory Committee
- O Issue of a final IFRS Accounting Standard

(2 marks)

---

10 Which **TWO** of the following statements would be an advantage of adopting IFRS Accounting Standards?

- ☐ It would be easier for investors to compare the financial statements of companies with those of foreign competitors
- ☐ Cross-border listing would be facilitated
- ☐ Accountants and auditors would have more defence in case of litigation
- ☐ The IFRS Accounting Standards can be more easily tailored to reflect the industries of the territory adopting them

(2 marks)

---

11 Which **TWO** of the following statements regarding systems of regulation of accounting are true?

- ☐ A principles-based system will require more detailed regulations than a rules-based system
- ☐ A rules-based system will tend to give rise to a larger number of IFRS Accounting Standards than a principles-based system
- ☐ A principles-based system seeks to cover every eventuality
- ☐ A principles-based system requires the exercise of more judgement in application than a rules-based system

(2 marks)

---

12 The process for developing an IFRS Accounting Standard involves a number of stages. During the early stages of a project, the International Accounting Standards Board (the Board) will undertake consultation on the key issues.

Which of the following is correct regarding the early stages of the process:

- O In the early stages of the project, the Board will issue a Discussion Paper to obtain views from the public
- O In the early stages of the project, the Board will consult with the Advisory Committee and IFRS Advisory Council to seek out the key issues

- ○ In the early stages of the project, the Board will issue a Discussion Paper then consult with the Advisory Committee
- ○ In the early stages of the project, the Board will issue an Exposure Draft to obtain views from the public **(2 marks)**

---

13 Historical cost accounting remains in use because of its practical advantages.

Which of the following is **NOT** an advantage of historical cost accounting?

- ○ Amounts of transactions are reliable and can be verified
- ○ Amounts in the statement of financial position can be matched to amounts in the statement of cash flows
- ○ It avoids the overstatement of profit which can arise during periods of inflation
- ○ It provides fewer opportunities for creative accounting than systems of current value accounting **(2 marks)**

---

14 Which of the following statements about the International Sustainability Standards Board (ISSB) is correct?

- ○ The ISSB will issue mandatory laws that companies complying with IFRS Accounting Standards will be required to apply.
- ○ The ISSB will initially focus on climate-related disclosures
- ○ The standards issued by the ISSB will replace those issued by the International Accounting Standards Board (the Board).
- ○ There has been no previous guidance for preparers of financial information in respect of sustainability disclosures **(2 marks)**

---

15 Drexler acquired an item of plant on 1 October 20X2 at a cost of $500,000. It has a useful life of five years (straight-line depreciation) and an estimated residual value of 10% of its historical cost or current cost as appropriate. As at 30 September 20X4, the manufacturer of the plant still makes the same item of plant and its current price is $600,000.

What is the correct carrying amount to be shown in the statement of financial position of Drexler as at 30 September 20X4 under the historical cost and current cost measurement bases?

Historical cost ($): (1) ▼

Current cost ($): (2) ▼

Pull down list 1

- 300,000
- 320,000

Pull down list 2

- 384,000
- 600,000

(2 marks)

---

16 Under the current value measurement basis, what is the definition of fulfilment value?

- ○ The amount of consideration received to incur the liability, less transaction costs

- O The price that would be paid to settle the liability at the measurement date
- O The consideration that would be received for incurring an equivalent liability at the measurement date
- O The present value of the estimated cash flows needed to fulfil a liability **(2 marks)**

---

17 Which of the following statements is an advantage of using the value in use measurement basis?

- O It assists a user to assess the future prospects of the business
- O Amounts used are objective and free from bias
- O It is an easily understood system of valuation
- O Amounts are reliable and can be verified to invoices and documents **(2 marks)**

---

18 Under the current cost measurement basis, what is the definition of the value in use measurement method?

- O Costs incurred at the time of acquisition
- O Present value of future cash flows, less costs of disposal
- O Open market value of the asset
- O Open market value of the asset, less the present value of the future cash outflows

(2 marks)

---

19 Which statement best describes the intention of the International Sustainability Standards Board (ISSB)?

- O To develop standards that result in a high-quality, comprehensive global baseline of sustainability disclosures focused on the needs of investors and the financial markets
- O To develop auditing standards to assist auditors who are providing an opinion on sustainability disclosures
- O To investigate complaints made against companies who are breaching local and international laws on environmental waste
- O To provide a framework for companies to follow when developing their own internal policies on sustainability **(2 marks)**

(Total = 22 marks)

Section B

Lisbon Co case **(18 mins)**

Information relevant to Questions 20–24

The accountant of Lisbon is considering a number of transactions and events and how they should be treated in accordance with the concepts and qualitative characteristics of financial information as set out in the *Conceptual Framework*.

During the year ended 31 March 20X6, Lisbon experienced the following transactions or events:

(1) Lisbon sold an asset to a finance company and immediately leased it back for the remainder of its useful life. The transaction met the criteria to be recognised as a sale under IFRS 15 *Revenue from Contracts with Customers*. The accountant determined that the transaction should be treated as a sale and leaseback in accordance with IFRS 16 *Leases* and has accounted for it accordingly.

(2) The company's statement of profit or loss, prepared using historical costs, showed a loss from operating its shops. Lisbon is aware that the increase in the value of its properties during the period far outweighs the operating loss.

(3) Inventory has historically been valued using the first in first out (FIFO) method but the accountant is considering changing to the weighted average (AVCO) method for the year to 31 March 20X6.

20 The accountant is aware that some members of the board of Lisbon have little understanding of accounting and is worried about presenting the financial statements at the board meeting.

In accordance with the *Conceptual Framework*, how should the accountant deal with this situation?

- O In doing the presentation the accountant should omit any complex issues, so that everybody can understand what they are saying
- O The accountant should open the presentation with the advice that some of them may not understand all of it
- O The accountant should classify, characterise and present the information clearly and precisely
- O The accountant should deliver their presentation just to those who are financially qualified **(2 marks)**

---

21 Which concept or qualitative characteristic has influenced the decision in (1) above?

- O Faithful representation
- O Verifiability
- O Accruals
- O Comparability **(2 marks)**

---

22 In looking at issue (2) above, the accountant decides that the properties should be revalued.

Which concept or qualitative characteristic has been applied in making this decision?

- O Materiality
- O Going concern
- O Relevance
- O Timeliness **(2 marks)**

23 Because of the loss arising from operating the shops, the accountant is considering whether Lisbon is a going concern. If it was decided that Lisbon was no longer a going concern at 31 March 20X6, which of the following is correct in accordance with the *Conceptual Framework*?

- O Financial statements do not need to be prepared
- O All the assets should be liquidated
- O The financial statements should be prepared on a different basis
- O The financial statements should be prepared as normal and the going concern status disclosed in the notes **(2 marks)**

---

24 In applying the enhancing qualitative characteristic of comparability, how should the change of inventory valuation basis be accounted for?

- O The change should be disclosed only
- O The financial statements for 31 March 20X6 should show both methods
- O The notes should show what the profit would have been if the change had not taken place
- O The financial statements for the prior period as shown at 31 March 20X6 should be restated using the weighted average basis **(2 marks)**

(Total = 10 marks)

PART B: ACCOUNTING FOR TRANSACTIONS IN FINANCIAL STATEMENTS (I)

Accounting for transactions in financial statements requires students to have a detailed understanding of the IFRS Accounting Standards. This first part of Part B covers the treatment of non-current assets and therefore focuses on IAS 16, IAS 36, IAS 38 and IAS 40. It is relevant to Chapters 3, 4 and 5 in the Workbook.

Ensure that this area is well revised as it is also relevant to lease accounting.

Section A questions

Questions 25–34: Tangible non-current assets (Chapter 3)

Questions 35–39: Intangible non-current assets (Chapter 4)

Questions 40–48: Impairment of assets (Chapter 5)

Section B questions on these topics are in Questions 49–78

Section A

Tangible non-current assets **(36 mins)**

25 Foster Co has built a new factory incurring the following costs:

	$'000
Land	1,200
Materials	2,400
Labour	3,000
Architect's fees	25
Surveyor's fees	15
Site overheads	300
Apportioned administrative overheads	150
Testing of fire alarms	10
Business rates for first year	12
	7,112

What will be the total amount capitalised in respect of the factory?

- O $6,640,000
- O $6,950,000
- O $7,112,000
- O $7,100,000

(2 marks)

---

26 Carriageways Co had the following bank loans outstanding during the whole of 20X8 which form the company's general borrowings for the year:

	$m
9% loan repayable 20X9	15
11% loan repayable 20Y2	24

Carriageways Co began construction of a qualifying asset on 1 April 20X8 and withdrew funds of $6 million on that date to fund the construction. On 1 August 20X8 an additional $2 million was withdrawn for the same purpose.

Calculate the borrowing costs which can be capitalised in respect of this project for the year ended 31 December 20X8.

- O $549,333
- O $480,000
- O $824,000
- O $533,333 **(2 marks)**

---

27 Leclerc Co has borrowed $2.4 million to finance the building of a factory. Construction is expected to take two years. The loan was drawn down on 1 January 20X9 and work began on 1 March 20X9. $1 million of the loan was not utilised until 1 July 20X9 so Leclerc was able to invest it until needed.

Leclerc Co is paying 8% on the loan and can invest surplus funds at 6%.

Calculate the borrowing costs to be capitalised for the year ended 31 December 20X9 in respect of this project.

- O $140,000
- O $192,000
- O $132,000
- O $160,000 **(2 marks)**

---

28 Which of the following statements is correct regarding investment properties in accordance with IAS 40 *Investment Property*?

(1) Transfers of IAS 16 property to or from an IAS 40 investment property should only be made when there is a change in their use.

(2) Transfers from an IAS 40 investment property to an IAS 16 property must be made at the fair value of the investment property at the date of the transfer.

(3) An entity should treat any difference between the measurement of an IAS 16 property and the measurement of an IAS 40 investment property at the date of transfer as an expense to the profit or loss.

- O Statement 1 only
- O Both statements 1 and 2
- O Both statements 2 and 3
- O Both statements 1 and 3 **(2 marks)**

---

29 Identify whether each of the following statements is true or false in accordance with IAS 40 *Investment Property*?

Following initial recognition, an investment property can be measured at either cost or fair value	**TRUE**	**FALSE**
If an investment property is held at fair value, this must be applied to all of the entity's investment properties	**TRUE**	**FALSE**
An investment property is initially measured at cost, including transaction costs	**TRUE**	**FALSE**
A gain or loss arising from a change in the fair value of	**TRUE**	**FALSE**

an investment property should be recognised in the revaluation surplus		

(2 marks)

---

30 Fido Feed Co has the following loans in place throughout the year ended 31 December 20X8 which constitute its general borrowings for the period.

	$m
10% bank loan	140
8% bank loan	200

On 1 July 20X8, $50 million was drawn down for the construction of a qualifying asset which was completed during 20X9.

What amount should be capitalised as borrowing costs at 31 December 20X8 in respect of this asset?

- O $2.0 million
- O $2.25 million
- O $4.4 million
- O $2.2 million

(2 marks)

---

31 Wetherby Co purchased a machine on 1 July 20X7 for $500,000. It is being depreciated on a straight-line basis over its useful life of ten years. Residual value is estimated at $20,000. On 1 January 20X8, following a change in legislation, Wetherby Co fitted a safety guard to the machine. The safety guard cost $25,000 and has a useful life of five years with no residual value.

What amount will be charged to profit or loss for the year ended 31 March 20X8 in respect of depreciation on this machine? (Enter your answer to the nearest whole $.)

$ [ ]

(2 marks)

---

32 Auckland Co purchased a machine for $60,000 on 1 January 20X7 and determined that it had a useful life of 15 years with nil residual value. On 31 March 20X9 it was revalued to $64,000 with no change in useful life.

What will be depreciation charge in relation to this machine in the financial statements of Auckland Co for the year ending 31 December 20X9? (Enter your answer to the nearest whole $.)

$ [ ]

(2 marks)

---

33 Carter Co vacated its head office building and let it out to a third party on 30 June 20X8. The building had an original cost of $900,000 on 1 January 20X0 and was being depreciated on a straight-line basis over 50 years. It was judged to have a fair value on 30 June 20X8 of $950,000. At the year-end date of 31 December 20X8 the fair value of the building was estimated at $1.2 million.

Carter Co uses the fair value model for investment property.

What amount will be shown in revaluation surplus at 31 December 20X8 in respect of this building? (Enter your answer to the nearest whole $.)

$ [ ] **(2 marks)**

---

34 Subsequent to initial recognition, investment properties held at fair value are not depreciated.

Required

Which of the following is a valid justification for investment properties held at fair value not being subject to deprecation, whilst property, plant and equipment held at fair value is subject to depreciation?

- O Investment properties don't generate income to match against any depreciation expense
- O You can't reliably measure the useful life of an investment property
- O Investment properties never decrease in value
- O An investment property is likely to increase in value so any residual value would be greater than it's carrying amount **(2 marks)**

(Total = 20 marks)

Intangible non-current assets (18 mins)

35 Sagan Co acquired a brand name with an estimated useful life of ten years on 1 January 20X2 for $10m. On 1 January 20X5 a brand specialist believed the brand to have a fair value of $14m. Sagan Co also ran a training course on 1 January 20X5 for all staff on how to use a new software system. This training cost Sagan Co $450,000. On average, the employees are expected to remain with Sagan Co for three years.

Required

How much should be recognised as an expense in the statement of profit or loss for the year ended 31 December 20X5 in respect of each item? ***(Mar/Jun 2022)***

Brand amortisation: [▼]

Training costs: [▼]

Pull down list

- $150,000
- $1m
- $2m
- $450,000

(2 marks)

---

36 Assoria Co had $20 million of capitalised development expenditure at cost brought forward at 1 October 20X7 in respect of products currently in production.

A new project began on 1 October 20X7. The research stage of the new project lasted until 31 December 20X7 and incurred $1.4 million of costs. From 1 January 20X8, the project incurred development costs of $800,000 per month. On 1 April 20X8 the directors of Assoria Co became confident that the project would be successful and yield a profit well in excess of costs. The project was still in development at 30 September 20X8. Capitalised development expenditure is amortised at 20% per annum using the straight-line method.

What amount will be charged to profit or loss for the year ended 30 September 20X8 in respect of research and development costs?

- O $8,280,000
- O $6,880,000
- O $7,800,000
- O $3,800,000

(2 marks)

---

37 Identify whether the following internally generated items are eligible or ineligible to be recognised as intangible assets in accordance with IAS 38 *Intangible Assets*? (Ignore the effect of business combinations.)

A customer list built up over the last ten years of trading updated for the customer's current preferences	**ELIGIBLE**	**INELIGIBLE**
Specialised tooling for a new product developed by the business	**ELIGIBLE**	**INELIGIBLE**
A working version of a new machine that uses new technology used for testing of the prototype apparatus	**ELIGIBLE**	**INELIGIBLE**
The title heading, font and design of the front page of a major broadsheet newspaper	**ELIGIBLE**	**INELIGIBLE**

(2 marks)

---

38 At 30 September 20X9, Sandown Co's trial balance showed a brand at cost of $30 million and accumulated amortisation on that brand brought forward at 1 October 20X8 of $9 million. Amortisation is based on a 10-year useful life. An impairment review on 1 April 20X9 concluded that the brand had a value in use of $12 million and a remaining useful life of three years. However, on the same date, Sandown Co received an offer to purchase the brand for $16 million and costs of $1m would be incurred in legal fees associated with the sale.

What should be the carrying amount of the brand in the statement of financial position of Sandown Co as at 30 September 20X9? (Enter your answer to the nearest $'000.)

$ [ ]

(2 marks)

---

39 Dempsey Co's year end is 30 September 20X5. Dempsey Co commenced the development stage of a project to produce a new pharmaceutical drug on 1 January 20X5. Expenditure of $40,000 per month was incurred until the project was completed on 30 June 20X5 when the drug went into immediate production. The directors became confident of the project's success on 1 March 20X5. The drug is expected to generate benefits for five years.

What is the carrying amount of any intangible asset recognised in respect of the project at 30 September 20X5 and what is the total amount Dempsey Co will charge to profit or loss for the year ended 30 September 20X5?

Select your answers from the options below and place them in the blank boxes.

Carrying amount of intangible asset at 30 September 20X5 = (1) ▼

Amount charged to profit or loss for period ending 30 September 20X5 =

(2) ▼

Pull down list 1

- $0
- $152,000
- $228,000
- $98,667

Pull down list 2

- $0
- $141,333
- $240,000
- $88,000

(2 marks)

(Total = 10 marks)

Impairment of assets **(32 mins)**

40 A cash-generating unit comprises the following assets:

	$'000
Building	700
Plant and equipment	200
Goodwill	90
Current assets	20
	1,010

Following an impairment review, it was discovered that an item of plant, carried at $40,000, is damaged and will have to be scrapped. The recoverable amount of the cash-generating unit is estimated at $750,000.

What will be the carrying amount of the building after the impairment loss has been recognised?

(to the nearest $'000)

- O $597
- O $577
- O $594
- O $548

(2 marks)

---

41 Complete the statement using the options provided. Select your answers from the options below and place them in the blank boxes.

The **recoverable amount** of an asset is the higher of [▼] and [▼] under IAS 36 *Impairment of Assets*.

Pull down list

- Fair value
- Fair value less costs of disposal
- Market value
- Value in use

(2 marks)

---

42 Lichen Co owns a machine that has a carrying amount of $85,000 at the year end of 31 March 20X9. Its market value is $78,000 and costs of disposal are estimated at $2,500. A new machine would cost $150,000. Lichen Co expects it to produce net cash flows of $30,000 per annum for the next three years. The cost of capital of Lichen Co is 8%.

What is the impairment loss on the machine to be recognised in the financial statements at 31 March 20X9? (Enter your answer to the nearest whole $.)

$ [ ] **(2 marks)**

---

43 IAS 36 *Impairment of Assets* suggests potential indicators of impairment.

Which **TWO** of the following would be **EXTERNAL INDICATORS** that one or more of an entity's assets may be impaired?

☐ An unusually significant fall in the market value of one or more assets

☐ Evidence of obsolescence of one or more assets

☐ A decline in the economic performance of one or more assets

☐ An increase in the market interest rates used to calculate value in use of the assets

(2 marks)

---

44 The following information relates to an item of plant owned by Bazaar Co:

(1) Its carrying amount in the statement of the financial position is $3 million.

(2) Bazaar Co has received an offer of $2.7 million from a company in Japan interested in buying the plant.

(3) The present value of the estimated cash flows from continued use of the plant is $2.6 million.

(4) The estimated cost of shipping the plant to Japan is $50,000.

What is the amount of the impairment loss that should be recognised in respect of the plant? (Enter your answer to the nearest whole $.)

$ [ ] **(2 marks)**

---

45 A business which comprises a single cash-generating unit has the following assets:

	$m
Goodwill	3
Patent	5
Property	10
Plant and equipment	15
Net current assets	

	$m
	2
	35

Following an impairment review it is estimated that the value of the patent is $2 million and the recoverable amount of the business is $24 million.

What is the carrying amount of the property following the impairment review?

- O $8 million
- O $10 million
- O $7.5 million
- O $5 million

(2 marks)

---

46 Riley Co acquired a non-current asset on 1 October 20W9 (ten years before 20X9) at a cost of $100,000 which had a useful life of ten years and a nil residual value. The asset had been correctly depreciated up to 30 September 20X4. At that date the asset was damaged and an impairment review was performed. On 30 September 20X4, the fair value of the asset less costs of disposal was $30,000 and the expected future cash flows were $8,500 per annum for the next five years. The current cost of capital is 10% and a five-year annuity of $1 per annum at 10% would have a present value of $3.79.

What amount would be charged to profit or loss for the impairment of this asset for the year ended 30 September 20X4?

- O $17,785
- O $20,000
- O $30,000
- O $32,215

(2 marks)

---

47 The net assets of Fyngle Co, a cash-generating unit (CGU), are:

	$
Property, plant and equipment	200,000
Allocated goodwill	50,000
Product patent	20,000
Net current assets (at net realisable value)	30,000
	300,000

An impairment review was carried out following adverse publicity received. The impairment review indicates that Fyngle Co has a recoverable amount of $200,000.

What would be the carrying amount of Fyngle Co's property, plant and equipment after the allocation of the impairment loss?

- O $154,545
- O $170,000
- O $160,000
- O $133,333

(2 marks)

---

48 Select whether each of the following statements is an indicator of impairment or is not an indicator of impairment under IAS 36 *Impairment of Assets*.

Advances in the technological environment in which an asset is employed has an adverse impact on its future use	**INDICATOR OF IMPAIRMENT**	**NOT AN INDICATOR OF IMPAIRMENT**
An increase in interest rates which increases the discount rate an entity uses	**INDICATOR OF IMPAIRMENT**	**NOT AN INDICATOR OF IMPAIRMENT**
The carrying amount of an entity's net assets is lower than the entity's number of shares in issue multiplied by its share price	**INDICATOR OF IMPAIRMENT**	**NOT AN INDICATOR OF IMPAIRMENT**
The estimated net realisable value of inventory has been reduced due to fire damage although this value is greater than its carrying amount	**INDICATOR OF IMPAIRMENT**	**NOT AN INDICATOR OF IMPAIRMENT**

(2 marks)

(Total = 18 marks)

Section B

Plethora plc case **(18 mins)**

Information relevant to questions 49–53

The draft financial statements of Plethora plc for the year to 31 December 20X9 are being prepared and the accountant has requested your advice on dealing with the following issues.

(1) Plethora plc has an administration building which it no longer needs. On 1 July 20X9, Plethora plc entered into an agreement to lease the building out to another company. The building cost $600,000 on 1 January 20X0 and is being depreciated over 50 years, based on the IAS 16 *Property, Plant and Equipment* cost model. Plethora plc applies the fair value model under IAS 40 *Investment Property* and the fair value of the building was assessed as $800,000 on 1 July 20X9. This valuation had not changed at 31 December 20X9.

(2) Plethora plc owns another building which has been leased out for a number of years. It had a fair value of $550,000 at 31 December 20X8 and $740,000 at 31 December 20X9.

(3) Plethora plc owns a retail business, which is considered a separate cash-generating unit, which suffered a difficult trading period in the previous year and was subject to an impairment review at 31 December 20X8. At that date, an impairment loss of $160,000 was recognised. The directors of Plethora plc believe the indicators of impairment have reversed by 31 December 20X9 and wish to reverse the previous impairment loss to the maximum extent possible.

Relevant financial information in respect of the retail business is as follows:

Asset	*Carrying amount at 31 December 20X8 before impairment*	*Impairment loss at 31 December 20X8*	*Estimated fair value at 31 December 20X9*	*Carrying amount at 31 December 20X9 had no impairment occurred*
Building	900	100	925	875
Plant and equipment	300	20	310	290
Goodwill	40	40	60	40

An impairment review has been carried out as at 31 December 20X9 and the recoverable amount of the cash-generating unit is estimated at $1.3 million.

49 What is the amount of the revaluation surplus that will be recognised in respect of the building in (1)? (Enter your answer to the nearest whole $.)

$ [ ] **(2 marks)**

---

50 In respect of the building in (2), how will the increase in value from $550,000 to $740,000 be accounted for?

- O Credited to profit or loss
- O Credited to the revaluation surplus
- O Credited to retained earnings
- O Credited to an investment property reserve **(2 marks)**

51 Using the pull-down list provided, select the amount at which an impaired asset is measured when an impairment has taken place?

▼

Pull down list

- Carrying amount
- Fair value
- Recoverable amount
- Value in use

(2 marks)

52 Which **TWO** of the following statements regarding the reversal of impairment losses are correct?

☐ The reversal of goodwill impairment should be recognised in other comprehensive income

☐ The reversal of impairment losses on revalued assets should be recognised in other comprehensive income

☐ An impairment loss can only be reversed if there is a change in the estimates used to determine the recoverable amount of the impaired assets

☐ Only impairment losses on non-current assets can be reversed **(2 marks)**

53 What will be the amount credited to the statement of profit or loss in respect of the reversal of the impairment loss in the year ended 31 December 20X9?

O $215,000

O $155,000

O $125,000

O $85,000 **(2 marks)**

(Total = 10 marks)

Linetti Co case (Mar/Jun 2019) (18 mins)

Information relevant to questions 54–58

During the year ended 31 December 20X8, Linetti Co built an extension to its head office. The costs associated with the head office extension are as follows:

	$m
Land acquisition	10.0
Fees for environmental certifications and building permits	0.5
Architect and engineer fees	1.0
Construction material and labour costs (including unused materials)	6.6

At 30 September 20X8, the date when the head office extension became available for use, the cost of unused materials on site amounted to $0.5 million. At that date, the total borrowing costs incurred on a loan which was used specifically to finance the head office extension amounted to $0.8 million.

Linetti Co also acquired 100% of a subsidiary, Scully Co, on 1 January 20X8. The carrying amount of the assets of Scully Co in the consolidated financial statements of the Linetti Group at 31 December 20X8, immediately before an impairment review, were as follows:

	$m
Goodwill	1.4
Brand name	2.0
Property, plant and equipment	6.0
Current assets (at recoverable amount)	2.4
	11.8

The recoverable amount of Scully Co was estimated at $9.6 million at 31 December 20X8 and the impairment of the investment in Scully Co was deemed to be $2.2 million.

54 For the year end 31 December 20X8, how much should be capitalised in respect of the construction of the extension to the head office building?

- O $18.4 million
- O $17.6 million
- O $18.9 million
- O $18.1 million **(2 marks)**

---

55 Linetti Co incurred further expenditure on the head extension after it had been completed.

Which of the following would qualify as capital expenditure?

- O Property insurance premiums incurred
- O Installation of new office fixtures and fittings
- O Marketing costs telling the public that the head office extension is operational
- O Maintenance and relocation of computers and related office equipment **(2 marks)**

---

56 At 31 December 20X9, the directors of Linetti Co decide to adopt the revaluation model of IAS 16 *Property, Plant and Equipment* for Linetti Co's property.

In accordance with IAS 16, which of the following statements is **NOT** true?

- O In subsequent years, the depreciation will be based on the revalued amount of the head office building as opposed to its cost
- O Any revaluation gain on the head office building is recognised in other comprehensive income and any revaluation loss is recognised in profit or loss
- O The original head office building and the new extension are revalued separately
- O The residual value and the useful life of the head office building must be reviewed each year **(2 marks)**

---

57 Assuming Scully Co represents a cash generating unit, what is the carrying amount of the brand at 31 December 20X8 following impairment review?

- O $1.2 million
- O $1.45 million
- O $1.73 million
- O $1.8 million **(2 marks)**

58 Which, if any, of the following statements regarding impairment reviews is/are correct?

(1) At the end of each reporting period, an entity should assess if there is any indication that assets have been impaired

(2) Annual impairment reviews are required on all intangible assets with indefinite lives

O 1 only

O 2 only

O Both 1 and 2

O Neither 1 nor 2 **(2 marks)**

(Total = 10 marks)

Elite Leisure Co case (18 mins)

The following scenario relates to questions 59–63.

Elite Leisure Co is a private limited liability company that operates a single cruise ship. The ship was acquired on 1 October 20W6 (ten years before 20X6). Details of the cost of the ship's components and the basis on which they are depreciated is as follows:

Component	*Original cost*	*Depreciation basis*
	$m	
Ship's fabric (hull, decks etc)	300	25 years straight-line
Cabins and entertainment area fittings	150	12 years straight-line
Propulsion system	100	Useful life of 40,000 hours

At 30 September 20X4 no further capital expenditure had been incurred on the ship.

The propulsion system has been used for 30,000 hours at 30 September 20X4. Due to the unreliability of the engines, a decision was taken in early October 20X4 to replace the whole of the propulsion system at a cost of $140 million. The useful life of the new propulsion system was 50,000 hours and, in the year, ended 30 September 20X5 the ship had used the system for 5,000 hours.

At the same time as the propulsion system replacement, Elite Leisure Co took the opportunity to do a limited upgrade to the facilities at a cost of $60 million and repaint the ship's fabric at a cost of $20 million. After the upgrade of the facilities, it was estimated that their remaining useful life was five years (from the date of the upgrade). For the purpose of calculating depreciation, all the work on the ship can be assumed to have been completed on 1 October 20X4. All residual values can be taken as nil.

59 At 30 September 20X4 the ship is eight years old. What is the carrying amount of the ship at that date?

O $279 million

O $275 million

O $229 million

O $254 million **(2 marks)**

60 What is the amount of depreciation that should be charged in respect of the propulsion system for the year ended 30 September 20X5? (Enter your answer to the nearest $m.)

$ [ ] **(2 marks)**

---

61 Ignoring depreciation, what is the charge to profit or loss for the year ended 30 September 20X5? (Enter your answer to the nearest whole $.)

$ [ ] **(2 marks)**

---

62 Elite Leisure Co's ship has to have a safety check carried out every five years at a cost of $50,000 in order to be licensed to operate. How should this be accounted for?

- O Set up a provision for the discounted present value and unwind over five years
- O Accrue the cost of the check over five years until it takes place
- O Charge $50,000 to profit or loss when incurred
- O Capitalise the cost when incurred and amortise over five years **(2 marks)**

---

63 Elite Leisure Co is being sued for $250,000 by a passenger who slipped on one of the gangways and twisted an ankle. The company's lawyer estimates that there is a 55% chance that it will lose the case. Legal costs for Elite Leisure Co will be $40,000.

Using the pull-down list provided, select the amount at which Elite Leisure Co provide in respect of this case.

[▼]

Pull down list

- $137,500
- $159,500
- $250,000
- $290,000

(2 marks)

(Total = 10 marks)

Advent Co case (18 mins)

The following scenario relates to questions 64–68

Advent Co is a publicly listed company. Details of Advent Co's non-current assets at 1 October 20X8 were:

	Land and building	*Plant*	*Telecommunications licence*	*Total*
	$m	$m	$m	$m
Cost/valuation	280	150	300	730
Accumulated depreciation/amortisation	(40)	(103)	(30)	(175)
Carrying amount	240	45	270	555

The following information is relevant:

(1) The land and building were revalued on 1 October 20X3 with $80 million attributable to the land and $200 million to the building. At that date the estimated remaining life of the building was 25 years. A further revaluation was not needed until 1 October 20X8 when the land and building were valued at $85 million and $180 million respectively. The remaining estimated life of the building at this date was 20 years.

(2) Plant is depreciated at 20% per annum on cost with time apportionment where appropriate. On 1 April 20X9, new plant costing $45 million was acquired. In addition, this plant cost $5 million to install and commission. No plant is more than four years old.

(3) The telecommunications licence was bought from the government on 1 October 20X7 and has a ten-year life. It is amortised on a straight-line basis. In September 20X9, a review of the sales of the products related to the licence showed them to be very disappointing. As a result of this review the estimated recoverable amount of the licence at 30 September 20X9 was estimated at only $100 million.

There were no disposals of non-current assets during the year to 30 September 20X9.

64 What is the carrying amount of the land and buildings at 30 September 20X9?

- O $256 million
- O $265 million
- O $240 million
- O $258 million

(2 marks)

---

65 What is the depreciation charge on the plant for the year ended 30 September 20X9?

- O $30 million
- O $25 million
- O $20 million
- O $35 million

(2 marks)

---

66 Having revalued its property Advent Co is required to make certain disclosures in respect of the revaluation.

Identify whether the following disclosures are, or are not required, in respect of revaluation.

The effective date of revaluation	**REQUIRED**	**NOT REQUIRED**
Professional qualifications of the valuer	**REQUIRED**	**NOT REQUIRED**
The basis used to revalue the assets	**REQUIRED**	**NOT REQUIRED**
The carrying amount of assets if no revaluation had taken place	**REQUIRED**	**NOT REQUIRED**

(2 marks)

---

67 What is the amount of the impairment loss on the licence? Select your answer from the pull-down list options below.

[▼]

Pull down list

- $100 million
- $140 million
- $170 million
- $240 million

(2 marks)

---

68 Advent Co's licence is now carried at its recoverable amount.

Complete the statement using the options provided.

The recoverable amount of an asset of an asset is the higher of [▼] and [▼].

Pull down list

- Carrying amount
- Carrying amount less costs of disposal
- Fair value less costs of disposal
- Value in use

(2 marks)

(Total = 10 marks)

Systria Co case (18 mins)

The following information is relevant to questions 69–73

Systria Co is preparing its financial statements for the year ended 31 December 20X7 and has a number of issues to deal with regarding non-current assets.

(1) Systria Co has suffered an impairment loss of $90,000 relating to one of its cash-generating units. The carrying amounts of the assets in the cash-generating unit prior to adjusting for impairment are:

	$'000
Goodwill	50
Patent	10
Land and buildings	100
Plant and machinery	50
Net current assets	10

The patent is now estimated to have no value.

(2) During the year to 31 December 20X7 Systria Co acquired Dominica for $10 million, its tangible assets being valued at $7 million and goodwill on acquisition being $3 million. Assets with a carrying amount of $2.5 million were subsequently destroyed. Systria Co has carried out an impairment review and has established that Dominica Co could be sold for $6 million, while its value in use is $5.5 million.

(3) A freehold property originally costing $100,000 with a 50-year useful life has accumulated depreciation to date of $20,000. The asset is to be revalued to $130,000 at 31 December 20X7.

69 What is the post-impairment carrying amount of plant and machinery in (1) above? (Enter your answer to the nearest whole $.)

$ [ ] **(2 marks)**

---

70 The finance director has been asked to report to the board on the reasons for the impairment review on the cash-generating unit. Which **TWO** of the following would be an internal indicator of impairment of an asset under IAS 36 *Impairment of Assets*?

☐ The market value of the asset has fallen significantly

☐ There are adverse changes to the use to which the asset is put

☐ The asset is fully depreciated

☐ The operating performance of the asset has declined **(2 marks)**

---

71 What is the carrying amount of the goodwill in (2) following the impairment review? Select your answer from the pull-down list options below.

[▼]

Pull down list

- $1.5 million
- $2 million
- $2.5 million
- $3 million

(2 marks)

---

72 Using the drag and drop options below, select the correct amounts to complete the double entry required to record the revaluation in (3).

		Debit
$20,000		Accumulated depreciation
$30,000		Property at cost
$50,000		Revaluation surplus
		Credit
		Accumulated depreciation
		Property at cost

	Revaluation surplus

(2 marks)

---

73 What will be the depreciation charge relating to the asset in (3) for the year ended 31 December 20X8?

- ○ $2,000
- ○ $2,600
- ○ $3,250
- ○ $2,750 **(2 marks)**

(Total = 10 marks)

Wilrob Co **(18 mins)**

Information relevant to questions 74–78.

Wilrob Co has the following research projects at 31 March 20X7:

- Project 324 – The project commenced on 1 April 20X6 and incurred total costs of $15m during the period to 31 December 20X6 on a pro-rata basis. On 30 June 20X6, the directors were confident that the project met the capitalisation criteria of IAS 38 *Intangible Assets*. The project was completed and began to generate revenue from 1 January 20X7. It is estimated that the project will generate revenue for five years.
- Project 325 – The project commenced on 1 September 20X6. Costs of $20,000 per month were incurred until 31 January 20X7 when the project was abandoned. The specialist equipment that had been purchased for Project 325 was transferred for use in another of Wilrob Co's research projects.
- Project 326 – The project commenced on 1 January 20X7. Costs of $40,000 per month were incurred until 31 August 20X7 when the directors increased the spend to $60,000 to complete the project quickly as a potential buyer had been identified on 20 July 20X7. The directors had not been confident of the success of the project until this point.

74 Which **TWO** of the following are required by IAS 38 *Intangible Assets* in relation to the amortisation of intangible assets (excluding goodwill)?

- ☐ Intangible assets should be amortised over the expected useful life or not at all if the useful life is deemed to be indefinite
- ☐ Intangible assets should not be amortised but instead reviewed for impairment losses only
- ☐ Intangible assets should be amortised on the basis of the expected pattern of consumption of the expected future economic benefits
- ☐ Intangible assets should not be amortised or impaired and instead simply carried forward at their original cost until sold or scrapped **(2 marks)**

---

75 Which **TWO** of the following statements are true in relation to IAS 38 *Intangible Assets*?

- ☐ IAS 38 requires the revaluation of intangible assets where a company has chosen to revalue its tangible non-current assets
- ☐ IAS 38 does not permit the revaluation of any intangible assets in any circumstances

☐ IAS 38 permits the revaluation of intangible assets only if there is an active market for such assets

☐ IAS 38 requires that the initial recognition of intangibles must be at cost **(2 marks)**

---

76 In accordance with IAS 38 *Intangible Assets*, what is charged to the statement of profit or loss for the year ended 31 March 20X7 in respect of project 324?

- O $5.5m
- O $6.5m
- O $7m
- O $10m

(2 marks)

---

77 In accordance with IAS 38 *Intangible Assets*, identify whether the following are true or false in respect of the accounting treatment of projects 325 and 326.

The cost for project 325 should be expensed in the statement of profit or loss for the year ended 31 March 20X7.	**TRUE**	**FALSE**
The specialist equipment that was purchased for project 325 should not be depreciated as it has only been used for abandoned or research projects.	**TRUE**	**FALSE**
The costs for project 326 should be included as an asset in the statement of financial position as at 31 March 20X7.	**TRUE**	**FALSE**

(2 marks)

---

78 During the year ended 31 March 20X8, Wilrob Co incurred the following costs:

(1) $400,000 in staff costs incurred in updating a computerised record of potential customers

(2) $800,000 for the purchase of a domain name for the website of a company making substantial online sales

(3) $4m for a patent purchased to improve the production process, with an expected useful life of three years

Which of the above costs would be capitalised as intangible assets in accordance with IAS 38 *Intangible Assets*? ***(ACCA, Examiners Report March/June 2021)***

- O 1 only
- O 3 only
- O 1 and 3 only
- O 1, 2 and 3

(2 marks)

(Total = 10 marks)

Part B: Accounting for transactions in financial statements (II)

The second part of Part B covers further assets and liabilities as well as income and expense items. Group accounting is also introduced.

Revenue can be a difficult topic. Ensure you read the question carefully to ensure you understand the scenario and the specific requirement. Accounting for government grants is, however, relatively straightforward.

Group accounting is covered across several chapters. You need to be able to calculate balances that would be presented in the group financial statements, so understanding the key calculations is important. The questions in this bank are an introduction to simple group accounting. There are further group accounting questions in Part D of this Practice and Revision Kit which cover Chapters 8–11.

Financial instruments can be seen as a complex area and you should use the questions in this bank to ensure you understand the key recognition and measurement rules for the different categories of financial assets and financial liabilities. Lease accounting questions require close reading to ensure that you understand what the question is asking. Ensure you know whether they are asking for the initial measurement or the carrying amount of the right-of-use asset or the lease liability. Also know when the optional recognition exemptions can be applied.

Questions on provisions and events after the reporting period may test whether the provision meets the requirements of IAS 37 or how to initially measure a provision. You may be expected to discount provisions to their present value, which can be tricky. Ensure also that you understand the link between provisions and property, plant and equipment. You need to understand whether events after the reporting period are adjusting or non-adjusting and whether disclosure is required.

Accounting for inventories and agriculture is generally straightforward. The requirements of IAS 12 regarding the accounting for basic taxation are unlikely to cause you many problems but deferred tax is more technical, particularly if revalued assets are involved as you will be expected to recognise deferred tax on those assets in the revaluation surplus.

Section A questions

Questions 79–93: Revenue (Chapter 6)

Questions 94–100: Introduction to groups (Chapter 7)

Questions 101–109: Financial instruments (Chapter 12)

Questions 110–121: Lease accounting (Chapter 13)

Questions 122–131: Provisions and events after the reporting period (Chapter 14)

Questions 132–140: Inventories and agriculture (Chapter 15)

Questions 141–148: Accounting for taxation (Chapter 16)

Section B questions on these areas are covered in questions 149–183

Section A

Revenue and government grants (54 mins)

79 Carraway Co entered into a contract on 1 January 20X5 to construct a factory for Seed Co.

The total contract price was $2.8m which is expected to generate a profit for Carraway Co. Seed Co obtains control of the factory as the asset is constructed.

Carraway Co has an enforceable right for payment in respect of the construction completed to date. The contract states that the performance obligations are measured according to certificates issued by the surveyor.

Carraway Co measures satisfaction of the performance obligations under the contract by reference to the value of work certified as complete. At 31 December 20X5, the contract was certified by the surveyor as 35% complete.

$800,000 has been invoiced to the customer but not yet paid.

Identify, by selecting the correct options below, whether a contract asset or contract liability will be recognised as at 31 December 20X5 and what the carrying amount will be in the statement of financial position as at that date.

	Asset or liability	Carrying amount
O	Contract asset	$180,000
O	Contract liability	$240,000

(2 marks)

---

80 America Co prepares its financial statement to 31 October each year. During the current year, America Co secured and received a government grant totalling $720,000 to support the digital upskilling of its workforce. $120,000 of the grant relates to investment in new IT equipment and the remainder is to support training across a two-year period from 1 April 20X5 to 31 March 20X7. The grant was received on 30 June 20X5. America Co fully intends to comply with the conditions of the grant. It purchased the new IT equipment on 1 April 20X5 as required and commenced training with immediate effect. America Co deducts grants relating to assets from the carrying amount of assets.

What amount should be included in non-current liabilities of America Co at the year end 31 October 20X5?

O $125,000

O $720,000

O $425,000

O $300,000 **(2 marks)**

---

81 On 1 October 20X2, Pricewell Co entered into a contract to construct a bridge. The total contract price was $50m and construction is expected to be completed on 30 September 20X4. The contract is expected to generate a profit for Pricewell Co. The customer obtains control of the bridge as construction takes place. Costs to date are:

	$m
Allocation of management time to obtain contract	2
Materials, labour and overheads	12
Depreciation of specialist plant and machinery	3

The value of the work completed at 31 March 20X3 has been agreed at $22m and the estimated cost to complete is $10m. Pricewell Co recognises satisfaction of performance obligations determined by the value of work completed to date.

What is the profit recognised in respect of the contract at 31 March 20X3?

O $5,000,000

O $7,000,000

O $25,000,000

O $Nil **(2 marks)**

82 The company recognises revenue on the basis of the costs incurred to date as a proportion of the total expected costs. The client gains the use of the asset during its construction.

The following details apply to a contract where performance obligations are satisfied over time at 31 December 20X5.

	$
Total contract revenue	120,000
Costs to date	48,000
Estimated costs to completion	48,000
Amounts invoiced	50,400
Amounts received from customers	40,000

What amount should be recognised as a contract asset in the statement of financial position as at 31 December 20X5?

- O $9,600
- O $12,000
- O $14,400
- O $50,400

(2 marks)

---

83 Broom Co receives a government grant of $1,500,000 on 1 July 20X5 allowing it to purchase machinery which also costs $1,500,000 on 1 July 20X5. The machinery is depreciated on a straight-line basis over its ten-year useful life. As Broom Co has incurred the expenditure on the asset, the accountant has recognised the full amount of the grant received as other income in the year to 31 December 20X5. Company policy is to account for all grants received as deferred income.

Identify the adjustment required to correctly account for the government grant at 31 December 20X5.

	Account	Amount
DEBIT	(1) ▼	(2) ▼
CREDIT	(1) ▼	(2) ▼

Pull down list 1

- Accrued income
- Deferred income
- Machinery cost
- Other income

Pull down list 2

- $1,425,000
- $1,500,000
- $150,000
- $75,000
- $Nil

(2 marks)

84 Batty Co has received a government grant of $400,000 on 1 January 20X5 to cover 50% of the cost of a new item of machinery. The grant was correctly recorded at that date.

The machinery will be depreciated over its useful life of five years and the residual value is estimated to be $25,000. Batty Co is expecting to meet all the performance obligations of the grant.

Using the drag and drop options below, select the double entries required to record the subsequent treatment of the grant in the financial statements of Batty Co during the year ended 31 December 20X5 and the depreciation charge for the year in relation to the machinery. The options may be used more than once.

	Debit	Credit
Other income		▼
Deferred income	▼	
Depreciation expense	▼	
Accumulated depreciation		▼

Pull down list

- $155,000
- $160,000
- $75,000
- $80,000

(2 marks)

---

85 On 25 June 20X9 Cambridge Co received an order from a new customer, Circus Co, for products with a sales value of $900,000. Circus Co enclosed a deposit with the order of $90,000.

On 30 June Cambridge Co had not completed credit checks on Circus Co and had not despatched any goods.

According to IFRS 15 *Revenue from Contracts with Customers*, how should Cambridge Co record this transaction in its financial statements for the year ended 30 June 20X9?

Select your answers from the options available (options may be used more than once and all three amount boxes must be completed).

Amount ($)		
900,000		Revenue
810,000		Current liability
90,000		Trade receivables
Nil		

(2 marks)

86 Repro Co, a company which sells photocopying equipment, has prepared its draft financial statements for the year ended 30 September 20X4. It has included the following transactions in revenue at the stated amounts below.

Which of these has been correctly included in revenue according to IFRS 15 *Revenue from Contracts with Customers*?

- O Agency sales of $250,000 on which Repro Co is entitled to a commission.
- O Sale proceeds of $20,000 for motor vehicles which were no longer required by Repro Co.
- O Sales of $150,000 on 30 September 20X4. The amount invoiced to and received from the customer was $180,000, which included $30,000 for ongoing servicing work to be done by Repro Co over the next two years.
- O Sales of $200,000 on 1 October 20X3 to an established customer which, (with the agreement of Repro Co), will be paid in full on 30 September 20X5. Repro Co has a cost of capital of 10%. **(2 marks)**

---

87 Yling Co entered into a contract which is expected to last 24 months on 1 January 20X4. The fixed price which has been agreed for the contract is $5m. At 30 September 20X4 the costs incurred on the contract were $1.6m and the estimated remaining costs to complete were $2.4m. Yling Co measures satisfaction of the performance obligations under the contract based on the percentage of the project certified as completed. At 30 September 20X4, the percentage certified as completed to date was 38%.

On 20 September 20X4 Yling Co received a payment from the customer of $1.74m which was equal to the total of the amounts invoiced to date.

What amount would be reported as a contract asset in Yling Co's statement of financial position as at 30 September 20X4?

- O Nil
- O $160,000
- O $1,000,000
- O $300,000 **(2 marks)**

---

88 Consignment inventory is an arrangement whereby inventory is held by one party but owned by another party. It is common in the motor trade.

Which **TWO** of the following indicate that the inventory in question is consignment inventory?

- ☐ Manufacturer can require the dealer to return the inventory
- ☐ Dealer has no right of return of the inventory
- ☐ Manufacturer bears obsolescence risk
- ☐ Dealer bears slow movement risk **(2 marks)**

---

89 Zayn Co spent $500,000 sending key staff on a one-day training course which took place on 1 January 20X6. Zayn Co is expected to benefit from this training for the next two years.

This training course was partly funded by a government scheme and Zayn Co received $50,000 from the government before the training commenced. The remaining balance of $50,000 is due to be received on 31 December 20X7. Current circumstances indicate that the receipt of the second instalment is virtually certain.

Selecting your answer from the pull-down list below, what amount should be charged to Zayn Co's statement of profit or loss for the year ended 31 December 20X6 to reflect the above transactions? ***(ACCA, Examiners Report June 2019)***

▼

Pull down list

- $150,000
- $200,000
- $400,000
- $450,000

(2 marks)

---

90 Newmarket Co's revenue as shown in its draft statement of profit or loss for the year ended 31 December 20X9 is $27m. This includes $8m for goods sold on 31 December 20X9 on which Newmarket Co will provide ongoing support services for two years after the sale.

The supply of the goods and the provision of services are separate performance obligations under the terms of IFRS 15 *Revenue from Contracts with Customers*.

The cost of providing support services is estimated at $800,000 per annum. Newmarket Co applies a 30% mark-up to all service costs.

At what amount should revenue be recognised in the statement of profit or loss of Newmarket Co for the year ended 31 December 20X9? (Ignore the effects of the time value of money and enter your answer to the nearest whole $.)

$ ______ **(2 marks)**

---

91 On 31 December 20X1 AB entered into a transaction to sell legal title to inventories which would take time to mature. The cost of the inventories at that date was $450,000. The inventories were sold to a financial institution for $420,000 with an option which allows AB to repurchase them on 31 December 20X3 for $463,050. At that date the selling price of the inventories would be approximately $540,000 and it was expected that AB would exercise the option.

How should the above transaction be accounted for in AB's financial statements for the year ended 31 December 20X1?

- O The inventory cost of $450,000 should be recognised in cost of sales and revenue of $420,000 should be recognised.
- O The inventories should be recorded in the statement of financial position at $420,000 and the $420,000 received should be reported as a liability. An inventory write-down of $30,000 should be reported in profit or loss.
- O The inventories should be recorded in the statement of financial position at $450,000 and the $420,000 received should be reported as a liability. There is no profit or loss effect.
- O The inventories should be recorded in the statement of financial position at $450,000 and the $420,000 received should be reported as a liability. Interest expense of $43,050 using the effective interest method should be reported in profit or loss.

(2 marks)

---

92 Under IFRS 15 Revenue from Contracts with Customers, which of the following is an indicator that a performance obligation has been satisfied at a point in time?

- ☐ The entity's performance does not create an asset with an alternative use to the entity and the entity has an enforceable right to payment for performance completed to date
- ☐ The approval of the contract creates enforceable rights and obligations in a given jurisdiction

- ☐ The customer has the significant risks and rewards of ownership of the asset
- ☐ The entity's performance creates or enhances an asset that the customer controls as the asset is created or enhanced
- ☐ The customer simultaneously receives and consumes the benefits provided by the entity's performance as the entity performs **(2 marks)**

---

93 Pearce Co sells $24,000 of goods to Level Co on 19 December 20X7. Pearce Co invoices Level Co on that date but it is agreed that delivery will be delayed until 20 January 20X8 as Level Co does not need the goods until then but has placed the order as these goods are in short supply. Pearce Co places the goods in a separate area of the warehouse and they are identified as waiting for delivery to Level Co.

As the customer has been invoiced, Pearce Co records this as a sale and trade receivable. The goods are included at cost in the stock take of Pearce Co as at 31 December 20X7 and recorded as part of closing inventory.

Pearce Co sells these goods at a margin of 15%.

Required

What entries to the financial statements does Pearce Co need to make as at 31 December 20X7?

- O Dr Revenue 24,000 Cr Trade receivable 24,000
- O Dr Trade receivable 24,000 Cr Revenue 24,000 Dr Inventory 20,400 Cr Cost of sales 20,400
- O Dr Cost of sales 20,400 Cr Inventory 20,400
- O Dr Cost of sales 24,000 Cr Inventory 24,000 **(2 marks)**

(Total = 30 marks)

Introduction to groups (25 mins)

94 On what basis may a subsidiary be excluded from consolidation in accordance with IFRS 10 *Consolidated Financial Statements*?

- O The activities of the subsidiary are dissimilar to the activities of the rest of the group
- O The subsidiary was acquired with the intention of reselling it after a short period of time
- O The subsidiary is based in a country with strict exchange controls which make it difficult for it to transfer funds to the parent
- O There is no basis on which a subsidiary may be excluded from consolidation **(2 marks)**

---

95 When a bargain purchase arises, IFRS 3 *Business Combinations* requires that the amounts involved in calculating the bargain purchase should first be reassessed.

When the amount of the bargain purchase has been confirmed, how should it be accounted for?

- O Charged as an expense in profit or loss
- O Capitalised and presented under non-current assets
- O Credited to profit or loss
- O Shown as a deduction from non-current assets **(2 marks)**

---

96 Which of the following is the criterion for the treatment of an investment as an associate?

- ○ Ownership of a majority of the equity shares
- ○ Ability to exercise control
- ○ Existence of significant influence
- ○ Exposure to variable returns from involvement with the investee **(2 marks)**

---

97 Which **TWO** of the following statements are correct when preparing consolidated financial statements?

- ☐ A subsidiary cannot be consolidated unless it prepares financial statements to the same reporting date as the parent
- ☐ A subsidiary with a different reporting date may prepare additional statements up to the group reporting date for consolidation purposes
- ☐ A subsidiary's financial statements can be included in the consolidation if the gap between the parent and subsidiary reporting dates is five months or less
- ☐ Where a subsidiary's financial statements are drawn up to a different reporting date from those of the parent, adjustments should be made for significant transactions or events occurring between the two reporting dates **(2 marks)**

---

98 IFRS 3 *Business Combinations* requires an acquirer to measure the assets and liabilities of the acquiree at the date of consolidation at fair value. IFRS 13 *Fair Value Measurement* provides guidance on how fair value should be established.

Identify whether the following factors are relevant or not relevant considerations when arriving at the fair value of a non-financial asset according to IFRS 13?

The characteristics of the asset	**RELEVANT**	**NOT RELEVANT**
The price paid to acquire the asset	**RELEVANT**	**NOT RELEVANT**
The principal or most advantageous market for the asset	**RELEVANT**	**NOT RELEVANT**
The highest and best use of the asset	**RELEVANT**	**NOT RELEVANT**

(2 marks)

---

99 An investor company assesses control to determine whether or not it is the parent of an investee company.

According to IFRS 10 *Consolidated Financial Statements*, which **THREE** of the following are required to determine whether an investor has control of an investee?
(ACCA, Examiners Report June 2019)

- ☐ The ability to use its power over the investee to affect the amount of the investor's returns
- ☐ Exposure to, or rights to, variable returns from its involvement with the investee
- ☐ Acquisition of 50% or more of the share capital
- ☐ Power over the investee **(2 marks)**

---

100 Petre Co owns 100% of the share capital of the following companies. The directors are unsure of whether the investments should be consolidated.

In which of the following circumstances would the investment **NOT** be consolidated?

- O Petre Co has decided to sell its investment in Alpha Co as it is loss-making; the directors believe its exclusion from consolidation would assist users in predicting the group's future profits
- O Beta Co is a bank and its activity is so different from the engineering activities of the rest of the group that it would be meaningless to consolidate it
- O Delta Co is located in a country where local accounting standards are compulsory and these are not compatible with IFRS Standards used by the rest of the group
- O Gamma Co is located in a country where a military coup has taken place and Petre Co has lost control of the investment for the foreseeable future **(2 marks)**

(Total = 14 marks)

Financial instruments **(32 mins)**

101 An 8% $30m convertible loan note was issued on 1 April 20X5 at par. Interest is payable in arrears on 31 March each year. The loan note is redeemable at par on 31 March 20X8 or convertible into equity shares at the option of the loan note holders on the basis of 30 shares for each $100 of loan. A similar instrument without the conversion option would have an interest rate of 10% per annum.

The present values of $1 receivable at the end of each year based on discount rates of 8% and 10% are:

		8%	*10%*
End of year	1	0.93	0.91
	2	0.86	0.83
	3	0.79	0.75
	Cumulative	2.58	2.49

What amount will be credited to equity on 1 April 20X5 in respect of this financial instrument?

- O $5,976,000
- O $1,524,000
- O $28,476,000
- O $30,000,000 **(2 marks)**

---

102 A 5% loan note was issued on 1 April 20X0 at its face value of $20m. Direct costs of the issue were $500,000. The loan note will be redeemed on 31 March 20X3 at a substantial premium. The effective interest rate applicable is 10% per annum.

At what amount will the loan note appear in the statement of financial position as at 31 March 20X2?

- O $21,000,000
- O $20,450,000
- O $22,100,000
- O $21,495,000 **(2 marks)**

103 Using the picklist options below, complete the statement to show how IFRS 9 *Financial Instruments* require investments in equity instruments to be measured and accounted for (in the absence of any election at initial recognition)?

(1) ▼	with changes going through	(2) ▼	.

Pull down list 1

- Amortised cost
- Fair value

Pull down list 2

- Other comprehensive income
- Profit or loss

(2 marks)

---

104 On 1 January 20X1, Penfold Co purchased a debt instrument at its fair value of $500,000. It had a principal amount of $550,000 and was due to mature in five years. The debt instrument carries fixed interest of 6% paid annually in arrears and has an effective interest rate of 8%. It is held at amortised cost.

At what amount will the debt instrument be shown in the statement of financial position of Penfold Co as at 31 December 20X2?

- O $514,560
- O $566,000
- O $564,560
- O $520,800

(2 marks)

---

105 On 1 July 20X7, Jacob Co purchased a five-year loan note investment with a par value of $7m. The investment was purchased at a 12% discount. The loan note has a coupon rate of 5% and an effective interest rate of 7%. Interest is receivable annually in arrears. Jacob Co has the intention of holding the loan note to receive the contractual cash flows.

How much finance income should be reported in the statement of profit or loss of the company for the year ended 30 June 20X9 (to the nearest $'000)? ***(Sep/Dec 2021)***

$ [ ]

(2 marks)

---

106 Which of the following is **NOT** classified as a financial instrument under IAS 32 *Financial Instruments: Presentation*?

- O Share options
- O Intangible assets
- O Trade receivables
- O Redeemable preference shares

(2 marks)

---

107 Dexon Co's draft statement of financial position as at 31 March 20X8 shows financial assets at fair value through profit or loss with a carrying amount of $12.5m as at 1 April 20X7.

These financial assets are held in a fund whose value changes directly in proportion to a specified market index. At 1 April 20X7 the relevant index was 1,200 and at 31 March 20X8 it was 1,296.

What amount of gain or loss should be recognised at 31 March 20X8 in respect of these assets? (Enter your answer to the nearest whole $.)

$ [ ] **(2 marks)**

---

108 On 1 January 20X8, Zeeper Co purchased 40,000 $1 listed equity shares at a price of $3 per share. An irrevocable election was made to recognise the shares at fair value through other comprehensive income. Transaction costs were $3,000. At the year end of 31 December 20X8 the shares were trading at $6 per share.

What amount in respect of these shares will be shown under 'investments in equity instruments' in the statement of financial position of Zeeper Co as at 31 December 20X8? (Enter your answer to the nearest whole $.)

$ [ ] **(2 marks)**

---

109 Zeta Co issues 6% redeemable preference shares on 31 December 20X3.

Required

Which of the following statements is true?

- O The issue is classified as equity because shares certificates are issued
- O The dividend payable on these shares will be included in the statement of changes in equity
- O The issue will be recorded by debiting investment and crediting bank
- O The dividend payable will be included in ZX's finance cost as a period expense

(2 marks)

(Total = 18 marks)

Lease accounting **(43 mins)**

110 On 1 January 20X6, Fellini Co entered into a contract for the right to use a machine for a four year period. The contract meets the definition of a lease under IFRS 16 *Leases*. Fellini Co paid a deposit of $700,000 on the commencement of the lease on 1 January 20X6 and a further 3 instalments of $700,000 are payable annually in advance. The present value of the future lease payments was $1,871,100 on commencement of the lease. The interest rate implicit in the lease is 6%.

What amount will appear under non-current liabilities in respect of this lease in the statement of financial position of Fellini Co at 31 December 20X6?

- O $700,000
- O $1,983,366
- O $1,283,366
- O $1,871,100

(2 marks)

---

111 Identify whether each of the following statements indicates or does not indicate that a contract contains a lease under IFRS 16 *Leases*?

The lessee obtains substantially all of the economic benefits from use of the asset	**INDICATES THAT THE CONTRACT CONTAINS A LEASE**	**DOES NOT INDICATE THAT THE CONTRACT CONTAINS A LEASE**
Ownership in the asset is transferred at the end of the lease term	**INDICATES THAT THE CONTRACT CONTAINS A LEASE**	**DOES NOT INDICATE THAT THE CONTRACT CONTAINS A LEASE**
The contract relates to an identified asset	**INDICATES THAT THE CONTRACT CONTAINS A LEASE**	**DOES NOT INDICATE THAT THE CONTRACT CONTAINS A LEASE**
If it suits them to do so, the lessor can substitute an identical asset	**INDICATES THAT THE CONTRACT CONTAINS A LEASE**	**DOES NOT INDICATE THAT THE CONTRACT CONTAINS A LEASE**

(2 marks)

---

112 Pebworth Co entered into a contract to acquire the right to use an item of plant for a period of three years from 1 April 20X7. The contract meets the definition of a lease under IFRS 16 *Leases*. The present value of the future lease payments on commencement of the lease was $15,462,000, which is also the initial carrying amount of the right-of-use asset. Pebworth Co will also make three rental payments of $6m per annum which are due to be paid in arrears on 31 March each year. The useful life of the plant is equal to the lease term. There is no option to buy the asset at the end of the lease term.

The interest rate implicit in the lease is 8% per annum.

What is the total charge to profit or loss in respect of this lease at 31 March 20X8?

- O $1,236,900
- O $5,154,000
- O $6,000,000
- O $6,390,900

(2 marks)

---

113 At what amount does IFRS 16 *Leases* require a lessee to measure a right-of-use asset acquired under a lease?

- O Lease liability + other direct costs + incentives received
- O Lease liability – other direct costs – amounts paid before or on commencement of the lease
- O Lease liability + other direct costs + amounts paid before or on commencement of the lease – incentives received
- O Lease liability – other direct costs – amounts paid before or on commencement of the lease + incentives received

(2 marks)

114 On 1 October 20X3, Fresco Co acquired the right to use an item of plant under a five-year contract. The contract meets the definition of a lease under IFRS 16 *Leases*. The terms of the contract required an immediate deposit of $2m with five payments of $6m paid annually in arrears commencing on 30 September 20X4. The present value of the future lease payments is $22,745,000 on commencement of the lease. The rate of interest implicit in the lease is 10% per annum.

What is the carrying amount of the lease current liability in Fresco Co's statement of financial position as at 30 September 20X4?

- O $1,901,950
- O $4,098,050
- O $6,000,000
- O $2,274,500 **(2 marks)**

---

115 The objective of IFRS 16 *Leases* is to prescribe the appropriate accounting treatment and required disclosures in relation to leases.

Which **TWO** of the following are among the criteria set out in IFRS 16 for an arrangement to be classified as a lease?

- ☐ The lessee has the right to substantially all of the economic benefits from use of the asset
- ☐ The lease term is for substantially all of the estimated economic life of the asset
- ☐ The agreement concerns an identified asset which cannot be substituted
- ☐ The lessor has the right to direct the use of the asset **(2 marks)**

---

116 Cornet Co has entered into an agreement for the right to use an asset for a period of eight years on 1 July 20X4. The useful life of the asset at that date is ten years. The lease requires annual payments of $750,000 in arrears. The present value of the future lease on commencement of the lease is $4,657,500. The interest rate implicit in the lease is 6%. Additionally, Cornet Co paid directly attributable costs of $37,500 on 1 July 20X4.

Select the total charge to the statement of profit or loss for the year ended 30 June 20X5 in respect of the right-of-use asset using the options in the pull-down list.
(ACCA, Examiners Report Dec 2018 (amended))

[▼]

Pull down list

- $1,029,450
- $279,450
- $586,875
- $866,325

(2 marks)

---

117 A sale and leaseback transaction involves the sale of an asset and the leasing back of the same asset.

If the arrangement meets the IFRS 15 *Revenue from Contracts with Customers* criteria to be recognised as a sale, how should any 'profit' on the sale be treated?

- O Recognise whole amount of profit immediately in profit or loss

- ○ Defer profit and amortise over the lease term
- ○ Recognise proportion relating to right-of-use retained
- ○ Recognise proportion relating to right-of-use transferred **(2 marks)**

---

118 During the year ended 30 September 20X4 Hyper Co entered into the following transactions:

On 1 October 20X3, Hyper Co entered into a contract to obtain the right to use an asset for a five-year period. The contract meets the definition of a lease under IFRS 16 *Leases*. An initial payment of $90,000 was made on commencement of the lease, being the first of five equal annual payments. The present value of the future lease payments on commencement of the lease was $250,000. The right-of-use asset has a five-year useful life. The lease has an implicit interest rate of 16%.

On 1 August 20X4, Hyper Co made a payment of $18,000 for a nine-month lease of an item of excavation equipment. Hyper wishes to utilise the exceptions available under IFRS 16 *Leases*.

What amount in total would be charged to Hyper Co's statement of profit or loss for the year ended 30 September 20X4 in respect of the above transactions? (Enter your answer to the nearest whole $.)

$ [ ] **(2 marks)**

---

119 On 1 January 20X6, Platinum Co sold its head office property, which had a carrying amount of $7,000,000, to a financial institution for a total of $8,000,000, which was its fair value on that date. The transaction constituted a sale in accordance with IFRS 15 *Revenue from Contracts with Customers*. The accountant of Platinum Co recognised the profit of $1,000,000 in other income. Platinum Co immediately entered into an agreement for the right to use the head office for a period of five years. Under the terms of the agreement, Platinum Co must make payments of $600,000 per annum payable annually in arrears. The present value of the future lease payments was $2,162,850 on commencement of the lease and the rate of interest implicit in the lease is 12%.

What will be the adjustment required to account for the gain on sale in profit or loss for the year ended 31 December 20X6? (Enter your answer to the nearest whole $.)

$ [ ] **(2 marks)**

---

120 On 1 April 20X5, Pennyroyal Co sold its property to a financial institution for $20,000,000 which was the fair value of the property at that date. The transaction constitutes a sale in accordance with IFRS 15 *Revenue from Contracts with Customers*. The property had a carrying amount of $18,000,000 and had an estimated remaining useful life of 10 years at the date of sale. Under the terms of the sale, Pennyroyal Co has the right to use the property for a four-year period commencing 1 April 20X5. The present value of the future payments under the lease have been correctly calculated as $7,092,000.

What is the amount of the gain that can be recognised in the statement of profit or loss in respect of this transaction for the year ended 31 March 20X6?

- ○ $709,200
- ○ $1,290,800
- ○ $2,000,000
- ○ $Nil **(2 marks)**

121 Jetsam Co entered into an agreement for the right to use an item of plant for a period of ten years from 1 April 20X0. The agreement required payments of $15,000 to be made annually in arrears. The present value of the future lease payments was estimated to be $100,650 at the inception of the lease and the rate of interest implicit in the lease was 8%. Both the lease term and the plant's estimated useful life was ten years.

Selecting your answer from the options below, what is the total charge to appear in the statement of profit or loss in respect of the lease for the year ended 31 December 20X0? ***(ACCA, Examiners Report Sep 2017, amended)***

[▼]

Pull down list

- $11,250
- $13,588
- $6,039
- $7,549

(2 marks)

(Total = 24 marks)

Provisions and events after the reporting period (36 mins)

122 Candel Co is being sued by a customer for $2m for breach of contract over a cancelled order. Candel Co has obtained legal opinion that there is a 20% chance that Candel Co will lose the case. Accordingly, Candel Co has provided $400,000 ($2m × 20%) in respect of the claim. The unrecoverable legal costs of defending the action are estimated at $100,000. These have not been provided for as the case will not go to court until next year.

What is the amount of the provision that should be made by Candel Co in accordance with IAS 37 *Provisions, Contingent Liabilities and Contingent Assets*?

$ [ ] **(2 marks)**

---

123 During the year Peterlee Co acquired an iron ore mine at a cost of $6m. In addition, when all the ore has been extracted (estimated ten years' time) the company will face estimated costs for landscaping the area affected by the mining that have a present value of $2m. These costs would still have to be incurred even if no further ore was extracted.

How should this $2m future cost be recognised in the financial statements?
(ACCA, Examiners Report June 2019)

- O Provision $2m and $2m capitalised as part of cost of mine
- O Provision $2m and $2m charged to operating costs
- O Accrual $200,000 per annum for next ten years
- O Should not be recognised as no cost has yet arisen **(2 marks)**

---

124 Select whether a provision is required or is not required in the financial statements of the following companies.

Aston Co has a company policy of cleaning up any environmental contamination caused by its operations, even though it is not legally obliged to do so	**PROVISION REQUIRED**	**NO PROVISION REQUIRED**
Brum Co has a fixed price contract to supply widgets to Erdington Co. Brum Co has calculated that it will cost more to manufacture the widgets than budgeted, which is more than the revenue agreed from Erdington Co	**PROVISION REQUIRED**	**NO PROVISION REQUIRED**
Coleshill Co is closing down a division. The board has prepared detailed closure plans which have not yet been communicated to customers and employees	**PROVISION REQUIRED**	**NO PROVISION REQUIRED**
Dudley Co has acquired a machine which requires the staff to be retrained on its safe operation. The staff training will occur in the next financial period	**PROVISION REQUIRED**	**NO PROVISION REQUIRED**

(2 marks)

---

125 On 1 January 20X5, Factman Co acquired a piece of equipment at a cost of $25m. The equipment has a useful life of five years and the company must decommission the equipment at the end of the five-year period. The estimated cost of this decommissioning in five years' time is $10m. Factman Co's cost of capital is 10% per annum. The present value of $1 receivable in five years' time at a discount rate of 10% per annum is $0.621. Factman Co has correctly capitalised the equipment and recognised a provision for decommissioning costs at the correct amount.

Required

What is the total charge to profit or loss relating to the equipment and decommissioning provision which will be required for the year ended 31 December 20X5 (to the nearest $'000) ***(Mar/Jun 2022)***

$ [ ]

(2 marks)

---

126 Identify whether the following statements are true or false in accordance with IAS 37 *Provisions, Contingent Liabilities and Contingent Assets.*

Provisions should be made for both constructive and legal obligations	**TRUE**	**FALSE**
Discounting may be used when estimating the amount of a provision	**TRUE**	**FALSE**
A restructuring provision must include the estimated costs of retraining or relocating continuing staff	**TRUE**	**FALSE**
A restructuring provision may only be made when a company has a detailed plan for the restructuring and has communicated to interested parties a firm intention to carry it out	**TRUE**	**FALSE**

(2 marks)

---

127 Eilish Co had a provision of $100,000 in its financial statements at 31 December 20X4 in relation to an ongoing court case. On 10 February 20X5, Eilish Co settled this case for $120,000.

What is the accounting entry required by Eilish Co on 10 February 20X5 in relation to this provision?

- O Debit Provision $100,000, Debit Profit or loss $20,000; Credit Cash $120,000
- O Debit Cash $120,000; Credit Provision $100,000, Credit Profit or loss $20,000
- O Debit Expense $120,000; Credit Provision $120,000
- O Debit Provision $120,000: Credit Expense $120,000 **(2 marks)**

---

128 On 1 October 20X3, Xplorer Co commenced drilling for oil from an undersea oilfield. The extraction of oil causes damage to the seabed which has a restorative cost (ignore discounting) of $10,000 per million barrels of oil extracted. Xplorer Co extracted 250 million barrels in the year ended 30 September 20X4.

Xplorer Co is also required to dismantle the drilling equipment at the end of its five-year licence. This has an estimated cost of $30m on 30 September 20X8. Xplorer Co's cost of capital is 8% per annum and $1 has a present value of 68 cents in five years' time.

What is the total provision (extraction plus dismantling) which Xplorer Co would report in its statement of financial position as at 30 September 20X4 in respect of its oil operations? (Enter your answer to the nearest whole $.)

$ [ ] **(2 marks)**

---

129 Hopewell Co sells a line of goods for which it provides a six-month warranty at no additional cost to the customer. The warranty guarantees the goods perform as expected and any defect arising during that period is repaired free of charge. Hopewell Co has calculated that if all the goods sold in the last six months of the year required repairs the cost would be $2m. If all of these goods had more serious faults and had to be replaced the cost would be $6m.

The normal pattern is that 80% of goods sold will be fault-free, 15% will require repairs and 5% will have to be replaced.

Using the pull-down list options, select what is the amount of the provision required.

[▼]

Pull down list

- $0.6 million
- $0.8 million
- $1.6 million
- $2 million

(2 marks)

---

130 Which **TWO** of the following events which occur after the reporting date of a company but before the financial statements are authorised for issue are classified as **ADJUSTING** events in accordance with IAS 10 *Events After the Reporting Period*?

- ☐ A change in tax rate announced after the reporting date, but affecting the current tax liability
- ☐ The discovery of a fraud which had occurred during the year
- ☐ The determination of the sale proceeds of an item of plant sold before the year end
- ☐ The destruction of a factory by fire **(2 marks)**

131 Coleridge Co is a manufacturing company.

The financial accountant of Coleridge Co is considering whether any of the events, which took place in April 20X5, require adjustment in the financial statements for the year ended 31 March 20X5

Which **TWO** of the following events require adjusting in the financial statements for the year ended 31 March 20X5, as required by IAS 10 *Events After the Reporting Period*?

☐ Thomas Co, a customer of Coleridge Co, which owes the company $200,000 at 31 March 20X5, entered insolvency on 3 April 20X5

☐ An employee has commenced legal proceedings against Coleridge Co following an industrial accident on 10 April 20X5. The company is expected to lose the case and estimates that damages of $350,000 will be paid to the employee

☐ Inventory that was held at cost of $200,000 on 31 March 20X5 was sold on 21 April 20X5 for $150,000

☐ The company had agreed the sale of the Wordsworth division at a board meeting on 25 March 20X5. The public announcement was made on 1 April 20X5 **(2 marks)**

(Total = 20 marks)

Inventories and agriculture (32 mins)

132 Caminas Co has the following products in inventory at the year end.

Product	*Quantity*	*Cost*	*Selling price*	*Selling cost*
A	1,000	$40	$55	$8
B	2,500	$15	$25	$4
C	800	$23	$27	$5

At what amount should total inventory be stated in the statement of financial position? Select your answers from the pull-down list provided.

[▼]

Pull down list

- $103,100
- $105,100
- $95,100
- $95,900

(2 marks)

---

133 At 31 December 20X4, Litch Co had, in inventory, 100 items of work in progress which had cost $14,900 to produce. It estimated that the work in progress would cost $13 per unit to complete, and that each unit would then sell for $166.

Direct selling costs are estimated at 2% of revenue.

In accordance with IAS 2 *Inventories*, what is the correct value of Litch Co's inventory as at 31 December 20X4? ***(ACCA Examiner's Report September/December 2020)***

O $14,900

O $16,268

O $16,200

O $14,968 **(2 marks)**

---

134 At what amount is a biological asset measured on initial recognition in accordance with IAS 41 *Agriculture*?

O Production cost

O Fair value

O Cost less estimated costs to sell

O Fair value less estimated costs to sell **(2 marks)**

---

135 Which of the following is **NOT** the outcome of a biological transformation according to IAS 41 *Agriculture*?

O Growth

O Harvest

O Procreation

O Degeneration **(2 marks)**

---

136 How is a gain or loss arising on a biological asset recognised in accordance with IAS 41 *Agriculture*?

O Included in profit or loss for the year

O Adjusted in retained earnings

O Shown under 'other comprehensive income'

O Deferred and recognised over the life of the biological asset **(2 marks)**

---

137 Identify whether the following statements about IAS 2 *Inventories* are correct or incorrect:

Production overheads should be included in cost on the basis of a company's actual level of activity in the period	CORRECT	INCORRECT
In arriving at the net realisable value of inventories, settlement discounts must be deducted from the expected selling price	CORRECT	INCORRECT
In arriving at the cost of inventories, FIFO, LIFO and weighted average cost formulas are acceptable	CORRECT	INCORRECT
It is permitted to value finished goods inventories at materials plus labour cost only, without adding production overheads	CORRECT	INCORRECT

(2 marks)

---

138 Bouani Co manufactures cycling equipment. It has a number of specialised frames in inventory which cost $20,000 to manufacture. These frames were manufactured following an order from a customer at an agreed selling price of $30,000. Due to recent technological advances, the current cost of manufacturing such frames is estimated to be $15,000.

Bouani Co also has inventory of 3,000 pedals at a cost of $20 each. These have become damaged. If the company spends $5,000 to repair all of them, these could be sold for $21 each.

Required

Which **TWO** of the following statements regarding Bouani Co's inventory are true? ***(Sep/Dec 2021)***

- ☐ The frames should be valued at $15,000
- ☐ The frames should be valued at $20,000
- ☐ The frames should be valued at $30,000
- ☐ The pedals should be valued at $60,000
- ☐ The pedals should be valued at $58,000
- ☐ The pedals should be valued at $65,000 **(2 marks)**

---

139 In preparing financial statements for the year ended 31 March 20X6, the inventory count was carried out on 4 April 20X6. The value of inventory counted was $36 million. Between 31 March and 4 April goods with a cost of $2.7 million were received into inventory and sales of $7.8 million were made at a mark-up on cost of 30%.

Using the pull-down list provided, select at what amount inventory should be stated in the statement of financial position as at 31 March 20X6?

[▼]

Pull down list

- $33.3 million
- $36.0 million
- $39.3 million
- $41.1 million

(2 marks)

---

140 At 31 March 20X7 Tentacle Co had 12,000 units of product W32 in inventory, included at cost of $6 per unit. During April and May 20X7 units of W32 were being sold at a price of $5.40 each, with sales staff receiving a 15% commission on the sales price of the product. The financial statements of Tentacle Co were approved by the Board on 14 July 20X7.

At what amount should inventory of product W32 be recognised in the financial statements of Tentacle Co as at 31 March 20X7? (Enter your answer to the nearest whole $.)

$ [ ] **(2 marks)**

(Total = 18 marks)

Accounting for taxation **(29 mins)**

141 Ullington Co's trial balance shows a debit balance of $2.1 million brought forward on current tax and a credit balance of $5.4 million brought forward on deferred tax. The tax charge for the current year is estimated at $16.2 million. The carrying amounts of net assets are $13 million in excess of their tax base, which includes a $3 million revaluation surplus on the first-time revaluation of buildings. The income tax and deferred tax rate is 30%.

What is the amount of income tax recognised in the statement of profit or loss of Ullington Co for the year?

O $15.6 million

- O $15.9 million
- O $16.8 million
- O $18.3 million **(2 marks)**

---

142 Jasper Orange Co's trial balance at 31 December 20X3 shows a debit balance of $700,000 on current tax and a credit balance of $8,400,000 on deferred tax. The directors have estimated the provision for income tax for the year at $4.5 million and the required deferred tax provision is $5.6 million, $1.2 million of which relates to a property revaluation.

What is the amount of income tax amount recognised in Jasper Orange Co's statement of profit or loss for the year ended 31 December 20X3?

- O $1 million
- O $2.4 million
- O $1.2 million
- O $3.6 million **(2 marks)**

---

143 The following information relates to an entity:

(1) At 1 January 20X8 the carrying amount of non-current assets exceeded their tax written down value by $850,000.

(2) For the year to 31 December 20X8 the entity claimed depreciation for tax purposes of $500,000 and charged depreciation of $450,000 in the financial statements.

(3) During the year ended 31 December 20X8 the entity revalued a property. The revaluation surplus was $250,000. There are no current plans to sell the property.

(4) The tax rate was 30% throughout the year.

What is the provision for deferred tax required by IAS 12 *Income Taxes* at 31 December 20X8?

- O $240,000
- O $270,000
- O $315,000
- O $345,000 **(2 marks)**

---

144 The statements of financial position of Nedburg Co include the following extracts:

Statements of financial position as at 30 September

	20X2	*20X1*
	$m	$m
Non-current liabilities		
Deferred tax	310	140
Current liabilities		
Taxation	130	160

The tax charge in the statement of profit or loss for the year ended 30 September 20X2 is $270 million.

What amount of tax was paid during the year to 30 September 20X2?

$ ____________ **(2 marks)**

145 The trial balance of Highwood Co at 31 March 20X6 showed credit balances of $800,000 on current tax and $2.6 million on deferred tax. A property was revalued during the year giving rise to deferred tax of $3.75 million. This has been included in the deferred tax provision of $6.75 million at 31 March 20X6.

The income tax liability for the year ended 31 March 20X6 is estimated at $19.4 million.

What is the amount of the income tax charge in the statement of profit or loss of Highwood at 31 March 20X6?

$ [ ] **(2 marks)**

---

146 Astral Co purchased an item of plant for $40,000 on 1 September 20X1. The plant has an estimated useful life of five years and an estimated residual value of $5,000. The plant is depreciated on a straight-line basis. Local tax law does not allow depreciation as an expense, but a tax allowance of 60% of the cost of the asset can be claimed in the year of purchase and 20% per annum on a reducing balance basis in the following years. The rate of income tax is 30%.

What charge or credit for deferred taxation should be recorded in Astral Co's statement of profit or loss for the year to 31 August 20X2? ***(ACCA, Examiners Report June 2018)***

- O $17,000 charge
- O $5,100 charge
- O $5,100 credit
- O $17,000 credit

(2 marks)

---

147 Isaac & Joseph Co purchased new machinery on 1 January 20X5 for $1,000,000. It has a residual value of $200,000, with the useful life deemed to be 8 years. The plant is depreciated on a straight-line basis.

Tax allowances of 50% of the cost of the asset can be claimed in the year of purchase, as depreciation is not allowed for tax purposes. The rate of income tax is 30%.

Identify by selecting the options provided below, whether a deferred tax asset or liability should be recognised at 31 December 20X5 and at what amount?

Deferred tax asset or liability	Amount
(1) ▼	(2) ▼

Pull down list 1

- Asset
- Liability

Pull down list 2

- $120,000
- $60,000
- $82,500

(2 marks)

---

148 The information below relates to the financial statements of Sheen Co as at 30 September 20X7:

	$
Carrying amount	
Plant (cost less depreciation)	110,000
Land (original cost $200,000)	280,000
Tax base	
Plant	90,000
Land	200,000
Tax rate	20%
Deferred tax liability	20,000
Revaluation surplus	64,000

Please identify whether the amount of the deferred tax liability and the Revaluation surplus are correct or incorrect. ***(Sep/Dec 2021)***

The amount of the deferred tax liability is	**CORRECT**	**INCORRECT**
The revaluation surplus is	**CORRECT**	**INCORRECT**

(2 marks)

(Total = 16 marks)

Section B

Derringdo Co case **(18 mins)**

Information relevant to questions 149–153

Derringdo Co is a broadband provider which receives government assistance to provide broadband to remote areas. Derringdo Co invested in a new server at a cost of $800,000 on 1 October 20X2. The server has an estimated useful life of ten years with a residual value equal to 15% of its cost. Derringdo Co uses straight-line depreciation on a time apportioned basis.

The company received a government grant of 30% of its cost price of the server at the time of purchase. The terms of the grant are that if the company retains the asset for four years or more, then no repayment liability will be incurred. Derringdo Co has no intention of disposing of the server within the first four years. Derringdo Co's accounting policy for capital-based government grants is to treat them as deferred income and release them to income over the life of the asset to which they relate.

149 What is the net amount that will be charged to operating expenses in respect of the server for the year ended 31 March 20X3?

- O $10,000
- O $28,000
- O $22,000
- O $34,000

(2 marks)

---

150 What amount will be presented under non-current liabilities at 31 March 20X3 in respect of the grant?

- O $228,000
- O $216,000
- O $240,000
- O $204,000

(2 marks)

---

151 Derringdo Co sells a package which gives customers a free laptop when they sign a two-year contract for the provision of broadband services. The laptop has a stand-alone price of $200 and the broadband contract is for $30 per month.

In accordance with IFRS 15 *Revenue from Contracts with Customers*, what amount will be recognised as revenue on each package in the first year?

Select the correct answer from the options below.

[▼]

Pull down list

- $158
- $281
- $439
- $461

(2 marks)

---

152 Determining the amount to be recognised in the first year is an example of which stage in the process of applying IFRS 15 *Revenue from Contracts with Customers*?

O Determining the transaction price
O Recognising revenue when a performance obligation is satisfied
O Identifying the separate performance obligations
O Allocating the transaction price to the performance obligations **(2 marks)**

---

153 Derringdo Co is carrying out a transaction on behalf of another entity and the finance director is unsure whether Derringdo Co should be regarded as an agent or a principal in respect of this transaction.

Which of the following would indicate that Derringdo Co is acting as an agent?

O Derringdo Co is primarily responsible for fulfilling the contract
O Derringdo Co is not exposed to credit risk for the amount due from the customer
O Derringdo Co is responsible for negotiating the price for the contract
O Derringdo Co will not be paid in the form of commission **(2 marks)**

(Total = 10 marks)

Campbell Co case (ACCA Examiner's Report Sep/Dec 2020) (18 mins)

Information relevant to questions 154–158.

The following details relate to three of Campbell Co's contracts:

Contract 1 has a total price of $9 million and commenced in 20X7. Total costs are expected to be $7 million. The progress towards completion is assessed at 90% at 31 December 20X8. Progress was measured at 20% for the year ended 31 December 20X7.

Contract 2 commenced in December 20X8 and is expected to generate a profit of $3 million. It is too early in the contract to assess progress towards completion. Campbell Co has spent $0.2 million so far, all of which is expected to be recoverable from the customer when Campbell Co sends its first invoice in 20X9.

Contract 3 relates to the sale of equipment to a customer for $2.36 million on 1 July 20X8. The sale included $0.4 million for installation of the equipment and $0.2 million relating to 12 months after-sales support. The equipment was installed on 1 July 20X8.

154 Identify whether the following statements are correct or incorrect in respect of how revenue should be recognised in accordance with IFRS 15 *Revenue from Contracts with Customers*?

Revenue should be recognised as an entity satisfies a performance obligation	CORRECT	INCORRECT
Progress towards completion on a contract should be measured solely on an input basis	CORRECT	INCORRECT

(2 marks)

---

155 What amount of revenue should be recognised in respect of Contract 1 in Campbell Co's statement of profit or loss for the year ended 31 December 20X8? (Enter your answer to the nearest whole $.)

$ [ ] **(2 marks)**

156 Which of the following items would **NOT** be recorded in the financial statements for 20X8 of Campbell Co in respect of Contract 2?

- O Revenue $0.2m
- O Cost of sales $0.2m
- O Contract asset $0.2m
- O Contract liability $0.2m **(2 marks)**

---

157 What amount of revenue should be recognised in respect of Contract 3 in Campbell Co's statement of profit or loss for the year ended 31 December 20X8?

- O $2.06m
- O $2.16m
- O $2.26m
- O $2.36m **(2 marks)**

---

158 Campbell Co offers its customers an accessory for the equipment that it sells in Contract 3. Campbell Co does not manufacture the accessory itself, but has an agreement with the manufacturer to sell the accessory on the manufacturer's behalf.

Campbell Co places the order with the manufacturer and the manufacturer delivers the accessory direct to the customer. The customer pays Campbell Co for the accessory and Campbell Co then deducts 3% commission before paying the manufacturer.

An accessory is delivered to one of Campbell Co's customers on 10 December 20X8, which the customer has accepted and will pay $50,000.

Which of the following correctly describes how Campbell Co should recognise this transaction?

- O $50,000 should be recognised as revenue by Campbell Co when the accessory has been delivered and accepted by the customer
- O $1,500 should be recognised as revenue by Campbell Co when the accessory has been paid for by the customer
- O $1,500 should be recognised as revenue by Campbell Co when the accessory has been delivered and accepted by the customer
- O $50,000 should be recognised as revenue by Campbell Co when the accessory has been paid for by the customer **(2 marks)**

(Total = 10 marks)

Apex Co case (18 mins)

The following scenario relates to questions 159–163.

Apex Co is a publicly listed supermarket chain. During the current year it started the building of a new store. The directors are aware that in accordance with IAS 23 *Borrowing Costs* certain borrowing costs have to be capitalised.

Details relating to construction of Apex Co's new store:

Apex Co issued a $10 million unsecured loan with a coupon (nominal) interest rate of 6% on 1 April 20X8. The loan is redeemable at a premium which means the loan has an effective finance cost of 7.5% per annum. The loan was specifically issued to finance the building of the new store which meets the definition of a qualifying asset in IAS 23. Construction of the store commenced on 1 May 20X8 and it was completed and ready for use on 28 February 20X9, but did not open for trading until 1 April 20X9.

159 Apex Co's new store meets the definition of a qualifying asset under IAS 23.

Which of the following is the correct description of a qualifying asset under IAS 23?

- O An asset that is ready for use or sale when purchased
- O An asset that takes a substantial period of time to get ready for its intended use or sale
- O An asset that is intended for use rather than sale
- O An asset that has been financed using a specific loan **(2 marks)**

---

160 Apex Co issued the loan stock on 1 April 20X8. Three events or transactions must be taking place for capitalisation of borrowing costs to commence in accordance with IAS 23. Which of the following is **NOT** one of these?

- O Expenditure on the asset is being incurred
- O Borrowing costs are being incurred
- O Physical construction of the asset is nearing completion
- O Necessary activities are in progress to prepare the asset for use or sale **(2 marks)**

---

161 What is the total of the finance costs which can be capitalised in respect of Apex Co's new store? (Enter your answer to the nearest whole $.)

$ [ ] **(2 marks)**

---

162 Rather than take out a loan specifically for the new store Apex Co could have funded the store from existing borrowings which are:

(1) 10% bank loan $50 million

(2) 8% bank loan $30 million

In this case it would have applied a 'capitalisation rate' to the expenditure on the asset. What would that rate have been?

- O 10%
- O 8.75%
- O 9%
- O 9.25% **(2 marks)**

---

163 If Apex Co had been able to temporarily invest the proceeds of the loan from 1 April to 1 May when construction began, how would the proceeds be accounted for?

- O Deducted from finance costs
- O Deducted from the cost of the asset
- O Recognised as investment income in the statement of profit or loss
- O Deducted from administrative expenses in the statement of profit or loss **(2 marks)**

(Total = 10 marks)

Bertrand Co case (18 mins)

Information relevant to questions 164–168

Bertrand Co issued $10 million convertible loan notes on 1 October 20X0 that carry a nominal interest (coupon) rate of 5% per annum. They are redeemable on 30 September 20X3 at par for cash or can be exchanged for equity shares in Bertrand Co on the basis of 20 shares for each $100 of loan. A similar loan note, without the conversion option, would have required Bertrand Co to pay an interest rate of 8%.

The present value of $1 receivable at the end of each year, based on discount rates of 5% and 8%, can be taken as:

		5%	8%
End of year	1	0.95	0.93
	2	0.91	0.86
	3	0.86	0.79
	cumulative	2.72	2.58

164 How should the convertible loan notes be accounted for?

- O As debt
- O As debt and equity
- O As equity
- O As debt until conversion, then as equity **(2 marks)**

---

165 What is the amount that will be recognised as finance costs for the year ended 30 September 20X1? (Enter your answer to the nearest whole $.)

$ [ ] **(2 marks)**

---

166 What is the amount that should be shown under liabilities at 30 September 20X1?

- O $9,425,000
- O $9,925,000
- O $9,690,000
- O Nil **(2 marks)**

---

167 If Bertrand Co had incurred transaction costs in issuing these loan notes, how would these have been accounted for?

- O Added to the proceeds of the loan notes
- O Deducted from the proceeds of the loan notes
- O Amortised over the life of the loan notes
- O Charged to finance costs **(2 marks)**

---

168 Bertrand Co also purchased a debt instrument which will mature in five years' time. Bertrand Co intends to hold the debt instrument to maturity to collect interest payments.

Complete the following statement using the options below.

This debt instrument will be measured as a financial [(1) ▼] at [(2) ▼] in the financial statements of Bertrand Co.

Pull down list 1

- Asset
- Liability

Pull down list 2

- Amortised cost
- Fair value
- Fair value through profit or loss

(2 marks)

(Total = 10 marks)

Fino Co case **(18 mins)**

Information relevant to questions 169–173

On 1 April 20X7, Fino Co entered into an agreement to gain the right to use plant for a period of three years. The agreement meets the definition of a lease in accordance with IFRS 16 *Leases*.

An initial payment of $100,000 was made on 1 April 20X7 and the present value of the future lease payments at that date is $173,500. Payments in respect of the lease are made in advance and are $100,000 per annum, commencing on 1 April 20X8. The rate of interest implicit in the lease is 10%. The lease does not transfer ownership of the plant to Fino Co by the end of the lease term and there is no purchase option available. Fino Co incurred initial direct costs of $20,000 to set up the lease and received lease incentives from the manufacturer totalling $7,000.

169 Over what period should Fino Co depreciate a right-of-use asset, according to IFRS 16 *Leases*?

O From the commencement of the lease to the end of the lease term

O From the commencement of the lease to the end of the useful life of the plant

O From the commencement of the lease to the longer of the end of the lease term and the end of the useful life of the plant

O From the commencement of the lease to the shorter of the end of the lease term and the end of the useful life of the plant **(2 marks)**

---

170 What is the initial cost of the right-of-use asset as at 1 April 20X7?

O $293,500

O $186,500

O $313,000

O $286,500 **(2 marks)**

---

171 The operations director has questioned why the lease payments cannot be simply charged to profit or loss.

In which **TWO** of the following situations would charging lease payments to profit or loss be the correct accounting treatment, assuming Fino Co takes advantage of any optional recognition exemptions available under IFRS 16 *Leases*? Select your answers from the drag and drop options provided.

Situations		Correct accounting treatment
Ownership is transferred at the end of the lease term		Option 1
The lease is for less than 12 months		Option 2
The leased asset has a low underlying value		
The leased asset has been specially adapted for the use of the lessee		

(2 marks)

---

172 Selecting your answer from the options provided, what is the carrying amount of the lease liability at 31 March 20X8?

[▼]

Pull down list

- $173,500
- $190,850
- $200,000
- $90,850

(2 marks)

---

173 On 1 October 20X7, Fino Co entered into a different lease agreement on another piece of equipment. The lease runs for ten months and payments of $1,000 per month are payable in arrears. As an incentive to enter into the lease, Fino received the first month rent free. Fino wishes to take advantage of the optional recognition exemptions under IFRS 16.

What amount should be recognised as payments under short-term leases in the year ended 31 March 20X8?

- O $5,000
- O $6,000
- O $4,500
- O $5,400

(2 marks)

(Total = 10 marks)

Julian Co case **(18 mins)**

Information relevant to questions 174–178

The carrying amount of Julian Co's property, plant and equipment at 31 December 20X3 was $310,000 and the tax written down value was $230,000.

The following data relates to the year ended 31 December 20X4:

(1) At the end of the year the carrying amount of property, plant and equipment was $460,000 and the tax written down value was $270,000. During the year some items were revalued upwards by $90,000. No items had previously required revaluation. In the tax jurisdiction in which Julian Co operates revaluations of assets do not affect the tax base of an asset or taxable profit. Gains due to revaluations are taxable on sale.

(2) Julian Co began development of a new product during the year and capitalised $60,000 in accordance with IAS 38 *Intangible Assets*. The expenditure was deducted for tax purposes as it was incurred. None of the expenditure had been amortised by the year end.

The corporate income tax rate is 30%. The current tax charge was calculated for the year as $45,000.

174 Julian Co's accountant is confused by the term 'tax base'. What is meant by 'tax base'?

- O The amount of tax payable in a future period
- O The tax regime under which an entity is assessed for tax
- O The amount attributed to an asset or liability for tax purposes
- O The amount of tax deductible in a future period

(2 marks)

---

175 Using the drag and drop options below, show the taxable temporary difference to be accounted for at 31 December 20X4 in relation to property, plant and equipment and development expenditure.

Nil

$60,000

$190,000

$270,000

	Property, plant and equipment
	Development expenditure

(2 marks)

---

176 What is the carrying amount of the revaluation surplus at 31 December 20X4?

- O $63,000
- O $90,000
- O $30,000
- O $27,000

(2 marks)

---

177 Selecting your answer from the options below, what amount will be shown as tax payable in the statement of financial position of Julian Co at 31 December 20X4?

[▼]

Pull down list

- $45,000
- $63,000
- $72,000
- $75,000

(2 marks)

---

178 Deferred tax assets and liabilities arise from taxable and deductible temporary differences.

Which of the following is **NOT** a circumstance giving rise to a temporary difference?

- O Depreciation accelerated for tax purposes
- O Development costs amortised in profit or loss but tax was deductible in full when incurred
- O Accrued expenses which have already been deducted for tax purposes
- O Revenue included in accounting profit when invoiced but only liable for tax when the cash is received **(2 marks)**

(Total = 10 marks)

Rainbird Co (18 mins)

Information relevant to question 179–183

Rainbird Co decided to reorganise a manufacturing facility during November 20X1 and commissioned a consulting engineer to carry out a feasibility study. A provision for the reorganisation was created at 31 December 20X1.

Staff functions will change following the reorganisation, so in December 20X1 Rainbird Co contracted with a training company to provide retraining to take place in January 20X2. A provision for this expenditure was created at 31 December 20X1.

Rainbird Co hopes that reorganising its manufacturing facility will improve quality control. It gives a one-year warranty with all products and the rate of returns under warranty is 12%. 5% of the returned items can be repaired at a cost of $5 (free of charge to the customer). The other 95% are scrapped and a full refund of $30 is given. Rainbird Co sold 525,000 units during the year to 31 December 20X1.

In five years' time Rainbird Co will have to dismantle its factory and return the site to the local authority. A provision was set up for the present value of the dismantling costs when the factory was first acquired. The opening balance on the provision at 1 January 20X1 was $2.63 million. Rainbird Co has a cost of capital of 8%.

179 Rainbird Co's accountant is preparing the financial statements for the year to 31 December 20X1 and is not too sure about the provisions set up for the reorganisation of the facility and the staff training.

Required

Which of these is a correct provision under IAS 37 *Provisions, Contingent Liabilities and Contingent Assets*?

- O The reorganisation
- O The staff training
- O The reorganisation and the staff training

O Neither the reorganisation nor the staff training **(2 marks)**

---

180 Rainbird Co's finance director is checking some of the financial estimates involved. In accordance with IAS 37, if the reporting entity is presently obliged to transfer economic benefit to another party, the occurrence is probable but the amount cannot be measured with sufficient reliability.

Required

Using the pull-down list below, select the correct option stating what this should give rise to in the financial statements.

[▼]

Pull down list

- A contingent asset
- A contingent liability
- A long-term liability
- A provision

(2 marks)

---

181 What is the amount of the provision that should be created at 31 December 20X1 for returns under warranty?

O $1,890,000

O $1,811,250

O $1,795,500

O $1,575,000 **(2 marks)**

---

182 What is the amount of the provision that should be carried forward at 31 December 20X1 for the dismantling of the factory?

O $2,630,000

O $2,419,600

O $2,435,185

O $2,840,400 **(2 marks)**

---

183 During January 20X2, before the financial statements of Rainbird Co for the year ended 31 December 20X1 had been finalised, a number of events took place.

Identify whether each of these events would require an adjustment to the financial statements as at 31 December 20X1 in accordance with IAS 10 *Events After the Reporting Period.*

Rainbird Co's board announced a plan to discontinue one of its operations and dispose of the plant. The loss on disposal is estimated at $2 million.	**REQUIRES ADJUSTMENT**	**DOES NOT REQUIRE ADJUSTMENT**
The employees of the operation to be discontinued commenced a case against Rainbird Co for constructive dismissal. The total cost could be $3 million.	**REQUIRES ADJUSTMENT**	**DOES NOT REQUIRE ADJUSTMENT**

A legal case for which Rainbird Co had provided \$1.7 million at 31 December 20X1 to cover possible damages was unexpectedly settled in its favour.	**REQUIRES ADJUSTMENT**	**DOES NOT REQUIRE ADJUSTMENT**
One of Rainbird Co's warehouses was destroyed by fire and half of the inventory on hand at 31 December 20X1, valued at \$2.5 million, was destroyed.	**REQUIRES ADJUSTMENT**	**DOES NOT REQUIRE ADJUSTMENT**

(2 marks)

(Total = 10 marks)

QUESTIONS

PART B: ACCOUNTING FOR TRANSACTIONS IN FINANCIAL STATEMENTS (III)

The final section of Part B covers reporting financial performance including the calculation of earnings per share. Reporting financial performance tests your knowledge on changing accounting policies or estimates in the financial statements, discontinued operations and held for sale assets and the accounting treatment for foreign exchange movements. You should note that discontinued operations is linked to the disposal of subsidiaries covered in Chapter 10 and you should be prepared to answer a question which combines these areas.

Section A questions

Questions 184–197: Reporting financial performance (Chapter 18)

Questions 198–205: Earnings per share (Chapter 19)

Section B questions on these areas are covered in questions 206–215

Section A

Reporting financial performance (50 mins)

184 Which of the following would be treated as a change of accounting policy under IAS 8 *Accounting Policies, Changes in Accounting Estimates and Errors*?

- O A change in valuation of inventory from a weighted average to a first-in-first-out (FIFO) basis
- O A change of depreciation method from straight line to reducing balance
- O Adoption of the revaluation model for non-current assets previously held at cost
- O Capitalisation of borrowing costs which have arisen for the first time **(2 marks)**

---

185 For an asset to be classified as 'held for sale' under IFRS 5 *Non-current Assets Held for Sale and Discontinued Operations* its sale must be 'highly probable'. Which of the following is **NOT** a requirement if the sale is to be regarded as highly probable?

- O Management must be committed to a plan to sell the asset
- O A buyer must have been located for the asset
- O The asset must be marketed at a reasonable price
- O The sale should be expected to take place within one year from the date of classification **(2 marks)**

---

186 Complete the statement using the options provided.

An asset classified as 'held for sale' should be measured at the lower of [▼] and [▼].

Pull down list

- Carrying amount
- Carrying amount less costs to sell
- Fair value less costs to sell
- Value in use

(2 marks)

187 Which of the following would be a change in accounting policy in accordance with IAS 8 *Accounting Policies, Changes in Accounting Estimates and Errors*?

- O Adjusting the financial statements of a subsidiary prior to consolidation as its accounting policies differ from those of its parent
- O A change in reporting depreciation charges as cost of sales rather than as administrative expenses
- O Depreciation charged on reducing balance method rather than straight line
- O Reducing the value of inventory from cost to net realisable value due to a valid adjusting event after the reporting period **(2 marks)**

---

188 Which of the following items is a change of accounting policy under IAS 8 *Accounting Policies, Changes in Accounting Estimates and Errors*?

- O Classifying commission earned as revenue in the statement of profit or loss, having previously classified it as other operating income
- O Switching to acquiring the right to use assets under leases when the previous policy was to purchase plant for cash
- O Changing the value of a subsidiary's inventory in line with the group policy for inventory valuation when preparing the consolidated financial statements
- O Revising the remaining useful life of a depreciable asset **(2 marks)**

---

189 As at 30 September 20X3 Dune Co's property in its statement of financial position was:

Property at cost (useful life 15 years)	$45 million
Accumulated depreciation	$6 million

On 1 April 20X4, Dune Co decided to sell the property. The property is being marketed by a property agent at a price of $42 million, which was considered a reasonably achievable price at that date. The expected costs to sell have been agreed at $1 million. Recent market transactions suggest that actual selling prices achieved for this type of property in the current market conditions are 10% less than the price at which they are marketed.

At 30 September 20X4 the property has not been sold.

At what amount should the property be reported in Dune Co's statement of financial position as at 30 September 20X4?

- O $41 million
- O $37.8 million
- O $36.8 million
- O $42 million **(2 marks)**

---

190 Steeplechase Co sold a machine to a Greek company which it agreed to invoice in €. The sale was made on 1 October 20X6 for €250,000. €125,000 was received on 1 November 20X6 and the balance is due on 1 January 20X7.

The exchange rate moved as follows:

1 October 20X6 – €0.91 to $1

1 November 20X6 – €0.95 to $1

31 December 20X6 – €0.85 to $1

At what amount will the receivable be shown in the financial statements at 31 December 20X6? (Enter your answer to the nearest whole $.)

$ ☐ **(2 marks)**

---

191 IAS 21 *The Effects of Changes in Foreign Exchange Rates* sets out how entities that carry out transactions in a foreign currency should measure the results of these transactions at the year end.

Using the pull-down list options provided, select which exchange rate should non-monetary items carried at historical cost be measured?

[▼]

Pull down list

- Average rate
- Closing rate
- Rate at beginning of the year
- Rate at date of transaction

(2 marks)

---

192 Miston Co buys goods priced at €50,000 from a Dutch company on 1 November 20X8. The invoice is due for settlement in two equal instalments on 1 December 20X8 and 1 January 20X9.

The exchange rate moved as follows:

1 November 20X8 – €1.63 to $1

1 December 20X8 – €1.61 to $1

31 December 20X8 – €1.64 to $1

What will be the net exchange gain or loss to be reported in the financial statements of Miston Co at 31 December 20X8? (Enter your answer to the nearest whole $.)

$ ☐ **(2 marks)**

---

193 Coppola Co has a factory with a carrying amount of $1.8 million as at 30 November 20X6. Management have agreed the sale of the factory to Francis Co, which is due to complete on 14 January 20X7. The sales contract was agreed and the decision to sell the factory announced on 1 December 20X6. Relevant information relating to the factory, which is correct both at 1 December 20X6 and 31 December 20X6 is as follows:

Fair value: $2.4 million

Value in use: $2.2 million

Costs to sell: $0.3 million

Depreciation for the factory in December 20X6 is calculated to be $0.2 million.

What is the carrying amount of the factory for inclusion in the financial statements of Coppola Co as at 31 December 20X6?

- O $1.6 million
- O $1.8 million
- O $1.9 million
- O $2.1 million

(2 marks)

194 According to IAS 8 *Accounting Policies, Changes in Accounting Estimates and Errors*, which is the correct accounting treatment to be adopted by a company reporting under IFRS Accounting Standards?

- O Changes in accounting estimates and errors should both be accounted for retrospectively
- O Changes in accounting estimates and errors should both be accounted for prospectively
- O Changes in accounting estimates should be accounted for retrospectively and errors accounted for prospectively
- O Changes in accounting estimates should be accounted for prospectively and errors accounted for retrospectively **(2 marks)**

---

195 During 20X7, Greetex Co discovered that $2.1 million of inventory recognised in the financial statements at 31 December 20X6 had in fact been sold before the year end. The following extracts from the financial statements for 20X6 (as reported) and 20X7 (draft) are available.

	20X6	20X7 (draft)
	$'000	$'000
Revenue	80,000	75,000
Cost of sales	(64,600)	(62,000)
Gross profit	15,400	13,000

The cost of sales for 20X7 includes the $2.1 million error in opening inventory.

What would be the revised cost of sales figures for Greetex Co as at 31 December 20X6 and 20X7?

Using the options below, click and drag the correct response for the cost of sales figures to be included in the financial statements as at 31 December 20X7.

	31 Dec 20X6	31 Dec 20X7
	$	$
Cost of sales	(1) ▼	(2) ▼

Pull down list 1

- 62,500
- 64,600
- 66,700

Pull down list 2

- 59,900
- 62,000
- 64,100

(2 marks)

---

196 Identify whether each of the following operations would be classified as a continuing or as a discontinued operation in accordance with IFRS 5 *Non-current Assets Held for Sale and Discontinued Operations*.

	Continuing	Discontinued
The operation is a subsidiary that was acquired exclusively with a view to resale	O	O
The operation meets the criteria to be held for sale but the sale has not been completed	O	O
The operation sold is a minor part of the business	O	O
The operation is loss making and the directors are currently considering whether to withdraw from the operation in the future	O	O

(2 marks)

---

197 Maitlis Co prepares its financial statements to 31 October each year. On 1 February 20X5, Maitlis Co met the criteria to classify its bakery division, a major line of business, as held for sale. It recognised a loss of $45,000 on that classification. Maitlis Co completed the disposal of the bakery division on 31 October 20X5. The carrying amount of the net assets of the bakery were $612,000 on the date of sale and Maitlis Co received proceeds of $700,000 on completion of the sale. The bakery made a loss of $34,000 in the period to 31 October 20X5. You can ignore the effects of taxation.

Required

What is the total amount of profit or loss on discontinued operations that should be presented on the face of the statement of profit or loss and other comprehensive income?

	$43,000	**Loss**
O	$9,000	Profit
O	$34,000	Loss
O	$88,000	Profit

(2 marks)

(Total = 28 marks)

Earnings per share **(29 mins)**

198 Barwell Co had 10 million ordinary shares in issue throughout the year ended 30 June 20X3. On 1 July 20X2, it had issued $2 million of 6% convertible loan stock, each $5 of loan stock convertible into 4 ordinary shares on 1 July 20X6 at the option of the holder.

Barwell Co had profit for the year ended 30 June 20X3 of $1,850,000. It pays tax on profits at 30%.

What was diluted earnings per share for the year?

- O $0.167
- O $0.185
- O $0.161
- O $0.17

(2 marks)

---

199 At 30 September 20X2 the trial balance of Cavern Co includes the following balances:

	$'000
Equity shares of 20c each	50,000
Share premium	15,000

Cavern Co has accounted for a fully subscribed rights issue of equity shares made on 1 April 20X2 of one new share for every four in issue at 42 cents each. This was the only share issue made during the year.

Using the drag and drop options below, show the balances on the share capital and share premium accounts at 30 September 20X1.

$'000		Balances
4,000		Share capital
11,250		Share premium
37,500		
40,000		

(2 marks)

---

200 Aqua Co has correctly calculated its basic earnings per share (EPS) for the current year.

Which **TWO** of the following items need to be additionally considered when calculating the diluted EPS of Aqua Co for the year?

☐ A 1 for 5 rights issue of equity shares during the year at $1.20 when the market price of the equity shares was $2.00

☐ The issue during the year of a convertible (to equity shares) loan note

☐ The granting during the year of directors' share options exercisable in three years' time

☐ Equity shares issued during the year as the purchase consideration for the acquisition of a new subsidiary company **(2 marks)**

---

201 Many commentators believe that the trend of earnings per share (EPS) is a more reliable indicator of underlying performance than the trend of net profit for the year.

Which of the following statements supports this view?

○ Net profit can be manipulated by the choice of accounting policies but EPS cannot be manipulated in this way

○ EPS takes into account the additional resources made available to earn profit when new shares are issued for cash, whereas net profit does not

○ The disclosure of a diluted EPS figure is a forecast of the future trend of profit

○ The comparative EPS is restated where a change of accounting policy affects the previous year's profits **(2 marks)**

202 At 1 January 20X8 Artichoke Co had 5 million $1 equity shares in issue. On 1 June 20X8, it made a 1 for 5 rights issue at a price of $1.50. The market price of the shares on the last day of quotation with rights was $1.80.

Total earnings for the year ended 31 December 20X8 was $7.6 million.

What was the earnings per share for the year?

- O $1.35
- O $1.36
- O $1.27
- O $1.06

(2 marks)

---

203 The weighted average number of ordinary shares that Fogarty Co has in issue for the year to 31 December 20X7 is 5,000,000.

On 1 January, Fogarty Co issued 500,000 share options to purchase one $1 ordinary share at $2.80 per share. These options are exercisable between 1 January 20X9 and 31 December 20Y0. The average market value of each $1 ordinary share of Fogarty Co during the year ended 31 December 20X7 is $3.50.

What is the weighted average number of shares to be used in the calculation of diluted earnings per share for the year ended 31 December 20X7?

- O 4.9 million
- O 5.1 million
- O 5.4 million
- O 5.5 million

(2 marks)

---

204 Plumstead Co had 4 million equity shares in issue throughout the year ended 31 March 20X7. On 30 September 20X7 it made a 1 for 4 bonus issue. Profit for the year ended 31 March 20X8 was $3.6 million, out of which an equity dividend of 20c per share was paid. The financial statements for the year ended 31 March 20X7 showed earnings per share (EPS) of $0.70.

What is the EPS for the year ended 31 March 20X8 and the restated EPS for the year ended 31 March 20X7? (Enter your answer to two decimal places.)

EPS 20X8: $ ☐

EPS 20X7: $ ☐

(2 marks)

---

205 Bollingbrook Co has earnings of $313,000 and 100,000 ordinary $1 shares in issue during 20X5. The company also has in issue $100,000 10% convertible loan stock which is convertible in one years' time at a rate of 3 ordinary shares for every $10 of stock. The tax rate is 30%.

What is the diluted earnings per share?

- O $2.41
- O $2.46
- O $2.48
- O $3.13

(2 marks)

(Total = 16 marks)

Section B

Tunshill Co case (Dec 2010 amended) (18 mins)

Information relevant to questions 206–210

The directors of Tunshill Co are disappointed by the draft profit for the year ended 30 September 20X3. The company's assistant accountant has suggested two areas where she believes the reported profit may be improved:

(1) A major item of plant that cost $20 million to purchase and install on 1 October 20X0 is being depreciated on a straight-line basis over a five-year period (assuming no residual value). The plant is wearing well and at the beginning of the current year (1 October 20X2) the production manager believed that the plant was likely to generate benefits over eight years in total (ie from the date of its purchase). The assistant accountant has calculated that, based on an eight-year life (and no residual value) the accumulated depreciation of the plant at 30 September 20X3 would be $7.5 million ($20 million / 8 years × 3). In the financial statements for the year ended 30 September 20X2, the accumulated depreciation was $8 million ($20 million / 5 years × 2). Therefore, by adopting an eight-year useful life, Tunshill Co can avoid a depreciation charge in the current year and instead credit $0.5 million ($8 million – $7.5 million) to profit or loss in the current year to improve the reported profit.

(2) Most of Tunshill Co's competitors value their inventory using the average cost (AVCO) basis, whereas Tunshill Co uses the first in first out (FIFO) basis. The value of Tunshill Co's inventory at 30 September 20X3 on the FIFO basis, is $20 million, however on the AVCO basis it would be valued at $18 million. By adopting the same method (AVCO) as its competitors, the assistant accountant says the company would improve its profit for the year ended 30 September 20X3 by $2 million. Tunshill Co's inventory at 30 September 20X2 was reported as $15 million, however on the AVCO basis it would have been reported as $13.4 million.

206 What is the nature of the change being proposed by the assistant accountant in (1) and how should it be applied?

- O Change of accounting policy: Retrospective application
- O Change of accounting policy: Prospective application
- O Change of accounting estimate: Retrospective application
- O Change of accounting estimate: Prospective application **(2 marks)**

---

207 Adjusting for the change of useful life, what will be the carrying amount of the plant at 30 September 20X3? (Enter your answer to the nearest whole $.)

$ [ ] **(2 marks)**

---

208 Which of the following would be treated as a change of accounting policy?

- O Tunshill Co has received its first government grant and is applying the deferred income method
- O Tunshill Co has changed the rate of depreciation used for its office equipment from 25% to 20% straight line basis
- O Tunshill Co has reclassified development costs from other operating expenses to cost of sales
- O Tunshill Co has increased its irrecoverable debt allowance from 10% to 12% **(2 marks)**

---

209 What will be the effect of the change in (2) on profits for the year ended 30 September 20X3?

- O Increased by $400,000
- O Reduced by $400,000
- O Increased by $1,600,000
- O Reduced by $1,600,000

(2 marks)

---

210 Using the drag and drop options below, select the correct account to show the accounting entry for the change in inventory value for the year ended 30 September 20X3?

Account		Debit/Credit
Cost of sales		Debit
Inventory		Credit
Revenue		

(2 marks)

(Total = 10 marks)

Hemlock Co case (18 mins)

Information relevant to questions 211–215

The directors of Hemlock Co are preparing the financial statements for the year ended 30 September 20X3. Hemlock Co is a publicly listed company.

(1) Most of Hemlock Co's competitors value their inventory using the average cost (AVCO) basis, whereas Hemlock Co uses the first in first out (FIFO) basis. The value of Hemlock Co's inventory at 30 September 20X3 on the FIFO basis, is $40 million, however on the AVCO basis it would be valued at $36 million. By adopting the same method (AVCO) as its competitors, the assistant accountant says the company would improve its profit for the year ended 30 September 20X3 by $4 million. Hemlock Co's inventory at 30 September 20X2 was reported as $30 million, however on the AVCO basis it would have been reported as $26.8 million.

(2) Hemlock Co sold a machine to Poisson SA, a French company which it agreed to invoice in €. The sale was made on 1 October 20X6 for €250,000. €155,000 was received on 1 November 20X6 and the balance is due on 1 January 20X7.

The exchange rate moved as follows:

1 October 20X6 – €0.85 to $1

1 November 20X6 – €0.84 to $1

31 December 20X6 – €0.79 to $1

(3) After correctly accounting for the information in (1) and (2), Hemlock Co has earnings of $9,160,000. It had 2,000,000 ordinary $1 shares in issue during the year to 30 September 20X3. Hemlock Co has an additional 1,000,000 shares under option at the year end. The fair value of the shares at that date is $12.00 per share and the exercise price for the options is $10.00 each.

211 At what amount will the receivable of €155,000 be shown in the financial statements at 31 December 20X6?

- O $130,200
- O $196,203
- O $183,253
- O $184,524 **(2 marks)**

---

212 Which of the following would be treated as a change of accounting policy?

- O Hemlock Co is adopting the revaluation policy for the first time for its tangible non-current assets
- O Hemlock Co has changed the rate of depreciation used for its office equipment from 30% to 20% straight-line basis
- O Hemlock Co has reclassified head office administration costs from cost of sales to other operating expenses
- O Hemlock Co has increased its allowance for irrecoverable debts from 10% to 12%

(2 marks)

---

213 What would be the effect on profits for the year ended 30 September 20X3 if Hemlock Co were to adopt the AVCO method of inventory valuation?

- O Increased by $800,000
- O Reduced by $800,000
- O Increased by $3,200,000
- O Reduced by $3,200,000 **(2 marks)**

---

214 The auditors of Hemlock Co have discovered a fundamental error in the prior year financial statements. The directors of Hemlock Co have agreed to correct the prior period error.

Which of the following are the disclosures which the directors should present in the financial statements?

(1) The nature of the error

(2) The amount of the correction for each item of the financial statements affected by the error and correction

- O Statement (1) only
- O Statement (2) only
- O Neither statement (1) or (2)
- O Both statements (1) and (2) **(2 marks)**

---

215 Calculate the diluted earnings per shares for Hemlock Co for the year ended 30 September 20X3. (Enter your answer to two decimal places.)

$ [ ] per share **(2 marks)**

(Total = 10 marks)

PART C: ANALYSING AND INTERPRETING THE FINANCIAL STATEMENTS OF SINGLE ENTITIES AND GROUPS

Analysing and interpreting financial statements is about more than simply calculating ratios. It is more important that you understand what the ratio tells you about the company or group and how different transactions and accounting policies can impact ratios.

One of the Section C questions will require the interpretation of the financial statements of single entities or groups. These questions will require the calculation of ratios and analysis of the performance and/or position of a company or group based on the ratios calculated and the information provided. It is essential that your discussion is relevant to the question as generic points are unlikely to score credit.

Section A questions

Questions 216–221: Interpretation of financial statements (Chapter 20)

Questions 222–229: Limitations of financial statements and interpretation techniques (Chapter 21)

Questions 230–237: Not-for-profit and public sector entities (Chapter 23)

Section B questions on these topics are in Questions 238–242

Section C questions are the constructed response questions worth 20 marks. Where the Examining Team's feedback is available (the question coming from a former exam), this feedback is given, together with top tips and easy marks.

Question 243 Woodbank Co

Question 244 Pinardi Co

Question 245 Funject Co

Question 246 Pastry Co

Question 247 Venus Co

Question 248 Mowair Co

Question 249 Perkins Co

Question 250 Pirlo Co

Question 251 Karl Co

Question 252 Kostner Co

Section A

Interpretation of accounting ratios and trends (22 mins)

216 Charlton Co has an average operating profit margin of 23% of which depreciation of plant and machinery accounts for 33% of the operating costs, as well as including 78% of the salaries cost within cost of sales. It has an average asset turnover of 0.8, which is similar to the averages for the industry.

The entity is most likely to be:

- O An architectural practice
- O A supermarket
- O An estate agent
- O A manufacturer

(2 marks)

---

217 Using the pull-down list provided, select the correct option to complete the following statement.

Reducing the [▼] will increase the length of a company's operating cycle.

Pull down list

- Inventory holding period
- Payables payment period
- Receivables collection period
- Time taken to produce goods

(2 marks)

---

218 In the year to 31 December 20X9 Weston Co pays an interim equity dividend of 3.4c per share and declares a final equity dividend of 11.1c. It has 5 million $1 shares in issue and the ex div share price is $3.50.

What is the dividend yield?

- O 4%
- O 24%
- O 3.2%
- O 4.1%

(2 marks)

---

219 Analysis of the financial statements of Capricorn Co at 31 December 20X8 yields the following information:

Gross profit margin	30%
Current ratio	2.14
Return on capital employed (ROCE)	16.3%
Asset turnover	4.19
Inventory turnover	13.9

What is the net profit margin?

- O 3.9%
- O 7.6%
- O 16.1%
- O 7.1%

(2 marks)

---

220 Camargue Co is a listed company with four million 50c ordinary shares in issue. The following extract is from its financial statements for the year ended 30 September 20X4.

STATEMENT OF PROFIT OR LOSS

	$'000
Profit before tax	900
Income tax expense	(100)
Profit for the year	800

At 30 September 20X4 the market price of Camargue Co's shares was $1.50. What was the P/E ratio on that date?

[ ]

(2 marks)

221 Extracts from the financial statements of Perseus Co are as follows:

Statement of profit or loss

	$'000
Operating profit	230
Finance costs	(15)
Profit before tax	215
Income tax	(15)
Profit for the year	200

Statement of financial position

	$'000
Ordinary shares	2,000
Revaluation surplus	300
Retained earnings	1,200
	3,500
10% loan notes	1,000
Current liabilities	100
Total equity and liabilities	4,600

What is the return on capital employed (ROCE)?

[ ]

(2 marks)

(Total = 12 marks)

Limitations of financial statements and interpretation techniques (29 mins)

222 Cyan Co carries its property at revalued amount. Property values have fallen during the current period and an impairment loss has been recognised on the property, however its carrying amount is still higher than its depreciated historical cost.

Complete the statement using the pull-down list below, showing the effect of the impairment on the return on capital employed (ROCE) and gearing ratios of Cyan Co.

The effect of this impairment will [▼] the ROCE ratio of Cyan Co, and [▼] its gearing ratio.

Pull down list

- Decrease
- Increase

(2 marks)

223 Magenta Ltd has a current ratio of 1.5, a quick ratio of 0.4 and a positive cash balance. If it purchases inventory on credit, what is the effect on these ratios?

	Current ratio	Quick ratio
O	Decrease	Decrease
O	Decrease	Increase
O	Increase	Decrease
O	Increase	Increase

(2 marks)

---

224 Fritwel Co has an asset turnover of 2.0 and an operating profit margin of 10%. It is launching a new product which is expected to generate additional sales of $1.6 million and additional profit of $120,000. It will require additional assets of $500,000.

Assuming there are no other changes to current operations, how will the new product affect these ratios?

Select the impact on the ratios below using the drag and drop options

Decrease		Operating profit margin
Increase		ROCE
No change		

(2 marks)

---

225 Which of the following is a plausible reason why a company's inventory holding period increases from one year to the next?

- O An increase in demand for its products
- O A reduction in selling prices
- O Obsolete inventory lines
- O Seasonal fluctuations in orders **(2 marks)**

---

226 Use of historical cost accounting means asset values can be reliably verified but it has a number of shortcomings which need to be considered when analysing financial statements.

Which of these is a possible result of the use of historical cost accounting during a period of inflation?

- O Overstatement of non-current asset values
- O Overstatement of profits
- O Understatement of interest costs
- O Understatement of return on capital employed (ROCE) **(2 marks)**

---

227 Directors will often take steps to reduce a company's gearing, for example if they are hoping to secure a bank loan.

Identify whether the following measures will increase, reduce or have no effect on gearing.

Renegotiating a loan to secure a lower interest rate	**INCREASE**	**REDUCE**	**NO EFFECT**
Applying the optional recognition exemption to a lease contract under IFRS 16 Leases	**INCREASE**	**REDUCE**	**NO EFFECT**
Repaying a loan just before the year end and taking it out again at the beginning of the next year	**INCREASE**	**REDUCE**	**NO EFFECT**
'Selling' an asset under a sale and leaseback agreement	**INCREASE**	**REDUCE**	**NO EFFECT**

(2 marks)

---

228 If a company wished to maintain the carrying amount in the financial statements of its non-current assets, which of the following would it be unlikely to do?

- O Sell a piece of equipment and enter into a short-term lease for similar equipment which meets the optional recognition exemption requirements, which the company has a policy of applying
- O Account for asset-based government grants using the deferred income approach
- O Revalue its properties
- O Change the depreciation method for new asset acquisitions from 25% diminishing balance to ten years straight line **(2 marks)**

---

229 Trent uses the formula: (trade receivables at year end/revenue for the year) × 365 to calculate how long on average (in days) its customers take to pay.

Which of the following would **NOT** affect the correctness of the above calculation of the average number of days a customer takes to pay?

- O Trent experiences considerable seasonal trading
- O Trent makes a number of cash sales through retail outlets
- O Reported revenue does not include a 15% sales tax whereas the receivables do include the tax
- O Trent factors with recourse the receivable of its largest customer **(2 marks)**

(Total = 16 marks)

Not-for-profit and public sector entities (29 mins)

230 Which of the following are unlikely to be stakeholders in a charity?

- O Taxpayers
- O Financial supporters
- O Shareholders
- O Government **(2 marks)**

231 The International Public Sector Accounting Standards Board regulates public sector entities and is developing a set of accounting standards which closely mirror IFRS Accounting Standards.

Which of these is the main concept which needs to be introduced into public sector accounting?

- O Materiality
- O Accruals
- O Relevance
- O Faithful representation **(2 marks)**

---

232 Public sector entities have performance measures laid down by government, based on Key Performance Indicators (KPIs). Which **THREE** of the following are likely to be financial KPIs for a local council?

- ☐ Rent receipts outstanding
- ☐ Interest cover
- ☐ Dividend cover
- ☐ Financial actuals against budget
- ☐ Return on capital employed **(2 marks)**

---

233 Which **TWO** of the ratios are **NOT** relevant for Yellow, a charity which operates from high street stores?

- ☐ Operating profit margin
- ☐ Inventory holding period
- ☐ Current ratio
- ☐ Earnings per share **(2 marks)**

---

234 Which of the following is the main aspect in which public sector bodies differ from charities?

- O Importance of budgeting
- O Funded by government
- O Performance measured by key performance indicators
- O No requirement to earn a return on assets **(2 marks)**

---

235 Although the objectives and purposes of not-for-profit entities are different from those of commercial entities, the accounting requirements of not-for-profit entities are moving closer to those entities to which IFRS Accounting Standards apply.

Which of the following IFRS requirements would **NOT** be relevant to a not-for-profit entity?

- O Preparation of a statement of cash flows
- O Requirement to capitalise a leased asset
- O Disclosure of dividends per share
- O Disclosure of non-adjusting events after the reporting date **(2 marks)**

---

236 Which **TWO** of the following statements about a not-for-profit entity are valid?

- ☐ There is no requirement to calculate an earnings per share figure as it is not likely to have shareholders who need to assess its earnings performance
- ☐ The revaluation of its property, plant and equipment is not relevant as it is not a commercial entity
- ☐ It prioritises non-financial KPIs over financial targets
- ☐ Its financial statements will not be closely scrutinised as it does not have any investors

(2 marks)

---

237 Cyan is a charity which operates high street charity shops. Its goods for sale comprise donations from the public and inventories purchased from suppliers on credit. It makes sales in its stores in cash only.

Which **TWO** of the following ratios are relevant for Cyan?

- ☐ Inventory holding period
- ☐ Return on capital employed
- ☐ Receivables collection period
- ☐ Payables payment period

(2 marks)

(Total = 16 marks)

Section B

Sandbag plc case **(18 mins)**

The following scenario relates to questions 238–242.

Sandbag plc is a listed manufacturing company. Its summarised statement of financial position is given below.

STATEMENT OF FINANCIAL POSITION AS AT 31 DECEMBER 20X4

	$m
Non-current assets	610
Inventories	96
Trade receivables	29
Current asset investments	5
Cash and cash equivalents	3
	133
	743
Equity and liabilities	
$1 ordinary shares	400
Retained earnings	190
	590
Non-current liabilities – loans	50
Trade and other payables	103
	743

238 What is Sandbag plc's current ratio at 31 December 20X4?

- O 0.37
- O 1.29
- O 0.87
- O 1.26 **(2 marks)**

---

239 The finance director of Sandbag plc is worried about its current ratio. He is considering a number of actions that he hopes will improve Sandbag plc's current ratio.

Which of the following would increase Sandbag plc's current ratio?

- O Offer a settlement discount to customers
- O Make a bonus issue of ordinary shares
- O Make a rights issue of ordinary shares
- O Sell current asset investments at the carrying amount **(2 marks)**

---

240 What is Sandbag plc's acid test (quick) ratio at 31 December 20X4? (Enter your answer to two decimal places)

(2 marks)

---

241 The finance director of Sandbag plc knows that the acid test ratio is below 1. He is planning two changes:

- Proposal 1: Offering a 2% early settlement discount to credit customers
- Proposal 2: Delaying payment to all trade payables by one extra month

Using the options below, match the effect the proposals would have on the acid test ratio (tokens can used more than once).

Increase ratio		Proposal 1
Decrease ratio		Proposal 2

(2 marks)

---

242 Sandbag plc is a manufacturing company. Which of the following ratios would best assess the efficiency of Sandbag plc?

- O Price/earnings ratio
- O Gearing ratio
- O Non-current asset turnover
- O Current ratio

(2 marks)

(Total = 10 marks)

Section C

243 Woodbank Co (Jun 2014 amended) (36 mins)

Shown below are the financial statements of Woodbank Co for its most recent two years:

STATEMENTS OF PROFIT OR LOSS FOR THE YEAR ENDED 31 MARCH

	20X4	20X3
	$'000	$'000
Revenue	150,000	110,000
Cost of sales	117,000	(85,800)
Gross profit	33,000	24,200
Distribution costs	(6,000)	(5,000)
Administrative expenses	(9,000)	(9,200)
Finance costs – loan note interest	(1,750)	(500)
Profit before tax	16,250	9,500
Income tax expense	(5,750)	(3,000)
Profit for the year	10,500	6,500

STATEMENTS OF FINANCIAL POSITION AS AT 31 MARCH

	20X4	20X3
	$'000	$'000
ASSETS		
Non-current assets		
Property, plant and equipment	118,000	85,000
Goodwill	30,000	–
	148,000	85,000
Current assets		
Inventories	15,500	12,000
Trade receivables	11,000	8,000
Cash and cash equivalents	500	5,000
	27,000	25,000
Total assets	175,000	110,000
EQUITY AND LIABILITIES		
Equity		
Equity shares of $1 each	80,000	80,000
Retained earnings	15,000	10,000
	95,000	90,000
Non-current liabilities		

	20X4	20X3
	$'000	$'000
10% loan notes	55,000	5,000
Current liabilities		
Trade payables	21,000	13,000
Current tax payable	4,000	2,000
	25,000	15,000
Total equity and liabilities	175,000	110,000

The following information is available:

(1) On 1 January 20X4, Woodbank Co acquired a controlling interest in Shaw Co for $50 million. It paid for the acquisition through the issue of additional 10% loan notes and by using some of its cash reserves. Shaw Co was an unincorporated entity and its results (for three months from 1 January 20X4 to 31 March 20X4) and net assets (including goodwill not subject to any impairment) are included in Woodbank Co's financial statements for the year ended 31 March 20X4. There were no other purchases or sales of non-current assets during the year ended 31 March 20X4.

(2) Extracts of the results (for three months) of the previously separate business of Shaw Co, which are included in Woodbank Co's statement of profit or loss for the year ended 31 March 20X4, are:

	$'000
Revenue	30,000
Cost of sales	(21,000)
Gross profit	9,000
Distribution costs	(2,000)
Administrative expenses	(2,000)

Required

(a) Calculate the equivalent ratios for Woodbank Co for the year ended 31 March 20X4.

(5 marks)

(b) Calculate, as far as the information permits, the equivalent ratios for Woodbank Co for the year ended 31 March 20X4 **excluding** the effects of the purchase of Shaw Co. **(3 marks)**

Ratio	Woodbank Co 20X3	Working	Woodbank Co 20X4	Working	Woodbank Co 20X4 excluding Shaw
Return on capital employed	10.5%				
Gross profit margin	22%				

Ratio	Woodbank Co 20X3	Working	Woodbank Co 20X4	Working	Woodbank Co 20X4 excluding Shaw
Profit before interest and tax margin	9.1%				
Current ratio	1.7:1				
Gearing (debt/(debt + equity))	5.3%				

(c) Assess the comparative financial performance and position of Woodbank Co for the year ended 31 March 20X4. Your answer should refer to the effects of the purchase of Shaw Co. **(12 marks)**

(Total = 20 marks)

244 Pinardi Group (36 mins)

This scenario relates to four requirements.

The Pinardi group operates in the fragrance and cosmetics industry. On 1 January 20X7 Pinardi Co disposed one of its subsidiaries, Silva Co, for cash of $42m. Silva Co manufactures jewellery and was sold because the Pinardi group wanted to exit this particular sector.

Extracts from the consolidated financial statements of the Pinardi group for the years ended 31 December 20X6 and 20X7 are as follows:

Statement of profit or loss

	20X7	20X6
	$'000	$'000
Revenue	98,300	122,400
Cost of sales	(47,600)	(71,800)
Gross profit	**50,700**	**50,600**
Operating expenses	(33,700)	(37,400)
Profit from operations	**17,000**	**13,200**
Finance costs	(3,200)	(5,500)
Profit before tax	**13,800**	**7,700**

Statement of financial position

	20X7	20X6
	$'000	$'000
Inventories	13,300	22,400
Cash	31,400	14,600

	20X7	20X6
	$'000	$'000
Non-current liabilities	42,000	61,000

The following information is relevant:

(1) The accounting assistant has not accounted for Silva Co as a discontinued operation because the disposal occurred on 1 January 20X7. No figures from Silva Co have been included in the 20X7 financial statements extracts above. The proceeds from the disposal have been recorded in cash, with all net assets and goodwill derecognised. The balancing figure was held in a suspense account.

(2) Pinardi Co acquired 100% of Silva Co on 1 January 20X1 and goodwill was calculated as $6m. The goodwill has been impaired by 30% in 20X5. The net assets at 1 January 20X7 were $35m.

(3) As part of the sales agreement, Pinardi group will receive an annual fee of $2m for the use of the Silva Co brand. The 20X7 annual fee has been included in the Pinardi group revenue for the year ended 31 December 20X7.

(4) Results obtained from Silva Co's individual published financial statements show the following key information:

	20X7	20X6
	$'000	$'000
Revenue	39,000	36,000
Gross profit	18,800	12,600
Profit from operations	8,000	6,000

(5) Prior to the disposal Silva Co used to use some property belonging to the Pinardi group. Following the disposal, the Pinardi group moved its cosmetic division into this property.

Previously, the cosmetic division had leased external facilities for $2.5m a year. At 1 January 20X7 the lease had ten years remaining. To exit the lease, the Pinardi group made a one-off payment of $3m to the lessor and recorded it as operating expenses.

(6) The Pinardi group acquires raw materials from overseas. In 20X6 the group recorded foreign exchange gains of $3m and in 20X7 the group made a foreign exchange loss of $1m. Both items were recognised within operating expenses.

Required

(a) Calculate the gain on disposal of Silva Co that would need to be included in the consolidated statement of profit or loss for the Pinardi group for the year ended 31 December 20X7. **(2 marks)**

(b) Explain whether or not the disposal of Silva Co is likely to constitute a discontinued operation and the correct accounting treatment for this. **(3 marks)**

(c) Calculate the following ratios, using the pre-formatted table, for the Pinardi group for 20X7 and 20X6:

- Gross profit margin;
- Operating profit margin;
- Interest cover; and
- Inventory turnover days.

(4 marks)

Ratio calculations

Ratio	Working	20X7	Working	20X6
Gross profit margin				
Operating profit margin				
Interest cover				
Inventory turnover days				

(d) Analyse the performance and position for the Pinardi group for the year ended 31 December 20X7 compared to the year ended 31 December 20X6. **(11 marks)**

(Total = 20 marks)

245 Funject Co (Mar/Jun 2017) (36 mins)

Funject Co has identified Aspect Co as a possible acquisition within the same industry. Aspect Co is currently owned by the Gamilton Group and the following are extracts from the financial statements of Aspect Co:

EXTRACT FROM THE STATEMENT OF PROFIT OR LOSS FOR THE YEAR ENDED 31 DECEMBER 20X4

	$'000
Revenue	54,200
Cost of sales	21,500
Gross profit	32,700
Operating expenses	11,700
Operating profit	21,000

STATEMENT OF FINANCIAL POSITION AS AT 31 DECEMBER 20X4

	$'000	$'000
Assets		
Non-current assets		24,400
Current assets		
Inventories	4,900	
Receivables	5,700	
Cash and cash equivalents	2,300	12,900
Total assets		37,300
Equity and liabilities		
Equity		
Equity shares		1,000
Retained earnings		8,000
		9,000
Liabilities		
Non-current liabilities		
Loan		16,700

	$'000	$'000
Current liabilities		
Trade payables	5,400	
Current tax payable	6,200	11,600
Total equity and liabilities		37,300

Additional information:

(1) On 1 April 20X4, Aspect Co decided to focus on its core business and so disposed of a non-core division. The disposal generated a loss of $1.5m which is included within operating expenses. The following extracts show the results of the non-core division for the period prior to disposal which were included in Aspect Co's results for 20X4:

	$'000
Revenue	2,100
Cost of sales	(1,200)
Gross profit	900
Operating expenses	(700)
Operating profit	200

(2) At present Aspect Co pays a management charge of 1% of revenue to the Gamilton Group which is included in operating expenses. Funject Co imposes a management charge of 10% of gross profit on all of its subsidiaries.

(3) Aspect Co's administration offices are currently located within a building owned by the Gamilton Group. If Aspect Co were acquired, the company would need to seek alternative premises. Aspect Co paid rent of $46,000 in 20X4. Commercial rents for equivalent office space would cost $120,000.

Required

(a) Redraft Aspect Co's statement of profit or loss for 20X4 to adjust for the disposal of the non-core division in note (1) and the management and rent charges which would be imposed per notes (2) and (3) if Aspect Co was acquired by Funject Co. **(4 marks)**

(b) Using the preformatted table provided below, calculate the equivalent 20X4 ratios for Aspect Co based on the restated financial information calculated in part (a).

Note. You should assume that any increase or decrease in profit as a result of your adjustments in part (a) will also increase or decrease cash. **(6 marks)**

Ratio calculations

	Industry KPIs 20X4	Working	Aspect Co 20X4
Gross profit margin	45%		
Operating profit margin	28%		
Receivables collection period	41 days		
Current ratio	1.6:1		
Acid test (quick) ratio	1.4:1		
Gearing (debt/equity)	240%		

(c) Using the ratios calculated in part (b), comment on Aspect Co's 20X4 performance and financial position compared to the industry average KPIs provided in the pre-formatted table.

(10 marks)

(Total = 20 marks)

246 Pastry Co (March/June 2021) (36 mins)

Pastry Co is considering the acquisition of a subsidiary in the catering industry. Two companies have been identified as potential acquisitions and extracts from the financial statements of Cook Co and Dough Co have been reproduced below:

STATEMENTS OF PROFIT OR LOSS FOR THE YEAR ENDED 30 SEPTEMBER 20X7

	Cook Co	*Dough Co*
	$'000	$'000
Revenue	21,500	16,300
Cost of sales	(14,545)	(8,350)
Gross profit	**6,955**	**7,950**
Operating expenses	(1,940)	(4,725)
Finance costs	(650)	(200)
Profit before tax	**4,365**	**3,025**
Income tax	(1,320)	(780)
Profit for the year	**3,045**	**2,245**

EXTRACTS FROM THE STATEMENTS OF FINANCIAL POSITION AS AT 30 SEPTEMBER 20X7

	Cook Co	*Dough Co*
	$'000	$'000
Non-current assets		
Property	22,250	68,500
Equity		
Equity shares of $1 each	1,000	1,000
Revaluation surplus	–	30,000
Retained earnings	18,310	2,600
Non-current liabilities		
Loan notes	7,300	5,200

Notes.

1 Both companies are owner-managed. Dough Co operates from expensive city centre premises, selling to local businesses and the public. Cook Co is a large wholesaler, selling to chains of coffee shops. Cook Co operates from a number of low-cost production facilities.

2 On 1 October 20X6, Dough Co revalued its properties for the first time, resulting in a gain of $30 million. The properties had a remaining useful life of 30 years at 1 October 20X6. Dough Co does not make a transfer from the revaluation surplus in respect of excess depreciation. Cook Co uses the cost model to account for its properties. Dough Co and Cook Co charge all depreciation expenses to operating expenses.

3 Cook Co charges the amortisation of its research and development to cost of sales, whereas Dough Co charges the same costs to operating expenses. These costs amounted to $1.2 million for Cook Co and $2.5 million for Dough Co.

4 The notes to the financial statements show that Cook Co paid its directors total salaries of $110,000 whereas Dough Co paid its directors total salaries of $560,000.

5 The following ratios have been correctly calculated in respect of Cook Co and Dough Co for the year ended 30 September 20X7:

	Cook Co	Dough Co
Gross profit margin	32.3%	48.8%
Operating profit margin	23.3%	19.8%
Return on capital employed	18.8%	8.3%

Required

(a) Adjust the relevant extracts fron Dough Co's financial statements to apply the same accounting policies as Cook Co and re-calculate Dough Co's ratios provided in note (5).

(6 marks)

(b) Based on these adjusted accounting ratios, compare the performance of the two companies. Your answer should comment on the difficulties of making a purchase decision based solely on the extracts of the financial statements and the information provided in notes (1) to (5).

(14 marks)

(Total = 20 marks)

247 Venus Group (36 mins)

This scenario relates to four requirements.

6 months

Venus Co acquired 70% of the equity share capital of Luto Co, its only subsidiary, on 1 January 20X8.

On reviewing the consolidated financial statements, the managing director of Venus Co was disappointed, commenting that he had expected to see higher gross profit for 20X8 due to the receipt of discounted purchases from Luto Co in the post-acquisition period. He has remarked that the acquisition of Luto Co has not had the positive impact he expected.

Extracts from the draft financial statements of the Venus Group and Venus Co (single entity) for the years ended 30 June 20X7 and 20X8 are:

Statement of profit or loss

	Venus Group (consolidated) 30 June 20X8	Venus Co (single entity) 30 June 20X7
	$'000	$'000
Revenue	39,000	32,000
Cost of sales	(26,500)	(21,000)
Gross profit	**12,500**	**11,000**
Net profit for the year	**9,800**	**8,900**
Profit attributable to:		
Owners of Venus Co	9,200	

	Venus Group (consolidated) 30 June 20X8	Venus Co (single entity) 30 June 20X7
	$'000	$'000
Non-controlling interest	600	

Statement of financial position

	Venus Group (consolidated) 30 June 20X8	Venus Co (single entity) 30 June 20X7
	$'000	$'000
Equity		
Share capital	30,000	20,000
Other components of equity (share premium)	35,000	5,000
Retained earnings	21,000	17,000
Non-controlling interest (NCI)	1,500	
	87,500	**42,000**

The acquisition of Luto Co has been accounted for correctly in the above financial statement extracts and the following notes are relevant:

(1) Luto Co recognised revenue of $5m in the post-acquisition period, which resulted in a profit of $2m.

(2) Since the acquisition, Venus Co is able to acquire goods from Luto Co at a discount. This has resulted in a saving of $500,000 for Venus Co in the post-acquisition period. At 30 June 20X8 Venus Co had no inventory that had been purchased from Luto Co.

(3) The consideration for the acquisition consisted of a share exchange and an additional $5m to be paid on 1 January 20X9. Venus Co has a cost of capital of 8% which is equivalent to a discount factor of 0.926.

(4) The fair values of Luto Co's assets at acquisition were equal to their carrying amounts, except for an item of plant. This plant had a remaining life of three years at the date of acquisition. Its fair value was $900,000 above its carrying amount. Venus Co's assets are held at historical cost.

(5) All revenue and expenses are deemed to accrue evenly throughout the year.

Required

(a) Based on the extracts provided, use the pre-formatted table to calculate the following ratios for Venus Co and the Venus Group for the years ended 30 June 20X8 and 30 June 20X7 respectively: Gross profit %, Net profit %, and Return on equity (equity should include NCI where applicable). **(3 marks)**

(b) (i) Complete the table provided to adjust Venus Co's consolidated profit for the year ended 30 June 20X8 in order to calculate the profit of Venus Co for that year as if the acquisition of Luto Co had not taken place. Your answer should take account of the information provided in the notes. Your answer should also recalculate the net profit %.

Note. The following preformatted table relates to this question and has been replicated in the response area: **(5 marks)**

		$'000
Venus Co consolidated profit for the year		9,800
Adjustment 1: Deduct Luto Co post-acquisition profit – Note (1)		(2,000)
Adjustment 2:	Note (2)	
Adjustment 3:	Note (3)	
Adjustment 4:	Note (4)	
Venus Co single entity net profit		

Net profit % working

(ii) Explain why consolidated financial statements, for example those of the Venus Group, are not comparable to those of a single entity, for example Venus Co. **(3 marks)**

(c) Based on your answers to parts (a) and (b), comment on the comparative performance of Venus Co for the years ended 30 June 20X7 and 20X8, specifically addressing the managing director's comments. **(9 marks)**

(Total = 20 marks)

248 Mowair Co (Sept/Dec 17) (36 mins)

Mowair Co is an international airline which flies to destinations all over the world. Mowair Co experienced strong initial growth but in recent periods the company has been criticised for under-investing in its non-current assets.

Extracts from Mowair Co's financial statements are provided below.

Statements of financial position as at 30 June

	20X7	*20X6*
	$'000	$'000
Assets		
Non-current assets		
Property, plant and equipment	317,000	174,000
Intangible assets (note ii)	20,000	16,000
	337,000	190,000
Current assets		
Inventories	580	490
Trade and other receivables	6,100	6,300
Cash and cash equivalents	9,300	22,100
Total current assets	15,980	28,890
Total assets	352,980	218,890
Equity and liabilities		
Equity		
Equity shares	3,000	3,000
Retained earnings	44,100	41,800

	20X7	20X6
	$'000	$'000
Revaluation surplus	145,000	Nil
Total equity	192,100	44,800
Liabilities		
Non-current liabilities		
6% loan notes	130,960	150,400
Current liabilities		
Trade and other payables	10,480	4,250
6% loan notes	19,440	19,440
Total current liabilities	29,920	23,690
Total equity and liabilities	352,980	218,890

Other EXTRACTS from Mowair Co's financial statements for the years ended 30 June

	20X7	20X6
	$'000	$'000
Revenue	154,000	159,000
Profit from operations	12,300	18,600
Finance costs	(9,200)	(10,200)
Cash generated from operations	18,480	24,310

The following information is also relevant:

(1) Mowair Co had exactly the same flight schedule in 20X7 as in 20X6, with the overall number of flights and destinations being the same in both years.

(2) In April 20X7, Mowair Co had to renegotiate its licences with five major airports, which led to an increase in the prices Mowair Co had to pay for the right to operate flights there. The licences with ten more major airports are due to expire in December 20X7, and Mowair Co is currently in negotiation with these airports.

Required

(a) Using the preformatted table provided below, calculate the required ratios for Mowair Co for the years ended 30 June 20X6 and 20X7. **(6 marks)**

	20X7	Workings	20X6	Workings
Operating profit margin				
Return on capital employed				
Net asset turnover				
Current ratio				
Interest cover				
Gearing				

	20X7	Workings	20X6	Workings
(Debt/Equity)				

Note. For calculation purposes, all loan notes should be treated as debt.

(b) Comment on the performance and position of Mowair Co for the year ended 30 June 20X7.

Note. Your answer should highlight any issues which Mowair Co should be considering in the near future. **(14 marks)**

(Total = 20 marks)

249 Perkins Co (Mar/Jun 18) (36 mins)

Below are extracts from the statements of profit or loss for the Perkins Group and Perkins Co for the years ending 31 December 20X7 and 20X6 respectively.

	20X7 *(Consolidated)*	*20X6* *(Perkins Co individual)*
	$'000	$'000
Revenue	46,220	35,714
Cost of sales	(23,980)	(19,714)
Gross profit	22,240	16,000
Operating expenses	(3,300)	(10,000)
Profit from operations	18,940	6,000
Finance costs	(960)	(1,700)
Profit before tax	17,980	4,300

The following information is relevant:

On 1 September 20X7, Perkins Co sold all of its shares in Swanson Co, its only subsidiary, for $28.64 million. At this date, Swanson Co had net assets of $26.1 million. Perkins Co originally acquired 80% of Swanson Co for $19.2 million, when Swanson Co had net assets of $19.8 million. Perkins Co uses the fair value method for valuing the non-controlling interest, which was measured at $4.9 million at the date of acquisition. Goodwill in Swanson Co has not been impaired since acquisition.

In order to compare Perkin Co's results for the years ended 20X6 and 20X7, the results of Swanson Co need to be eliminated from the above consolidated statements of profit or loss for 20X7. Although Swanson Co was correctly accounted for in the group financial statements for the year ended 31 December 20X7, a gain on disposal of Swanson Co of $9.44 million is currently included in operating expenses. This reflects the gain which should have been shown in Perkins Co's individual financial statements.

In the year ended 31 December 20X7, Swanson Co had the following results:

	$m
Revenue	13.50
Cost of sales	6.60
Operating expenses	2.51
Finance costs	1.20

During the period from 1 January 20X7 to 1 September 20X7, Perkins Co sold $1 million of goods to Swanson Co at a margin of 30%. Swanson Co had sold all of these goods on to third parties by 1 September 20X7.

Swanson Co previously used space in Perkins Co's properties, which Perkins Co did not charge Swanson Co for. Since the disposal of Swanson Co, Perkins Co has rented that space to a new tenant, recording the rental income in operating expenses.

The following ratios have been correctly calculated based on the above financial statements:

	20X7 (Consolidated)	*20X6 (Perkins Co individual)*
Gross profit margin	48.1%	44.8%
Operating margin	41%	16.8%
Interest cover	19.7 times	3.5 times

Required

(a) Calculate the gain on disposal which should have been shown in the consolidated statement of profit or loss for the Perkins group for the year ended 31 December 20X7. **(5 marks)**

(b) Remove the results of Swanson Co and the gain on disposal of the subsidiary to prepare a revised statement of profit or loss for the year ended 31 December 20X7 for Perkins Co only. **(4 marks)**

(c) Calculate the equivalent ratios to those given for Perkins Co for 20X7 based on the revised figures in part (b) of your answer. **(2 marks)**

(d) Using the ratios calculated in part (c) and those provided in the question, comment on the performance of Perkins Co for the years ended 31 December 20X6 and 20X7. **(9 marks)**

(Total = 20 marks)

250 Pirlo Co (Mar/Jun 2019 amended) (36 mins)

The consolidated statements of profit or loss for the Pirlo group for the years ended 31 December 20X9 and 20X8 are shown below.

	20X9	*20X8*
	$'000	$'000
Revenue	213,480	216,820
Cost of sales	(115,620)	(119,510)
Gross profit	97,860	97,310
Operating expenses	(72,360)	(68,140)
Profit from operations	25,500	29,170
Finance costs	(17,800)	(16,200)
Investment income	2,200	2,450
Profit before tax	9,900	15,420
Share of profit of associate	4,620	3,160
Tax expense	(2,730)	(3,940)
Profit for the year	11,790	14,640

Attributable to:

Shareholders of Pirlo Co	8,930	12,810
Non-controlling interest	2,860	1,830

The following information is relevant:

(1) On 31 December 20X9, the Pirlo group disposed of its entire 80% holding in Samba Co, a software development company, for $300m. The Samba Co results have been fully consolidated into the consolidated financial statements above. Samba Co does not represent a discontinued operation.

(2) The proceeds from the disposal of Samba Co have been credited to a suspense account and no gain/loss has been recorded in the financial statements above.

(3) Pirlo Co originally acquired the shares in Samba Co for $210m. At this date, goodwill was calculated at $70m. Goodwill has not been impaired since acquisition, and external advisers estimate that the goodwill arising in Samba Co has a value of $110m at 31 December 20X9.

(4) On 31 December 20X9, Samba Co had net assets with a carrying amount of $260m. In addition to this, Samba Co's brand name was valued at $50m at acquisition in the consolidated financial statements. This is not reflected in Samba Co's individual financial statements, and the value is assessed to be the same at 31 December 20X9.

(5) Samba Co is the only subsidiary in which the Pirlo group owned less than 100% of the equity. The Pirlo group uses the fair value method to value the non-controlling interest. At 31 December 20X9, the non-controlling interest in Samba Co is deemed to be $66m.

(6) Until December 20X8, Pirlo Co rented space in its property to a third party. This arrangement ended and, on 1 January 20X9, Samba Co's administrative department moved into Pirlo Co's property. Pirlo Co charged Samba Co a reduced rent. Samba Co's properties were sold in April 20X9 at a profit of $2m which is included in administrative expenses.

(7) On 31 December 20X9, the employment of the two founding directors of Samba Co was transferred to Pirlo Co. From the date of disposal, Pirlo Co will go into direct competition with Samba Co. As part of this move, the directors did not take their annual bonus of $1m each from Samba Co. Instead, they received a similar 'joining fee' from Pirlo Co, which was paid to them on 31 December 20X9. These individuals have excellent relationships with the largest customers of Samba Co, and are central to Pirlo Co's future plans.

(8) Samba Co's revenue remained consistent at $26m in both 20X9 and 20X8 and Samba Co has high levels of debt. Key ratios from the Samba Co financial statements are shown below:

	20X9	20X8
Gross profit margin	81%	80%
Operating profit margin	66%	41%
Interest cover	1.2 times	1.1 times

Required

(a) Calculate the gain/loss on the disposal of Samba Co which will be recorded in: **(4 marks)**

(i) The individual financial statements of Pirlo Co; and

(ii) The consolidated financial statements of the Pirlo Group.

(b) Calculate ratios equivalent to those provided in note (viii) for the Pirlo Group for the years ended 31 December 20X9 and 20X8. No adjustment is required for the gain/loss on disposal from (a). **(3 marks)**

(c) Briefly explain the conditions that the directors of Pirlo would have considered in determining whether Samba Co was a discontinued operation and briefly explain the impact on the group financial statements if they had determined that Samba Co was a discontinued operation.

(3 marks)

(d) Comment on the performance and interest cover of the Pirlo Group for the years ended 31 December 20X9 and 20X8. Your answer should comment on:

- The overall performance of the Pirlo Group;
- How, once accounted for, the disposal of Samba Co will impact on your analysis; and
- The implications of the disposal of Samba Co for the future results of the Pirlo Group.

(10 marks)

(Total = 20 marks)

251 Karl Co (September/December 2020) (36 mins)

At 1 January 20X8, the Karl group consisted of the parent, Karl Co, and two wholly-owned subsidiaries. There were no intra-group transactions during the year.

The sale of one of the subsidiaries, Sinker Co, was completed on 31 December 20X8 when Karl Co sold its entire holding for $20 million cash. Sinker Co had net assets of $29 million at the date of disposal. The sale does not meet the definition of a discontinued operation and has been correctly accounted for in the consolidated financial statements. The gain/loss on disposal of Sinker Co is included in administrative expenses.

Karl Co had originally purchased Sinker Co on 1 January 20X2 for $35 million. The fair value and carrying amount of net assets of Sinker Co at the date of acquisition were $28 million. Goodwill was considered to be impaired by 70% at 31 December 20X8.

Extracts from the consolidated financial statements for the years ended 31 December 20X8 and 20X7 are shown below:

EXTRACTS FROM THE STATEMENTS OF PROFIT OR LOSS FOR THE YEAR ENDED 31 DECEMBER

	Consolidated 20X8	*Consolidated 20X7*
	$m	$m
Revenue	289	272
Cost of sales	(165)	(140)
Gross profit	**124**	**132**
Administrative expenses	(45)	(23)
Distribution costs	(15)	(13)
Operating profit / (loss)	**64**	**96**

EXTRACTS FROM THE STATEMENTS OF FINANCIAL POSITION AS AT 31 DECEMBER

	Consolidated 20X8	Consolidated 20X7
	$m	$m
Current assets	112	125
Equity	621	578
Non-current liabilities	100	150
Current liabilities	36	161

The following information is also relevant:

(1) The majority of non-current liabilities is comprised of bank loans.

(2) Sales of Sinker Co represented 14% of the total group sales for 20X8, however, in March 20X8, Sinker Co lost a significant customer contract resulting in a number of redundancies. These redundancy costs amounted to $15 million and are included in administrative expenses. Overall, Sinker Co made an operating loss of $17 million.

(3) The Karl group manufactures food packaging. The inventory included in the above consolidated statement of financial position is:

Group inventory at

	$m
31 December 20X8	65
31 December 20X7	78

(4) At 31 December 20X8, Sinker Co had inventory of $42 million.

Required

(a) Calculate the gain/loss arising on the disposal of Sinker Co in the consolidated financial statements of the Karl group. **(4 marks)**

(b) Based on the financial statements provided, calculate the following ratios and comment on the financial performance and position of the Karl group for the years ended 31 December 20X8 and 20X7:

(1) Gross profit margin;

(2) Operating profit margin;

(3) Return on capital employed;

(4) Current ratio; and

(5) Gearing ratio (debt/debt + equity)).

Note. A maximum of 5 marks is available for the calculation of ratios. **(13 marks)**

(c) Comment on how the sale of Sinker Co will affect the comparability of the consolidated financial statements for the years ended 31 December 20X7 and 20X8. **(3 marks)**

(Total = 20 marks)

252 Kostner Co (36 mins)

Statement of cash flows for Kostner Co for the year ended 31 December 20X8

	$'000	$'000
Cash flows from operating activities		
Profit before taxation	350	
Adjustments for:		
Depreciation	600	
Profit on disposal of PPE	(3,000)	
Interest expense	270	
	(1,810)	
(Increase) decrease in inventories	(838)	
(Increase) decrease in trade & other receivables	(722)	
Increase (decrease) in provisions	50	

	$'000	$'000
Increase (decrease) in trade payables	710	
Cash used in operations	(2,610)	
Interest paid	(300)	
Income taxes paid	(472)	
Net cash from operating activities		(3,382)
Cash flows from investing activities		
Interest received	40	
Proceeds from disposal of property	9,900	
Purchase of property, plant and equipment	(800)	
Net cash from investing activities		9,140
Cash flows from financing activities		
Proceeds from long term borrowings	1,100	
Proceeds from issue of share capital	1,500	
Payments under leases	(2,440)	
Net cash from financing activities		160
Net increase in cash and cash equivalents		5,918
Cash and cash equivalents at beginning of period		(2,500)
Cash and cash equivalents at end of period		3,418

Extract of the statement of profit or loss for the year ended 31 December 20X8

	31 December 20X8	*31 December 20X7*
	$'000	$'000
Revenue	3,206	3,107
Cost of sales	(807)	(745)
Gross profit	2,399	2,362
Administration costs	(379)	(350)
Other operating expenses	(1,470)	(920)
Operating profit	550	1,092
Interest paid	(270)	(20)
Interest received	40	39
Profit before taxation	320	1,111

Kostner Co runs a small number of gym and leisure facilities in the south-west of England.

The following information is also provided regarding the company:

- Inventories held by the gyms are mainly consumables such as towels, drinks and snacks which are all available for purchase by the clients. During December, Kostner purchased a new range of high protein recovery drinks, ProBizz. Marty Grosman, the Purchases Manager, helped Kostner obtain a 'great margin' on the drinks by buying in bulk. Revenue from consumables has remained relatively static year on year.

- Gym members pay an annual subscription by monthly direct debit. New members must pay a non-refundable joining fee which is recognised immediately in the financial statements.
- Other revenue comes from Kostner licensing out its brand of bespoke fitness classes, the 'TotemPower', based on a core strength workout using poles. The licence is capitalised and reviewed for impairment on an annual basis.
- During September, it was decided to rent out some of the unused studio space for freelance gym instructors to use to put on specialist group classes such as Pump Strength, Hi-Intensity Workout, PilaYoga and Free Dance. This has proved very popular, with the freelancers being invoiced in arrears. This amount was outstanding at year end as the credit controller had been on long term sick leave.
- There was an inaugural fitness festival to attract clients to the gyms in the new year which was held at the South Kimble gym in December, income of $325,000 from this event is currently outstanding from the organisers. This debt is expected to be recovered in full.
- There is a provision in the accounts for a legal claim made against Kostner from a client who injured herself on a faulty piece of equipment. The provision in the accounts recognises that the claim is likely to succeed and is close to settlement at the year end.

Breakdown of the revenue

	20X8	20X7
	$'000	$'000
Fitness festival	325	-
TotemPower	280	260
Rental of rooms	300	-
Membership & sundries	2,301	2,847
Total revenue	3,206	3,107

Required

(a) Interpret the profitability and cash flow of Kostner Co using the information provided. Highlight any areas of concern for the management team supporting your answer with relevant evidence. **(15 marks)**

(b) Compare the usefulness of information from the statement of cash flows with that obtained from the statement of profit or loss extract. **(5 marks)**

(Total = 20 marks)

PART D: PREPARATION OF FINANCIAL STATEMENTS (I)

Section C of the exam will include a question on the preparation of financial statements for single entities or groups. You may be asked to prepare a single entity statement of profit or loss and other comprehensive income or a statement of financial position. You may be also asked to prepare a statement of changes in equity for a single entity or extracts from the single entity statement of cash flows. In respect of group accounting, you may be asked to prepare a consolidated statement of profit or loss and other comprehensive income or a consolidated statement of financial position for a simple group. The FR syllabus defines a simple group as a parent and up to two subsidiaries controlled by the parent, and one associate of the parent.

Section A questions

Questions 253–266: Consolidated statement of financial position (Chapter 8)

Questions 267–274: Consolidated statement of profit or loss and other comprehensive income (Chapter 9)

Questions 275–279: Disposals of subsidiaries (Chapter 10)

Questions 280–287: Accounting for associates (Chapter 11)

Questions 288–292: Presentation of published financial statements (Chapter 17)

Questions 293–297: Statement of cash flows (Chapter 22)

Section B questions on these topics are in questions 298–327

Section C questions on these topics are in questions 328–337

Section A

Consolidated statement of financial position (50 mins)

253 Witch Co acquired 70% of the 200,000 equity shares of Wizard Co, its only subsidiary, on 1 April 20X8 when the retained earnings of Wizard Co were $450,000. The carrying amounts of Wizard Co's net assets at the date of acquisition were equal to their fair values.

Witch Co measures non-controlling interest at fair value, based on share price. The market value of Wizard Co shares at the date of acquisition was $1.75.

At 31 March 20X9 the retained earnings of Wizard Co were $750,000. At what amount should the non-controlling interest appear in the consolidated statement of financial position of Witch Co at 31 March 20X9?

$ [ ] **(2 marks)**

---

254 Cloud Co obtained a 60% holding in the 100,000 $1 shares of Mist Co on 1 January 20X8. Cloud Co paid $250,000 cash immediately with an additional $400,000 payable on 1 January 20X9 and one share in Cloud Co for each two shares acquired. Cloud Co has a cost of capital of 8% and the market value of its shares on 1 January 20X8 was $2.30.

What was the total consideration paid for Cloud Co's share of Mist Co?

- O $689,370
- O $719,000
- O $758,370
- O $788,000 **(2 marks)**

---

255 On 1 June 20X1, Premier Co acquired 80% of the equity share capital of Sandford Co. At the date of acquisition the fair values of Sandford Co's net assets were equal to their

carrying amounts with the exception of its property. This had a fair value of $1.2 million BELOW its carrying amount. The property had a remaining useful life of eight years.

What effect will any adjustment required in respect of the property have on group retained earnings at 30 September 20X1?

$ [ ] [ ] **(2 marks)**

---

256 On 1 August 20X7, Patronic Co purchased 18 million of the 24 million $1 equity shares of Sardonic Co. The acquisition was through a share exchange of two shares in Patronic Co for every three shares in Sardonic Co. The market price of a share in Patronic Co at 1 August 20X7 was $5.75. Patronic Co will also pay in cash on 31 July 20X9 (two years after acquisition) $2.42 per acquired share of Sardonic Co. Patronic Co's cost of capital is 10% per annum.

What is the amount of the consideration attributable to Patronic Co for the acquisition of Sardonic Co?

- O $105 million
- O $139.5 million
- O $108.2 million
- O $103.8 million

(2 marks)

---

257 On 1 April 20X0, Picant Co acquired 75% of Sander Co's equity shares by means of a share exchange and an additional amount payable on 1 April 20X1 that was contingent upon the post-acquisition performance of Sander Co. At the date of acquisition Picant Co assessed the fair value of this contingent consideration at $4.2 million but by 31 March 20X1 it was clear that the amount to be paid would be only $2.7 million.

Using the drag and drop options below, demonstrate how Picant Co would account for this $1.5 million adjustment in its financial statements as at 31 March 20X1?

Account		
Current liabilities		Debit
Goodwill		Credit
Retained earnings		

(2 marks)

---

258 Crash Co acquired 80% of Bang Co's 100,000 $1 ordinary shares for $800,000 when the retained earnings of Bang Co were $570,000.

Bang Co also has an internally developed customer list which has been independently valued at $90,000.

The directors of Crash Co are deciding whether to recognise non-controlling interest at fair value or at its share of the net assets of Bang Co at the date of acquisition. The fair value of the non-controlling interest in Bang Co was judged to be $220,000 at the date of acquisition.

What was the goodwill arising on the acquisition of Bang Co if the NCI is measured at fair value or as a proportionate share of the net assets at acquisition?

Fair value	Share of net assets
▼	▼

Pull down list

- $192,000
- $260,000
- $264,000
- $350,000

(2 marks)

---

259 Tazer Co, a parent company, acquired Lowdown Co, an unincorporated entity, for $2.8 million. A fair value exercise performed on Lowdown Co's net assets at the date of purchase showed:

	$'000
Property, plant and equipment	3,000
Identifiable intangible asset	500
Inventories	300
Trade receivables less payables	200
	4,000

How should the purchase of Lowdown be reflected in Tazer Co's consolidated statement of financial position?

- O Record the net assets at the carrying amounts shown above and credit profit or loss with $1.2 million
- O Record the net assets at the carrying amounts shown above and credit Tazer Co's consolidated goodwill with $1.2 million
- O Derecognise the identifiable intangible asset, record the remaining net assets at the carrying amounts shown above and credit profit or loss with $700,000
- O Record the purchase as a financial asset investment at $2.8 million **(2 marks)**

---

260 Pratt Co acquired two subsidiaries in the year ended 31 December 20X5. Pratt Co values non-controlling interests at fair value.

On 1 January 20X5, Pratt Co acquired 80% of the equity shares of Sam Co. Goodwill at the date of acquisition was correctly calculated as $20,000. The goodwill of Sam Co was not impaired in the year ended 31 December 20X5.

In reviewing the fair value of Sam Co's net assets at acquisition, Pratt Co concluded that property, plant and equipment, with a remaining life of five years, had a fair value of $5,000 in excess of its carrying amount.

On 1 April 20X5, Pratt Co acquired 75% of the equity shares of Tait Co. Goodwill at the date of acquisition was correctly calculated as $50,000. At 31 December 20X5, the goodwill in Tait Co was impaired by 40%.

Sam Co has not incorporated these adjustments into its individual financial statements.

What is the total charged to group retained earnings at 31 December 20X5 as a result of these consolidation adjustments?

- $15,800
- $21,000
- $15,750
- $16,800

(2 marks)

---

261 Platt Co has owned 60% of the issued equity share capital of Serpi Co for many years. At 31 October 20X7, the individual statements of financial position included the following:

	Platt Co	*Serpi Co*
	$	$
Current assets	700,000	500,000
Current liabilities	300,000	200,000

Neither had a bank overdraft at 31 October 20X7.

During the year ended 31 October 20X7, Platt Co made $100,000 sales on credit to Serpi Co. Serpi Co had one-quarter of these goods in inventory at 31 October 20X7. Platt Co makes a 20% gross profit margin on all sales.

On 31 October 20X7, Serpi Co sent a cheque for $50,000 to pay all of the outstanding balance due to Platt Co. Platt Co did not receive this cheque until 2 November 20X7.

Platt Co's policy for in-transit items is to adjust for them in the parent company.

In respect of current assets and current liabilities, what amounts will be reported in Platt Co's consolidated statement of financial position at 31 October 20X7?

- Current assets $1.197 million and current liabilities $0.5 million
- Current assets $1.145 million and current liabilities $0.45 million
- Current assets $1.195 million and current liabilities $0.45 million
- Current assets $1.195 million and current liabilities $0.5 million

(2 marks)

---

262 Boat Co acquired 60% of Anchor Co on 1 January 20X4. At the date of acquisition, the carrying amount of Anchor Co's net assets were the same as their fair values, with the exception of an item of machinery which had a carrying amount of $90,000, a fair value of $160,000 and a remaining useful life of five years. Non-controlling interests are valued at fair value.

What is the journal entry required to reflect this fair value adjustment in the consolidated statement of financial position of Boat Co as at 31 December 20X6?

			$	**$**
O	Debit	Retained earnings	25,200	
	Debit	Non-controlling interest	16,800	
			28,000	
	Debit	Property, plant and equipment		70,000
	Credit	Goodwill		
O	Debit	Retained earnings	8,400	
	Debit	Non-controlling interest	5,600	
			56,000	
	Debit	Property, plant and equipment		70,000
	Credit	Goodwill		

			$	$
O	Debit	Retained earnings	57,600	
	Debit	Non-controlling interest	38,400	
	Debit	Property, plant and equipment	64,000	
	Credit	Goodwill		160,000
O	Debit	Retained earnings	42,000	
	Debit	Property, plant and equipment	28,000	
	Credit	Goodwill		70,000

(2 marks)

---

263 On 1 July 20X5, Pull Co acquired 80% of the equity of Sat Co. At the date of acquisition, goodwill was calculated as $10,000 and the non-controlling interest was measured at fair value. In conducting the fair value exercise on Sat Co's net assets at acquisition, Pull Co concluded that property, plant and equipment with a remaining life of ten years had a fair value of $300,000 in excess of its carrying amount. Sat Co had not incorporated this fair value adjustment into its individual financial statements.

At the reporting date of 31 December 20X5, the goodwill was fully impaired. For the year ended 31 December 20X5, Sat Co reported a profit for the year of $200,000.

What is the Pull Group profit for the year ended 31 December 20X5 that is attributable to non-controlling interests?

O $16,000

O $12,000

O $35,000

O $15,000 **(2 marks)**

---

264 Zebra Co acquired 75% of the 2 million issued $1 ordinary shares of Penguin Co on 1 January 20X2 for $3,700,000 when Penguin Co's retained earnings were $1,770,000. Zebra Co has no other subsidiaries.

Zebra Co elected to measure non-controlling interests in Penguin Co at their fair value of $1,140,000 at the acquisition date.

An impairment review performed on 31 December 20X3 indicated that goodwill on the acquisition of Penguin Co had been impaired by $100,000. No impairment was recognised in the year ended 31 December 20X2.

Which **THREE** of the following statements are true in respect of the non-controlling interest to be included in the consolidated statement of financial position of the Zebra group for the year ended 31 December 20X3?

☐ Non-controlling interest would be higher if the proportionate method was used

☐ It will be included at its fair value on acquisition plus share of post-acquisition earnings of Penguin Co.

☐ It will be included as a separate component of equity.

☐ 25% of the impairment in the goodwill arising on acquisition will be debited to it.

☐ It will be included in the non-current liabilities of the Zebra group. **(2 marks)**

265 Platinum Co acquired 80% of the ordinary share capital of Palladium Co on 1 April 20X0 by means of cash and contingent consideration. At this date, Platinum Co assessed the fair value of contingent consideration at $250,000. Platinum Co measures non-controlling interest at fair value at the date of acquisition, which was estimated to be $100,000 the goodwill arising on acquisition was $300,000.

The following figures for Palladium Co are relevant:

	$'000
Ordinary shares of $1 each at acquisition	500
Retained earnings/(losses) at 1 January 20X0	(300)
Profit for the year ended 31 December 20X0	120

The profits for Palladium Co have accrued evenly throughout the year.

What was the cash consideration paid by Platinum Co for the investment in Palladium Co? ***(ACCA Financial Reporting March/June 2021 Examiner's report)***

$ [ ] **(2 marks)**

---

266 Indicate, by selecting the relevant boxes in the table, whether the following statements are true or false in relation to accounting for the acquisition of a subsidiary. ***(ACCA Financial Reporting March/June 2021 Examiner's report)***

Where a parent company is satisfied that there has been a gain on a bargain purchase (negative goodwill), it should be recognised in the consolidated statement of profit or loss immediately	**TRUE**	**FALSE**
If the liabilities of the acquired entity are overstated, then goodwill will also be overstated	**TRUE**	**FALSE**

(2 marks)

(Total = 28 marks)

Consolidated statement of profit or loss and other comprehensive income (29 mins)

267 Paprika Co purchased 75% of the equity share capital of Salt Co on 30 April 20X4. Non-controlling interests are measured at fair value.

The cost of sales of both companies for the year ended 30 April 20X6 are as follows:

	Paprika	*Salt*
	$	$
Cost of sales	60,000	100,000

The following information is provided:

(1) Salt Co had machinery included in its net assets at acquisition with a carrying amount of $120,000 but a fair value of $200,000. The machinery had a remaining useful life of eight years at the date of acquisition. All depreciation is charged to cost of sales.

(2) During the year, Salt Co sold some goods to Paprika Co for $32,000 at a margin of 25%. Three quarters of these goods remained in inventory at year end.

What is the cost of sales in Paprika Co's consolidated statement of profit or loss for the year ended 30 April 20X6?

- O $144,000
- O $132,000
- O $176,000
- O $140,000 **(2 marks)**

---

268 Hillusion Co acquired 80% of Skeptik Co on 1 July 20X2. In the post-acquisition period Hillusion Co sold goods to Skeptik Co at a price of $12 million. These goods had cost Hillusion Co $9 million. During the year to 31 March 20X3 Skeptik Co had sold $10 million (at cost to Skeptik Co) of these goods for $15 million.

How will this affect group cost of sales in the consolidated statement of profit or loss of Hillusion Co for the year ended 31 March 20X3?

- O Increase by $11.5 million
- O Increase by $9.6 million
- O Decrease by $11.5 million
- O Decrease by $9.6 million **(2 marks)**

---

269 On 1 July 20X7, Spider Co acquired 60% of the equity share capital of Fly Co and on that date made a $10 million loan to Fly Co at a rate of 8% per annum.

What will be the effect on group retained earnings at the year-end date of 31 December 20X7 when this intragroup transaction is cancelled?

- O Group retained earnings will increase by $400,000
- O Group retained earnings will be reduced by $240,000
- O Group retained earnings will be reduced by $160,000
- O There will be no effect on group retained earnings **(2 marks)**

---

270 Wiley Co acquired 80% of Coyote Co on 1 January 20X8. At the date of acquisition Coyote Co had a building which had a fair value $22 million and a carrying amount of $20 million. The remaining useful life of the building was 20 years.

Coyote Co's profit for the year to 30 June 20X8 was $1.6 million which accrued evenly throughout the year.

Wiley Co measures non-controlling interest at fair value. At 30 June 20X8 it estimated that goodwill in Coyote Co was impaired by $500,000.

What is the total comprehensive income attributable to the non-controlling interest at 30 June 20X8?

- O $40,000
- O $50,000
- O $187,500
- O $150,000 **(2 marks)**

---

271 Basil Co acquired 60% of Parsley Co on 1 March 20X9. In September 20X9 Basil Co sold $46,000 worth of goods to Parsley Co. Basil Co applies a 30% mark-up to all its sales. 25% of these goods were still held in inventory by Parsley Co at the end of the year.

An extract from the draft statements of profit or loss of Basil Co and Parsley Co at 31 December 20X9 is:

	Basil Co	Parsley Co
	$	$
Revenue	955,000	421,500
Cost of sales	(407,300)	(214,600)
Gross profit	547,700	206,900

All revenue and costs arise evenly throughout the year.

What will be shown as gross profit in the consolidated statement of profit or loss of Basil Co for the year ended 31 December 20X9?

$ ______ **(2 marks)**

---

272 Premier Co acquired 80% of Sanford Co on 1 June 20X1. Sales from Sanford Co to Premier Co throughout the year ended 30 September 20X1 were consistently $1 million per month. Sanford Co made a mark-up on cost of 25% on these sales. At 30 September 20X1 Premier Co was holding $2 million inventory that had been supplied by Sanford Co in the post-acquisition period.

By how much will the unrealised profit decrease the profit attributable to the non-controlling interest for the year ended 30 September 20X1?

$ ______ **(2 marks)**

---

273 Brigham Co has owned 70% of Dorset Co for many years. It also holds a $5 million 8% loan note from Dorset Co. The financial statements of Dorset Co show a profit for the year ended 31 December 20X6 of $1.3 million.

Brigham Co acquired 80% of the equity shares in York Co on 1 July 20X6. The financial statements of York Co show a profit for the year ended 31 December 20X6 of $2.4 million.

The profits of all group companies accrue evenly across the year.

What is the amount attributable to the non-controlling interests in the consolidated statement of profit or loss? (Enter your answer to the nearest $'000)

$ ______ ,000 **(2 marks)**

---

274 Pearl Co has controlled an 80% owned subsidiary, Silver Co, for many years. Silver Co sold goods to Pearl Co for $120,000 at a mark-up of 20% during the year. Pearl Co had sold half of these goods by the year end.

Required

Which of the following statements regarding intra-group transactions in the consolidated financial statements are true or false? ***(Mar-Jun 2022)***

Revenue must be reduced by a total of $120,000	**TRUE**	**FALSE**
Cost of sales must be reduced by a total of $110,000	**TRUE**	**FALSE**
Non-controlling interest must be reduced by $2,000	**TRUE**	**FALSE**

(2 marks)

(Total = 16 marks)

Disposals of subsidiaries **(18 mins)**

275 On 1 January 20X3, Westbridge Co acquired all of Brookfield Co's 100,000 $1 shares for $300,000. The goodwill acquired in the business combination was $40,000, of which 50% had been written off as impaired by 31 December 20X5. On 31 December 20X5 Westbridge Co sold all of Brookfield Co's shares for $450,000 when Brookfield Co had retained earnings of $185,000.

Using the pull-down list provided, select which is the correct answer for the profit on disposal that should be included in the consolidated financial statements of Westbridge Co?

[▼]

Pull down list

- $145,000
- $165,000
- $245,000
- $330,000

(2 marks)

---

276 On 1 January 20X8, Lentil Co acquired all of Chickpea Co's 100,000 $1 shares for $400,000. The goodwill acquired in the business combination was $60,000, of which 40% had been written off as impaired by 31 December 20X8. On 31 December 20X5 Lentil Co sold all of Chickpea Co's shares for $680,000 when Chickpea Co had retained earnings of $215,000.

What is the profit on disposal that should be included in the individual entity financial statements of Lentil Co?

$ [ ] **(2 marks)**

---

277 Alderminster Co acquired a 70% holding in Bidford Co on 1 January 20X4 for $600,000. At that date the fair value of the net assets of Bidford Co was $700,000. Alderminster Co measures non-controlling interest at its share of net assets.

On 31 December 20X6 Alderminster Co sold all its shares in Bidford Co for $950,000. At that date the fair value of Bidford Co's net assets was $850,000. Goodwill was not impaired.

What was the profit or loss on disposal to be recognised in the consolidated financial statements of Alderminster Co?

[(1) ▼] [(2) ▼]

Pull down list 1

- $135,000
- $200,000
- $245,000
- $355,000

Pull down list 2

- Loss

- Profit

(2 marks)

---

278 Jalapeno Co is preparing its consolidated financial statements for the year ended 31 December 20X7. Jalapeno Co acquired a 75% holding in Habanero Co on 1 January 20X4 for consideration of $580,000. The fair value of the net assets of Habanero Co was $640,000 at that date. The goodwill of Habanero Co was impaired by 20% in the current year; it was not previously impaired. Jalapeno Co also acquired a holding of 70% of the shares in Bonnet Co on 1 January 20X5 with goodwill of $50,000 arising on acquisition. The goodwill in Bonnet Co has not been impaired. Jalapeno Co sold its entire holding of Bonnet Co on 31 December 20X7.

Jalapeno Co measures non-controlling interests at acquisition as a share of net assets.

What is the carrying amount of goodwill to be recognised in the consolidated financial statements of Jalapeno Co at 31 December 20X7?

$ [ ]

(2 marks)

---

279 At 1 January 20X2, the Dug Group consisted of Dug Co, the parent company, and its two wholly-owned subsidiaries Russel Co and Karl Co. There were no intra-group transactions during the year to 31 December 20X2.

Dug Co sold its entire holding of Russel Co for cash consideration of $50 million on 31 December 20X2. Dug Co had net assets of $39 million at the date of disposal. Dug Co had originally purchased Russel Co on 1 January 20X1 for consideration of $28 million when the net assets of Russel Co were $22 million. The goodwill was impaired by 50% in the year to 31 December 20X2.

What is the profit or loss recognised in the consolidated statement of profit or loss on the disposal of Russel Co? (You should enter a loss as a negative number.)

$ [ ] [ ]

(2 marks)

(Total = 10 marks)

Accounting for associates **(29 mins)**

280 On 1 October 20X8, Pacemaker Co acquired 30 million of Vardine Co's 100 million shares in exchange for 75 million of its own shares. The fair value of Pacemaker Co's shares at the date of this share exchange was $1.60 each.

Vardine Co's profit is subject to seasonal variation. Its profit for the year ended 31 March 20X9 was $100 million. $20 million of this profit was made from 1 April 20X8 to 30 September 20X8.

Pacemaker Co has one subsidiary and no other investments apart from Vardine Co.

What amount will be shown as 'investment in associate' in the consolidated statement of financial position of Pacemaker Co as at 31 March 20X9?

- O $144 million
- O $150 million
- O $78 million
- O $126 million

(2 marks)

281 Jarvis Co owns 30% of McLintock Co. During the year to 31 December 20X4 McLintock Co sold $2 million of goods to Jarvis Co, of which 40% were still held in inventory by Jarvis at the year end. McLintock Co applies a mark-up of 25% on all goods sold.

What effect would the above transactions have on group inventory at 31 December 20X4?

- O Debit group inventory $48,000
- O Debit group inventory $160,000
- O Credit group inventory $48,000
- O No effect on group inventory

(2 marks)

---

282 Ulysses Co owns 25% of Grant Co, which it purchased on 1 May 20X8 for $5 million. At that date Grant Co had retained earnings of $7.4 million. At the year-end date of 31 October 20X8 Grant Co had retained earnings of $8.5 million after paying out a dividend of $1 million. On 30 September 20X8, Grant Co sold $600,000 of goods to Ulysses Co, on which it made 30% profit. Ulysses Co had not resold these goods by 31 October.

At what amount will Ulysses Co report its investment in Grant Co in its consolidated statement of financial position at 31 October 20X8?

- O $5,000,000
- O $5,275,000
- O $5,230,000
- O $4,855,000

(2 marks)

---

283 On 1 February 20X3, Pinot Co acquired 30% of the equity shares of Noir Co, its only associate, for $10 million in cash. The profit for the year of Noir Co for the year to 30 September 20X3 was $6 million. Profits accrued evenly throughout the year. Noir Co made a dividend payment of $1 million on 1 September 20X3. At 30 September 20X3 Pinot Co decided that an impairment loss of $700,000 should be recognised on its investment in Noir Co.

What amount will be shown as 'investment in associate' in the statement of financial position of Pinot Co as at 30 September 20X3?

$ [ ]

(2 marks)

---

284 Ruby Co owns 30% of Emerald Co and exercises significant influence over it. Emerald Co reports a profit of $1,980,000 in its individual financial statements for the year ended 30 September 20X7. During the year, Emerald Co sold goods to Ruby Co for $160,000. Emerald Co applies a one-third mark-up on cost. Ruby Co still had 25% of these goods in inventory at the year end.

What amount should be recognised as the share of profit from the associate in the consolidated statement of profit or loss of Ruby Co for the year ended 30 September 20X7?

$ [ ]

(2 marks)

---

285 Chloe Co owns 40% of Amy Co and exercises significant influence over it. During the year, Chloe Co sold goods to Amy Co, earning a margin of 30% on the sale. Amy Co still had half of these goods in inventory at the year end.

Identify the correct adjustments to eliminate the unrealised profit in inventories.

Cost of sales		DR
Investment in associate		CR
Share of profit of associate		
Inventories		

(2 marks)

---

286 Identify **TWO** associate companies of Zuckal Co (identify one from each group).
(ACCA Examiner's Report, September/December 2020)

Associate 1	Associate 2
(1) ▼	(2) ▼

Pull down list 1

- Acquisition of 10% of Artles Co. Zuckal Co has no representation on the board or Artles Co. All decisions are made at board level.
- Acquisition of 40% of Bandoka Co. Due to an agreement with other shareholders, Zuckal Co effectively holds 52% of the voting rights.
- Acquisition of 50% of Castur Co. Zuckal Co has appointed two of the five board members.

Pull down list 2

- Acquisition of 15% of Furnitt Co. Zuckal Co can appoint one of Furnitt Co's five board members. No party can appoint more than two.
- Acquisition of 21% of Dunnatonn Co. The other 79% of Dunnatonn Co is owned by Yentee Co, a company with no links to Zuckal Co.
- Acquisition of 70% of Eahnn Co. Zuckal Co has been able to direct the operating activities of Eahnn Co for many years, and has exercised that right.

(2 marks)

---

287 Alpha Co acquired 80% of the ordinary share capital of Bravo Co on 1 September 20X4 and 40% of the ordinary share capital of Charlie Co a number of years ago.

On 30 November 20X4, Alpha Co sold goods to Bravo Co, making a profit of $2,000. Half of these items remained in inventory at the year end. The profit for the year ended 31 December 20X4 for each company is:

	Alpha Co ($)	Bravo Co ($)	Charlie Co ($)
Profit for the year	80,200	51,900	86,800

Required

What is the amount of profit attributable to the equity shareholders of Alpha Co in the consolidated statement of profit or loss for the year ended 31 December 20X4?

$ [ ] **(2 marks)**

(Total = 16 marks)

Presentation of published financial statements (18 mins)

288 Which of the following would not **NECESSARILY** lead to a liability being classified as a current liability?

- O The liability is expected to be settled in the course of the entity's normal operating cycle
- O The liability has arisen during the current accounting period
- O The liability is held primarily for the purpose of trading
- O The liability is due to be settled within 12 months after the end of the reporting period

(2 marks)

---

289 Which of the following would be shown in the 'other comprehensive income' section of the statement of profit or loss and other comprehensive income?

- O An increase in valuation on an investment property
- O Profit on sale of an investment
- O Receipt of a government grant
- O A revaluation surplus of a factory building **(2 marks)**

---

290 Using the pull-down list provided which of the following are **NOT** items required by IAS 1 *Presentation of Financial Statements* to be shown on the face of the statement of financial position?

[▼]

Pull down list

- Government grants
- Intangible assets
- Inventories
- Provisions

(2 marks)

---

291 How does IAS 1 *Presentation of Financial Statements* define the 'operating cycle' of an entity?

- O The time between acquisition of assets for processing and delivery of finished goods to customers
- O The time between delivery of finished goods and receipt of cash from customers
- O The time between acquisition of assets for processing and payment of cash to suppliers
- O The time between acquisition of assets for processing and receipt of cash from customers **(2 marks)**

292 Where are equity dividends paid presented in the financial statements?

- O As a deduction from retained earnings in the statement of changes in equity
- O As a liability in the statement of financial position
- O As an expense in profit or loss
- O As a loss in 'other comprehensive income' **(2 marks)**

(Total = 10 marks)

Statement of cash flows **(18 mins)**

293 Extracts from the statements of financial position of Nedburg Co are as follows.

Statements of financial position as at 30 September

	20X2	*20X1*
	$m	$m
Equity		
Ordinary shares of $0.50 each	750	500
Share premium	350	100
Retained earnings	1,980	1,740

On 1 October 20X1, a bonus issue of one new share for every ten held was made, financed from share premium. This was followed by a further issue for cash.

The statement of profit or loss of Nedburg Co shows a profit for the year of $480,000.

Using the pull-down list available, what amount will appear under 'cash flows from financing activities' in the statement of cash flows of Nedburg Co for the year ended 30 September 20X2 in respect of share issues?

[▼]

Pull down list

- $160 million
- $210 million
- $500 million
- $660 million

(2 marks)

294 The statement of financial position of Pinto Co at 31 March 20X7 showed property, plant and equipment with a carrying amount of $1,860,000. At 31 March 20X8 it had increased to $2,880,000.

During the year to 31 March 20X8, plant with a carrying amount of $240,000 was sold at a loss of $90,000, depreciation of $280,000 was charged and $100,000 was added to the revaluation surplus in respect of property, plant and equipment.

What amount should be presented in 'investing activities' in the statement of cash flows of Pinto Co for the year ended 31 March 20X8 as cash paid to acquire property, plant and equipment?

- O $1,640,000
- O $1,440,000
- O $1,260,000
- O $1,350,000

(2 marks)

---

295 The following information is available for the property, plant and equipment of Fry Co as at 30 September:

	20X4	*20X3*
	$'000	$'000
Carrying amounts	23,400	14,400

The following items were recorded during the year ended 30 September 20X4:

(1) Depreciation charge of $2.5 million

(2) An item of plant with a carrying amount of $3 million was sold for $1.8 million

(3) A property was revalued upwards by $2 million

(4) Environmental provisions of $4 million relating to property, plant and equipment were capitalised during the year

What amount would be shown in Fry Co's statement of cash flows for purchase of property, plant and equipment for the year ended 30 September 20X4?

- O $8.5 million
- O $12.5 million
- O $7.3 million
- O $10.5 million

(2 marks)

---

296 The carrying amount of property, plant and equipment was $410 million at 31 March 20X1 and $680 million at 31 March 20X2. Right of use assets are included within property, plant and equipment.

During the year, property with a carrying amount of $210 million was revalued to $290 million. The company entered into lease arrangements during the year. The lease liability was initially measured as $12 million. Direct costs of $1 million were paid to arrange the lease and a deposit of $5 million was paid to secure the lease. The total depreciation charge for the year was $115 million. There were no disposals.

What amount will appear in the statement of cash flows for the year ended 31 March 20X2 in respect of purchases of property, plant and equipment?

$ [ ]

(2 marks)

---

297 Extracts from Deltoid Co's statements of financial position are as follows:

STATEMENT OF FINANCIAL POSITION AS AT 31 MARCH

	20X1	*20X0*
	$'000	$'000
Non-current assets		
Property, plant and equipment		
Right-of-use asset	6,500	2,500

	20X1	20X0
	$'000	$'000
Non-current liabilities		
Lease liability	4,800	2,000
Current liabilities		
Lease liability	1,700	800

Right-of-use assets are initially measured equal to the initial amount of the lease liability, other than to correctly account for direct costs of $50,000 which were incurred on the arrangement of new lease contracts. During the year to 31 March 20X1 depreciation charged on right-of-use assets was $1,800,000.

What amount will be shown in the statement of cash flows of Deltoid Co for the year ended 31 March 20X1 in respect of payments made under leases?

$ ____________ **(2 marks)**

(Total = 10 marks)

Section B

Root Co and Branch Co case (18 mins)

Information relevant to questions 298–302

On 1 April 20X7, Root Co acquired 116 million of Branch Co's 145 million ordinary shares for an immediate cash payment of $210 million and issued at par one 10% $100 loan note for every 200 shares acquired.

At the date of acquisition Branch Co owned a recently built property that was carried at its depreciated construction cost of $62 million. The fair value of this property at the date of acquisition was $82 million and it had an estimated remaining useful life of 20 years.

Branch Co also had an internally developed brand which was valued at the acquisition date at $25 million with a remaining life of 10 years.

The inventory of Branch Co at 31 March 20X9 includes goods supplied by Root Co for a sale price of $56 million. Root adds a mark-up of 40% on cost to all sales.

298 What is the total amount of the consideration transferred by Root Co to acquire the investment in Branch Co? (Give your answer in millions.)

$ [ ] million **(2 marks)**

---

299 What will be the amount of the adjustment to group retained earnings at 31 March 20X9 in respect of the movement on the fair value adjustments?

- O $7 million
- O $3.5 million
- O $5.6 million
- O $2.8 million

(2 marks)

---

300 What is the amount of the unrealised profit arising from intragroup trading? (Give your answer in millions).

$ [ ] [ ] **(2 marks)**

---

301 Using the drag and drop options available, show how should the unrealised profit be posted?

Accounts		
Cost of sales		Debit
Inventories		Credit
Non-controlling interest		
Non-current assets		

(2 marks)

---

302 Branch Co has recently lost some large contracts and the directors of Root Co are wondering if Branch Co can be excluded from consolidation next year.

Which of the following situations would allow a subsidiary to be excluded from consolidation?

- O The activities of the subsidiary are significantly different to the activities of the rest of the group
- O Control of the subsidiary has been lost
- O Control of the subsidiary is only intended to be temporary
- O The subsidiary operates under long-term restrictions which prevent it from transferring funds to the parent **(2 marks)**

(Total = 10 marks)

Port Co and Alfred Co case (18 mins)

Information relevant to questions 303–307

On 1 November 20X4, Port Co purchased 75% of the equity of Alfred Co for $650,000. The consideration was 35,000 $1 equity shares in Port Co with a fair value of $650,000.

Noted below are extracts from the draft statements of profit or loss for Port Co and its subsidiary Alfred Co for the year ending 31 December 20X4 along with the draft statements of financial position as at 31 December 20X4.

The profits of Alfred Co have been earned evenly throughout the year.

DRAFT STATEMENTS OF PROFIT OR LOSS FOR THE YEAR ENDING 31 DECEMBER 20X4 (EXTRACT)

	Port Co	*Alfred Co*
	$'000	$'000
Gross profit	364	240
Profit for the year	330	96

DRAFT STATEMENTS OF FINANCIAL POSITION AS AT 31 DECEMBER 20X4 (EXTRACTS)

	Port Co	*Alfred Co*
	$'000	$'000
Equity		
$1 Equity shares	200	100
Share premium	500	85
Retained earnings	2,900	331
Revaluation surplus	30	–
	3,630	516

Port Co has not accounted for the issue of its own shares or for the acquisition of the investment in Alfred Co.

303 Using the drag and drop options below, show the balances on the share capital and share premium accounts at 31 December 20X4.

Share capital	Share premium
$	$
▼	▼

Pull down list

- 1,115,000
- 235,000
- 335,000
- 585,000

(2 marks)

---

304 What are the net assets of Alfred Co at acquisition?

$ [ ] **(2 marks)**

---

305 The accountant of Port Co is finalising the consolidated financial statements. Which **TWO** of the following statements are true regarding consolidated financial statements?

☐ The non-controlling interest share of profit is part of the consolidated statement of profit or loss

☐ Goodwill on acquisition should be amortised over a period not exceeding 20 years

☐ If a subsidiary is acquired during the year, its results are apportioned over the year of acquisition

☐ Only the group share of the subsidiary's non-current assets is shown in the statement of financial position **(2 marks)**

---

306 What is the amount of group gross profit for the year ended 31 December 20X4?

$ [ ] **(2 marks)**

---

307 What is group retained earnings at 31 December 20X4?

O $2,912,000

O $2,916,000

O $2,972,000

O $2,996,000 **(2 marks)**

(Total = 10 marks)

Polestar Co case **(18 mins)**

The following scenario relates to questions 308–312.

On 1 April 20X3, Polestar Co acquired 75% of the 12 million 50 cent equity shares of Southstar Co. Polestar Co made an immediate cash payment of $1.50 per share. The statements of profit or loss for the year ended 30 September 20X3 show revenue for Polestar Co and Southstar Co as $110 million and $66 million respectively. Revenue accrued evenly over the year.

Additional information:

(1) At the date of acquisition, the fair values of Southstar Co's assets were equal to their carrying amounts with the exception of right-of-use property held under a lease agreement. This had a fair value of $2 million above its carrying amount and a remaining lease term of ten years at that date. All depreciation is included in cost of sales.

(2) Contingent consideration was estimated to be $1.8 million at 1 April 20X3, but by 30 September 20X3 due to continuing losses, its value was estimated at only $1.5 million. The contingent consideration has not been recorded by Polestar Co and the directors expect the acquisition to be a bargain purchase.

(3) Polestar sold materials at their cost of $4 million to Southstar Co in June 20X3. Southstar Co processed all of these materials at an additional cost of $1.4 million and sold them back to Polestar Co in August 20X3 for $9 million. At 30 September 20X3 Polestar Co had $1.5 million of these goods still in inventory. There were no other intragroup sales.

(4) Polestar Co's policy is to value the non-controlling interest at fair value at the date of acquisition. Southstar Co's share price of $1.20 per share at that date can be deemed to be representative of the fair value of the shares held by the non-controlling interest. The retained earnings of Southstar at the acquisition date were $14.3 million.

308 What was the fair value of Southstar Co's net assets at the acquisition date? Submit your answer to one decimal place.

$ [ ] million **(2 marks)**

---

309 What is consolidated revenue for the year ended 30 September 20X3?

- O $130 million
- O $143 million
- O $163 million
- O $156 million **(2 marks)**

---

310 Due to lower-than-expected profits of the acquired company, Southstar Co, the estimated value of the contingent consideration has fallen from $1.8 million to $1.5 million.

Using the drag and drop options below, show how this be accounted for in Polestar Co.

Account		
Goodwill		Debit
Liability		Credit
Profit or loss		

(2 marks)

---

311 What is the amount of the adjustment to profit attributable to the non-controlling interest in respect of unrealised profit?

$ [ ]

(2 marks)

---

312 Polestar Co measures the non-controlling interest in Southstar Co at fair value. Which of the following applies when non-controlling interest is measured at fair value?

- O The non-controlling interest will be allocated its share of any negative goodwill
- O The non-controlling interest will be allocated the whole of the pre-acquisition profits
- O The non-controlling interest will be allocated its share of any goodwill impairment
- O If the subsidiary's share price falls, the non-controlling interest will be adjusted

(2 marks)

(Total = 10 marks)

Plateau Co case (18 mins)

The following information relates to questions 313–317.

On 1 October 20X6, Plateau Co acquired the following non-current investments:

- Three million equity shares in Savannah Co by an exchange of one share in Plateau Co for every two shares in Savannah Co plus $1.25 per acquired Savannah Co share in cash. The market price of each Plateau Co share at the date of acquisition was $6 and the market price of each Savannah Co share at the date of acquisition was $3.25.
- 30% of the equity shares of Axle Co at a cost of $7.50 per share in cash.

Only the cash consideration of the above investments has been recorded by Plateau Co.

Extracts from the summarised draft statements of financial position of the three companies at 30 September 20X7 are:

	Plateau Co	*Savannah Co*	*Axle Co*
	$'000	$'000	$'000
Equity shares of $1 each	10,000	4,000	4,000
Retained earnings			
– at 30 September 20X6	16,000	6,000	11,000
– for year ended 30 September 20X7	9,250	2,900	5,000
	35,250	12,900	20,000

The following information is relevant:

(1) At the date of acquisition Savannah Co had five years remaining of an agreement to supply goods to one of its major customers. The agreement has been consistently renewed when it expires. The directors of Plateau Co estimate that the value of this customer-based contract has a fair value of $1 million and an indefinite life and has not suffered any impairment.

(2) During the year ended 30 September 20X7 Savannah Co sold goods to Plateau Co for $2.7 million. Savannah Co had marked up these goods by 50% on cost. Plateau Co had a third of the goods still in its inventory at 30 September 20X7. There were no intragroup payables/receivables at 30 September 20X7.

(3) It is the group policy to value non-controlling interest at acquisition at full (or fair) value. For this purpose the share price of Savannah Co at the acquisition date should be used.

313 What is the total of the consideration paid by Plateau Co for Savannah Co?

- O $3,750,000
- O $9,750,000
- O $12,750,000
- O $21,750,000

(2 marks)

---

314 How should the customer contract in note (1) be accounted for?

- O Should not be recognised as item is internally generated
- O Group share of 75% should be recognised and not amortised
- O Should be recognised at $1 million and not amortised
- O Should be recognised at $1 million and amortised over five years

(2 marks)

---

315 What amount will be shown as non-controlling interest in the consolidated statement of financial position at 30 September 20X7?

- O $3,900,000
- O $3,250,000
- O $3,225,000
- O $3,975,000

(2 marks)

---

316 What amount will be shown in the consolidated statement of financial position at 30 September 20X7 in respect of the investment in Axle Co?

$ [ ]

(2 marks)

---

317 Plateau Co is negotiating a contract to supply goods to Axle Co in the coming year (ended 30 September 20X8) at 20% profit.

How will the unrealised profit on the sale of these goods be eliminated from the consolidated financial statements for the year ended 30 September 20X8? Select your answers from the drag and drop options provided.

Account		
Group inventory		Debit
Investment in associate		Credit
Share of profit of associate		
Cost of sales		

(2 marks)

(Total = 10 marks)

Pinto Co case (18 mins)

The following scenario relates to questions 318–322.

Pinto Co is a publicly listed company. The following financial statements of Pinto Co are available:

STATEMENT OF PROFIT OR LOSS AND OTHER COMPREHENSIVE INCOME FOR YEAR ENDED 31 MARCH 20X8 (EXTRACT)

	$'000
Profit before tax	440
Income tax expense	(160)
Profit for the year	280
Other comprehensive income	
Gains on property revaluation	100
Total comprehensive income	380

STATEMENTS OF FINANCIAL POSITION (EXTRACTS) AS AT

		31 March 20X8		*31 March 20X8*
	$'000	$'000	$'000	$'000
Non-current assets (Note (1))				
Property, plant and equipment		2,880		1,860
Investment property		420		400
		3,300		2,260
Equity				

		31 March 20X8		31 March 20X8
	$'000	$'000	$'000	$'000
Retained earnings		990		860
Non-current liabilities				
Deferred tax	50	50	30	430
Current liabilities				
Trade payables	1,610		1,270	
Current tax payable	150		–	

The following supporting information is available:

(1) An item of plant with a carrying amount of $240,000 was sold at a loss of $90,000 during the year. Depreciation of $280,000 was charged (to cost of sales) for property, plant and equipment in the year ended 31 March 20X8.

(2) Pinto Co uses the fair value model in IAS 40 Investment Property. Pinto Co sold investment property for $160,000 on 1 February 20X8. Its fair value at 1 April 20X7 was $140,000. Other movements in the carrying amount of investment property were due to fair value adjustments.

You are preparing a statement of cash flows for Pinto Co for the year to 31 March 20X8.

318 What is the amount of tax that Pinto Co either received or paid during the year?

O $60,000 paid

O $60,000 received

O $10,000 paid

O $10,000 received **(2 marks)**

---

319 What is the net cash used in investing activities?

$ [ ] **(2 marks)**

---

320 What was the amount of the dividend paid in the year?

O $150,000

O $250,000

O $50,000

O $310,000 **(2 marks)**

---

321 Under which **TWO** classification(s) can dividends paid be shown in the statement of cash flows?

☐ Investing activities

☐ Financing activities

☐ Operating activities

☐ Movement in payables **(2 marks)**

322 Which of the following items will **NOT** be adjusted against Pinto Co's profit before tax in arriving at net cash from operating activities?

- O The increase in trade payables
- O The proceeds from sale of plant
- O The increase in the warranty provision
- O The investment income **(2 marks)**

(Total = 10 marks)

Woolf Co case (18 mins)

The following scenario relates to questions 323–327.

The following extracts are from the draft financial statements of Woolf Co for the year ended 31 December 20X7:

	31 Dec 20X6	*31 Dec 20X7*
	$'000	$'000
Current liabilities		
Government grants	400	600
Lease liabilities	800	900
Non-current liabilities		
Government grants	900	1,400
Lease liabilities	1,700	2,000

	$'000
Interest received	40
Profit before taxation	50

The following supporting information is available:

(1) Woolf Co initially measured right-of-use assets acquired under lease contracts arranged during the year at $1,540,000. The amount was calculated as the initial measurement of the lease liability adjusted to take account of direct costs incurred of $40,000.

(2) Woolf Co purchased a factory during the year which qualified the company to receive government grants of $950,000, which was included within liabilities on receipt. Total depreciation recognised in profit before taxation was $2,200,000.

(3) The net movement in working capital balances resulted in an outflow of $100,000 over the course of the year.

323 Using the pull-down list provided, select the correct amount paid in respect of lease liabilities for the year ended 31 December 20X7.

[▼]

Pull down list

- $1,100,000
- $1,140,000

- $1,900,000
- $400,000

(2 marks)

---

324 Insofar as the information allows, what is the cash from operations figure for inclusion in the statement of cash flows for Woolf Co at 31 December 20X7?

O Cash inflow of $1,860,000

O Cash inflow of $2,110,000

O Cash inflow of $2,360,000

O Cash inflow of $3,060,000 **(2 marks)**

---

325 Which of the following statements provides a plausible reason for the movement in the working capital balances of Woolf Co during the year?

(1) A decrease in inventories due to a successful year end warehouse sale

(2) A decrease in trade receivables due to the recruitment of an experienced credit controller

(3) A decrease in trade payables due to Woolf Co seeking prompt payment discounts instead of utilising the full credit period terms

O Option (1) only

O Option (2) only

O Option (1) and (2)

O Option (3) only **(2 marks)**

---

326 Which of the following cash flows would **NOT** be included under cash flows from financing activities?

O Cash proceeds from issuing ordinary share capital

O Cash proceeds from repayments of lease liabilities

O Cash proceeds from the sale of a factory

O Cash payments from the issue of debentures by the company **(2 marks)**

---

327 IAS 20 *Government Grants and Disclosure of Government Assistance* allows two choices for the presentation of government grants relating to assets.

Which of the following accounting treatments would be valid options for Woolf Co to adopt in respect of the grant received for the factory unit?

(1) Recognise the income from the grant as deferred income

(2) Deduct the grant in arriving at the carrying amount of the asset acquired

(3) Present the whole grant as a separate credit in the statement of profit or loss within 'other income'

O Option (1) only

O Option (2) only

O Options (1) and (2)

O Option (3) **(2 marks)**

(Total = 10 marks)

Section C

328 Pedantic Co (Dec 2008 amended) (36 mins)

On 1 April 20X8, Pedantic Co acquired 60% of the equity share capital of Sophistic Co in a share exchange of two shares in Pedantic Co for three shares in Sophistic Co. At that date the retained earnings of Sophistic Co were $5 million. The issue of shares has not yet been recorded by Pedantic Co. At the date of acquisition shares in Pedantic Co had a market value of $6 each. Below are the summarised draft statements of financial position of both companies.

STATEMENTS OF FINANCIAL POSITION AS AT 30 SEPTEMBER 20X8

	Pedantic Co	Sophistic Co
	$'000	$'000
Assets		$'000
Non-current assets		
Property, plant and equipment	40,600	12,600
Current assets	16,000	6,600
Total assets	56,600	19,200
Equity and liabilities		
Equity shares of $1 each	10,000	4,000
Retained earnings	35,400	6,500
	45,400	10,500
Non-current liabilities		
10% loan notes	3,000	4,000
Current liabilities	8,200	4,700
Total equity and liabilities	56,600	19,200

The following information is relevant:

(1) At the date of acquisition, the fair values of Sophistic's assets were equal to their carrying amounts with the exception of an item of plant, which had a fair value of $2 million in excess of its carrying amount. It had a remaining life of five years at that date (straight-line depreciation is used). Sophistic Co has not adjusted the carrying amount of its plant as a result of the fair value exercise.

(2) Sales from Sophistic Co to Pedantic Co in the post-acquisition period were $8 million. Sophistic Co applied a mark-up on cost of 40% on these sales. Pedantic Co had sold $5.2 million (at cost to Pedantic Co) of these goods by 30 September 20X8.

(3) Sophistic Co's trade receivables at 30 September 20X8 include $600,000 due from Pedantic Co which did not agree with Pedantic Co's corresponding trade payable. This was due to cash in transit of $200,000 from Pedantic Co to Sophistic Co. Both companies have positive bank balances.

(4) Pedantic Co has a policy of accounting for any non-controlling interest at full fair value. The fair value of the non-controlling interest in Sophistic Co at the date of acquisition was estimated to be $5.9 million. Consolidated goodwill was not impaired at 30 September 20X8.

Required

(a) Prepare the consolidated statement of financial position for Pedantic Co as at 30 September 20X8. **(16 marks)**

(b) Pedantic Co has been approached by a potential new customer, Trilby Co, to supply it with a substantial quantity of goods on three-month credit terms. Pedantic Co is concerned at the risk that such a large order represents in the current difficult economic climate, especially as Pedantic Co's normal credit terms are only one month's credit. To support its application for credit, Trilby has sent Pedantic Co a copy of Tradhat Co's most recent audited consolidated financial statements. Trilby Co is a wholly owned subsidiary within the Tradhat Co group. Tradhat Co's consolidated financial statements show a strong statement of financial position including healthy liquidity ratios.

Comment on the importance that Pedantic Co should attach to Tradhat Co's consolidated financial statements when deciding on whether to grant credit terms to Trilby Co. **(4 marks)**

(Total = 20 marks)

329 Gold Co (March/June 2021) (36 mins)

On 1 January 20X2, Gold Co acquired 90% of the 16 million $1 equity share capital of Silver Co. Gold Co issued three new shares in exchange for every five shares it acquired in Silver Co. Additionally Gold Co will pay further consideration on 31 December 20X2 of $2.42 per share acquired. Gold Co's cost of capital is 10% per annum and the discount factor at 10% for one year is 0.9091. At the date of acquisition, shares in Gold Co and Silver Co had fair values of $8.00 and $3.50 respectively.

Statement of profit or loss for the year ended 30 September 20X2

	Gold Co	Silver Co
	$'000	$'000
Revenue	103,360	60,800
Cost of sales	(81,920)	(41,600)
Gross profit	**21,440**	**19,200**
Distribution costs	(2,560)	(2,980)
Administrative expenses	(6,080)	(3,740)
Investment income	800	–
Finance costs	(672)	–
Profit before tax	**12,928**	**12,480**
Income tax expense	(4,480)	(2,560)
Profit for the year	**8,448**	**9,920**

The following information is relevant:

(1) At 1 October 20X1, the retained earnings of Silver Co were $56 million.

(2) At the date of acquisition, the fair value of Silver Co's assets were equal to their carrying amounts with the exception of two items:

- An item of plant had a fair value of $2.6 million above its carrying amount. The remaining life of the plant at the date of acquisition was three years. Depreciation is charged to cost of sales.
- Silver Co had a contingent liability which Gold Co estimated to have a fair value of $850,000. This has not changed as at 30 September 20X2.

Silver Co has not incorporated these fair value changes into its financial statements.

(3) Gold Co's policy is to value the non-controlling interest at fair value at the date of acquisition. For this purpose, Silver Co's share price at that date can be deemed to be representative of the fair value of the shares held by the non-controlling interest.

(4) Sales from Gold Co to Silver Co in the post-acquisition period had consistently been $600,000 per month. Gold Co made a mark-up on cost of 25% on these sales. Silver Co had $1.2 million of these goods in inventory as at 30 September 20X2.

(5) Gold Co's investment income is a dividend received from its investment in a 40% owned associate which it has held for several years. The associate made a profit of $3 million for the year ended 30 September 20X2.

(6) On 1 October 20X1 Gold Co issued 100,000 $100 6% convertible loan notes at par value, with interest payable annually in arrears over a five-year term. The equivalent rate for non-convertible loan notes was 8%. Gold Co has recorded the loan notes as a liability at par value and charged the annual 6% interest to finance costs.

Rate	Discount factors in Year 5	Annuity factors for 5 years
6%	0.747	4.212
8%	0.681	3.993

(7) At 30 September 20X2 no impairment to goodwill is required.

(8) Profits accrue evenly throughout the year unless otherwise stated.

Required

(a) Calculate the goodwill arising on the acquisition of Silver Co. **(6 marks)**

(b) Prepare the consolidated statement of profit or loss for Gold Co for the year ended 30 September 20X2. **(14 marks)**

Note. All workings should be done to the nearest $'000.

(Total = 20 marks)

330 Paradigm Co (Dec 2011 amended) (36 mins)

On 1 October 20X2, Paradigm Co acquired 75% of Strata Co's equity shares by means of a share exchange of two new shares in Paradigm Co for every five acquired shares in Strata Co. In addition, Paradigm Co issued to the shareholders of Strata Co a $100 10% loan note for every 1,000 shares it acquired in Strata Co. Paradigm Co has not recorded any of the purchase consideration, although it does have other 10% loan notes already in issue.

The market value of Paradigm Co's shares at 1 October 20X2 was $2 each.

The summarised statements of financial position of the two companies at 31 March 20X3 are:

	Paradigm Co	Strata Co
	$'000	$'000
ASSETS		
Non-current assets		
Property, plant and equipment	47,400	25,500
Financial asset: equity investments (Note (1))	7,500	3,200
	54,900	28,700
Current assets		

	Paradigm Co	Strata Co
	$'000	$'000
Inventories (Note (2))	17,400	8,400
Trade receivables (Note (3))	14,800	9,000
Bank	5,100	–
Total assets	92,200	46,100
EQUITY AND LIABILITIES		
Equity		
Equity shares of $1 each	40,000	20,000
Retained earnings/(losses) – at 1 April 20X2	19,200	(4,000)
– for year ended 31 March 20X3	7,400	8,000
	66,600	24,000
Non-current liabilities		
10% loan notes	8,000	–
Current liabilities		
Trade payables (Note (3))	17,600	13,000
Bank overdraft	–	9,100
Total equity and liabilities	92,200	46,100

The following information is relevant:

(1) At the date of acquisition, Strata Co produced a draft statement of profit or loss which showed it had made a net loss for the year of $2 million at that date. Paradigm Co accepted this figure as the basis for calculating the pre- and post-acquisition split of Strata Co's profit for the year ended 31 March 20X3.

Also at the date of acquisition, Paradigm Co conducted a fair value exercise on Strata Co's net assets which were equal to their carrying amounts (including Strata Co's financial asset equity investments) with the exception of an item of plant which had a fair value of $3 million below its carrying amount. The plant had a remaining estimated useful life of three years at 1 October 20X2.

Paradigm Co's policy is to value the non-controlling interest at fair value at the date of acquisition. For this purpose, a share price for Strata Co of $1.20 each is representative of the fair value of the shares held by the non-controlling interest.

(2) Each month since acquisition, Paradigm Co's sales to Strata Co were consistently $4.6 million. Paradigm Co had marked these up by 15% on cost. Strata Co had one month's supply ($4.6 million) of these goods in inventory at 31 March 20X3. Paradigm Co's normal mark-up (to third party customers) is 40%.

(3) Strata Co's current account balance with Paradigm Co at 31 March 20X3 was $2.8 million, which did not agree with Paradigm Co's equivalent receivable due to a payment of $900,000 made by Strata Co on 28 March 20X3, which was not received by Paradigm Co until 3 April 20X3.

(4) The financial asset equity investments of Paradigm Co and Strata Co are carried at their fair values as at 1 April 20X2. As at 31 March 20X3, these had fair values of $7.1 million and $3.9 million respectively.

(5) There were no impairment losses within the group during the year ended 31 March 20X3.

Required

Prepare the consolidated statement of financial position for Paradigm Co as at 31 March 20X3.

(Total = 20 marks)

331 Viagem Co (Dec 2012 amended) (36 mins)

On 1 January 20X2, Viagem Co acquired 90% of the equity share capital of Greca Co in a share exchange in which Viagem Co issued two new shares for every three shares it acquired in Greca Co. Additionally, on 31 December 20X2, Viagem Co will pay the shareholders of Greca Co $1.76 per share acquired. Viagem Co's cost of capital is 10% per annum.

At the date of acquisition, shares in Viagem Co and Greca Co had a market value of $6.50 and $2.50 each respectively.

Statements of profit or loss for the year ended 30 September 20X2

	Viagem Co	Greca Co
	$'000	$'000
Revenue	64,600	38,000
Cost of sales	(51,200)	(26,000)
Gross profit	13,400	12,000
Distribution costs	(1,600)	(1,800)
Administrative expenses	(3,800)	(2,400)
Investment income	500	–
Finance costs	(420)	–
Profit before tax	8,080	7,800
Income tax expense	(2,800)	(1,600)
Profit for the year	5,280	6,200
Equity as at 1 October 20X1		
Equity shares of $1 each	30,000	10,000
Retained earnings	54,000	35,000

The following information is relevant:

(1) At the date of acquisition the fair values of Greca Co's assets were equal to their carrying amounts with the exception of two items:

(i) An item of plant had a fair value of $1.8 million above its carrying amount. The remaining life of the plant at the date of acquisition was three years. Depreciation is charged to cost of sales.

(ii) Greca Co had a contingent liability which Viagem Co estimated to have a fair value of $450,000. This has not changed as at 30 September 20X2.

Greca Co has not incorporated these fair value changes into its financial statements.

(2) Viagem Co's policy is to value the non-controlling interest at fair value at the date of acquisition. For this purpose, the market value of Greca Co's shares at that date can be deemed to be representative of the fair value of the shares held by the non-controlling interest.

(3) Sales from Viagem Co to Greca Co throughout the year ended 30 September 20X2 had consistently been $800,000 per month. Viagem Co made a mark-up on cost of 25% on these sales. Greca Co had $1.5 million of these goods in inventory as at 30 September 20X2.

(4) Viagem Co's investment income is a dividend received from its investment in a 40% owned associate which it has held for several years. The associate's profit for the year ended 30 September 20X2 was $2 million.

(5) Although Greca Co has been profitable since its acquisition by Viagem Co, the market for Greca Co's products has been badly hit in recent months and Viagem Co has calculated that the goodwill has been impaired by $2 million as at 30 September 20X2.

Required

(a) Calculate the goodwill arising on the acquisition of Greca Co. **(6 marks)**

(b) Prepare the consolidated statement of profit or loss for Viagem Co for the year ended 30 September 20X2. **(14 marks)**

(Total = 20 marks)

332 McIlroy Co (36 mins)

At 1 October 20X7, McIlroy Co had an 80% holding in Spieth Co and a 65% holding in Clarke Co.

On 30 September 20X8, McIlroy sold all of its 65,000 $1 shares in Clarke Co for $582,000. No accounting entries have been made to record the disposal, other than to record the disposal proceeds in a suspense account. The disposal is the final part of a plan by McIlroy Co to dispose of Clarke Co's operations because it operates in separate business sector to the other companies in the group. Clarke Co's retained earnings at 1 October 20X7 were $286,000. McIlroy Co measures all non-controlling interests using the proportionate method.

The draft individual statements of profit or loss of the three companies are shown below:

Draft statements of profit or loss for the year ended 30 September 20X8

	McIlroy Co	Spieth Co	Clarke Co
	$	$	$
Revenue	3,463,760	828,000	1,939,520
Cost of sales	(1,558,690)	(402,400)	(878,830)
Gross profit	1,905,070	425,600	1,060,690
Administrative expenses	(486,700)	(103,580)	(421,380)
Operating profit	1,418,370	322,020	639,310
Investment income	318,000)	–	–
Profit before tax	1,736,370	322,020	639,310
Income tax expense	(302,000)	(74,700)	(201,910)
Profit for the year	1,434,370	247,320	437,400

The draft individual statements of financial position at 30 September 20X8 for McIlroy Co and Spieth Co show:

	McIlroy Co	Spieth Co
	$	$
Equity		
Ordinary share capital ($1)	500,000	200,000
Retained earnings	3,419,310	581,580

Additional information

(1) McIlroy Co acquired its holding in Spieth Co on 1 October 20X4 when Spieth Co's retained earnings were $180,600. The fair values of Spieth Co's net assets at the date of acquisition were the same as their carrying amounts, with the exception of equipment which was estimated to have a fair value of $80,000 in excess of its carrying amount. The equipment had a remaining useful life of eight years at the date of acquisition. Depreciation is presented within administrative expenses. McIlroy Co had determined that the goodwill recognised on the acquisition of Spieth Co has been impaired by $30,000 in the current year.

(2) McIlroy Co acquired its holding in Clarke Co several years ago for $268,000 when Clarke Co's retained earnings were $174,200. The fair values of Clarke Co's net assets at the date of acquisition were the same as their carrying amounts. The goodwill in Clarke Co was impaired by $25,000 in the year ended 30 September 20X7. No further impairment of the goodwill in Clarke Co is required in the current year.

(3) During the year Spieth Co sold goods to McIlroy Co for $54,000 earning a gross margin of 20%. At the year-end McIlroy Co had half of these goods in inventory.

(4) McIlroy paid a dividend of $2.10 per share in the current year. Spieth Co paid a dividend of $1.50 per share during the current year. Clarke Co did not pay a dividend.

(5) Clarke Co is considered a discontinued operation of McIlroy Co in accordance with IFRS 5 *Non-current Assets Held for Sale and Discontinued Operations*.

Required

(a) Explain why Clarke Co is considered a discontinued operation of McIlroy Co. **(3 marks)**

(b) Prepare the consolidated statement of profit of loss for McIlroy Co for the year ended 30 September 20X8. **(13 marks)**

(c) Calculate the consolidated retained earnings balance as at 30 September 20X8. **(4 marks)**

(Total = 20 marks)

333 Plastik Co (Dec 2014 amended) (36 mins)

On 1 January 20X4, Plastik Co acquired 80% of the equity share capital of Subtrak Co. The consideration was satisfied by a share exchange of two shares in Plastik Co for every three acquired shares in Subtrak Co. At the date of acquisition, shares in Plastik Co and Subtrak Co had a market value of $3 and $2.50 each respectively. Plastik Co will also pay cash consideration of 27.5 cents on 1 January 20X5 for each acquired share in Subtrak Co. Plastik Co has a cost of capital of 10% per annum. None of the consideration has been recorded by Plastik Co.

Below are the summarised draft financial statements of both companies.

Statements of profit or loss and other comprehensive income for the year ended 30 September 20X4

	Plastic Co	Subtrak Co
	$'000	$'000
Revenue	62,600	30,000
Cost of sales	(45,800)	(24,000)
Gross profit	16,800	6,000
Distribution costs	(2,000)	(1,200)
Administrative expenses	(3,500)	(1,800)
Finance costs	(200)	–
Profit before tax	11,100	3,000
Income tax expense	(3,100)	(1,000)

	Plastic Co	Subtrak Co
	$'000	$'000
Profit for the year	8,000	2,000
Other comprehensive income:		
Gain on revaluation of property	1,500	–
Total comprehensive income	9,500	2,000

Statements of financial position as at 30 September 20X4

	Plastik Co	Subtrak Co
	$'000	$'000
ASSETS		
Non-current assets		
Property, plant and equipment	18,700	13,900
Current assets		
Inventories (Note (2))	4,300	1,200
Trade receivables	5,700	2,500
Cash and cash equivalents	–	300
	10,000	4,000
Total assets	28,700	17,900
EQUITY AND LIABILITIES		
Equity		
Equity shares of $1 each	10,000	9,000
Revaluation surplus (Note (1))	2,000	–
Retained earnings	6,300	3,500
	18,300	12,500
Non-current liabilities		
10% loan notes (Note (2))	2,500	1,000
Current liabilities		
Trade payables (Note (4))	3,400	3,600
Bank	1,700	–
Current tax payable	2,800	800
	7,900	4,400
Total equity and liabilities	28,700	17,900

The following information is relevant:

(1) At the date of acquisition, the fair values of Subtrak Co's assets and liabilities were equal to their carrying amounts with the exception of Subtrak Co's property which had a fair value of $4 million above its carrying amount. For consolidation purposes, this led to an increase in depreciation charges (in cost of sales) of $100,000 in the post-acquisition period to 30 September 20X4. Subtrak Co has not incorporated the fair value property increase into its entity financial statements.

The policy of the Plastik Co group is to revalue all properties to fair value at each year end. On 30 September 20X4, the increase in Plastik Co's property has already been recorded, however, a further increase of $600,000 in the value of Subtrak Co's property between its value at acquisition and 30 September 20X4 has not been recorded.

(2) Sales from Plastik Co to Subtrak Co throughout the year ended 30 September 20X4 had consistently been $300,000 per month. Plastik Co made a mark-up on cost of 25% on all these sales. $600,000 (at cost to Subtrak Co) of Subtrak Co's inventory at 30 September 20X4 had been supplied by Plastik Co in the post-acquisition period.

(3) Plastik Co's policy is to value the non-controlling interest at fair value at the date of acquisition. For this purpose Subtrak Co's share price at that date can be deemed to be representative of the fair value of the shares held by the non-controlling interest.

(4) Due to recent adverse publicity concerning one of Subtrak Co's major product lines, the goodwill which arose on the acquisition of Subtrak Co has been impaired by $500,000 as at 30 September 20X4. Goodwill impairment should be treated as an administrative expense.

(5) Assume, except where indicated otherwise, that all items of income and expenditure accrue evenly throughout the year.

Required

(a) Calculate the goodwill arising on the acquisition of Subtrak Co on 1 January 20X4. **(4 marks)**

(b) Calculate the following amounts for presentation in the consolidated statement of financial position: **(6 marks)**

(i) Group retained earnings

(ii) Non-controlling interest

(c) Prepare the consolidated statement of profit or loss and other comprehensive income for Plastik Co for the year ended 30 September 20X4. **(10 marks)**

(Total = 20 marks)

334 Laurel Co (36 mins)

Laurel Co has two subsidiaries, Hardy Co and Stan Co, and one associate, Comic Co. It is preparing its consolidated financial statements for the year to 31 December 20X9.

The statements of financial position of the four companies at 31 December 20X9 are set out below:

	Laurel Co	Hardy Co	Stan Co	Comic Co
	$m	$m	$m	$m
Non-current assets				
Property, plant and equipment	220	160	140	78
Investments	370	–	–	–
	590	160	140	78
Current assets				
Inventories	384	234	58	122
Trade receivables	275	166	124	67
Cash at bank	42	10	28	34
	701	410	210	223

	Laurel Co	Hardy Co	Stan Co	Comic Co
	$m	$m	$m	$m
	1,291	570	350	301
Equity				
Share capital – $1 ordinary shares	500	96	100	80
Share premium	46	3	–	–
Retained earnings	288	128	76	97
	834	227	176	177
Current liabilities				
Trade payables	457	343	174	124
	1,291	570	350	301

You are also given the following information:

(1) Laurel Co acquired 80% of the ordinary share capital of Hardy Co for $160m when the retained earnings of Hardy Co were $64m. The fair values of Hardy Co's assets were equal to their carrying amounts at the date of acquisition. Group policy is to measure non-controlling interests at fair value at the date of acquisition. The fair value of the non-controlling interests in Hardy Co on 1 January 20X7 was calculated as $39m.

(2) Laurel Co acquired 60% of the ordinary share capital of Stan Co for $140m on 1 January 20X7 when the retained earnings of Stan Co were $42m. At the date of acquisition, Stan Co owned some items of equipment with a carrying amount of $45m, which had had a fair value of $57m. These assets were originally purchased by Stan Co on 1 January 20X5 and are being depreciated over six years. The fair value of the non-controlling interests in Stan Co was $35m.

(3) On 1 January 20X8, Laurel Co acquired 40% of the ordinary share capital of Comic Co for $70m. The retained earnings of Comic Co were $24m at the date of acquisition.

(4) On 30 November 20X9, Laurel Co sold some goods to Hardy Co for cash for $32m. These goods had originally cost $22m and none had been sold by the year end. On 10 December 20X9 Laurel Co also sold goods to Comic Co for cash for $22m. These goods originally cost $10m and Comic Co had sold half by the year end.

(5) Cumulative impairment losses on recognised goodwill in Hardy Co amounted to $15 million at 31 December 20X9. Impairment losses on goodwill in Stan Co are $6m to the same date. No impairment losses have been necessary to date relating to the investment in the associate.

Required

Prepare a consolidated statement of financial position for the Laurel Group as at 31 December 20X9.

(Total = 20 marks)

335 Paladin Co (Dec 2011 amended) (36 mins)

On 1 October 20X0, Paladin Co secured a majority equity shareholding in Saracen Co on the following terms.

An immediate payment of $4 per share on 1 October 20X0; and a further amount deferred until 1 October 20X1 of $5.4 million.

The immediate payment has been recorded in Paladin Co's financial statements, but the deferred payment has not been recorded. Paladin Co's cost of capital is 8% per annum, giving the deferred payment a current cost at 1 October 20X0 of $5 million.

On 1 February 20X1, Paladin Co also acquired 25% of the equity shares of Augusta Co paying $10 million in cash.

The summarised statements of financial position of the three companies at 30 September 20X1 are:

	Paladin Co	Saracen Co	Augusta Co
	$'000	$'000	$'000
Assets			
Non-current assets			
Property, plant and equipment	40,000	31,000	30,000
Intangible assets	7,500	–	–
Investments – Saracen Co (8 million shares at $4 each)	32,000	–	–
– Augusta Co	10,000	–	–
	89,500	31,000	30,000
Current assets			
Inventories	11,200	8,400	10,000
Trade receivables	7,400	5,300	5,000
Cash and cash equivalents	3,400	–	2,000
Total assets	111,500	44,700	47,000
Equity and liabilities			
Equity			
Equity shares of $1 each	50,000	10,000	10,000
Retained earnings – at 1 October 20X0	25,700	12,000	31,800
– for year ended 30 September 20X1	9,200	6,000	1,200
	84,900	28,000	43,000
Non-current liabilities			
Deferred tax	15,000	8,000	1,000
Current liabilities			
Bank	–	2,500	–
Trade payables	11,600	6,200	3,000
Total equity and liabilities	111,500	44,700	47,000

The following information is relevant:

(1) Paladin Co's policy is to value the non-controlling interest at fair value at the date of acquisition. The directors of Paladin Co considered the fair value of the non-controlling interest in Saracen Co to be $7 million.

(2) At the date of acquisition, the fair values of Saracen Co's property, plant and equipment was equal to its carrying amount with the exception of Saracen Co's plant which had a fair value of $4 million above its carrying amount. At that date the plant had a remaining life of four years. Saracen Co uses straight-line depreciation for plant assuming a nil residual value.

Also at the date of acquisition, Paladin Co valued Saracen Co's customer relationships as a customer base intangible asset at fair value of $3 million. Saracen Co has not accounted for this asset. Trading relationships with Saracen Co's customers last on average for six years.

(3) At 30 September 20X1, Saracen Co's inventory included goods bought from Paladin Co (at cost to Saracen Co) of $2.6 million. Paladin Co had marked up these goods by 30% on cost. Paladin Co's agreed current account balance owed by Saracen Co at 30 September 20X1 was $1.3 million.

(4) Impairment tests were carried out on 30 September 20X1 which concluded that consolidated goodwill was not impaired, but, due to disappointing earnings, the value of the investment in Augusta Co was impaired by $2.5 million.

(5) Assume all profits accrue evenly through the year.

Required

Prepare the consolidated statement of financial position for Paladin Co as at 30 September 20X1.

(Total = 20 marks)

336 Dargent Co (Mar/Jun 2017) (36 mins)

On 1 January 20X6, Dargent Co acquired 75% of Latree Co's equity shares by means of a share exchange of two shares in Dargent Co for every three Latree Co shares acquired. On that date, further consideration was also issued to the shareholders of Latree Co in the form of $100 8% loan notes for every 100 shares acquired in Latree Co. None of the purchase consideration, nor the outstanding interest on the loan notes at 31 March 20X6, has yet been recorded by Dargent Co. At the date of acquisition, the share price of Dargent Co and Latree Co is $3·20 and $1·80 respectively.

The summarised statements of financial position of the two companies as at 31 March 20X6 are:

	Dargent Co	Latree Co
	$'000	$'000
Assets		
Non-current assets		
Property, plant and equipment (note (1))	75,200	31,500
Investment in Amery Co at 1 April 20X5 (note (4))	4,500	–
	79,700	31,500
Current assets		
Inventory (note (3))	19,400	18,800
Trade receivables (note (3))	14,700	12,500
Bank	1,200	600
	35,300	31,900
Total assets	115,000	63,400
Equity and liabilities		
Equity		
Equity shares of $1 each	50,000	20,000
Retained earnings – at 1 April 20X5	20,000	19,000
– for year ended 31 March 20X6	16,000	8,000
	86,000	47,000

	Dargent Co	Latree Co
	$'000	$'000
Non-current liabilities		
8% loan notes	5,000	–
Current liabilities (note (3))	24,000	16,400
	29,000	16,400
Total equity and liabilities	115,000	63,400

The following information is relevant:

(1) At the date of acquisition, the fair values of Latree Co's assets were equal to their carrying amounts. However, Latree Co operates a mine which requires to be decommissioned in five years' time. No provision has been made for these decommissioning costs by Latree Co. The present value (discounted at 8%) of the decommissioning is estimated at $4 million and will be paid five years from the date of acquisition (the end of the mine's life).

(2) Dargent Co's policy is to value the non-controlling interest at fair value at the date of acquisition. Latree Co's share price at that date can be deemed to be representative of the fair value of the shares held by the non-controlling interest.

(3) The inventory of Latree Co includes goods bought from Dargent Co for $2.1 million. Dargent Co applies a consistent mark-up on cost of 40% when arriving at its selling prices.

On 28 March 20X6, Dargent Co despatched goods to Latree Co with a selling price of $700,000. These were not received by Latree Co until after the year end and so have not been included in the above inventory at 31 March 20X6.

At 31 March 20X6, Dargent Co's records showed a receivable due from Latree Co of $3million, this differed to the equivalent payable in Latree Co's records due to the goods in transit.

The intra-group reconciliation should be achieved by assuming that Latree Co had received the goods in transit before the year end.

(4) The investment in Amery Co represents 30% of its voting share capital and Dargent Co uses equity accounting to account for this investment. Amery Co's profit for the year ended 31 March 20X6 was $6 million and Amery Co paid total dividends during the year ended 31 March 20X6 of $2 million. Dargent Co has recorded its share of the dividend received from Amery Co in investment income (and cash).

(5) All profits and losses accrued evenly throughout the year.

(6) There were no impairment losses within the group for the year ended 31 March 20X6.

Required

Prepare the consolidated statement of financial position for Dargent Co as at 31 March 20X6.

(Total = 20 marks)

337 Party Co (Sep/Dec 2017) (36 mins)

The following are the draft statements of financial position of Party Co and Streamer Co as at 30 September 20X5:

	Party Co	Streamer Co
	$'000	$'000
ASSETS		
Non-current assets		
Property, plant and equipment	392,000	84,000

	Party Co	Streamer Co
	$'000	$'000
Investments	120,000	–
	512,000	84,000
Current assets	94,700	44,650
Total assets	606,700	128,650
EQUITY AND LIABILITIES		
Equity		
Equity shares	190,000	60,000
Retained earnings	210,000	36,500
Revaluation surplus	41,400	4,000
	441,400	100,500
Non-current liabilities		
Deferred consideration	28,000	–
Current liabilities	137,300	28,150
Total equity and liabilities	606,700	128,650

The following information is relevant:

(1) On 1 October 20X4, Party Co acquired 80% of the share capital of Streamer Co. At this date the retained earnings of Streamer Co were $34 million and the revaluation surplus stood at $4 million. Party Co paid an initial cash amount of $92 million and agreed to pay the owners of Streamer Co a further $28 million on 1 October 20X6. The accountant has recorded the full amounts of both elements of the consideration in investments. Party Co has a cost of capital of 8%. The appropriate discount rate is 0.857.

(2) On 1 October 20X4, the fair values of Streamer Co's net assets were equal to their carrying amounts with the exception of some inventory which had cost $3 million but had a fair value of $3.6 million. On 30 September 20X5, 10% of these goods remained in the inventories of Streamer Co.

(3) During the year, Party Co sold goods totalling $8 million to Streamer Co at a gross profit margin of 25%. At 30 September 20X5, Streamer Co still held $1 million of these goods in inventory. Party Co's normal margin (to third party customers) is 45%.

(4) The Party group uses the fair value method to value the non-controlling interest. At acquisition the non-controlling interest was valued at $15 million.

Required

(a) Prepare the consolidated statement of financial position of the Party group as at 30 September 20X5. **(15 marks)**

(b) Party Co has a strategy of buying struggling businesses, reversing their decline and then selling them on at a profit within a short period of time. Party Co is hoping to do this with Streamer Co.

As an adviser to a prospective purchaser of Streamer Co, explain any concerns you would raise about making an investment decision based on the information available in the Party Group's consolidated financial statements in comparison to that available in the individual financial statements of Streamer Co. **(5 marks)**

(Total = 20 marks)

QUESTIONS

338 Fresco Co (Jun 2012 amended) (36 mins)

The following trial balance as at 31 March 20X2 has been extracted from the cloud accounting software used by Fresco Co:

	$'000	$'000
Equity shares of 50 cents each (Note (1))		45,000
Share premium (Note (1))		5,000
Retained earnings at 1 April 20X1		5,100
Freehold property (12 years) at cost (Note (2))	48,000	
Plant and equipment – at cost (Note (2))	47,500	
Accumulated depreciation of freehold property at 1 April 20X1		16,000
Accumulated depreciation of plant and equipment at 1 April 20X1		33,500
Inventories at 31 March 20X2	25,200	
Trade receivables (Note (3))	28,500	
Cash and cash equivalents		1,400
Deferred tax (Note (4))		3,200
Trade payables		27,300
Revenue		350,000
Cost of sales	298,700	
Lease payments (Note (2))	8,000	
Distribution costs	16,100	
Administrative expenses	26,900	
Bank interest	300	
Current tax (Note (4))	800	
Suspense account (Note (1))		13,500
	500,000	500,000

The following notes are relevant:

(1) The suspense account represents the corresponding credit for cash received for a fully subscribed rights issue of equity shares made on 1 January 20X2. The terms of the share issue were one new share for every five held at a price of 75 cents each. The price of the company's equity shares immediately before the issue was $1.20 each.

(2) Non-current assets:

Fresco Co decided to revalue its freehold property on 1 April 20X1. The directors accepted the report of an independent surveyor who valued the freehold property at $36 million on that date. Fresco Co has not yet recorded the revaluation. The remaining life of the freehold property is eight years at the date of the revaluation. Fresco Co makes an annual transfer to retained profits to reflect the realisation of the revaluation surplus. In Fresco Co's tax jurisdiction the revaluation does not give rise to a deferred tax liability.

On 1 April 20X1, Fresco Co acquired the right to use an item of plant under an agreement that meets the definition of a lease under IFRS 16 *Leases*. The rate of interest implicit in the lease agreement is 10% per annum. The lease payments in the trial balance represent an initial deposit of $2 million paid on 1 April 20X1 and the first annual rental of $6 million paid on 31 March 20X2. The lease agreement requires four further annual payments of $6 million on 31 March each year, starting 31 March 20X3. The present value of the future lease payments on inception of the lease is $23 million. The useful life of the plant is five years.

Plant and equipment (other than the leased plant) is depreciated at 20% per annum using the reducing balance method.

No depreciation has yet been charged on any non-current asset for the year ended 31 March 20X2. Depreciation is charged to cost of sales.

(3) In March 20X2, Fresco Co's internal audit department discovered a fraud committed by the company's credit controller who did not return from a foreign business trip. The outcome of the fraud is that $4 million of the company's trade receivables have been stolen by the credit controller and are not recoverable. Of this amount, $1 million relates to the year ended 31 March 20X1 and the remainder to the current year. Fresco Co is not insured against this fraud.

(4) Fresco Co's income tax calculation for the year ended 31 March 20X2 shows a tax refund of $2.4 million. The balance on current tax in the trial balance represents the under/over provision of the tax liability for the year ended 31 March 20X1. At 31 March 20X2, Fresco Co had taxable temporary differences of $12 million (requiring a deferred tax liability). The income tax rate of Fresco Co is 25%.

Required

(a) Prepare the statement of profit or loss and other comprehensive income for Fresco Co for the year ended 31 March 20X2. **(8 marks)**

(b) Prepare the statement of financial position of Fresco Co as at 31 March 20X2. **(12 marks)**

(Total = 20 marks)

339 Loudon Co (September/December 2020) (36 mins)

Loudon Co has extracted a draft statement of profit or loss for the year ended 30 September 20X8 (before any adjustments required by Notes (1) to (4) below) from its accounting software. The draft profit has been added to retained earnings and the summarised trial balance of Loudon Co as at 30 September 20X8 is:

	$'000	$'000
Equity shares of $1 each		10,000
Retained earnings as at 30 September 20X8 (draft)		4,122
Office building at cost	20,000	
Factories cost 1 October 20X7 (Note (2))	40,000	
Office building accumulated depreciation 1 October 20X7		4,000
Factories accumulated depreciation 1 October 20X7		11,100
Environmental provision 1 October 20X7 (Note (3))		1,228
Current liabilities		34,500
Current assets	14,700	
Proceeds of 5% loan note (Note (1))		5,000
Deferred tax		1,500
Interest paid (Note (1))	250	
Suspense account (Note (2))		3,500

	$'000	$'000
	74,950	74,950

The following notes are relevant:

(1) **Loan note**

A 5% loan note was issued on 1 October 20X7 at its face value of $5m. Direct costs of the issue amounted to $0.125m and were charged to profit or loss. The loan will be redeemed in five years' time at a substantial premium which gives an effective interest rate of 8%. The annual repayments of $250,000 ($5m at 5%) are paid on 30 September each year.

(2) **Non-current assets**

Loudon Co acquired an office building for $20m on 1 October 20X2 with an estimated useful life of 25 years. Depreciation is charged on a pro-rata basis. On 1 April 20X8, the building was deemed to be impaired as its fair value was estimated to be $12m. At that date the estimated remaining life was revised to 12 years. Ignore the deferred tax consequences of this revaluation. Loudon Co had ten factories. On 1 October 20X7 Loudon Co sold one of its factories with a carrying amount of $3m (cost $5m and accumulated depreciation $2m) for $3.5m. The proceeds were credited to the suspense account.

No depreciation has yet been charged on any non-current asset for the year ended 30 September 20X8. The factories are depreciated at 15% per annum using the reducing balance method.

(3) **Environmental provision**

Loudon Co has an obligation to clean-up environmental damage caused at one of its factory sites during 20X7. The clean-up is due to take place at the end of the factory's useful life. The liability has been accounted for appropriately and the balance at 1 October 20X7 represents the correct present value at that date. Loudon Co has a cost of capital of 5%.

(4) **Deferred tax**

At 30 September 20X8, the tax written down value of property, plant and equipment was $25m. The income tax rate applicable to Loudon Co is 20%.

Required

(a) Prepare a schedule of adjustments required to the retained earnings of Loudon Co as at 30 September 20X8 as a result of the information in Notes (1) to (4). **(8 marks)**

(b) Prepare the statement of financial position of Loudon Co as at 30 September 20X8.

Note. The notes to the statement of financial position are not required. All calculations should be rounded to the nearest $'000. **(12 marks)**

(Total = 20 marks)

340 Print Co **(36 mins)**

This scenario relates to two requirements.

Print Co is a manufacturing company and has the following trial balance at 30 June 20X2:

	$'000	$'000
Equity shares of $1 each		29,600
Other components of equity (share premium)		15,500
Retained earnings at 30 June 20X1		11,470
Plant and machinery (Note (5))		
Cost	16,200	

	$'000	$'000
Accumulated depreciation at 30 June 20X1		7,290
Land – at cost	45,000	
Bank loan (repayable 20X5) (Note (1))		30,000
Trade and other receivables	25,010	
Trade and other payables		4,170
Cash at bank	4,700	
Revenue		97,400
Production costs	60,150	
Administrative expenses	29,570	
Distribution costs	7,200	
Finance costs	750	
Inventory at 30 June 20X1	6,850	
	195,430	**195,430**

The following additional information is available:

(1) On 1 January 20X2 Print Co raised funds of $30m. The full amount was recorded in the nominal ledger as a bank loan. The funds actually consisted of a bank loan of $16m and $14m from the issue of seven million $1 ordinary shares. Interest is payable on the loan at 5% per annum. An accrual for six months interest has been included in trade and other payables and recognised as a finance cost. However, the calculation of interest was incorrectly based on the nominal ledger loan balance at 30 June 20X2.

(2) Inventories at 30 June 20X2 were initially valued at a total cost of $5.7m. This includes 700 units with a cost of $1,400 per unit. In order to sell these items, they need an additional process that costs $400 per unit, at which point they can then be sold for $1,600 per unit.

(3) At 30 June 20X2, Print Co has a contract to purchase 22,500 electrical components over the next three years at a cost of $450 each. These purchases are made at a constant rate. These components are no longer required for their initial purpose but do have an alternative use, which will require additional manufacturing costs of $600 per component. Thereafter, each component can then be sold for $900. Alternatively, Print Co could cancel the contract immediately by paying a penalty of $4m. Any adjustment resulting from this information should be made to administration expenses. Ignore discounting.

(4) On 1 July 20X1, the directors of Print Co decided to sell a piece of machinery and the asset met the criteria to be classified as held for sale at that date. The machine, which cost $2.4m, had a carrying amount of $1.5m at 1 July 20X1. At that date its fair value less costs to sell was $1.14m. The machine was sold for $1.1m after selling costs on 1 July 20X2. No adjustments have been made to take account of classifying the machine as held for sale.

(5) Print Co's policy is to depreciate plant and machinery at 15% per annum on cost and to present the depreciation charge in cost of sales.

(6) The income tax refund for the year has been estimated to be $2.53m.

Required

(a) Prepare the statement of profit or loss for Print Co for the year ended 30 June 20X2.

(8 marks)

(b) Prepare the statement of financial position for Print Co as at 30 June 20X2. **(12 marks)**

(Total = 20 marks)

341 Xtol Co (Jun 2014 amended) (36 mins)

The following trial balance relates to Xtol Co at 31 March 20X4:

	$'000	$'000
Revenue		490,000
Cost of sales	290,600	
Distribution costs	33,500	
Administrative expenses	36,800	
Loan note interest and dividends paid (Notes (4) and (5))	13,380	
Bank interest	900	
Freehold property at cost	100,000	
Plant and equipment at cost (Note (2))	155,500	
Accumulated depreciation at 1 April 20X3:		
Freehold property		25,000
Plant and equipment		43,500
Inventories at 31 March 20X4	61,000	
Trade receivables	63,000	
Trade payables		32,200
Bank		5,500
Equity shares of 25 cents each (Note (3))		56,000
Share premium		25,000
Retained earnings at 1 April 20X3		26,080
5% convertible loan note (Note (4))		50,000
Current tax (Note (6))	3,200	
Deferred tax (Note (6))		4,600
	757,880	757,880

The following notes are relevant:

(1) Revenue includes an amount of $20 million for cash sales made through Xtol Co's retail outlets during the year on behalf of Francais. Xtol Co, acting as agent, is entitled to a commission of 10% of the selling price of these goods. By 31 March 20X4, Xtol Co had remitted to Francais $15 million (of the $20 million sales) and recorded this amount in cost of sales.

(2) Plant and equipment is depreciated at 12½% per annum on the reducing balance basis. All amortisation and depreciation of non-current assets is charged to cost of sales. Freehold property is depreciated over 20 years.

(3) On 1 August 20X3, Xtol Co made a fully subscribed rights issue of equity share capital based on two new shares at 60 cents each for every five shares held. The issue has been fully recorded in the trial balance figures.

(4) On 1 April 20X3, Xtol Co issued a 5% $50 million convertible loan note at par. Interest is payable annually in arrears on 31 March each year. The loan note is redeemable at par or convertible into equity shares at the option of the loan note holders on 31 March 20X6. The interest on an equivalent loan note without the conversion rights would be 8% per annum.

The present values of $1 receivable at the end of each year, based on discount rates of 5% and 8%, are:

		5%	8%
End of year	1	0.95	0.93
	2	0.91	0.86
	3	0.86	0.79

(5) An equity dividend of 4 cents per share was paid on 30 May 20X3 and, after the rights issue, a further dividend of 2 cents per share was paid on 30 November 20X3.

(6) The balance on current tax represents the under/over provision of the tax liability for the year ended 31 March 20X3. A provision of $28 million is required for current tax for the year ended 31 March 20X4 and at this date the deferred tax liability was assessed at $8.3 million.

Required

(a) Prepare the statement of profit or loss for Xtol Co for the year ended 31 March 20X4. **(8 marks)**

(b) Prepare the statement of financial position for Xtol Co for the year ended 31 March 20X4. **(12 marks)**

(Total = 20 marks)

342 Mims Co (36 mins)

This scenario relates to three requirements.

The following is an extract from the trial balance of Mims Co for the year ended 31 December 20X5:

	$'000	$'000
Revenue		24,300
Cost of sales	11,600	
Administrative expenses	10,900	
Distribution costs	7,300	
Income tax (note (3))	140	
Deferred tax liability 1 January 20X5 (note (3))		7,700
Provision at 1 January 20X5 (note (2))		4,600
Retained earnings 1 January 20X5		43,200
Equity share capital ($1) at 1 January 20X5		60,000
Intangible assets (note (6))	3,300	
Investment property (note (5))	19,000	
Finance costs	1,400	
Investment income		500
Suspense account		46,500

The following information is relevant:

(1) Mims Co noted there was an error in the inventory count at 31 December 20X4, meaning that the closing inventory balance in the 20X4 financial statements was overstated by $0.7m. No entries have yet been made to correct this error.

(2) The provision relates to a court case in existence since December 20X4. Mims Co settled this case on 31 December 20X5 for $6m. The full amount was credited correctly to cash, with a corresponding debit entry being made in the suspense account.

(3) The income tax figure in the trial balance relates to the under/over provision from the previous year. The current year tax is estimated to be a tax refund of $1.2m. In addition to this, the deferred tax liability at 31 December 20X5 is estimated to be $8.2m.

(4) On 30 September 20X5, Mims Co made a 1-for-4 rights issue. The exercise price was $3.50 per share. The proceeds were correctly accounted for in cash, with a corresponding credit entry being made in the suspense account.

(5) Mims Co acquired an investment property for $20m cash on 1 January 20X5 and decided to use the fair value model to account for investment properties. As the property is expected to have a 20-year useful life, depreciation was recorded on this basis. The fair value of the property at 31 December 20X5 has been assessed at $22m but no accounting has taken place in relation to this. All depreciation and amortisation is charged on a pro-rata basis to administrative expenses. There were no other acquisitions or disposals of non-currents assets.

(6) Mims Co incurred a number of expenses in relation to brands during the year and has capitalised the following costs as intangible assets:

- $1.3m cash was paid on 1 April 20X5 to promote one of its major brands which is deemed to have an indefinite life.
- $2m cash was paid on 1 October 20X5 to acquire a brand from one of its competitors. Mims Co expect the brand to have a useful life of five years. Mims Co intends to sell it after five years. At the point of sale, it is estimated that the value of the brand will have increased and so no amortisation has been accounted for in the current year.

(7) Mims Co paid a dividend of $0.04 per share on all existing shares 31 December 20X5, recording the dividend paid in administrative expenses.

Required

(a) Prepare the statement of profit or loss for Mims Co for the year ended 31 December 20X5.

(12 marks)

(b) Prepare the statement of changes in equity for Mims Co for the year ended 31 December 20X5. **(5 marks)**

(c) Prepare the following extracts from the statement of cash flows for Mims Co for the year ended 31 December 20X5:

- Cash flows from investing activities; and
- Cash flows from financing activities.

(3 marks)

(Total = 20 marks)

343 Atlas Co (36 mins)

The following trial balance relates to Atlas Co at 31 March 20X3.

		$'000	$'000
Equity shares of 50 cents each			50,000
Share premium			20,000
Retained earnings at 1 April 20X2			11,200
Land and buildings – at cost (land $10 million) (Note (1))		60,000	
Plant and equipment – at cost (Note (1))		94,500	
Accumulated depreciation at 1 April 20X2:	– buildings		20,000

	$'000	$'000
– plant and equipment		24,500
Inventories at 31 March 20X3	43,700	
Trade receivables	42,200	
Bank		6,800
Deferred tax (Note (2))		6,200
Trade payables		35,100
Revenue		550,000
Cost of sales	411,500	
Distribution costs	21,500	
Administrative expenses	30,900	
Dividends paid	20,000	
Bank interest	700	
Current tax (Note (2))		1,200
	725,000	725,000

The following notes are relevant:

(1) Non-current assets:

On 1 April 20X2, the directors of Atlas Co decided that the financial statements would show an improved position if the land and buildings were revalued to market value. At that date, an independent valuer valued the land at $12 million and the buildings at $35 million and these valuations were accepted by the directors. The remaining life of the buildings at that date was 14 years. Atlas Co does not make a transfer to retained earnings for excess depreciation. Ignore deferred tax on the revaluation surplus.

Plant and equipment is depreciated at 20% per annum using the reducing balance method and time apportioned as appropriate. All depreciation is charged to cost of sales, but none has yet been charged on any non-current asset for the year ended 31 March 20X3.

(2) Atlas Co estimates that an income tax provision of $27.2 million is required for the year ended 31 March 20X3 and at that date the liability to deferred tax is $9.4 million. The movement on deferred tax should be taken to profit or loss. The balance on current tax in the trial balance represents the under/over provision of the tax liability for the year ended 31 March 20X2.

Required

(a) Prepare the statement of profit or loss and other comprehensive income for Atlas Co for the year ended 31 March 20X3. **(8 marks)**

(b) Prepare the statement of financial position of Atlas Co as at 31 March 20X3. **(10 marks)**

(c) Calculate basic earnings per share for the year ended 31 March 20X3. **(2 marks)**

(Total = 20 marks)

344 Moby Co (Dec 2013 amended) (36 mins)

The following trial balance as at 30 September 20X3 has been extracted from Moby Co's accounting software:

	$'000	$'000
Revenue		227,800

	$'000	$'000
Cost of sales	164,500	
Distribution costs	13,500	
Administrative expenses	16,500	
Bank interest	900	
Dividend	2,000	
Lease rental paid on 30 September 20X3 (Note (2))	9,200	
Land ($12 million) and building ($48 million) at cost (Note (2))	60,000	
Owned plant and equipment at cost (Note (2))	65,700	
Right-of-use asset – leased plant at initial carrying amount (note (ii))	35,000	
Accumulated depreciation at 1 October 20X2:		
Building		10,000
Owned plant and equipment		17,700
Leased plant		7,000
Inventories at 30 September 20X3	26,600	
Trade receivables	38,500	
Balance on contract (Note (1))	4,000	
Bank		5,300
Insurance provision (Note (3))		150
Deferred tax (Note (4))		8,000
Lease liability at 1 October 20X2 (Note (2))		29,300
Trade payables		21,300
Current tax (Note (4))		1,050
Equity shares of 20 cents each		45,800
Share premium		3,200
Loan note (Note (5))		40,000
Retained earnings at 1 October 20X2	–	19,800
	436,400	436,400

The following notes are relevant:

(1) The following amounts are relevant to the contract:.

Cost incurred to date	$8 million
Value of invoices issued (work certified)	$10 million

The contract commenced on 1 October 20X2 and is for a fixed price of $25 million. Performance obligations are satisfied over time. Moby Co's policy is to recognise satisfaction of performance obligations on such contracts based on a stage of completion given by the work certified as a percentage of the contract price. Moby has invoiced work to the value of $4 million in the year and has not yet received any payments from the customer.

(2) Non-current assets:

Moby Co decided to revalue its land and buildings for the first time on 1 October 20X2. A qualified valuer determined the relevant revalued amounts to be $16 million for the land and $38.4 million for the building. The building's remaining life at the date of the revaluation was 16 years. This revaluation has not yet been reflected in the trial balance figures. Moby Co does not make a transfer from the revaluation surplus to retained earnings in respect of the realisation of the revaluation surplus. Deferred tax is applicable to the revaluation surplus at 25%.

The right-of-use asset relates to leased plant was acquired on 1 October 20X1 under a five-year agreement which meets the definition of a lease under IFRS 16 *Leases*. The carrying amount of the leased plant in the trial balance is equal to the present value of the future lease payments at the lease inception date. The rentals are $9.2 million per annum payable on 30 September each year. The rate of interest implicit in the lease is 10% per annum. The useful life of the leased plant was 7 years.

Owned plant and equipment is depreciated at 12.5% per annum using the reducing balance method.

No depreciation has yet been charged on any non-current asset for the year ended 30 September 20X3. All depreciation is charged to cost of sales.

(3) On 1 October 20X2, Moby Co received a renewal quote of $400,000 from the company's property insurer. The directors were surprised at how much it had increased and believed it would be less expensive for the company to 'self-insure'. Accordingly, they charged $400,000 to administrative expenses and credited the same amount to the insurance provision. During the year, the company incurred $250,000 of expenses relating to previously insured property damage which it has debited to the provision.

(4) A provision for income tax for the year ended 30 September 20X3 of $3.4 million is required. The balance on current tax represents the under/over provision of the tax liability for the year ended 30 September 20X2. At 30 September 20X3 the tax base of Moby Co's net assets was $24 million less than their carrying amounts. This does not include the effect of the revaluation in note 2 above. The income tax rate of Moby Co is 25%.

(5) The $40 million loan note was issued at par on 1 October 20X2. No interest will be paid on the loan; however it will be redeemed on 30 September 20X5 for $53,240,000, which gives an effective finance cost of 10% per annum.

(6) A share issue was made on 31 December 20X2 of 4 million shares for $1 per share. It was correctly accounted for.

Required

Required

(a) Prepare the statement of profit or loss and other comprehensive income for Moby Co for the year ended 30 September 20X3. **(13 marks)**

(b) Prepare the statement of changes in equity for Moby Co for the year ended 30 September 20X3. **(7 marks)**

(Total = 20 marks)

345 Haverford Co (Mar/Jun 2018) (36 mins)

Below is the trial balance for Haverford Co at 31 December 20X7:

	$'000	$'000
Property – carrying amount 1 January 20X7 (Note (4))	18,000	
Ordinary shares $1 at 1 January 20X7 (Note (3))		20,000
Other components of equity (Share premium) at 1 January 20X7 (note (iii))		3,000

	$'000	$'000
Revaluation surplus at 1 January 20X7 (Note (4))		800
Retained earnings at 1 January 20X7		6,270
Draft profit for the year ended 31 December 20X7		2,250
4% Convertible loan notes (Note (1))		8,000
Dividends paid	3,620	
Cash received from contract customer (Note (2))		1,400
Cost incurred on contract to date (Note (2))	1,900	
Inventories (Note (5))	4,310	
Trade receivables	5,510	
Cash	10,320	
Current liabilities		1,940
	43,660	43,660

The following notes are relevant:

(1) On 1 January 20X7, Haverford Co issued 80,000 $100 4% convertible loan notes. The loan notes can be converted to equity shares on 31 December 20X9 or redeemed at par on the same date. An equivalent loan without the conversion rights would have required interest of 6%. Interest is payable annually in arrears on 31 December each year. The annual payment has been included in finance costs for the year. The present value of $1 receivable at the end of each year, based on discount rates of 4% and 6%, are:

	4%	6%
End of year 1	0.962	0.943
End of year 2	0.925	0.890
End of year 3	0.889	0.840

(2) During the year, Haverford Co entered into a contract to construct an asset for a customer. Control of the asset transfers to the customer as it is completed and Haverford Co does not have an alternative use for the asset. Haverford Co measures satisfaction of performance obligations over time by way of reference to certified work completed. The contract had a total price of $14 million. The costs to date of $1.9 million are included in the above trial balance. Costs to complete the contract are estimated at $7.1 million.

At 31 December 20X7, the contract is was independently certified as be 40% complete. To date, Haverford Co has invoiced $1.4 million to the customer and this is shown in the above trial balance.

(3) Haverford Co made a 1 for 5 bonus issue on 31 December 20X7, which has not yet been recorded in the above trial balance. Haverford Co intends to utilise the share premium as far as possible in recording the bonus issue.

(4) Haverford Co's property had previously been revalued upwards, leading to the balance on the revaluation surplus at 1 January 20X7. The property had a remaining life of 25 years at 1 January 20X7.

At 31 December 20X7, the property was valued at $16 million.

No entries have yet been made to account for the current year's depreciation charge or the property valuation at 31 December 20X7. Haverford Co does not make an annual transfer from the revaluation surplus in respect of excess depreciation.

(5) It has been discovered that inventory totalling $0.39 million had been omitted from the final inventory count in the above trial balance.

Required

(a) Calculate the adjusted profit for Haverford Co for the year ended 31 December 20X7. **(6 marks)**

(b) Prepare the statement of changes in equity for Haverford Co for the year ended 31 December 20X7. **(6 marks)**

(c) Prepare the statement of financial position for Haverford Co as at 31 December 20X7. **(8 marks)**

(Total = 20 marks)

346 Flamingo Co (36 mins)

You are the assistant accountant at Flamingo Co responsible for preparing the statement of cash flows for the year ended 30 June 20X2.

The draft statement of cashflows has been extracted from the computerised accounting system, however there is a discrepancy between the cash and cash equivalents figure at 30 June 20X2 presented in the draft statement of cash flows and the cash and equivalents figure presented in the statement of financial position.

You have been provided with the following information:

Extract from draft statement of cash flows for the year ended 30 June 20X2

	$	$
Net cash from operating activities		1,697,785
Cash flows from investing activities		
Purchase of property, plant and equipment	(2,150,700)	
Net cash used in investing activities		(2,150,700)
Cash flows from financing activities		
Proceeds from issue of ordinary share capital	1,000,000	
Proceeds from issue of borrowings	300,000	
Net cash from financing activities		1,300,000
Net increase in cash and cash equivalents		847,085
Cash and cash equivalents at beginning of period		112,800
Cash and cash equivalents at end of period		959,885

Extracts from the statement of financial position as at 30 June 20X2

	20X2	20X1
	$	$
Non-current assets		
Property, plant and equipment	7,979,100	5,828,400
Right of use assets	535,000	0
Current assets		
Cash and cash equivalents	346,885	112,800
Equity		

	20X2	20X1
	$	$
Ordinary share capital ($1 shares)	3,000,000	2,400,000
Share premium account	600,000	200,000
Retained earnings	2,522,905	1,917,560
Revaluation surplus	200,000	0
Non-current liabilities		
Lease obligations	446,000	0
Current liabilities		
Lease obligations	69,000	0

The statement of financial position extract above has been correctly prepared and does not need adjusting for the additional information below:

(1) A share issue at market price was made on 1 January 20X2. The statement of cash flows has been prepared assuming this was the only movement in share capital in the year, however a 1 for 6 bonus issue of ordinary shares was made out of retained earnings prior to the cash share issue.

(2) 'Purchase of property, plant and equipment' had been calculated by taking the movement between the opening and closing balances property, plant and equipment balances presented in the statement of financial position. Depreciation relating to property, plant and equipment of $260,000 was expensed to the statement of profit or loss in the year and the revaluation surplus in 20X2 relates to the revaluation of land. Depreciation has not been adjusted for in calculating net cash from operating activities. Flamingo Co disposed of property, plant and equipment which had a carrying amount of $782,000 for proceeds of $825,000 on 1 July 20X1. The profit on disposal has not been adjusted for in calculating net cash from operating activities.

(3) Flamingo Co entered into a lease agreement on 1 February 20X2. The right of use asset was initially measured correctly at $540,000 on commencement of the lease. Flamingo Co incurred expenses of $20,000 directly relating to the arrangement of the lease. The right of use asset was depreciated by $5,000 in the year which has not been adjusted for in calculating net cash from operating activities.

(4) The lease obligations relate solely to the right of use asset referred to in (3) above. Interest paid in respect of lease obligations has been correctly adjusted for in calculating net cash from operating activities.

(5) Flamingo Co reported a profit of $912,345 in the year.

Required

(a) Prepare a revised extract from Flamingo Co's statement of cash flows for the year ended 31 December 20X2. **(14 marks)**

(b) Explain whether the information in the statement of cash flows might be considered more useful than the information provided by the statement of profit or loss and the statement of financial position. **(6 marks)**

(Total = 20 marks)

347 Dickson Co (36 mins)

Below are the statements of financial position of Dickson Co as at 31 March 20X8 and 31 March 20X7, together with the statement of profit or loss and other comprehensive income for the year ended 31 March 20X8.

	20X8	20X7
	$'000	$'000
Non-current assets		
Property, plant and equipment	799	657
Right-of-use asset	126	80
Development expenditure	290	160
	1,215	897
Current assets		
Inventories	360	227
Trade receivables	274	324
Investments	143	46
Cash and cash equivalents	29	117
	806	714
Total assets	2,021	1,611
Equity	$'000	$'000
Share capital – $1 ordinary shares	500	400
Share premium	350	100
Revaluation surplus	160	60
Retained earnings	229	255
	1,239	815
Non-current liabilities		
6% debentures	150	100
Lease liabilities	100	80
Deferred tax	48	45
	298	225
Current liabilities		
Trade payables	274	352
Lease liabilities	17	12
Current tax	56	153
Debenture interest	5	–
Bank overdraft	132	54
	484	571
Total equity and liabilities	2,021	1,611

Statement of profit or loss and other comprehensive income

	$'000
Revenue	1,476
Cost of sales	(962)
Gross profit	514
Other expenses	(157)
Finance costs	(15)
Profit before tax	342
Income tax expense	(162)
Profit for the year	180
Other comprehensive income:	
Gain on revaluation of property, plant and equipment	100
Total comprehensive income for the year	280

Notes.

1 During 20X8, amortisation of $60,000 was charged on development projects.

2 During 20X8, items of property, plant and equipment with a carrying amount of $103,000 were sold for $110,000. Profit on sale of these items was netted off against 'other expenses'.

Depreciation charged in the year on property, plant and equipment totalled $47,000.

Dickson Co acquired a new right-of-use asset which was initially measured equal to the initial amount of the lease liability of $56,000. Depreciation on right-of-use assets has been correctly calculated as $10,000 for the year. Lease payments are made in arrears on the last day of each accounting period.

3 During the year Dickson Co made a 1 for 8 bonus issue, capitalising its retained earnings, followed by a rights issue.

4 The current asset investments are government bonds and management has decided to classify them as cash equivalents.

5 The new debentures were issued on 1 April 20X7. Finance cost includes debenture interest and lease finance charges only.

6 Dickson Co has a net cash generated from operating activities of $40,000.

Required

(a) Prepare an extract from the statement of cash flows for Dickson Co showing the net cash generated by or used from both investing activities and financing activities. **(10 marks)**

(b) Explain to the board of directors of Dickson Co what information is included in the statement of cash flows that cannot be obtained from reviewing the other primary financial statements. **(3 marks)**

(c) Discuss Dickson Co's performance for the year with reference to the profit for the year and the extract from the statement of cash flows prepared in (a). **(7 marks)**

(Total = 20 marks)

Answers

PART A: THE CONCEPTUAL AND REGULATORY FRAMEWORK FOR FINANCIAL REPORTING

Section A

Conceptual Framework

1 The correct answer is: A present economic resource controlled by an entity as a result of past events. An economic resource is a right that has the potential to produce economic benefits

Conceptual Framework, para. 4.3-4.4

2 The correct answer is: Carter has estimated the tax charge on its profits for the year just ended as $165,000

The licence payment could be avoided by ceasing manufacture.

The fall in value of the investment is a loss chargeable to profit or loss.

Planned expenditure does not constitute an obligation.

3 The correct answer is: The present value of the future cash flows obtainable from the continued use of the asset and its ultimate disposal

4 The correct answers are:

- It is principles-based rather than rules-based but it is not an IFRS Accounting Standard
- If it is revised it will not automatically lead to changes to the IFRS Accounting Standard

The Conceptual Framework is principles-based rather than rules-based and its purpose is to assist the International Accounting Standards Board (Board) to develop IFRS Accounting Standards. The Conceptual Framework is not an IFRS Accounting Standard and nothing in the Conceptual framework overrides any IFRS Accounting Standard or any requirement in an IFRS Accounting Standard. The *Conceptual Framework* may be revised from time to time on the basis of the Board's experience of working with it, but such revisions will not automatically lead to changes to the IFRS Accounting Standards. Any decision to amend an IFRS Accounting Standard would require the Board to go through its due process for adding a project to its agenda and developing an amendment to that IFRS Accounting Standard.

5 The correct answer is: Consistency

Consistency is an important part of the qualitative characteristic of comparability, but it is not the same thing. Comparability of financial statements is aided by the consistency of policies and methods used, either between companies within the same industry or within the same company, between different years.

6 The correct answers are:

- To assist preparers to develop consistent accounting policies when no IFRS Accounting Standard applies to a particular event
- To assist in determining the treatment of items not covered by an existing IFRS Accounting Standard

It is not to be authoritative where a specific IFRS Accounting Standard conflicts with the *Conceptual Framework* as the *Conceptual Framework* will be overridden if there is a specific IFRS Accounting Standard. Whenever there is a conflict between an IFRS Accounting Standard and the *Conceptual Framework*, the IFRS Accounting Standard takes precedence. Nor is it to issue rules regarding the accounting treatment of elements in the financial statements, as the *Conceptual Framework* is a principles-based format, not a prescriptive, rules-based approach.

7 The correct answer is: (1) and (4)

A secret formula for the manufacture of a best-selling sauce. The recipe is kept secure at the company premises and known only by the company directors.

A receivable from a customer which has been sold (factored) to a finance company. The finance company has full recourse to the company for any losses.

The receivable has been factored with recourse so should continue to be recognised as an asset. The company selling the receivable still retains control over that debt, not the factoring company.

8 The correct answer is: Neither 1 nor 2

The *Conceptual Framework* states that permitting alternative accounting treatments for the same economic phenomenon diminishes comparability (para. 2.29) and it also states that comparability does not equal uniformity (para. 2.27).

Regulatory framework

9 The correct answer is: Publication of an Exposure Draft

An Exposure Draft will be published following the review of Discussion Paper comments.

10 The correct answers are:

- It would be easier for investors to compare the financial statements of companies with those of foreign competitors
- Cross-border listing would be facilitated

Adopting IFRS Accounting Standards improves the comparability of the financial statements. Many territories now have either adopted or require listed companies to adopt IFRS Accounting Standards, this means a more consistent approach across the global listing exchanges, in theory, meaning that the company will not have to report in local GAAP removing one barrier to listing abroad if they are already adopting IFRS Accounting Standards.

Accountants and auditors may have **less** defence in case of litigation as they will not be able to demonstrate that they followed some precise rule, but will instead have to defend their application of judgement.

One potential downside of adopting IFRS Accounting Standards is that they are standardised and cannot be amended easily to reflect local industries. One way a country can do this is by converging their local national accounting standards with IFRS Accounting Standards, albeit with the ability to make amendments to reflect local industries.

11 The correct answers are:

- A rules-based system will tend to give rise to a larger number of IFRS Accounting Standards than a principles-based system
- A principles-based system requires the exercise of more judgement in application than a rules-based system

12 The correct answer is: In the early stages of the project, the Board will consult with the Advisory Committee and IFRS Advisory Council to seek out the key issues

The Advisory Committee and IFRS Advisory Council will review and decide upon the key issues prior to issuing a Discussion Paper which will seek out public comments. An Exposure Draft will pull together the key responses following the public comments and seek out additional clarification prior to any IFRS Accounting Standard being issued.

13 The correct answer is: It avoids the overstatement of profit which can arise during periods of inflation

Historical cost accounting does not avoid the overstatement of profit which arises during periods of inflation, which is why alternative models have been proposed.

14 The correct answer is: The ISSB will initially focus on climate-related disclosures

The ISSB has stated that it will initially focus on climate-related disclosures due to the urgent need for information on climate-related matters..

15 Historical cost ($): 320,000

Current cost ($): 384,000

	Historical cost	Current cost
	$	$
Cost/valuation	500	600
Depreciation ((500,000 × 90%) /5) × 2	(180)	
Depreciation ((600,000 × 90%) /5) × 2		(216)
Carrying amount	320	384

16 The correct answer is: The present value of the estimated cash flows needed to fulfil a liability

Fulfilment value is the present value of the amount of cash, or other economic resources, that the entity expects to be obliged to transfer to settle the liability.

17 The correct answer is: It assists a user to assess the future prospects of the business

The others are benefits of historical cost accounting.

18 The correct answer is: Present value of future cash flows, less costs of disposal

Costs incurred at the time of acquisition is historical cost. Open market value of the asset is fair value. Open market value less the present value of the future cash outflows is not a measurement under the *Conceptual Framework*.

19 The correct answer is: To develop standards that result in a high-quality, comprehensive global baseline of sustainability disclosures focused on the needs of investors and the financial markets

Section B

Lisbon Co case

20 The correct answer is: The accountant should classify, characterise and present the information clearly and precisely

The *Conceptual Framework* requires information to be presented in a manner that is clear and understandable, but without omitting complex issues.

21 The correct answer is: Faithful representation

The substance of the transaction is that a sale and leaseback has taken place and the transaction should be accounted for as such rather than a sale being recognised.

22 The correct answer is: Relevance

The historical cost of the properties will be less relevant than their current value.

23 The correct answer is: The financial statements should be prepared on a different basis

The basis of valuation of assets will be affected.

24 The correct answer is: The financial statements for the prior period as shown at 31 March 20X6 should be restated using the weighted average basis

This is a change of accounting policy so the information will be amended retrospectively. As such, the prior period financial statements should be restated.

Section A

Tangible non-current assets

25 The correct answer is: $6,950,000

	$'000
Land	1,200
Materials	2,400
Labour	3,000
Architect's fees	25
Surveyor's fees	15
Site overheads	300
Testing fire alarms	10
	6,950

$6,640,000 includes everything up to surveyor's fees but omits the site overheads and the costs of testing the fire alarms.

$7,112,000 includes all costs including administrative overheads and business rates which cannot be capitalised.

$7,100,000 wrongly includes the administrative overheads.

26 The correct answer is: $549,333

Weighted average capitalisation rate =

(9% × 15 / 39) + (11% × 24 / 39) = 3.5% + 6.8% = 10.3%

		$
Borrowing costs =	$6m × 10.3% × 9/12	463,500
+	$2m × 10.3% × 5/12	85,833
		549,333

$480,000 uses the 9% interest rate instead of calculating the weight average cost of borrowing.

$824,000 does not pro-rate for 9 months and 5 months respectively.

$533,333 uses a simple average of 10% instead of the weighted average.

27 The correct answer is: $140,000

	$
Borrowing costs March – December ($2.4m × 8% × 10/12)	160,000
Less investment income ($1m × 6% × 4/12)	(20,000)
	140,000

$192,000 ignores pro-rating and does not deduct the investment income.

$132,000 ignores pro-rating

ANSWERS

$160,000 correctly pro-rates the borrowing costs but does not deduct the investment income.

28 The correct answer is: Both statements 1 and 2

Transfers should only be made when there is a change in use of the property. (IAS 40: para. 57)

Transfers from an IAS 40 investment property to an IAS 16 property must be made at the fair value of the investment property at the date of the transfer. (IAS 40: para. 60)

An entity should treat any difference at the transfer date from a capitalised property (treated under IAS 16) when transferred to an investment property as a revaluation under IAS 16. (IAS 40: para. 61)

29 The correct answers are:

Following initial recognition, an investment property can be measured at either cost or fair value	**TRUE**	
If an investment property is held at fair value, this must be applied to all of the entity's investment properties	**TRUE**	
An investment property is initially measured at cost, including transaction costs	**TRUE**	
A gain or loss arising from a change in the fair value of an investment property should be recognised in the revaluation surplus		**FALSE**

The gain or loss arising from a change in the fair value of an investment property should be recognised in profit or loss not the revaluation surplus.

30 The correct answer is: $2.2 million

Weighted capitalisation rate =

(10% × 140/340) + (8% × 200/340) = 4.1% + 4.7% = 8.8%

$50 million × 8.8% × 6/ 12 = $2.2 million

$2.0 million assumes the cheaper 8% borrowing rate.

$2.25 million assumes a simple average of 9%.

$4.4 million does not pro-rate for 6 months.

31 $ 37,250

	$'000
Machine ((500,000 – 20,000) / 10 × 9/12)	36,000
Safety guard ((25,000/5) × 3/12)	1,250
	37,250

32 $ 4,765

The machine has been owned for 2 years 3 months, so the remaining useful life at 31 March 20X9 was 12 years 9 months.

Prior to revaluation it was being depreciated at $4,000 pa (60,000 / 15), so the charge for the first three months of 20X9 was $1,000 (4,000 × 3/12).

The machine will now be depreciated over the remaining 12 years 9 months = 153 months. So the charge for the remaining 9 months of 20X9 is $3,765 (64,000 × 9/153).

So total depreciation for the year ended 31.12.X9 is (1,000 + 3,765) = $4,765

33 $ 203,000

Prior to 30 June 20X8, the building was classified as property, plant and equipment and was accounted for under IAS 16. When the building was let out to a third party, there was a change in usage and it was transferred to an investment property, and so is accounted for under IAS 40. IAS 40 requires that assets must be measured at fair value at the date of transfer ($950,000 in the question) and be accounted for as a revaluation gain, recognised as a revaluation surplus.

	$
Cost 1.1.X0	900,000
Depreciation to 30.6.X8 (900,000 × 8.5 / 50)	(153,000)
Carrying amount 30.6.X8	747,000
Revaluation surplus	203,000
Fair value 30.6.X8	950,000

The increase of ($1,200,000 – $950,000) = $250,000 arising between 30.6.X8 and 31.12.X8 will be credited to profit or loss in accordance with IAS 40.

34 The correct answer is: An investment property is likely to increase in value so any residual value would be greater than it's carrying amount

Investments properties are held to earn rentals, capital appreciation or both. It is not true to say they don't generate income – there might be fair value gains or rental income or both. It is possible to measure the useful life of an investment property. Although investment properties are likely to increase in value, their value may decrease.

Intangible non-current assets

35 Brand amortisation: $1m

Training costs: $450,000

In accordance with IAS 38 *Intangible Assets*, the revaluation model for intangible assets can only be applied when an active market exists upon which fair value can be based. IAS 38 specifically states that an active market cannot exist for brands.

On this basis, despite a valuer believing that the brand is worth $14m, it should continue to be recognised at its cost of $10m and be amortised over 10 years, resulting in an amortisation expense in the year ended 31 December 20X5 of $1m ($10m x 1/10 years).

The costs of staff training are specifically identified in IAS 38 as being an example of expenditure that is not part of the cost of an intangible asset. Although an entity may have a team of skilled staff and may be able to identify incremental staff skills leading to the future economic benefits from training, there is not sufficient control over such economic benefits for an intangible asset to be recognised.

36 The correct answer is: $7,800,000

	$
Research costs	1,400,000
Expensed development Jan–Mar (800 × 3)	2,400,000
Depreciation on capitalised amount b/f (20m × 20%)	4,000,000
	7,800,000

$8,280,000 includes depreciation on the development costs capitalised in the current year. Note that no depreciation is charged on the new project as it is still in development.

$6,880,000 includes depreciation on the development costs capitalised in the current year and does not write off the research costs.

$3,800,000 does not include the depreciation costs.

37 The correct answers are:

A customer list built up over the last ten years of trading updated for the customer's current preferences		**INELIGIBLE**
Specialised tooling for a new product developed by the business	**ELIGIBLE**	
A working version of a new machine that uses new technology used for testing of the prototype apparatus	**ELIGIBLE**	
The title heading, font and design of the front page of a major broadsheet newspaper		**INELIGIBLE**

Per IAS 38, development costs allowable for capitalisation include 'the design, construction and operation of a pilot plant that is not of a scale economically feasible for commercial production' (the working version of the new machine) and 'the design of tools, jigs, moulds and dies involving new technology' (specialised tooling) (IAS 38: paras. 57–62). Mastheads (the heading across a newspaper) and customer lists cannot be recognised expenditure on these items cannot be distinguished from the costs of developing the business as a whole. IAS 38 specifically prohibits these items from being capitalised (IAS 38: paras. 63-64).

38 $ 12,500

	$'000
Recoverable amount – fair value less costs of disposal	15,000
Less depreciation 1.4.X9 – 30.9.X9 (15m / 3 × 6/12)	(2,500)
	12,500

The recoverable amount is the higher of the fair value less costs of disposal of $15,000 (16,000 – 1,000) and the value in use of $12,000.

Assets continue to be depreciated after they have been impaired.

39 Carrying amount of intangible asset at 30 September 20X5 = $152,000

Amount charged to profit or loss for period ending 30 September 20X5 = $88,000

Working

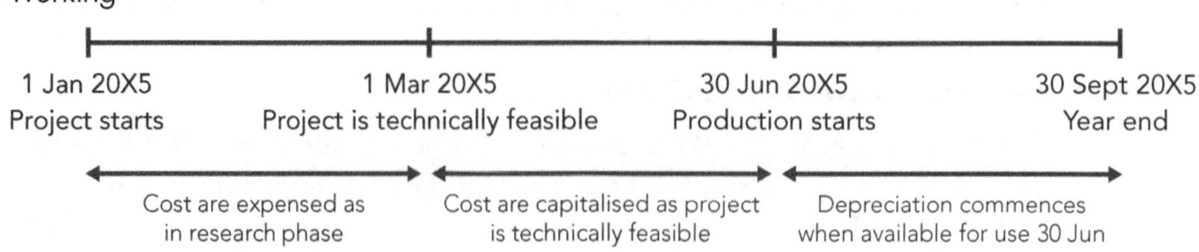

	$
Capitalised as an intangible asset from 1 March – 30 June 20X5 (40,000 × 4)	160,000
Amortisation of asset from 1 July 20X5	(8,000)

	$
(160,000/5 years × 3/12)	
Carrying amount of the asset at 30 September 20X5	152,000
Expenses for January and February 20X4 (2 × 40,000)	80,000
Amortisation expense for the period	8,000
Expenses taken to the statement of profit or loss	88,000

Impairment of assets

40 The correct answer is: $594

	$'000
Total impairment (1,010 – 750)	260
Goodwill	(90)
Damaged plant	(40)
Balance to allocate	130

The remaining $130,000 will be allocated pro rata as follows:

	Building	*Plant*
	$'000	$'000
	700	160
Impairment	(106)	(24)
	594	136

41 The **recoverable amount** of an asset is the higher of [fair value less costs of disposal] and [value in use] under IAS 36 *Impairment of Assets.*

42 $ [7,687]

Fair value less costs of disposal (78,000 – 2,500) = $75,500

Value in use

	$
30,000 × 1 / 1.08	27,778
30,000 × 1 / 1.08^2	25,720
30,000 × 1 / 1.08^3	23,815
	77,313

ANSWERS

Recoverable amount is $77,313 and carrying amount is $85,000, so impairment is $7,687.

43 The correct answers are:

- An unusually significant fall in the market value of one or more assets
- An increase in the market interest rates used to calculate value in use of the assets

The other options are internal indicators of impairment.

44 $ 350,000

	$
Fair value less costs of disposal (2.7m – 50,000)	2,650,000
Value in use	2,600,000
Carrying amount	3,000,000
Recoverable amount	2,650,000
Impairment loss	350,000

45 The correct answer is: $8 million

	$m	$m	$m
Goodwill	3	(3)	–
Patent	5	(3)	2
Property	10	(2)	8
Plant and equipment	15	(3)	12
Current assets	2	–	2
	35	(11)	24

The goodwill is written off, the patent is written down and the remaining $5m impairment is allocated pro rata to the property and the plant and equipment.

$10 million does not allocate any of the impairment loss to the property.

$7.5 million allocates the remaining $5m impairment equally to property and plant and equipment

$5 million allocates all of the remaining impairment against property.

46 The correct answer is: $17,785

	$
Carrying amount (100,000 × 5/10)	50,000
Fair value less costs to sell	30,000
Value in use (8,500 × 3.79)	32,215

Recoverable amount is $32,215 and impairment loss = 50,000 – 32,215 = $17,785

$20,000 takes the recoverable amount to be the lower of the value in use and the fair value less costs to sell.

$30,000 takes the recoverable amount to be the lower of the value in use and the fair value less costs to sell and uses this as the amount of the impairment.

$32,215 assumes the recoverable amount to be the amount of impairment.

47 The correct answer is: $154,545

	Net assets prior to impairment	Impairment	Impaired net assets
	$	$	$
Property, plant and equipment	200,000	(45,455)	154,545
Goodwill	50,000	(50,000)	–
Product patent	20,000	(4,545)	15,455
Net current assets	30,000	–	30,000
	300,000	(100,000)	200,000

Goodwill is written off in full and the balance of the loss is pro-rated between PPE and the patent.

48 The correct answers are:

Advances in the technological environment in which an asset is employed has an adverse impact on its future use	**INDICATOR OF IMPAIRMENT**	
An increase in interest rates which increases the discount rate an entity uses	**INDICATOR OF IMPAIRMENT**	
The carrying amount of an entity's net assets is lower than the entity's number of shares in issue multiplied by its share price	**INDICATOR OF IMPAIRMENT**	
The estimated net realisable value of inventory has been reduced due to fire damage although this value is greater than its carrying amount		**NOT AN INDICATOR OF IMPAIRMENT**

The estimated net realisable value of inventory that has been reduced due to fire damage but the value is greater than its carrying amount is **not** an indicator of impairment. If the NRV of inventory is greater than its carrying amount, then no impairment has arisen.

Section B

Plethora plc case

49 $ 314,000

Building transferred to investment property

	$'000
Original cost	600
Depreciation 1.1.X0 to 1.7.X9 ((600 / 50) × 9.5)	(114)
Carrying amount at 1.7.X9	486
Revaluation surplus	314
Fair value	800

50 The correct answer is: Credited to profit or loss

The increase in value in this case of $190,000 (740,000 – 550,000) will be credited to profit or loss in accordance with IAS 40.

51 Recoverable amount

If the asset has been impaired, it must have been written down to its recoverable amount. This is the higher of fair value less costs of disposal and value in use.

52 The correct answers are:

- The reversal of impairment losses on revalued assets should be recognised in other comprehensive income
- An impairment loss can only be reversed if there is a change in the estimates used to determine the recoverable amount of the impaired assets

Impairment losses in respect of goodwill cannot be subsequently reversed. Whilst IAS 36 does not apply to inventories, it does not scope out other current assets.

53 The correct answer is: $85,000

Impairment losses on assets, other than goodwill, can be reversed up to the maximum of what the asset would have been carried at had no impairment occurred.

Asset	*Carrying amount at 31 December 20X8 before impairment*	*Impairment loss at 31 December 20X8*	*Carrying amount at 31 December 20X8 AFTER impairment*	*Carrying amount at 31 December 20X9 had no impairment occurred*	*Reversal of imp. loss*
	$'000	$'000	$'000	$'000	$'000
Building	900	100	800	875	75
Plant and equipment	300	20	280	290	10
Goodwill	40	40	Nil	40	Nil
Total					85

Linetti Co case

54 The correct answer is: $18.4 million

This is calculated as $10m + $0.5m + $1m + $6.6m less unused materials of $0.5m plus borrowing costs of $0.8m.

$17.6 million does not include the borrowing costs which can be capitalised.

$18.9 million includes the $0.5 million of unused materials.

$18.1 million includes the unused materials but does not include the borrowing costs.

55 The correct answer is: Installation of new office fixtures and fittings

Insurance premiums are expensed as they form part of the normal costs of using the head office. Marketing costs are specifically disallowed by IAS 16. The maintenance costs of the computers are expensed as they are normal costs of operating the computers.

56 The correct answer is: The original head office building and the new extension are revalued separately

The extension is part of the original building, and therefore the building must be revalued as one asset.

57 The correct answer is: $1.8 million

The impairment loss for the CGU is $2.2m ($11.8m – $9.6m). The impairment loss is initially allocated to the goodwill balance of $1.4m. The unallocated impairment loss is $0.8m. This is allocated to the brand and PPE based on their carrying amounts:

		Allocation of impairment
	$m	$m
Brand	2	(0.2)
PPE	6	(0.6)
Total	8	(0.8)

The value of the brand is therefore $1.8m (2m – 0.2m).

58 The correct answer is: Both 1 and 2

Both of the actions are required on an annual basis (IAS 36: paras. 9 and 10).

Elite Leisure Co case

59 The correct answer is: $279 million

	Cost	*Dep'n period*	*Dep'n to date*	*Carrying amount*
	£m			$m
Ships fabric	300	8/25	(96)	204
Cabins etc	150	8/12	(100)	50
Propulsion	100	30/40 hrs	(75)	25
				279

60 $ 14 million

$14m = (140m × 5,000/50,000)

61 $ 45 million

$45m = (Repainting $20m + Loss on disposal $25m)

62 The correct answer is: Capitalise the cost when incurred and amortise over five years

ANSWERS

IAS 16 paragraph 13–14 refers specifically to when assets may require substantial inspections and/or overhauls on a periodic basis: "When each major inspection is performed, its cost is recognised in the carrying amount of the item of property, plant and equipment as a replacement" (IAS 16: para. 13).

63 $290,000

(250 + 40)

At 55% losing the case is 'probable' so must be provided for.

Advent Co case

64 The correct answer is: $256 million

		$m
Land		85
Building	180 × 19/20	171
		256

$265 million ignores the effect of depreciation in the current year.

$240 million does not apply the revaluation in the current year.

$258 million depreciates the building over the 25 years useful life at the date of the previous valuation.

65 The correct answer is: $35 million

		$m
Existing plant	150 × 20%	30
New plant	50 × 20% × 6/12m	5
		35

66 The correct answers are:

The effective date of revaluation	**REQUIRED**	
Professional qualifications of the valuer		**NOT REQUIRED**
The basis used to revalue the assets	**REQUIRED**	
The carrying amount of assets if no revaluation had taken place	**REQUIRED**	

There is no requirement to disclose the professional qualifications of the valuer.

67 $140 million

	$m
Balance 1.10.X8	270
Depreciation to 30.9.X9	(30)
	240
Impairment loss (β)	(140)
Recoverable amount	100

68 The recoverable amount of an asset of an asset is the higher of fair value less costs of disposal and value in use.

As stated in IAS 36 *Impairment of Assets*, para. 22. The other options are not in line with the accounting standard.

Systria Co case

69 $ 40,000

	Original	Impairment	
	$'000	$'000	
Goodwill	50	(50)	
Patent	10	(10)	
Land and buildings	100	(20)	*Remaining 30*
Plant and machinery	50	(10)	*pro rata*
Net current assets	10	–	
		(90)	

70 The correct answers are:

- There are adverse changes to the use to which the asset is put
- The operating performance of the asset has declined

Depreciation is irrelevant and the other options are an external indicator of impairment.

71 $1.5 million

ANSWERS

Recoverable amount is $6 million, leaving an impairment loss of $4 million.

$2.5 million will be allocated to the destroyed assets and the remaining $1.5 million written off against goodwill.

$3 million – $1.5 million = $1.5 million.

72 The correct answers are:

	Debit
$20,000	Accumulated depreciation
$30,000	Property at cost
	Revaluation surplus
	Credit
	Accumulated depreciation
	Property at cost
$50,000	Revaluation surplus

The depreciation is written off and the balance added to the cost of the property.

73 The correct answer is: $3,250

Depreciation to date of $20,000 means the property has 40 years of useful life left at the revaluation date. Depreciation will be $130,000/40.

Wilrob Co

74 The correct answers are:

- Intangible assets should be amortised over the expected useful life or not at all if the useful life is deemed to be indefinite
- Intangible assets should be amortised on the basis of the expected pattern of consumption of the expected future economic benefits

75 The correct answers are:

- IAS 38 permits the revaluation of intangible assets only if there is an active market for such assets
- IAS 38 requires that the initial recognition of intangibles must be at cost

76 The correct answer is: $5.5m

The $15m of project costs incurred between 1 April 20X6 and 31 December 20X6 cover a nine-month period. As the project did not meet the capitalisation criteria of IAS 38 until 30 June 20X6, this means that any costs related to the first three months of the year (1 April 20X6 – 30 June 20X6) were research expenditure which should be charged to the statement of profit or loss: $15m × 3/9 months = $5m.

Therefore, the remaining $10m ($15m × 6/9 months) would be capitalised as development expenditure. As the project was completed and began to generate revenue from 1 January 20X7, the capitalised development expenditure should then be amortised from that date over its useful life of five years. This requires an amortisation expense for three months (1 January 20X7 – 31 March 20X7) which should be charged to the statement of profit or loss: $10m / 5 years × 3/12 months = $0.5m.

Therefore, the total charge to the statement of profit or loss in respect of project 324 for the year ended 31 March 20X7 is $5.5m.

Research $5m + amortisation $0.5m = $5.5m

77 The correct answers are:

The cost for project 325 should be expensed in the statement of profit or loss for the year ended 31 March 20X7.	**TRUE**	
The specialist equipment that was purchased for project 325 should not be depreciated as it has only been used for abandoned or research projects.		**FALSE**
The costs for project 326 should be included as an asset in the statement of financial position as at 31 March 20X7.		**FALSE**

78 The correct answer is: 1 and 3 only

An intangible asset can be recognised when it meets: (1) the definition of an intangible asset; and (2) the recognition criteria.

Both the domain name and the patent meet the definition of being intangible assets and the cost of each can clearly be measured reliably. Based on the information available, it appears that economic benefits will flow to the entity through revenue from online sales (domain name) and production cost savings (patent). Internally generated customer lists are specifically excluded by IAS 38 from being recognised as intangible assets (along with other items such as internally generated brands). This is because any expenditure incurred on such items cannot be distinguished from the cost of developing the business as a whole.

ANSWERS

Section A

Revenue and government grants

79 The correct answer is:

Asset or liability	**Carrying amount**
Contract asset	$180,000

	$
Revenue recognised $2,800,000 ×35%	980,000
Less amounts invoiced to date	(800,000)
Contract asset	180,000

80 The correct answer is: $125,000

The $120,000 relating to the purchase of IT equipment can be recognised as income immediately as the terms of that portion of the grant have already been satisfied.

The remaining $600,000 should be initially deferred and then released to income on a monthly basis as the condition of the grant, being to provide training, are satisfied. The receipt date of the government grant is not relevant, the terms of the grant are being complied with from 1 April 20X5 and therefore grant income can be recognised from that date. At 31 October 20X5, the remaining term attached to the training grant is 17 months, of which 12 months are current and 5 months are non-current.

The non-current liability is therefore measured as $600,000 × 5/24 months = $125,000

$720,000 is the full amount of the grant

$425,000 is the full amount of the liability

$300,000 is the current portion of the liability

81 The correct answer is: $7,000,000

	$'000
Contract revenue recognised	22,000
Costs to date	(12,000)
Depreciation of specialist plant	(3,000)
Profit recognised at 31 March 20X3	7,000

$5,000,000 incorrectly deducts the management time in calculating profit; but costs that would have been incurred regardless of whether the contract was obtained are recognised as an expense as incurred.

$25,000,000 incorrectly reflects total expected profit.

$Nil assumes that no profit or loss can be recognised to date.

82 The correct answer is: $9,600

	$
Revenue recognised ($120,000 × 50% (W))	60,000

	$
Amounts invoiced	(50,400)
Contract asset	9,600

Working

Costs to date	$48,000
Costs to complete	$48,000
Percentage completion	50%

$12,000 is the profit that can be recognised rather than the contract asset (50% × ($120,000 – $96,000)).

$14,400 is the trade receivables balance ($50,400 – $40,000).

$50,400 is the total amount invoiced.

83

	Account	Amount
DEBIT	Other income	$1,425,000
CREDIT	Deferred income	$1,425,000

	$
Grant received and recognised in other income 1.7.X5	1,500,000
Recognised year to 31.12.X5 (1,500,000 / 10yrs × 6/12m)	(75,000)
Amount to be deferred	1,425,000

84

	Debit	Credit
Other income		$80,000
Deferred income	$80,000	
Depreciation expense	$155,000	
Accumulated depreciation		$155,000

Working

Grant is 50% of the asset, so the asset cost is $400,000 × 2 = $800,000

The depreciation is $800,000 – $25,000/5 years = $155,000

The grant is recognised as deferred income on the SOFP and released to the profit or loss in the same manner as the depreciation (over 5 years, therefore $400,000/5 years = $80,000).

85 The correct answers are:

Amount ($)	
Nil	Revenue
90,000	Current liability

ANSWERS

Nil	Trade receivables

No sale has taken place as control of the goods has not been transferred (so revenue will be nil), but Cambridge Co must show that it is holding $90,000 which belongs to Circus Co.

86 The correct answer is: Sales of $150,000 on 30 September 20X4. The amount invoiced to and received from the customer was $180,000, which included $30,000 for ongoing servicing work to be done by Repro Co over the next two years.

The amount to recognise in revenue is $150,000 as the performance obligations relating to servicing have not yet been satisfied and therefore the amount of $30,000 will be recognised as a contract liability.

87 The correct answer is: $160,000

Contract asset:

	$'000
Revenue recognised to date ($5m × 38%)	1,900
Less amounts invoiced	(1,740)
	160

$Nil is incorrect as it refers to trade receivables rather than contract asset.

$1,000,000 is incorrect as it is the total profit for the contract.

$300,000 is incorrect as it is the profit that can be recognised at 30 September 20X4.

88 The correct answers are:

- Manufacturer can require the dealer to return the inventory
- Manufacturer bears obsolescence risk

These both indicate that the manufacturer retains ownership of the inventory. The other options would indicate that the risks and rewards have been transferred to the dealer.

89 $400,000

An asset is defined as 'a present economic resource controlled by the entity as a result of past events' (*Conceptual Framework*). The staff training does not meet the definition of an asset because the employer does not control its employees; the employer cannot control whether or not an employee chooses to leave employment. If an employee leaves, the employer will not receive the full benefit of the staff training. If the staff training is not an asset, then $500,000 should be charged in full to profit or loss in the year in which it is incurred and cannot be spread across two years. As the second instalment of the government grant is virtually certain then the full $100,000 can be offset against the $500,000 staff training costs.

90 $ 24,920,000

	$'000
Revenue per draft profit or loss	27,000
Service and support costs (800 × 2 × 130%)	(2,080)
	24,920

91 The correct answer is: The inventories should be recorded in the statement of financial position at $450,000 and the $420,000 received should be reported as a liability. There is no profit or loss effect.

The transaction is entered into on the last day of the financial year and is, in substance, a financing transaction as AB can repurchase the inventories in two years later at a higher amount that includes interest for the two years.

92 The correct answers are:

- The approval of the contract creates enforceable rights and obligations in a given jurisdiction
- The customer has the significant risks and rewards of ownership of the asset

The other three are all indicators that a performance obligation is satisfied over time rather than at a point in time.

Other indicators that a performance obligation is satisfied at a point in time include (but are not limited to):

- The entity has a present right to payment for the asset
- The customer has legal title to the asset
- The entity has transferred physical possession of the asset
- The customer has accepted the asset

93 The correct answer is: Dr Cost of sales 20,400 Cr Inventory 20,400

This transaction is a bill and hold arrangement. Since there is a substantive reason for the bill and hold (the customer wants to secure the scarce item but does not want to take delivery yet) and the goods have been identified as belonging to the customer and are ready for delivery, revenue can be recognised. Revenue has been recognised so there is no adjustment to revenue or trade receivables. However, since revenue has been recognised then the cost must be included in cost of sales not part of closing inventory. Therefore, an adjustment is needed.

Introduction to groups

94 The correct answer is: There is no basis on which a subsidiary may be excluded from consolidation

95 The correct answer is: Credited to profit or loss

IFRS 3 requires a bargain purchase to be credited to profit or loss as it is an economic gain. If the consideration is higher than the net assets being purchased, that would constitute goodwill (not taking the debit to the profit and loss). By taking the bargain purchase to the profit and loss immediately, IFRS 3 aims to restrict any excess being carried forwards.

96 The correct answer is: Existence of significant influence

The other options indicate control over a subsidiary as set out by IAS 27 *Consolidated and Separate Financial Statements.*

97 The correct answers are:

- A subsidiary with a different reporting date may prepare additional statements up to the group reporting date for consolidation purposes
- Where a subsidiary's financial statements are drawn up to a different reporting date from those of the parent, adjustments should be made for significant transactions or events occurring between the two reporting dates

The allowable gap between reporting dates is three months, not five. IAS 27 allows subsidiaries to have non-coterminous year ends, provided several criteria are met, including stating reasons why the financial year end is different to the parent.

98 The correct answers are:

The characteristics of the asset	**RELEVANT**	

ANSWERS

The price paid to acquire the asset		**NOT RELEVANT**
The principal or most advantageous market for the asset	**RELEVANT**	
The highest and best use of the asset	**RELEVANT**	

The price paid to acquire the asset is the historical cost of the asset. Fair value looks at the future benefits which are expected to flow from the asset, as opposed to what was paid in the past.

IFRS 13 will take into account assumptions that market participants may use when establishing a fair value for the asset.

99 The correct answers are:

- The ability to use its power over the investee to affect the amount of the investor's returns
- Exposure to, or rights to, variable returns from its involvement with the investee
- Power over the investee

In accordance with IFRS 10, paragraph 7.

IFRS 10 makes no reference to a holding of more than 50% of the equity shares of an investee company.

100 The correct answer is: Gamma Co is located in a country where a military coup has taken place and Petre Co has lost control of the investment for the foreseeable future

Consolidation is not appropriate in this case as the parent has lost control.

Financial instruments

101 The correct answer is: $1,524,000

	$'000
Interest years 1–3 (30m × 8% × 2.49)	5,976
Repayment year 3 (30m × 0.75)	22,500
Debt component	28,476
Equity option (β)	1,524
	30,000

$5,976,000 is the present value of the future interest payments.

$28,476,000 is the debt component.

$30,000,000 is the total amount raised on the issue.

102 The correct answer is: $21,495,000

	$'000
Proceeds (20m – 0.5m)	19,500
Interest 10%	1,950
Interest paid (20m × 5%)	(1,000)
Balance 31 March 20X1	20,450
Interest 10%	2,045
Interest paid (20m × 5%)	(1,000)

	$'000
	21,495

103 Fair value with changes going through profit or loss.

Fair value through OCI would be correct if an election had been made to recognise changes in value through other comprehensive income. Amortised cost is used for debt instruments, not equity instruments.

104 The correct answer is: $514,560

	$
1 January 20X1	500,000
Interest 8%	40,000
Interest received (550,000 × 6%)	(33,000)
31 December 20X1	507,000
Interest 8%	40,560
Interest received	(33,000)
31 December 20X2	514,560

105 $ 437,000

The investment would initially be recorded at its fair value plus any transaction costs. As the $7m loan note was purchased at a 12% discount and no transaction costs are included in the question, this means that the investment would be recorded on 1 July 20X7 at its fair value of $6,160,000 ($7m × 88%)

Year ended	Opening balance $'000	Effective interest (7%) $'000	Nominal interest (5%) $'000	Closing balance $'000
30 June 20X8	6,160	431	(350)	6,241
30 June 20X9	6,241	437	(350)	6,328

106 The correct answer is: Intangible assets

These do not give rise to a present right to receive cash or other financial assets. The other options are financial instruments.

107 $ 1,000,000

	$'000
$12,500 × 1,296 / 1,200	13,500
Carrying amount	(12,500)
Gain	1,000

108 $ 240,000

	$
40,000 shares @ $6	240,000

Transaction costs are added to the initial cost but omitted from subsequent measurement.

109 The correct answer is: The dividend payable will be included in ZX's finance cost as a period expense

Financial instruments are recognised according to their substance, not their legal form. These redeemable preference shares have an obligation to pay cash; thus they must be classified as a liability, irrespective of the fact they are named shares and may have share certificates attached to them. The dividend or cost attached to the share should be treated in the same way as the share itself. If the share is classified as a liability, the dividends will be treated as finance costs in the SPLOCI not as a deduction from retained earnings.

Lease accounting

110 The correct answer is: $1,283,366

	$
PV of future lease payments	1,871,100
Interest at 6% (6% × $1,871,100)	112,266
Balance of the lease liability at 31 Dec 20X6	1,983,366
Current	700,000
Non-current	1,283,366
	1,983,366

$700,000 is the current portion of the lease liability.

$1,983,336 is the total amount of the liability.

$1,871,100 is the opening balance.

111 The correct answers are:

The lessee obtains substantially all of the economic benefits from use of the asset	INDICATES THAT THE CONTRACT CONTAINS A LEASE	
Ownership in the asset is transferred at the end of the lease term	INDICATES THAT THE CONTRACT CONTAINS A LEASE	
The contract relates to an identified asset	INDICATES THAT THE CONTRACT CONTAINS A LEASE	
If it suits them to do so, the lessor can substitute an identical asset		DOES NOT INDICATE THAT THE CONTRACT CONTAINS A LEASE

The lessee does not have right of use of an identified asset as the lessor has substitution rights.

112 The correct answer is: $6,390,900

	$	Finance charge
Initial liability (PV of future cash flows)	15,462,000	
Interest 8% ($15.462m × 8%)	1,236,960	1,236,960
Payment	(6,000,000)	
Total lease liability at 31.3.X8	10,698,960	

Depreciation is charged based on the shorter of the lease term and the useful life, which are both three years in this case.

	$
Initial measurement of right-of-use asset	15,462,000
Depreciation charge 15,462,000/3	(5,154,000)
Carrying amount	10,308,000

Charge to the profit and loss is $5,154,000 +$1,236,960 = $6,390,900

$1,236,960 only charges the finance cost.

$5,154,000 is only the depreciation charged.

$6,000,000 is just the payment made.

113 The correct answer is: Lease liability + other direct costs + amounts paid before or on commencement of the lease – incentives received

114 The correct answer is: $4,098,050

	$
Present value of the future lease payments at 1 October 20X3	22,745,000
Interest at 10%	2,274,500
Less payment in arrears	(6,000,000)
Lease liability as at 30 Sept 20X4	19,019,500

Extend the calculation to work out the lease liability at the end of the next period:

	$
B/fwd	19,019,500
Interest at 10%	1,901,950
Payment in arrears	(6,000,000)
Lease liability at 30 Sept 20X5	14,921,450
Calculation of current liability (19,019,500 – 14,921,450)	4,098,050

$1,901,950 is only the interest charge for the next period.

$6,000,000 is just the cash payment to be made, not the liability.

$2,274,500 is the interest charge for the first period only.

115 The correct answers are:

- The lessee has the right to substantially all of the economic benefits from use of the asset
- The agreement concerns an identified asset which cannot be substituted

The lease term does not have to be for substantially all of the estimated useful life of the asset. If the lessor has the right to direct the use of the asset, the lessee does not have right of use, so it is not a lease within the scope of IFRS 16.

116 $866,325

	$
Cost 1 July 20X4 ($4,657,500 + $37,500)	4,695,000
Depreciation to 30 June 20X5 ($4,695,000/8)	586,875

Lease liability at 1 July 20X4 6% interest = $4,657,500 × 6% = $279,450

Total charge to the SOPL (279,450 + 586,875) = $866,325

117 The correct answer is: Recognise proportion relating to right-of-use transferred

118 $ 112,000

	$
Lease interest (250,000 × 16%)	40,000
Plant depreciation ((250,000 + 90,000) / 5)	68,000
Short-term lease (18,000 × 2/9)	4,000
Total charge to profit or loss	112,000

119 $ 270,356

Only the gain on the rights transferred to the financial institution can be recognised in profit or loss. As the accountant has recognised the total gain of $1,000,000 in other income, an adjustment is required to remove the gain on the rights retained.

	$
Total gain (8,000,000 – 7,000,000)	1,000,000
Gain on rights retained (1,000,000 × 2,162,850 / 8,000,000)	270,356
Gain on rights transferred (1,000,000 – 270,356) (P/L)	729,644

120 The correct answer is: $1,290,800

Only the gain in respect of the rights transferred to the financial institution can be recognised in profit or loss.

	$
Total gain (20,000,000 – 18,000,000)	2,000,000
Gain on rights retained (2,000,000 × 7,092,000/20,000,000)	709,200
Gain on rights transferred (2,000,000 – 709,200)	1,290,800

121 $13,588

		$
Depreciation for the year	100,650/10	10,065
Finance cost for the year	100,650 × 8%	8,052
Total charge for the year		18,702

Apportion for the year as acquired part way through the accounting period.

1 April – 31 December = 9 months so 9/12 × \$18,702 = \$13,588

Provisions and events after the reporting period

122 \$ 100,000

Loss of the case is not 'probable', so no provision is made, but the legal costs will have to be paid so should be provided for.

123 The correct answer is: Provision \$2m and \$2m capitalised as part of cost of mine

\$2m should be provided for and capitalised as part of the cost of the mine. It will then be depreciated over the useful life.

124 The correct answers are:

Aston Co has a company policy of cleaning up any environmental contamination caused by its operations, even though it is not legally obliged to do so	**PROVISION REQUIRED**	
Brum Co has a fixed price contract to supply widgets to Erdington Co. Brum Co has calculated that it will cost more to manufacture the widgets than budgeted, which is more than the revenue agreed from Erdington Co	**PROVISION REQUIRED**	
Coleshill Co is closing down a division. The board has prepared detailed closure plans which have not yet been communicated to customers and employees		**NO PROVISION REQUIRED**
Dudley Co has acquired a machine which requires the staff to be retrained on its safe operation. The staff training will occur in the next financial period		**NO PROVISION REQUIRED**

Aston Co will create a provision for the present value of the environmental clear up cost – they have a probable outflow of costs (the decommissioning costs) and there is a present obligation (as they have a policy of cleaning up, it is a constructive obligation as opposed to a legal obligation).

Brum Co has discovered that the cost of supply exceeds the expected revenue from the contract. This is an example of an onerous contract. A provision should be recognised that is the unavoidable costs of meeting the contract with Erdington Co (the lower of the cost of fulfilling the contract or penalties from the failure to fulfil the contract). These costs are not stated in the question, but that would be the basis for the calculation of the provision.

Coleshill Co has not communicated the plans officially so the decision could still be reversed. Although no provision is required in the financial statements, it would be disclosed in a note to the accounts if material as it might affect the going concern of the company.

Dudley Co has acquired a machine which requires the staff to be retrained on its safe operation. The staff training will happen in the next financial period. Provisions as a result of the training of staff are forbidden by IAS 37 as the company does not have control over the staff (they can leave at any time).

125 \$ 3,863,000

The decommissioning provision should have been capitalised as part of the cost of the equipment at its present value of \$6,210,000 (\$10m × 0.621) on 1 January 20X5.

This means that the depreciation for the year ended 31 December 20X5 would have been \$6,242,000 ((\$25m + \$6.21m) × 1/5 years)

In addition to the depreciation of the equipment, the discount on the decommissioning provision would need to be unwound and a finance cost of \$621,000 (\$6,210,000 × 10%) should be recognised in the statement of profit or loss.

Therefore, the total charge to profit or loss relating to the equipment and decommissioning provision required for the year ended 31 December 20X5 would be $6,863,000 ($6,242,000 depreciation + $621,000 finance cost)

126 The correct answers are:

Provisions should be made for both constructive and legal obligations	**TRUE**	
Discounting may be used when estimating the amount of a provision	**TRUE**	
A restructuring provision must include the estimated costs of retraining or relocating continuing staff		**FALSE**
A restructuring provision may only be made when a company has a detailed plan for the restructuring and has communicated to interested parties a firm intention to carry it out	**TRUE**	

127 The correct answer is: Debit Provision $100,000, Debit Profit or loss $20,000; Credit Cash $120,000

The provision is a liability and therefore a credit balance. On settlement, the provision must be reversed with a debit. An expense of $100,000 was previously recognised in 20X4 when the original provision was created, so therefore only the extra $20,000 paid needs to be recognised as an expense in profit or loss in 20X5. Cash is an asset and therefore a debit balance. It is reduced by the amount paid with a credit entry.

128 $ 24,532,000

	$'000
Restoration of seabed (10,000 × 250)	2,500
Dismantling of equipment (30m × 0.68)	20,400
Unwinding of discount (20,400 × 8%)	1,632
	24,532

129 $0.6 million

	$m
$2 million × 15%	0.3
$6 million × 5%	0.3
	0.6

130 The correct answers are:

- The discovery of a fraud which had occurred during the year
- The determination of the sale proceeds of an item of plant sold before the year end

These both provide evidence of conditions that existed at the end of the reporting period. The other options refer to conditions which arose after the reporting period and are therefore non-adjusting events according to IAS 10 *Events After the Reporting Period*.

131 The correct answers are:

- Thomas Co, a customer of Coleridge Co, which owes the company $200,000 at 31 March 20X5, entered insolvency on 3 April 20X5
- Inventory that was held at cost of $200,000 on 31 March 20X5 was sold on 21 April 20X5 for $150,000

Both of these events give additional information about the value of assets which were included in the financial statements of Coleridge at 31 March 20X5. The inventory is required to be held at the lower of cost or net realisable value, and the receivable requires to be reduced by $200,000 as the amount will not be recovered.

The factory accident occurred after the year end, so is not an adjusting event.

The sale of the Wordsworth division, although it was decided prior to the year end, was not a commitment at the year end. However, it may be required to disclose these two events if they are material.

Inventories and agriculture

132 $95,100

Product		$
A	1,000 × 40	40,000
B	2,500 × 15	37,500
C	800 × 22	17,600
		95,100

133 The correct answer is: $14,900

	$
Cost	14,900
NRV (100 units × ($166 – $13) – ($166 × 2%)) = 100 × ($153 - $3.32)	14,968
Lower	14,900

134 The correct answer is: Fair value less estimated costs to sell

IAS 41 *Agriculture* requires biological assets to be measured on initial recognition at fair value less estimated costs to sell.

135 The correct answer is: Harvest

Harvest is an intervention, not a biological process. Growth, procreation and degeneration are natural biological processes.

136 The correct answer is: Included in profit or loss for the year

A gain or loss on a biological asset is included in profit or loss for the year.

137 The correct answers are:

Production overheads should be included in cost on the basis of a company's actual level of activity in the period		**INCORRECT**
In arriving at the net realisable value of inventories, settlement discounts must be deducted from the expected selling price		**INCORRECT**
In arriving at the cost of inventories, FIFO, LIFO and weighted average cost formulas are acceptable		**INCORRECT**
It is permitted to value finished goods inventories at materials plus labour cost only, without adding production overheads		**INCORRECT**

Production overheads are allocated on the basis of a company's normal level of activity. Settlement discounts are not deducted to arrive at NRV. The LIFO formula is not allowed under IAS 2 *Inventories*. Valuation of finished goods should include production overheads.

138 The correct answers are:

- The frames should be valued at $20,000
- The pedals should be valued at $58,000

One of the basic principles from IAS 2 is that inventory should be measured at the lower of cost and net realisable value (NRV).

The frames had cost Bouani $20,000 to manufacture and these were included in inventory at this amount. The question does not indicate any selling costs which will be incurred so NRV must be the $30,000 agreed selling price. This means that the frames should continue to be carried at $20,000, being the lower of cost and NRV. The fact that the frames could now be manufactured for $15,000 is not relevant.

The cost of the pedals is $60,000 (3,000 pedals × $20). The NRV would be $58,000 ([3,000 pedals × $21] less $5,000 costs to repair). As the pedals are currently being held at a cost of $60,000, the carrying amount should now be reduced to the lower NRV amount

139 $39.3 million

	$m
Per inventory count	36.0
Received after year end	(2.7)
Sold after year end (7.8m / 1.3)	6.0
	39.3

140 $ 55,080

NRV – (12,000 × (5.4 × 85%)) = $55,080

The inventory at year end should be held at the lower of cost and net realisable value ($5.40 – ($5.40 × 15%) = $4.59 per unit, giving 12,000 × $4.59 = $55,080.

As information has come to light after the year end but before the approval of the financial statements and the inventory was held at the year end, the value should be restated to its net realisable value less selling costs.

Accounting for taxation

141 The correct answer is: $15.9 million

	$'000
Charge for year	16,200
Under-provision	2,100
P/L adjustment re: deferred tax (W)	(2,400)
Profit or loss charge	15,900

Working

	$'000
Provision needed (13m × 30%)	3,900
Provision b/f	(5,400)
Reduce provision	(1,500)
Amount to revaluation surplus (3m × 30%)	900

	$'000
Amount to profit or loss	(2,400)

142 The correct answer is: $1.2 million

	$'000
Prior year under-provision	700
Current provision	4,500
Movement of deferred tax (8.4 – 5.6)	(2,800)
Deferred tax on revaluation surplus	(1,200)
Income tax expense	1,200

143 The correct answer is: $345,000

	$'000
B/f	850
Year to 31.12.X8 (500 – 450)	50
Revaluation surplus	250
	1,150
× 30%	345

144 $ 130 million

	$m
B/f (140 + 160)	300
Charge for year	270
C/f (310 + 130)	(440)
Tax paid	130

145 $ 19 million

	$'000
Current charge	19,400
Over-provision	(800)
Deferred tax (W)	400
	19,000

Working

	$'000
Required provision	6,750
Less revaluation	(3,750)
	3,000
Balance b/f	(2,600)

ANSWERS

	$'000
Charge to income tax	400

146 The correct answer is: $5,100 charge

As the tax base is less than the carrying amount for accounting purposes (more tax benefit has been taken), then a provision is required.

Carrying amount (accounting)

	$'000
Cost of asset	40,000
Depreciation charge (40,000 – 5,000)/5 years	(7,000)
Carrying amount at 31 August 20X2	33,000
Tax base	
Cost of asset	40,000
Less Y1 tax depreciation at 60% 40,000 × 0.6	(24,000)
	16,000
Difference $33,000 – $16,000	17,000
Tax provision 0.3 × $17,000	5,100

147

Deferred tax asset or liability	Amount
Liability	$120,000

As the tax base is less than the accounting carrying amount (more tax benefit has been taken), then deferred tax liability is required:

Carrying amount	$'000
Cost of asset	1,000
Residual value	(200)
Depreciable value	800
Depreciation charge 800/8 years	(100)
Carrying amount at 31 December 20X5 (1,000 – 100)	900
Tax base	
Cost of asset	1,000
Less Y1 tax allowance at 50%	(500)
	500
Difference $900,000 – $500,000	400
Tax liability 30% × $400,000	120

148 The correct answers are:

The amount of the deferred tax liability is	CORRECT	

The revaluation surplus is	**CORRECT**	

Deferred tax liability

	Carrying amount ($)	Tax base ($)	Taxable temporary difference ($)	Deferred tax at 20% ($)
Plant	110,000	90,000	20,000	4,000 liability
Land	280,000	200,000	80,000	16,000 liability
				20,000 liability

Revaluation surplus

	$
Revaluation gain ($280,000 - $200,000)	80,000
Less associated deferred tax (per above)	(16,000)
Total revaluation surplus	64,000

Section B

Derringdo Co case

149 The correct answer is: $22,000

	$
Operating expenses	
Depreciation charge (800,000 × 85% × 10% × 6/12)	34,000
Release of grant (240,000 × 10% × 6/12)	(12,000)
	22,000

150 The correct answer is: $204,000

	$
Deferred income	
Grant received ($800,000 × 30%)	240,000
Release for this year ($240,000 × 10% × 6/12)	(12,000)
Total balance at year end	228,000
Presentation	
Current liability ($240,000 × 10%)	24,000
Non-current liability (balance)	204,000
	228,000

151 $439

	$
Year 1	
Laptop (W)	158
Broadband (562 (W) /2)	281
	439

Working

	$	%	$
Laptop	200	22	158
Broadband (30 × 12 × 2)	720	78	562
	920	100	720

152 The correct answer is: Recognising revenue when a performance obligation is satisfied

153 The correct answer is: Derringdo Co is not exposed to credit risk for the amount due from the customer

The other options would all suggest that Derringdo Co was the principal.

BPP

Campbell Co case

154 The correct answers are:

Revenue should be recognised as an entity satisfies a performance obligation	**CORRECT**	
Progress towards completion on a contract should be measured solely on an input basis		**INCOMPLETE**

155 $ 6.3m

	$m
Total revenue 31 December 20X8 ($9m × 90%)	8.1
Recognised in the period to 31 December 20X7 ($9m × 20%)	1.8
Amount recognised in the current year	6.3

156 The correct answer is: Contract liability $0.2m

Revenue will be recognised to the level of recoverable costs where the progress cannot be measured. Therefore $0.2 million should be recognised as Revenue and cost of sales. As no invoice has yet been issues a contract asset will be recognised for $0.2 million.

157 The correct answer is: $2.26m

The after sales support will be recognised over the 12-month period. As Campbell Co has already provided six months of support, $0.1 million can be recognised meaning that $2.26 million can be recognised overall ($2.36 million – $0.1 million).

158 The correct answer is: $1,500 should be recognised as revenue by Campbell Co when the accessory has been delivered and accepted by the customer

Campbell Co is acting as an agent as the equipment accessory is delivered directly to the customer from the manufacturer. Only the 3% commission should be recognised as revenue (3% × $50,000 = $1,500). As the customer has taken delivery and accepted the price of $50,000, the revenue can be recognised at that point.

Apex Co case

159 The correct answer is: An asset that takes a substantial period of time to get ready for its intended use or sale

(IAS 23: para. 5)

160 The correct answer is: Physical construction of the asset is nearing completion

IAS 23 has no requirements in respect of the stage of completion of the asset

161 $ 625,000

$625,000 = (($10m 7.5%) × 10/12)

162 The correct answer is: 9.25%

	%
10% × 50/80	6.25
8% × 30/80	3.00
	9.25

163 The correct answer is: Recognised as investment income in the statement of profit or loss

ANSWERS

The investment proceeds were earned before construction began, so are not deducted from the borrowing costs which are being capitalised.

Bertrand Co case

164 The correct answer is: As debt and equity

165 $ 735,000

	$'000
Interest payable ($10m × 5% × 2.58*)	1,290
Capital repayable ($10m × 0.79)	7,900
Debt element	9,190
Finance costs for year = 9,190 × 8%	735

166 The correct answer is: $9,425,000

	$'000
1 October 20X0	9,190
Finance charge 8%	735
Interest paid (10,000 × 5%)	(500)
Balance 30 September 20X1	9,425

167 The correct answer is: Deducted from the proceeds of the loan notes

The effective interest rate is then applied to the net amount.

168 This debt instrument will be measured as a financial asset at amortised cost in the financial statements of Bertrand Co.

Fino Co case

169 The correct answer is: From the commencement of the lease to the shorter of the end of the lease term and the end of the useful life of the plant

170 The correct answer is: $286,500

	$
Present value of future lease payments	173,500
Payments made on the commencement of the lease	100,000
Initial direct costs	20,000
Less: Lease incentives	(7,000)
Initial cost of the right of use asset	286,500

171 The correct answers are:

Situations	Correct accounting treatment
The lease is for less than 12 months	Option 1
The leased asset has a low underlying value	Option 2

Where the agreement is for less than 12 months or the underlying asset is of low value, lease payments can be charged directly to profit or loss, in accordance with the optional recognition exemptions available in IFRS 16.

172 $190,850

	$
Present value of future cash flows at 1.4.X7	173,500
Interest accrued 1.4.X7 – 31.3.X8 ($173,500 × 10%)	17,350
Lease liability as at 31.3.X8	190,850

$173,500 does not factor in the interest charge, $200,000 is the future instalment payments. $90,850 takes the correct calculation of the interest but then deducts the payment which is not due until the following day (1 April 20X8).

173 The correct answer is: $5,400

((9,000/10) × 6) = $5,400

Julian Co case

174 The correct answer is: The amount attributed to an asset or liability for tax purposes

175 The correct answers are:

$190,000	Property, plant and equipment
$60,000	Development expenditure

PPE ($460,000 – $270,000). Development expenditure is in line with IAS 38 and is per the question.

176 The correct answer is: $63,000

The revaluation surplus is carried net of deferred tax.

	$
Revaluation	90,000
Deferred tax (90,000 × 30%)	(27,000)
Carrying amount of revaluation surplus	63,000

177 $45,000

The tax charge for the year.

178 The correct answer is: Accrued expenses which have already been deducted for tax purposes

They will not give rise to a temporary difference.

Rainbird Co

179 The correct answer is: Neither the reorganisation nor the staff training

The reorganisation cannot be provided for because it has only gone as far as a feasibility study.

Staff training is not a valid provision as IAS 37 paragraph 81 specifically forbids costs relating to retraining or relocating staff to be provided for in restricting provisions.

180 A contingent liability

The outcome is probable but cannot be reliably measured.

181 The correct answer is: $1,811,250

Total returns = 525,000 × 12% = 63,000

Expected cost

	$
63,000 × 95% × 30	1,795,500
63,000 × 5% × 5	15,750
	1,811,250

182 The correct answer is: $2,840,400

$2.63 million × 108% = $2,840,400. This is the unwinding of the discount.

183 The correct answers are:

Rainbird Co's board announced a plan to discontinue one of its operations and dispose of the plant. The loss on disposal is estimated at $2 million.		DOES NOT REQUIRE ADJUSTMENT
The employees of the operation to be discontinued commenced a case against Rainbird Co for constructive dismissal. The total cost could be $3 million.		DOES NOT REQUIRE ADJUSTMENT
A legal case for which Rainbird Co had provided $1.7 million at 31 December 20X1 to cover possible damages was unexpectedly settled in its favour.	REQUIRES ADJUSTMENT	
One of Rainbird Co's warehouses was destroyed by fire and half of the inventory on hand at 31 December 20X1, valued at $2.5 million, was destroyed.		DOES NOT REQUIRE ADJUSTMENT

Only the legal case requires adjustment because it provides evidence regarding conditions that existed at the end of the reporting period ie, the legal case that was ongoing.

The other events have all taken place after the reporting period.

PART B: ACCOUNTING FOR TRANSACTIONS IN FINANCIAL STATEMENTS (III)

Section A

Reporting financial performance

184 The correct answer is: A change in valuation of inventory from a weighted average to a first-in-first-out (FIFO) basis

A change of depreciation method is treated as a change of accounting estimate. Adoption of the revaluation method is dealt with under IAS 16. Application of a new accounting policy (such as capitalisation of borrowing costs) for transactions that did not previously occur is not a change in accounting policy according to IAS 8.

185 The correct answer is: A buyer must have been located for the asset

It is not necessary for a buyer to have been located for the asset, only that the sale is 'highly probable' and a buyer is being actively sought by organisation (IFRS 5: para. 8).

186 An asset classified as 'held for sale' should be measured at the lower of [carrying amount] and [fair value less costs to sell].

As the assets are to be sold, value in use is not relevant and recoverable amount will be fair value less costs to sell.

187 The correct answer is: A change in reporting depreciation charges as cost of sales rather than as administrative expenses

This is a change in presentation which will affect calculation of gross profit and will be retrospectively adjusted when presenting comparatives. A and D are simply adjustments made during preparation of the financial statements, C is a change of accounting estimate.

188 The correct answer is: Classifying commission earned as revenue in the statement of profit or loss, having previously classified it as other operating income

This is a change in presentation so qualifies as a change in accounting policy.

189 The correct answer is: $36.8 million

Selling price of $42 million × 90% less costs to sell.

$41 million is the selling price less costs to sell.

$37.8 million ignores the costs to sell.

$42 million is the selling price.

190 $ [147,059]

€125,000/0.85

191 [Rate at date of transaction]

192 $ [98 loss]

Date	Rate	$	€	Gain/(loss)
1/11	1.63	30,675	50,000	
1/12	1.61	(15,528)	(25,000)	(191)
31/12	1.64	15,244	25,000	93
				(98)

ANSWERS

193 The correct answer is: $1.8 million

The factory is a held for sale asset from 1 December 20X6 and is therefore measured at the lower of its carrying amount and its fair value less costs to sell (IFRS 5: para. 15).

The fair value less costs to sell ($2.4 million – $0.3 million = $2.1 million) is greater than the carrying amount of $1.8 million and therefore no impairment is recognised on initial recognition of the held for sale asset on 1 December 20X6. As the information is the same at 31 December 20X6, no subsequent adjustment is required.

$1.6 million is the carrying amount less depreciation of $0.2 million, however, once the factory is classified as held for sale, depreciation is no longer charged and therefore the depreciation for December does not require to be accounted for.

$1.9 million is the value in use less costs of disposal, but this is not a valid measurement of the asset under IFRS 5.

194 The correct answer is: Changes in accounting estimates should be accounted for prospectively and errors accounted for retrospectively

Changes in accounting estimates do not affect previous periods and are therefore not corrections of errors. IAS 8 does give examples on what constitutes changes in accounting policy and what is defined as an estimate. A change in the basis of measuring an asset, for example, such as inventory being measured on a FIFO basis instead of the weighted average cost, will be a change in accounting policy, not a change in estimate.

195

	31 Dec 20X6	31 Dec 20X7
	$	$
Cost of sales	66,700	59,900

Working

Cost of sales

	20X6	20X7
	$'000	$'000
As stated in question	64,600	62,000
Inventory adjustment	2,100	(2,100)
	66,700	59,900

The $2.1m was included in closing inventory at 31 December 20X6 in error. If the closing inventory decreases to remove the effect of the error, the cost of sales will increase by the same amount.

The opening inventory at 1 January 20X7 also included the $2.1m in error. A decrease in opening inventory to remove the effect of the error will decrease cost of sales by the same amount.

196 The correct answers are:

- The operation is a subsidiary that was acquired exclusively with a view to resale - **Discontinued**
- The operation meets the criteria to be held for sale but the sale has not been completed - **Discontinued**
- The operation sold is a minor part of the business - **Continuing**
- The operation is loss making and the directors are currently considering whether to withdraw from the operation in the future - **Continuing**

To be presented as a discontinued operation, the operation must be sold or held for sale and:

(1) represent a major line of business or geographical location;

(2) is part of a single coordinated plan to dispose of a major line of business or geographical area;

(3) is a subsidiary acquired with a view to resale.

197 The correct answer is:

$43,000	**Loss**
$9,000	Profit

The profit or loss on discontinued operations will comprise:

- The loss on classification as held for sale = ($45,000).
- The gain on disposal of the net assets = $88,000 (700,000 – 612,000).
- The loss made by the bakery = ($34,000).
- The net profit on discontinued operations is therefore $9,000 (-45,000 + 88,000 – 34,000).

Earnings per share

198 The correct answer is: $0.167

	$'000
Earnings on dilution:	
Basic	1,850
Add back interest (2,000 × 6% × 70%)	84
	1,934

	'000
Shares on dilution:	
Existing	10,000
Conversion (2m × 4/5)	1,600
	11,600

Basic EPS = 1,850 / 10,000 = $0.185

Diluted EPS = 1,934 / 11,600 = $0.167

199 The correct answers are:

$'000	Balances
40,000	Share capital
4,000	Share premium

	Share capital	Share premium
	$'000	$'000
Balance 30 September X2 (250m shares)	50,000	15,000
Rights issue:		

ANSWERS

	Share capital	Share premium
	$'000	$'000
Share capital (50m × 20c)	(10,000)	
Share premium (50m × 22c)	–	(11,000)
Balance 30 September X1 (200m shares)	40,000	4,000

200 The correct answers are:

- The issue during the year of a convertible (to equity shares) loan note
- The granting during the year of directors' share options exercisable in three years' time

The convertible loan note and the share options should be taken into account when calculating diluted EPS.

201 The correct answer is: EPS takes into account the additional resources made available to earn profit when new shares are issued for cash, whereas net profit does not

202 The correct answer is: $1.35

TERP

5 × 1.8 =	9.0	
1 × 1.5 =	1.5	
	10.5 / 6	= $1.75

Shares

	$'000
5,000 × 5/12 × 1.8 / 1.75	2,143
6,000 × 7/12	3,500
	5,643

EPS = 7,600 / 5,643 = $1.35

203 The correct answer is: 5.1 million

Calculate the shares that are treated as being issued for nil consideration:

No. of shares under option		500,000
No. of shares that would have been issued at the average market price	(500,000 × $2.80) / 3.50	(400,000)
No. of shares treated as issued for nil consideration		100,000

Shares used in EPS calculation = 5,000,000 + 100,000 = 5.1m

204 EPS 20X8: $ 0.72

EPS 20X7: $ 0.56

Workings

1 ***Calculation of the effect of the bonus issue on the weighted average of shares***

	Number of shares	Time apportioned	Bonus fraction	Weighted average
1/4/X7	4,000,000	6/12	5/4	2,500,000
30/09/X7 Bonus issue (1 for 4)	1,000,000			
	5,000,000			2,500,000
				5,000,000

2 ***Calculation of EPS for the year ended 31 March 20X8***

	Shares
	$'000
B/f 1 April 20X7	4,000
Bonus issue (1 for 4)	1,000
C/f 31 March 20X8	5,000

EPS 20X8 = 3.6 / 5 = $0.72

3 ***Calculation of the (restated) EPS for the year ended 31 March 20X7***

Restated EPS 20X7 = $0.70 × 4,000 / 5,000 = $0.56 (after taking into account the effect of the bonus issue of shares in September 20X7)

205 The correct answer is: $2.46

Working

Additional shares resulting from conversion $100,000/$10 × 3 shares = 30,000 shares

Total dilutive number of shares	100,000 + 30,000 = 130,000
Revised earnings	$313,000 + (10% × $100,000 × 70%) = $320,000
Diluted earnings per share	$320,000/130,000 = $2.46

$2.41 ignores the interest saving after conversion ($313,000/130,000 = $2.41)

$2.48 ignores the tax effect on the interest saving after conversion ($323,000/130,000 = $2.48)

$3.13 ignores the increase in shares and calculates the basic earnings per share ($313,000/100,000 = $3.13)

Section B

Tunshill Co case

206 The correct answer is: Change of accounting estimate: Prospective application

This is a change of accounting estimate so does not need to be retrospectively applied.

207 $ 10,000,000

	$m
Original cost 1 October 20X0	20
Two years depreciation ((20/5) × 2)	(8)
Carrying amount at 1 October 20X2	12
Depreciation to 30 September 20X3 (12/6)	(2)
Carrying amount at 30 September 20X3	10

208 The correct answer is: Tunshill Co has reclassified development costs from other operating expenses to cost of sales

This is a change in presentation so it is a change of accounting policy.

209 The correct answer is: Reduced by $400,000

	FIFO	AVCO	Current year profit
	$m	$m	$m
Year to 30 September 20X2	15	13.4	(1.6)
B/f 1 October 20X2			1.6
Year to 30 September 20X3	20	18	(2.0)
At 30 September 20X3			(0.4)

The net effect at 30 September 20X3 of this proposal will be to reduce current year profits by $400,000.

210 The correct answers are:

Account	Debit/Credit
Cost of sales	Debit
Inventory	Credit

The credit entry reduces inventory.

Hemlock Co case

211 The correct answer is: $196,203

The receivable is a monetary asset and is therefore retranslated at the closing rate at year end $155,000/0.79.

212 The correct answer is: Hemlock Co has reclassified head office administration costs from cost of sales to other operating expenses

This is a change in presentation, so it is a change in accounting policy.

213 The correct answer is: Reduced by $800,000

In 20X2 closing inventory is $3.2 million lower ($30m – $26.8m), so cost of sales in 20X2 will be higher and the profit will therefore be lower. So in 20X2, profit, retained earnings and inventory would all be decreased by $3.2 million.

In 20X3 opening inventory is $3.2 million lower and closing inventory is $4 million lower. Cost of sales in 20X3 will therefore increase by $0.8 million and so profit will be reduced by $0.8 million.

214 The correct answer is: Both statements (1) and (2)

IAS 8 states that the nature and the amount of the error should be disclosed, detailing each of the lines affected by the adjustment and the error.

215 $ 4.23 per share

	Weighted average number of shares
Ordinary shares	2,000,000
Shares under option	1,000,000
Equivalent at fair value (1,000,000 × 10.00/12.00)	(833,333)
	2,166,667
DEPS (9,160,000 / 2,166,667)	$4.23 per share

ANSWERS

PART C: ANALYSING AND INTERPRETING THE FINANCIAL STATEMENTS OF SINGLE ENTITIES AND GROUPS

Section A

Interpretation of accounting ratios and trends

216 The correct answer is: A manufacturer

The low asset turnover suggests a capital-intensive industry. The high percentage of depreciation supports this theory that the business has a large amount of non-current assets. This rules out the estate agency or architectural practice. Supermarkets can also be capital-intensive but tend to operate on low profit margins, and the cost of sales personnel costs would be included within administrative and sales costs, rather than the cost of manufacturing the product itself, as in a manufacturing industry.

217 Reducing the [payables payment period] will increase the length of a company's operating cycle.

This will reduce working capital and means that it will take longer to build up working capital needed for production. The other options will all speed up the operating cycle.

218 The correct answer is: 4.1%

Working: (Dividends (3.4 + 11.1) / Share price) × 100 = 14.5 / 350 × 100 = 4.1%

219 The correct answer is: 3.9%

Profit margin is a component of ROCE: Profit margin × Asset turnover = ROCE

Working

16.3% / 4.19 = 3.9%

220 [7.5]

Working

EPS = 800 / 4,000 = $0.20. P/E ratio = 150 / 20 = 7.5

221 [5.1%]

	$'000
Profit before interest and tax	230
Capital employed (3,500 + 1,000)	4,500
	= 5.1%

Limitations of financial statements and interpretation techniques

222 The effect of this impairment will [increase] the ROCE ratio of Cyan Co, and [increase] its gearing ratio.

Capital employed (assets) would decrease, increasing ROCE. The impairment loss will reduce equity (revaluation surplus) and so increase gearing.

223 The correct answer is:

Current ratio	Quick ratio
Decrease	Decrease

The value of the inventory will be added to both current assets and current liabilities. It will add proportionately more to liabilities and so reduce the current ratio. The effect on the quick ratio will be even greater as inventory is excluded from assets.

224 The correct answers are:

Decrease	Operating profit margin
Increase	ROCE

The new product will have an operating profit of 120 / 1,600 = 7.5%, so will reduce the current margin. It will have a ROCE of 120 / 500 = 24%, higher than the current 20%.

225 The correct answer is: Obsolete inventory lines

Obsolete goods can lead to a build-up of unsold inventory, thereby increasing the holding period. A reduction in selling price or an increase in demand could increase sales leading to a fall in the holding period. Seasonal fluctuations will change the holding period throughout the year but should not affect the year-on-year picture.

226 The correct answer is: Overstatement of profits

The use of historical cost accounting during a period of inflation can lead to overstatement of profits. Non-current assets carried at historical cost may be presented at a value well below their fair value, leading to understated depreciation and consequently overstated profits. This can be compounded by the use of FIFO, if inventory is held at an original cost which is significantly below replacement cost. The charge to cost of sales will be understated and profit overstated.

The use of historical cost accounting will lead to understatement rather than overstatement of non-current asset values and will not affect interest costs. It is likely to lead to overstatement rather than understatement of ROCE.

227 The correct answers are:

Renegotiating a loan to secure a lower interest rate			**NO EFFECT**
Applying the optional recognition exemption to a lease contract under IFRS 16 Leases		**REDUCE**	
Repaying a loan just before the year end and taking it out again at the beginning of the next year		**REDUCE**	
'Selling' an asset under a sale and leaseback agreement		**REDUCE**	

228 The correct answer is: Sell a piece of equipment and enter into a short-term lease for similar equipment which meets the optional recognition exemption requirements, which the company has a policy of applying

This would be an unlikely transaction as it would remove the asset from the statement of financial position. The short-term recognition exemption being applied to the replacement equipment would mean it is not recognised on the statement of financial position.

The deferred income approach to accounting for government grants leaves the carrying amount of the asset intact, rather than deducting the amount of the grant from the asset amount.

Revaluing assets is the obvious way of increasing the carrying amount of assets.

Under the diminishing balance method, more depreciation is charged in the earlier years of the life of an asset, so a change to 10% straight line would reduce the depreciation charge for the first few years. Of course, this effect is only temporary as the charge will catch up after a few years.

229 The correct answer is: Trent factors with recourse the receivable of its largest customer

A receivable factored with recourse will still be included in trade receivables at the year end. Seasonal trading will create particular distortion if the busiest period is just before the year end. Cash sales will need to be removed from the calculation and an adjustment will have to be made for sales tax.

Not-for-profit and public sector entities

230 The correct answer is: Shareholders

Charities do not usually have shareholders, in the commercial sense of the term.

231 The correct answer is: Accruals

Public sector accounting needs to move from cash-based accounting to application of the accruals concept.

232 The correct answers are:

- Rent receipts outstanding
- Interest cover
- Financial actuals against budget

A local council would not pay dividends and would be unlikely to measure ROCE, which deals with return to investors.

233 The correct answers are:

- Operating profit margin
- Earnings per share

Charities do not operate with a view to earning a profit and do not have shareholders.

Inventory holding period is relevant to a charity as the charity will generate funds based on the inventory it sells. The current ratio will also be relevant as to remain viable, the charity must be able to pay any liabilities as they fall due.

234 The correct answer is: Funded by government

Public sector bodies have a major advantage not generally enjoyed by charities – government funding.

235 The correct answer is: Disclosure of dividends per share

Not-for-profit entities do not have share capital so dividends per share is not relevant. The other requirements could be relevant to a not-for-profit entity.

236 The correct answers are:

- There is no requirement to calculate an earnings per share figure as it is not likely to have shareholders who need to assess its earnings performance
- It prioritises non-financial KPIs over financial targets

The objectives of a not-for-profit entity do not include making a profit so it would not calculate earnings per share or report to shareholders. However, it is likely to have to account to the trustees of the Board of the charity or entity using non-financial KPIs. For example, a hospital may account for mortality rates, or a children's charity show the numbers of children assisted during the period.

237 The correct answers are:

- Inventory holding period
- Payables payment period

Cyan holds inventory for resale and therefore the inventory holding period is relevant. It purchases inventory from suppliers and therefore the payables payment period is also relevant.

ROCE is not relevant for a charity and as sales are all in cash, there will be no receivables balance.

Section B

Sandbag plc case

238 The correct answer is: 1.29

Current ratio = current assets/current liabilities = 133/103 = 1.29

239 The correct answer is: Make a rights issue of ordinary shares

This would increase both cash and share capital, increasing current assets without incurring any additional liabilities.

Offering a settlement discount to customers would make cash received lower than receivables which would decrease the current ratio.

Making a bonus issue of shares would generate no cash at all and would not affect the current ratio.

Selling current asset investments would simply replace one current asset with another, at the same amount.

240 | 0.36 |

Acid test ratio = (current assets – inventories)/current liabilities = (133 – 96)/103 = 0.36

241 The correct answers are:

Decrease ratio	Proposal 1
Increase ratio	Proposal 2

Proposal 1 will cause the acid test ratio to fall because, although receivables will convert into cash more quickly, the amount of cash received will be less than the amount of the receivables. Current assets will fall without any change in current liabilities, so the acid test ratio will fall.

Proposal 2 will cause the acid test ratio to rise, by delaying the reduction in cash that would occur by paying suppliers. Since the acid test ratio is less than 1, anything that prevents an equal fall in current assets and current liabilities will boost the ratio.

242 The correct answer is: Non-current asset turnover

A manufacturing company will have high non-current assets (factory, plant and machinery), so this ratio will measure how efficiently it is using its non-current assets to generate revenue.

The P/E ratio is a measure of market confidence in the future of the entity. Gearing relates to long-term solvency and the current ratio relates to liquidity.

Section C

243 Woodbank Co

Text reference

Chapter 20.

Top tips

The question makes it very clear where your analysis should be heading – the **effect** of the purchase of Shaw Co – so concentrate on this and review the information from this angle.

Easy marks

Calculating the ratios should be easy marks, but remember to show your workings.

Examining Teams' comments

Many candidates paid too little attention to the incremental effect of the acquisition of Shaw Co and few commented on the fact that profit or loss only included the results of Shaw Co for three months. This led a lot of candidates to conclude that the acquisition was not advantageous, which is not the conclusion borne out by taking into account the expected profits of Shaw over 12 months.

Marking guide	Marks
(c) 1 mark per valid point (including 8 for ratios)	12
Total	20

(a) and

(b)

Ratio	Woodbank Co 20X3	Working	Woodbank Co 20X4	Working	Woodbank Co 20X4 excluding Shaw
Return on capital employed	10.5%	(16,250 + 1,750) / (95,000 + 55,000)	12%	(18,000 – 5,000)/(150,000 – 50,000)	13%
Gross profit margin	22%	33,000/150,000	22%	(33,000 – 9,000)/(150,000 – 30,000)	20%
Profit before interest and tax margin	9.1%	(16,250 + 1,750) /150,000	12%	(18,000 – 5,000)/(150,000 – 30,000)	10.8%
Current	1.7:1	27,000/25,000	1.08:1	N/A	N/A

ANSWERS

Ratio	Woodbank Co 20X3	Working	Woodbank Co 20X4	Working	Woodbank Co 20X4 excluding Shaw
ratio					
Gearing (debt/(debt + equity))	5.3%	55,000 / (55,000 + 95,000)	36.7%	N/A	N/A

(c) **Analysis of performance and position**

The acquisition of Shaw Co has materially affected the results of Woodbank Co for the year ended 31 March 20X4. In order to make a meaningful comparison of the performance of Woodbank Co during the year to 31 March 20X4 with its performance during the year to 31 March 20X3, it is necessary to isolate the effects of the acquisition and consider how Woodbank Co's performance would have looked without Shaw Co.

Profitability

Shaw Co has contributed positively to profitability with both the gross profit margin and profit before interest and tax margin both being higher after the acquisition. However, the $50 million of loan notes which financed the acquisition have increased capital employed and so exerted a downward pull on ROCE. With Shaw Co, ROCE is 12%. Without Shaw Co it would have been 13%. This is likely to be due to only three months profits of Shaw Co being included in PBIT. If 12 months' profits were used, we could expect the return to be correspondingly higher.

Woodbank Co's individual gross profit has declined by 2% since 20X3. While revenue has risen by 9%, cost of sales has increased by 11%. However, Woodbank Co has done well at keeping down expenses and its PBIT margin without Shaw Co (10.8%) would have been up on 20X3 (9.1%). It is important to remember that Shaw Co was only owned for the final three months of the financial year, not much time for the additional assets to show a return. It is likely that the acquisition will enhance profitability to a greater extent over the next 12 months.

Liquidity

The current ratio of Woodbank Co has fallen from 1.7:1 to 1.08:1. This is a steep drop. We can see immediately that cash reserves have declined by $4.5 million, which is likely to be due to using cash reserves to partly fund the acquisition of Shaw Co. Trade payables have increased by $8 million. This suggests that Woodbank Co is having trouble paying its suppliers on time or that Shaw had a large amount of trade payables which have now been consolidated within the group. The retained earnings balance shows that Woodbank Co paid a dividend of $5.5 million during 20X4. This was perhaps unwise when working capital was needed to finance expansion and pay the additional loan interest. Had the dividend not been paid the current ratio for 20X4 would be 1.3:1 – still a fall from 20X3, but less alarming.

Gearing

Gearing has risen from 5.3% to 36.7%, attributable to an additional $50 million loan notes issued to finance the acquisition of Shaw Co. The interest payments each year will be $5.5 million which is the same as the amount of the dividend paid in 20X4. Shareholders may expect to receive less in future years as the servicing of the debt will take priority, but had the acquisition been funded by a share issue their returns would have been diluted. Gearing of 36.7% is still within acceptable limits and future good returns from the acquisition will build up retained earnings and keep gearing in check.

Conclusion

Woodbank Co's performance would have been broadly comparable to the previous year had no acquisition taken place. The acquisition of Shaw Co has had a detrimental effect on liquidity and gearing for 20X4 but appears from three months results to have the capacity to significantly increase profits for Woodbank Co. It seems likely that over a longer period this will also improve liquidity and gearing, giving an overall positive result for shareholders.

244 Pinardi Group

Text references

Chapters 20 and 21

Top tips

Use the proforma provided for ratios and show all your workings. If you show your workings, marks may be awarded for your approach even if the final answer is not correct. This is not possible if you simply include yours final answer.

Easy marks

Most candidates find ratio calculations relatively easy and many candidates score full marks in this area.

Examiner comments

You should refer to the full examiners' comments which are available on the ACCA website (www.accaglobal.com).

The examining team noted that many scripts continue to provide superficial, 'textbook' answers that do not draw on any of the information from the scenario. Candidates should note that these types of answers will attract little, if any, marks. To earn marks in this type of question it is essential that candidates use the scenario to provide a rationale for the changes in the performance and position. This scenario was not short of clues, one of the biggest being the disposal of Silva Co, so it was surprising that many answers failed to consider this at all.

Marking guide	Marks	
(a) Calculations	2	
		2
(b) Explanation	3	
		3
(c) Ratios	4	
		4
(d) Analysis	11	
		11
Total		20

(a) **Gain on disposal**

	$'000
Proceeds	42,000
Less: Net assets at disposal	(35,000)
Less: Goodwill at disposal (W)	(4,200)
Gain on disposal	2,800

ANSWERS

Working

Goodwill at disposal

	$'000
Goodwill at acquisition	6,000
Less: Impairment (6,000 × 30%)	(1,800)
Unimpaired goodwill at disposal	4,200

(b) **Explanation of Silva Co disposal**

Silva Co is likely to meet the criteria as it is a separate major line of operations which has been disposed of during the year.

As a discontinued operation, the results would be removed and presented separately on the face of the statement of profit or loss together with the gain (post-tax) on disposal of $2.8m.

As Silva Co was sold on 1 January 20X7, there are no results to incorporate for the current year. However, the results of 20X6 should be shown as a discontinued operation for comparative purposes.

(c) **Ratio calculations**

Ratio	Working	20X7	Working	20X6
Gross profit margin	(50,000/98,300) × 100	51.6%	(50,600/122,400) × 100	41.3%
Operating profit margin	(17,000/98,300) × 100	17.3%	(13,200/122,400) × 100	10.8%
Interest cover	(17,000/3,200)	5.3 times	(13,200/5,500)	2.4 times
Inventory turnover days	(13,300/47,600) × 365	102 days	(22,400/71,800) × 365	114 days

(d) **Analysis**

Performance

The overall revenue is down by $24m, which may be largely due to the disposal of Silva Co, which is in the 20X6 results but contributed no revenue in 20X7.

Last year, Silva Co contributed $36m in revenue. Removing this from the 20X6 results shows that there has been a like-for-like increase of $11.9m (($122.4m – $36) – $98.3m) from the fragrance and cosmetics divisions.

The gross profit margin is up significantly from 20X6 to 20X7, from 41% to 52%. We can see that the gross profit margin of Silva Co in 20X6 was only 35% ($12.6m/$36m), so the other parts of the group were able to generate higher gross profit margins historically.

The operating profit margin has increased, although not quite as dramatically as the increase in gross profit margin. In fact, the operating expenses have only decreased by $3.7m, despite the $24.1m decrease in revenue. There are some factors to consider within the operating expenses for 20X7. There is a one-off exit fee of $3m for the cosmetics division to exit the lease. While this is expensive, the division would have been paying $25m over 10 years so will ultimately save a significant amount of money.

In addition to this, the effects of foreign exchange gains and losses are included in the operating expenses line. In 20X6, there was a gain of $3m but in 20X7 there was a loss of $1m, which will have reduced operating profit. This shows that the Pinardi group has quite large exposure to foreign currency risk.

The interest cover has increased from 2.4 to 5.3 during the year, which is a combination of both an increase in operating profits and a decrease in finance costs. The finance costs are likely to have decreased due to the exit from the lease.

Position

The decrease in non-current liabilities is likely to be partly due to the removal of the lease liability for the cosmetics division, which had 10 years remaining.

Some of the non-current liabilities may also have been paid off from the proceeds from the sale of Silva Co. Silva Co was sold for $42m, but cash has only increased by around $17m. Therefore, the Pinardi group may have used some of the cash to reduce the non-current liabilities in the group.

It is also worth noting that in 20X6 the assets and liabilities would have included the Silva Co figures. It may have been that Silva Co had significant non-current liabilities which were removed when it was sold.

The inventory turnover figure shows that the Pinardi group is able to turn over inventory more quickly than previously. The inventory days are high, but the nature of the Pinardi group products will mean that they are not immediately perishable, so this is unlikely to be a significant concern.

In 20X6, the Pinardi group inventory turnover period would have included the figures relating to Silva Co. The removal of this seems to show that the inventory turnover period relating to cosmetics and fragrance is lower than that of the jewellery sector.

Conclusion (marks awarded for sensible conclusion)

Whilst Silva Co does generate profits, the disposal seems to have been a good move. Silva Co's results have actually improved since disposal, showing it is not a struggling business. The additional focus on the remaining divisions has generated more profits for the Pinardi group, particularly now the cosmetics division is utilising the group property and no longer requiring leased premises.

Other comments which candidates may produce which could be given credit

It should be noted that there is now $2m revenue relating to the use of the Silva Co name, which will be there each year. Removing this for comparability shows that the like-for-like increase in revenue is $10m.

The inclusion of the $2m income from Silva Co with no cost of sales will have increased the gross profit margin. Even removing this reduces it to 50.6% and so has not accounted for a significant movement.

Whilst cash has only increased by $17m despite the $42m sale, it may have been that Silva Co had a significant amount of cash in the bank, which was removed from the group when Silva Co was disposed of.

The exclusion of the $36m revenue and $6.6m operating expenses of Silva Co from the 'continuing operations' consolidated statement of profit or loss for 20X6 suggests that operating expenses as a percentage of revenue in 20X6 were 35.6% (30,800 [37,400 – 6,600]/86,400 [122,400 – 36,000]), which is actually higher than that for 20X7 (34.2%). On a like-for-like basis this, along with the improvement in the gross profit margin, this suggests a better financial performance for the Pinardi group without Silva Co.

245 Funject Co

Text references

Chapters 20 and 21

Top Tips

Clearly laying out the calculations for the restated profit or loss and the ratios is vital. You should ensure you show your workings or underlying formula for all ratio calculations performed. Remember to state whether an adjustment makes an increase or decrease in profit (show decreases in brackets). Ensure that you link your discussion back to the scenario in order to score well in the explanations.

Easy marks

Calculation of ratios, remember to use the preformatted response area provided and show your workings (as the revised figures were used, it was imperative to show the workings or zero marks were given). A mark is always given for stating a conclusion and you should aim to remember to include a conclusion at the end of your discussion

Examining Team's comments

Most answers confined themselves to giving a textbook based explanation of what the ratio told users and whether the company's ratio was higher or lower than the industry average. Some answers went on to suggest whether the company ratios were better or worse than the industry averages, but very few provided any further analysis. Better answers referred to the differing performance of the division disposed of and its impact on the company's results.

Marking guide		Marks	
(a)	Adjustment to revenue and cost of sales	1	
	Disposal of non-core division	1	
	Management charge (remove old, add new)	1	
	Rent expense (remove current, add commercial)	1	
			4
(b)	Calculation of ratios	6	
			6
(c)	Profitability comments	5	
	Liquidity comments	3	
	Gearing comments	1	
	Conclusion	1	
			10
Total			20

(a) **Restated financial information**

Statement of profit or loss

	20X4
	$'000
Revenue (54,200 – 2,100 (Note 1))	52,100
Cost of sales (21,500 – 1,200 (Note 1)	(20,300)
Gross profit	31,800
Operating expenses (W)	(12,212)
Profit before tax	19,588

Working

Restatement of operating expenses

	20X4
	$'000
As per question	11,700

	20X4
	$'000
Less: expenses relating to non-core division	(700)
loss on disposal of non-core division	(1,500)
Gamilton Group management charge (54,200 × 1%)	(542)
Add: Funject management charge (31,800 × 10%)	3,180
Less: rent charged by Gamilton Group	(46)
Add: commercial rent	120
	12,212

(b) Profit has decreased from $21,000,000 to $19,588,000 and the resulting journal entry will be ($'000s):

Debit Retained earnings (21,000 – 19,588)	$1,412	
Credit Cash		$1,412

Ratio calculations

	Industry KPIs 20X4	Working	Aspect Co 20X4
Gross profit margin	45%	31,800/52,000 × 100	61%
Operating profit margin	28%	19,588/52,100 × 100	38%
Receivables collection period	41 days	(5,700/52,100) × 365	40
Current ratio	1.6:1	(12,900 – 1,412)/11,600	1:1
Acid test (quick) ratio	1.4:1	(12,900 – 4,900 – 1,412)/(11,600)	0.57:1
Gearing (debt/equity)	240%	16,700 / (9,000 – 1,412)	220%

(c) **Commentary on performance**

Profitability

The discontinued operation had a gross profit % (GP%) of 43% (900/2,100 × 100) and an operating profit % (OP%) of 10% (200/2,100 × 100). Before adjusting for the disposal, Aspect Co has a GP% of 60%. After an adjustment has been made to reflect the disposal, Aspect Co's GP% is 61% which is higher than the industry average of 45%. Thus, it would appear that the disposal of the non-core division has had a positive impact on the GP% of Aspect Co. Such a positive comparison of the GP% to the industry average would suggest that Aspect Co has negotiated a very good deal with its suppliers for the cost of goods in comparison to its competitors; the GP% is 16% (61 – 45) higher than the industry average.

However, when considering the OP%, the financial statements have been adjusted to reflect:

(1) the disposal of the discontinued operation;

(2) a new management charge which would be imposed by Funject Co; and

(3) commercial rent charges.

These adjustments result in an OP% of 38%. So, although the OP% is still 10% (38 – 28) higher than the industry average, it would appear that some of the advantage of having such a good deal with its suppliers is lost when operating costs are incurred. The OP% does not outperform the industry average to the same extent that GP% did. Although the management charge will be eliminated as an intra-group transaction on consolidation, it will

ANSWERS

still have an impact in the individual financial statements of Aspect Co. However, there is no indication of what this charge is for and whether or not it represents a market value for these costs. The rent of $120,000 is deemed to be a fair market value which would indicate that the previous rent charge of $46,000 was artificially low. If Funject Co acquires Aspect Co, it may wish to capitalise on the relationship which Aspect Co has with its supplier of goods but it might also need to investigate the composition of operating costs other than those described above to see if any of these can be avoided/reduced.

Liquidity

Aspect Co's receivables collection period appears to be comparable with the KPIs provided (40 days in comparison to 41 days). Terms of trade of 30 days are quite reasonable (though this usually depends on the type of business) and so there are no causes for concern here.

Given that Aspect Co's receivables collection period is comparable to the industry average, the difference in the current ratio (1·1:1 in comparison to 1·6:1) can only be explained by either lower current assets other than receivables (for example, cash) or higher current liabilities. As Aspect Co's cash balance does not appear to be low ($2·3m), this suggests that its liabilities might be higher than average. Perhaps Aspect Co's favourable relationship with its suppliers also extends to longer than average credit terms. As Aspect Co's acid (quick) ratio (0·57:1) is much less than the industry average (1·4:1), this would also suggest that Aspect Co is holding a higher than average level of inventory. This may raise a concern about Aspect Co's ability to sell its inventory. There is also a current tax bill to consider. Indeed, if Aspect Co were asked to settle its current liabilities from merely its receivables and bank, it would be unable to do so. Perhaps Funject Co may wish to further investigate the procedures associated with the purchase and holding of Aspect Co's inventory prior to a takeover. As a parent company, Funject Co should be able to influence these procedures and have more control over the levels of inventory held.

Gearing

Aspect Co appears to be highly geared but perhaps this is not a huge cause for concern because it appears to be a highly geared industry (220% compared to 240%). It may be that the proceeds from the sale of the non-core division can be/were used to pay down loans. As the gearing for the industry is higher than that of Aspect Co, it may be that Aspect Co could still increase borrowings in future. If so, Aspect Co may need to increase working capital efficiency and reduce costs in order to generate enough cash to service higher borrowings.

Conclusion

Overall, Aspect's statement of financial position gives little cause for concern; the profitability margins appear to be healthy although further investigations of operating costs and working capital efficiency may be required. More information also needs to be obtained about the nature of the business and perhaps the financial statements of several years (as opposed to one) might also be beneficial.

246 Pastry Co

Text references

Chapters 20 and 21.

Top Tips

You have been given the ratios before adjustment and are asked to recalculate them after making adjustments for consistent accounting policies. You need to find an efficient way to process any adjustments in respect of the accounting policies and calculating the ratios as the requirement is only worth six marks. The CBE version of the question available on the ACCA website (www.accaglobal.com) contains a pre-formatted response area which would help with your approach. You must ensure your analysis uses information provided in the question in order that your answer has sufficient depth. The Examiner's report for this question states that rote learned answers to ratio analysis will not score credit.

Easy marks

The calculation of ratios should be well practiced and should be relatively easy.

Examining Team's comments

Most candidates scored poorly on this question due to poor exam technique, either due to not addressing the requirements or not using the information in the scenario.

Marking guide		Marks
(a) Adjustment of financial statements	3	
Ratio calculations	3	
		6
(b) Analysis – 1 mark per well explained point	14	
		14
Total		20

(a) Adjusted financial statement extracts and ratios for Dough Co

	As per question	*Adjustment*	*Adjusted*
	$'000	$'000	$'000
SOPL:			
Revenue	16,300		16,300
Cost of sales	(8,350)	(2,500)	(10,850)
Gross profit	7,950		5,450
Operating expenses	(4,725)	1,000 2,500	(1,225)
Profit from operations	3,225		4,225
SOFP:			
Property	68,500	(30,000) 1,000	39,500
Equity shares	1,000		1,000
Revaluation surplus	30,000	(30,000)	Nil
Retained earnings	2,600	1,000	3,600
Loan notes	5,200		5,200

	Cook Co	*Dough Co (original)*	*Workings*	*Dough Co (restated)*
Gross profit margin	32.3%	48.8%	5,450/16,300 × 100	33.4%
Operating profit margin	23.3%	19.8%	4,225/16,300 × 100	25.9%
ROCE	18.8%	8.3%	4,225/(4,600 + 5,200) × 100	43.1%

If Dough Co accounted for properties under the cost model:

- Depreciation would reduce by $1,000,000 ($30 million/30 years) making operating expenses $3,725,000, and profit from operations $4,225,000.
- Retained earnings would increase by $1,000,000 to $3,600,000.
- Revaluation surplus of $30 million would be removed.
- Property would decrease by $29 million ($30 million less extra depreciation).

If Dough Co accounted for amortisation in cost of sales:

- Cost of sales would increase by $2.5 million, making gross profit $5,450,000.
- Operating expenses would decrease by $2.5 million, but profit from operations would remain at $4,225,000

(b) Cook Co may be a slightly larger company, having made more sales and profits during the year. Initially, it appears that Dough Co makes a significantly higher margin than Cook Co (48.8% compared to 32.3%), which suggests that it is much more profitable to sell as a retailer rather than wholesale.

However, this is misleading as the higher gross profit margin is largely due to the accounting policy of where amortisation is charged. Once the figures are adjusted to make the two companies comparable, the two gross profit margins are much closer (33.4% and 32.3%).

Even with this adjustment, Dough Co still makes a higher gross profit margin, suggesting that the relatively high-cost properties are still producing a good return. Looking at the operating profit margin, it appears that Cook Co makes a significantly higher margin, suggesting a greater cost control (23.3% compared to 19.8%). Once the adjustments for the different accounting policies are taken into account, it can be seen that the margins are much more comparable (23.3% and 25.9%). Without further information on the operating expenses, it is difficult to draw too many conclusions about the cost management of the two companies. The one thing which can be noted is the higher payment of salaries in Dough Co compared to Cook Co. As both companies are owner managed, it may be that Cook Co's management are taking a lower level of salaries in order to show increased profits.

Alternatively, it could be that the Dough Co management are taking salaries which are too high, at the expense of the growth of the business. The low level of retained earnings suggests that Dough Co's owners may not leave much money in the business for growing the company.

ROCE

When looking at the return on capital employed, the initial calculations show that Cook Co is making a much more impressive return from its long-term funding (18.8% compared to 8.3%). This is completely reversed when the revaluation surplus is removed from Dough Co's figures, as Dough Co makes a return of almost twice that of Cook Co (18.8% and 43.1%).

This return is not due to high operating profits, as the margins of the two companies are similar, with Dough Co actually making lower profits from operations.

The reason for the high return on capital employed is that Dough Co has a much better asset turnover than Cook Co. This is not because Dough Co is generating more sales, as these are lower than Cook Co. The reason is that Dough Co has a significantly lower equity balance, due to having extremely low retained earnings relative to Cook Co.

Difficulties

Without examining the market value of Cook Co's properties, it will be difficult to assess which company is likely to cost more to purchase. Basing any investment decision on a single year's financial statements is difficult, as the impact of different accounting policies is difficult to assess. From the information provided, it is unclear whether Cook Co's directors are taking an unrealistically low salary, or whether Dough Co's directors are taking vastly greater salaries than average.

Conclusion

Overall, both companies appear to be profitable and have performed well. Looking at previous years' financial statements of both entities will enable us to make a much clearer investment decision, as will looking at the notes to the accounts to assess the accounting policies applied by each company.

247 Venus Group

Text reference

Chapters 20 and 21.

Top Tips

You must refer to the scenario when interpreting the ratios. The examiners have reported several times that credit will only be awarded to candidates who apply their answers to the scenario and that marks will not be awarded for generic discussion of each ratio.

Easy marks

Well prepared candidates should be able to score well in the ratio calculations.

Examiner comments

The analysis and interpretation of a group is an important area of the syllabus and will continue to be examined. As in previous examination sessions, most candidates failed to score high marks on this question. The reason for this seemed to be poor exam technique by not addressing the requirement or not adequately using the information in the scenario.

Weaker candidates appear to have grasped the message about the importance of using the scenario but now copy out sections of the requirement into the answer. This repetition of the scenario will not gain marks as the examination team are looking for individuals to use that information to explain the impact on the entity. The lowest performing candidates continue to make the same mistakes, either ignoring the scenario completely and giving 'textbook' answers about what the movements in the ratios could mean or simply putting extremely brief answers

Marking guide	Marks	
(a) Ratios	3	
		3
(b) (i) Venus Co profit	5	
		5
(ii) Comparability	3	
		3
(c) Performance and conclusion	9	
		9
Total		20

(a)

	Workings	20X8	Workings	20X7
		%		%
Gross profit	12,500/39,000 × 100	32.1	11,000/32,000 × 100	34.4
Net profit	9,800/39,000 × 100	25.1	8,900/32,000 × 100	27.8
Return on equity	9,800/87,500 × 100	11.2	8,900/42,000 × 100	21.2

(b) (i)

	$'000
Venus Co consolidated profit for the year	9,800
Adjustment 1: Deduct Luto Co post-acquisition profit – Note (1)	(2,000)
Adjustment 2: Deduct savings due to discounts received from Luto Co – Note (2)	(500)
Adjustment 3: Add back unwinding of discount on deferred consideration (W) – Note (3)	185
Adjustment 4: Add back fair value adjustment depreciation (900/3 × 6/12) – Note (4)	150
Venus Co single entity net profit	7,635
Net profit % working: 7,635/(39,000 - 5,000 post-acquisition revenue) × 100	22.5%

Working

	$'000
Discount unwound (5m × 0.926 × 8% × 6/12)	185
Alternatively	
Discount unwound ((5m/1.08) × 8% × 6/12)	*185*

(ii) **Comparability**

It is not possible to compare consolidated financial statements with those of a single entity for a number of reasons which include:

The results in a consolidated statement of profit or loss include not only the income and expenses of the parent, but also the income and expenses of any subsidiaries for the period during the year that they are controlled by the parent.

Transactions between the parent and its subsidiaries, like intra-group sales, will be eliminated on consolidation but will remain in the single entity statement of profit or loss.

The consolidated statement of financial position includes all of the assets and liabilities controlled by the parent at the year end, including those of its subsidiaries.

Equity in consolidated financial statements will be increased by the addition of the non-controlling interest and the post-acquisition retained earnings from subsidiaries.

Intra-group balances are removed on consolidation; however, the single entity financial statements will include items like intra- group loans, intra-group receivables and intra-group payables.

(c) **Performance**

Despite the increase in revenue, profit attributable to the owners of Venus Co has increased by only $0.3m ($9.2m – $8.9m) following the acquisition.

As Luto Co has made a profit of $2m, this suggests that Venus Co has made a smaller profit than in the previous year.

The disappointing gross profit noted by the managing director and the resulting fall in the gross profit % will be partly due to a loss of profitability in Venus Co's own business.

Venus Co's 20X8 net profit without Luto Co would have been down on 20X7 by $2.165m ($9.8m – $7.635m (part (b))) and the net profit % would have fallen to 22.5%. Venus Co has maintained its profit at a comparable level to the previous year only through the contribution of its subsidiary. This shows that the profits of Luto Co have had a positive impact on the group.

The acquisition has led to a significant deterioration in return on equity (ROE) (11.2% compared to 21.2%). This is not so much due to the net profit %, which is down by less than three percentage points (27.8% – 25.1%), but to the increase in equity ($87.5m compared to $42m).

The acquisition has increased share capital and share premium and brought in non-controlling interests (NCI). The financial statements show the whole share issue and NCI but only six months' group trading, which will have a negative impact on ROE.

Managing director's (MD's) comments

The MD is incorrect to be disappointed in the performance of the subsidiary as it has had an overall positive impact on group performance (see performance comments above), which should increase when a full year's results are consolidated in 20X9.

The MD was expecting to see a favourable effect on gross profit due to the new discount from Luto Co. This has no effect on the consolidated financial statements, or the ratios based on the consolidated financial statements, as intra-group trading is eliminated on consolidation.

Conclusion

It does not appear that the disappointing results for the year to 30 June 20X8 can be attributed to the acquisition, as the results of Venus Co would have been down on the previous year if the acquisition had not taken place.

Additional points which could have been made:

There may also be synergies arising from the acquisition which will reduce operating costs in future years but have not yet had time to fully emerge.

It is also relevant to note that while Luto Co's assets have undergone a fair value uplift, the non-current assets of Venus Co are carried at historical cost, which can have the effect of inflating ROE. If Venus Co's assets were fair valued, this would probably increase equity and also reduce earnings through a higher depreciation charge.

248 Mowair Co

Text references

Chapters 20 and 21.

Top Tips

In explaining the ratios, it is important to consider the context of the scenario and not simply explain what the ratio shows. This question gives suitable headings as part B asks for commentary on the 'performance' and 'position' of the business. As this is a discussion question, it is expected that the candidate can supply a suitable conclusion, even if only a short paragraph or couple of sentences as this shows an understanding of the whole question and that the candidate can pull their answer together.

Easy marks

Ensure workings (or underlying formula) are shown for the calculation of the ratios (which is generally performed well by candidates). Marks are awarded not just for the ratio answers, but also for the workings behind them.

Examining Team's comments

The Examining Team are looking for meaningful use of the scenario, not just stating that ratios have improved/worsened, there needs to be relevant suggested reasons why these changes may have occurred. Calculation of ratios was performed well, however, candidates are not using all the information provided in the question when answering the analysis question in part (b).

Marking guide	Marks

(a) Ratio calculations	6	
		6
(b) Performance	6	
Position	4	
Future issues of concern	3	
Conclusion	1	
		14
Total		20

(a)

	20X7	Workings	20X6	Workings
Operating profit margin	8.0%	(12,300/154,000) × 100	11.7%	(18,600/159,000) × 100
Return on capital employed	3.6%	(12,300/(192,100 + 130,960 + 19,440)) × 100	8.7%	(18,600/(44,800 + 150,400 + 19,440)) × 100
Net asset turnover	0.45 times	154,000/(192,100 + 130,960 + 19,440)	0.74 times	159,000/(44,800 + 150,400 + 19,440)
Current ratio	0.53:1	15,980/29,920	1.22:1	28,890/23,690
Interest cover	1.3 times	12,300/9,200	1.8 times	18,600/10,200
Gearing (Debt/Equity)	78.3%	((130,960 + 19,440)/192,100) × 100	379.1%	((150,400 + 19,440)/44,800) × 100

Note. For calculation purposes, all loan notes should be treated as debt.

(b) **Performance**

Mowair Co's revenue has declined in the year. As Mowair Co has had exactly the same number of flights in the year, the decline must be due to either lower numbers of passengers or from Mowair Co reducing the price on certain flights. To substantiate this, it would be helpful to see the number of passengers who have flown on Mowair Co flights during the year.

In addition to the decline in revenue, there has been a decline in the operating profit margin in the year. As the number of flights operated by Mowair Co has remained the same, it would appear that a number of the costs incurred by Mowair Co on operating the airline will be relatively fixed and may not have changed significantly during the year. It has been noted that there has been an increase in cost of licences charged by airports during the year, which would again cause the operating profit margin to fall as amortisation would be higher. This only occurred in April 20X7, so the full impact will not actually be felt until next year.

In addition to this, it important to note that there are numerous contracts up for renewal in the next year. This could lead to higher prices for using the airports, and may even result in Mowair Co being unable to use those airports in future. If this is the case, it may have a significant impact on the revenue for the business, as these are described as major airports, which will have the higher levels of demand.

Return on capital employed has declined significantly in the year. There are two major reasons for this. First, there has been a decline in the profit from operations, as discussed above. In addition to this, Mowair Co has revalued its non-current assets in the year. This means that there is a large revaluation surplus in 20X7 which was not present in 20X6. This will have the effect of reducing the return on capital employed due to there being a much larger total balance in equity. If the return on capital employed is calculated without this, it would be 6·2%, which still represents a decline in performance.

Looking at the net asset turnover, this has declined dramatically from 0·74 times to 0·45 times. This will again be affected by the revaluation surplus, making the two years incomparable. If this is removed from the calculation, the net asset turnover increases to 0·78 times. This is a slight increase in performance. This increase has not come from increased revenue, as it can be seen that revenue has fallen by $5 million. Rather, this increase has come from the decrease in capital employed. This arises from the reduction in the loan notes, which appear to have a significant amount repaid annually.

Position

The value of non-current assets has risen sharply in the year, by $147 million. A large proportion of that will be due to the revaluation which has taken place, leading to an increase of $145 million. This suggests that Mowair Co has acquired some new assets in the year, but it is unclear what these are. They may be replacement components on aircraft, as it is unlikely to be significant enough to be an actual new aircraft itself.

The level of debt in the business is a concern, as this makes up a significant portion of the entity's financing, and appears to incur a large annual repayment. The reduction in the current ratio can be attributed to the large decrease in cash, which is likely to be due to the debt repayments made.

It is worth noting that Mowair Co is almost completely funded by debt, with a relatively small amount held in share capital. Therefore, there is an opportunity for a new investor to consider putting more money into the business in the form of shares and the company then repaying some of the loans held by Mowair Co. As Mowair Co is currently repaying $19 million a year on the loans, it may be more sensible to repay these if possible, freeing up a lot more cash for growing the business or to be returned annually in the form of dividends, also saving $9 million a year in interest.

Issues to consider in the future

There are a number of things to consider regarding the future performance of Mowair Co. The first of these is the ten major licences which are due for renegotiation with airports. If the price is raised on these, then this will lead to reduced profits being made by Mowair Co in future periods.

The debt appears to be being repaid in annual instalments of $19 million, meaning that Mowair Co needs to generate sufficient cash to repay that each year, before returning any profit to the owner. In addition to this, the $9 million interest means that the business appears currently unable to return any cash to investors.

Finally, Mowair Co's business model is heavily dependent on large, expensive items of non-current assets. It has been noted that there has been criticism of under-investment in these, so this could lead to large potential outlays in the near future to replace assets.

Conclusion

Mowair Co has not shown a weakened performance in the current year, but appears to be a profitable business at its core. The major issue with the business is the level of debt, which is resulting in $19 million annual repayments and $9 million annual interest. Any new investor who was able to reduce these amounts as part of any future purchase, would put the business in a much stronger cash position.

249 Perkins Co

Text references

Chapters 20 and 21.

Top Tips

Start with the calculations in the order they are presented in the requirement. Ensure that the time apportionment is correctly calculated for the number of months that the subsidiary is owned. Use the headings given in the question when structuring the narrative answer, and consider what the calculated ratios represent (for example, liquidity) and so what those ratios have informed the user of the financial statements.

Easy marks

Ensure workings (or underlying formula) are shown for the calculation of the ratios (which is generally performed well by candidates). Marks are awarded not just for the ratio answers, but also for the workings behind them.

Examining Team's comments

Once again, the Examining Team have indicated that narrative analysis is brief or not relevant to the scenario, for example, omitting the disposal of the subsidiary. The loss on disposal is generally performed well, but be careful to ensure time-apportionment of the results on the subsidiary when completing the statement of profit or loss.

Marking guide		Marks	
(a)	Proceeds	0.5	
	Goodwill	2.5	
	Net assets	0.5	
	NCI	1.5	
			5
(b)	Revenue and COS	2	
	Other costs	2	
			4
(c)	Ratios	4	
			2
(d)	Gross profit margin	2	
	Operating profit margin	5	
	Interest cover	1	
	Conclusion	1	
			9
Total			20

(a) Gain on disposal in Perkins group consolidated statement of profit or loss

	$'000
Proceeds	28,640
Less: Goodwill (W1)	(4,300)
Less: Net assets at disposal	(26,100)
Add: NCI at disposal (W2)	6,160
	4,400

Workings

1 ***Goodwill***

	$'000
Consideration	19,200
NCI at acquisition	4,900
Less: Net assets at acquisition	(19,800)
	4,300

2 ***NCI at disposal***

	$'000
NCI at acquisition	4,900
20% × (26,100 – 19,800)	(1,260)
	6,160

(b) Adjusted P/L extracts:

	$'000
Revenue (46,220 – 9,000 (S × 8/12) + 1,000 (intra-group))	38,220
Cost of sales (23,980 – 4,400 (S × 8/12)) [see Note]	(19,580)
Gross profit	18,640
Operating expenses (3,300 – 1,673 (S × 8/12) + 9,440 profit on disposal)	(11,067)
Profit from operations	7,573
Finance costs (960 – 800 (S × 8/12))	(160)

Note. Originally, the intra-group sale resulted in $1 million turnover and $0.7 million costs of sales. These amounts were recorded in the individual financial statements of Perkins Co. On consolidation, the $1 million turnover was eliminated – this needs to be added back. The corresponding $1 million COS consolidation adjustment is technically made to Swanson Co's financial statements and so can be ignored here.

(c) Ratios of Perkins Co, eliminating impact of Swanson Co and the disposal during the year

	20X7 recalculated	*Working (see P/L above)*	*20X7 original*	*20X6*
Gross profit margin	48.8%	18,640/38,220	48.1%	44.8%
Operating margin	19.8%	7,573/38,220	41%	16.8%
Interest cover	47.3 times	7,573/160	19.7 times	3.5 times

(d) **Analysis of Perkins Co**

Gross profit margin

In looking at the gross margin of Perkins Co, the underlying margin made by Perkins Co is higher than in 20X6.

After the removal of Swanson Co's results, this continues to increase, despite Swanson Co having a gross margin of over 50%. It is possible that Swanson Co's gross profit margin was artificially inflated by obtaining cheap supplies from Perkins Co.

Perkins Co makes a margin of 48.8%, but only sold goods to Swanson at 30%.

ANSWERS

Operating margin

The operating margin appears to have increased significantly on the prior year. It must be noted that this contains the profit on disposal of Swanson Co, which increases this significantly.

Removing the impact of the Swanson Co disposal still shows that the margin is improved on the prior year, but it is much more in line.

Swanson Co's operating margin is 32.6%, significantly higher than the margin earned by Perkins Co, again suggesting that a profitable business has been sold. This is likely to be due to the fact that Swanson Co was able to use Perkins Co's facilities with no charge, meaning its operating expenses were understated compared to the market prices.

It is likely that the rental income earned from the new tenant has helped to improve the operating margin, and this should increase further once the tenant has been in for a full year.

Interest cover

Initially, the interest cover has shown good improvement in 20X7 compared to 20X6, as there has been a significant increase in profits. Even with the profit on disposal stripped out, the interest cover would still be very healthy.

Following the removal of Swanson Co, the interest cover is improved further. This may be because the disposal of Swanson Co has allowed Perkins Co to repay debt and reduce the interest expense incurred.

Conclusion

Swanson Co seems to have been a profitable company, which raises questions over the disposal. However, some of these profits may have been derived from favourable terms with Perkins Co, such as cheap supplies and free rental. It is worth noting that Perkins Co now has rental income in the year. This should grow in future periods, as this is likely to be a full year's income in future periods.

250 Pirlo Co

Marking guide		Marks
(a) Disposal	4	
		4
(b) Ratios	3	
		3
(c) Discontinued operations	3	
		3
(d) Revenue/margins	5	
Other and conclusion	5	
		10
Total		20

(a) (i) Individual financial statements of Pirlo Co

	$'000
Sales proceeds	300,000
Cost of investment	(210,000)
Gain on disposal	90,000

(ii) Consolidated financial statements of the Pirlo Group

	$'000
Sales proceeds	300,000
Less: goodwill	(70,000)
Less: net assets ($260m + $50m FV)	(310,000)
Add: NCI	66,000
Loss on disposal	(14,000)

(b) Key ratios

	20X9	*20X8*
Gross profit margin	45.8%	44.9%
	(97,860/213,480) × 100%	(97,310/216,820) × 100%
Operating margin	11.9%	13.5%
	(25,500/213,480) × 100%	(29,170/216,820) × 100%
Interest cover	1.43	1.8
	(25,500/17,800)	(29,170/16,200)

(c) The directors of Pirlo Co have determined that Samba Co is not a discontinued operation. In determining this outcome, the directors would have considered whether the operation:

- Represents either a separate major line of business or a geographical area of operations
- Is part of a single co-ordinated plan to dispose of a separate major line of business or geographical area of operations; or
- Is a subsidiary acquired exclusively with a view to resale and the disposal involves loss of control.

If Samba Co had been considered a discontinued operation, the net amount of the post-tax profit or loss of Samba Co and the loss on disposal of Samba Co would be presented separately on the face of the consolidated statement of profit or loss and other comprehensive income.

(d) **Comment on the performance**

The revenue for the group for the year has actually declined in the year. The scenario states that the Samba Co revenue has remained the same in both years, so this decrease appears to represent a decline from the remaining companies in the group.

Whilst there has been an overall decline in revenue, the gross profit margin has improved in 20X9 (44.9% increased to 45.8%). Samba Co has a significantly higher gross profit margin (81%) in relation to the rest of the group, suggesting that the rest of the Pirlo Group operates at a lower gross profit margin.

The operating profit margin of the group has deteriorated in 20X9 (13.5% has decreased to 11.9%). This is initially surprising due to the significant increase in the operating profit margin of Samba Co (41% has increased to 66%). However, the increase in Samba Co's operating profit margin may not represent a true increase in performance in Samba Co due to the following:

- Samba Co has recorded a $2m profit on disposal of its properties, which will inflate its profit from operations in 20X9.
- In addition to this, Samba Co has been charged a lower rate of rent by Pirlo Co, which may also have the impact of making the profit from operations in 20X9 higher than the previous period if the rent is lower than the depreciation Samba Co would have recorded.

This concern is further enhanced when the share of the profit of the associate is considered. This has contributed $4.6m to the profit for the year, which is nearly 40% of the overall profit of the group.

The combination of these factors raises concerns over the profitability of Pirlo Co and any other subsidiaries in the group, as it appears to be loss making. Some of these losses will have been made through the loss of rental income through the new arrangement.

The joining fee paid to Samba Co's previous directors is a one-off cost paid by Pirlo Co. Consequently, it is included in the consolidated statement of profit or loss for the year ended 31 December 20X9. A similar amount was paid by Samba Co in the form of an annual bonus in the year ended 20X8. Therefore, 20X8 and 20X9 are comparable but the joining fee represents a cost saving for Pirlo Co in future years.

The decline in interest cover appears to be driven by both the decrease in profit from operations and an increase in finance costs. As Samba Co has a large amount of debt, and much lower interest cover than the group, this should increase in future periods.

The disposal of Samba Co appears to be surprising, given that it generates the high margins compared to the rest of the group. The loss on disposal of Samba Co should be brought into the consolidated statement of profit or loss. This would reduce profit from operations by a further $14m and would reduce the operating profit margin further to 5.4%.

The sale of Samba Co at a loss is very surprising given that it appears to contribute good results and has a history of strong performance. Whilst selling Samba Co at a loss may be a strange move, Pirlo Co may believe that the real value of the Samba Co business has been secured by employing the two founding directors.

Conclusion

The disposal of Samba Co does not appear to be a good move, as the Pirlo group seems to be losing its most profitable element. The Pirlo Co directors seem to have made a risky decision to move into the software development industry as a competitor of Samba Co.

251 Karl Co

Text references

Chapters 20 and 21.

Top Tips

The question doesn't specifically ask you to calculate goodwill, but you should know that it is an important part of the disposal calculation so don't miss it out. Ensure your analysis refers to information in the scenario.

Easy marks

The calculation of ratios should be reasonably easy. Ensure you show your workings.

Examining Team's comments

The Examining Team have indicated candidates failed to score well in this question, mainly due to not addressing all of the requirements and/or not referring to the information in the question when performing analysis.

Marking guide	Marks	
(a) Disposal loss	4	
		4
(b) Ratio calculations	5	
Analysis	8	
		13
(c) Comparability	3	
		3

Marking guide	Marks
Total	20

(a) **Loss on disposal**

The loss on disposal in the consolidated financial statements is:

	$m
Proceeds	20
Less: net assets	(29)
Less: carrying amount of goodwill (W1)	(2.1)
Loss on disposal	(11.1)

Working

Goodwill

	$m
FV/cost of investment	35
Less net assets at acquisition	(28)
Goodwill at acquisition	7
Goodwill impairment (70%)	(4.9)
Carrying amount of goodwill	2.1

(b) **Ratios and commentary**

	20X8	20X7
Profitability ratios		
Gross profit margin	**42.9%** ($124m / $289m × 100)	**48.5%** ($132m / $272m × 100)
Operating profit margin	**22.1%** ($64m / $289m × 100)	**35.3%** ($96m / $272m × 100)
ROCE (operating profit / equity + NCL)	**8.9%** ($64m / ($621m + $100m)	**13.2%** ($96m / ($578m + $150m)
Liquidity ratios		
Current ratio	**3.1:1** $112m / $36m	**0.8:1** $125m / $161m
Gearing (debt / debt + equity)	**13.9%** 100/100 + 621	**20.6%** 150/150 + 578

Financial performance

Consolidated revenue has increased from 20X7 to 20X8, despite the loss of Sinker Co's significant customer contract three months into the financial year. This might suggest that an increase in the revenue of Karl (or its other subsidiary, or both) has more than compensated for Sinker Co's lost revenue. However, even though the group revenue has increased, the gross profit margin has fallen by 5.6% and the group cost of sales is higher than 20X7. This is likely

ANSWERS

to have been impacted by the poor financial performance of Sinker Co. Alternatively, it may be that the sales mix of the group has changed.

As sales of Sinker Co represent 14% of the total group sales, this poor performance will also have impacted on the group operating margin. Operating profit margin has dropped significantly from 35.3% to 22.1%. Administrative expenses have almost doubled from $23 million for the year ended 31 December 20X7 to $45 million for the year ended 31 December 20X8. Part of this increase will be due to the $11.1 million loss on disposal of Sinker Co. The administrative expenses will also have increased as a result of the $15 million staff redundancy costs and impairment of goodwill.

ROCE has fallen from 13.2% to 8.9%, but this figure is hard to interpret, as the return includes the results of Sinker Co (including the loss on disposal and impairment of goodwill) but the capital employed does not include the capital of Sinker Co due to the disposal at the year end. The operating loss made by Sinker Co of $17 million, plus the loss on disposal of $11.1 million and impairment of $4.9 million will have reduced operating profit. Although it is a simplification, removing these balances would result in a group ROCE of 12.9% ($64m + ($17m + $11m + $4.9m))/(($621m + $17m + $11.1m + $4.9m) + $100m) which is more in line with the 20X7 figure.

Financial position

The current ratio shows considerable improvement for the year ended 20X8, following the disposal of Sinker Co. The group was in a net current liability position at the end of 20X7. This would suggest that Sinker Co may have had a large bank overdraft balance or high levels of payables at 31 December 20X8. It would appear that the sale of Sinker Co has improved the liquidity of the group.

It should be noted that 20X8 group current assets of $112 million will include the $20 million consideration for Sinker Co. This could be used to settle some of the long-term debt. Bank loans have already decreased by at least $50 million. There is no information about the long-term loans of Sinker Co.

Gearing has been reduced during the year from 20.6% to 13.9% but, without further information on Sinker Co's non-current liabilities, it is very difficult to tell if this is a result of the disposal or whether Karl Co has simply repaid debt during the year.

Conclusion

The inclusion of Sinker Co in the consolidated statement of profit or loss does not appear to have had an adverse impact on revenue generation but, now that Karl Co has disposed of the poorly performing subsidiary, it might be able to better control costs, thereby improving gross and operating profit margins. Sinker Co appears to have been a drain on the liquidity of the group, and the position of the group appears to be much healthier following the disposal of Sinker Co.

(c) The results of Karl Co and its two subsidiaries, including Sinker Co, will have been consolidated in the group financial statements for the year ended 31 December 20X7 but only in the consolidated statement of profit or loss for the year ended 31 December 20X8.

So, 20X8 will not be directly comparable to 20X7 because Karl Co sold its holding in Sinker Co on the last day of the year ended 31 December 20X8. This means that the consolidated statement of financial position at 31 December 20X8 will have been prepared on a different basis to that of 20X7. The results of Sinker Co for the year ended 31 December 20X8 will be included in the 20X8 consolidated statement of profit or loss (SOPL). Because Sinker Co was disposed on the last day of the financial year, its results for the full year will be included, and therefore, with the exception of the loss on disposal, the figures in the consolidated SOPL will be comparable to those of the previous year. The loss on disposal is included within administrative expenses in the consolidated SOPL for the year ended 31 December 20X8 which explains why this balance is significantly higher than in the previous year.

Operating profit of the group for the year ended 31 December 20X8 will be distorted by this loss. The consolidated statement of financial position as at 31 December 20X8 will not include the assets and liabilities of Sinker Co as the net assets are no longer controlled by Karl at that date.

Therefore, the consolidated assets and liabilities will not be directly comparable year on year.

252 Kostner Co

Note. More points have been made to cover the type of answers which may be given, not all are required to make the maximum score of 15 marks. Marking allocation is 5 marks on profitability and 5 marks on liquidity with a further 5 marks commenting on overall performance, interactions and recommendations for management with any suitable conclusions).

(a) **Performance**

Profitability

- Although revenue has increased year on year, management should review the individual revenue streams to assess whether there are any areas of concern.
- Membership and sundries have seen the largest decrease year on year in revenue, and as the information has stated that revenue from consumables has remained static, the fall must be attributed to membership subscriptions. As this is the core of the business, management need to assess why the income is dropping so drastically. From a strategic point, there may be an issue with the quality of the freelance trainers who are renting the studio rooms, and it is recommended that the members who are cancelling their subcriptions be asked for their reasoning to ascertain the issues.
- Membership revenue may also be affected as the revenue is not split between the non-refundable joining fee and the regular subscriptions. There may be a decrease in attracted new members hence the reduction in revenue.
- The new sports drink, ProBizz was bought at a heavily discounted rate by buying in bulk prior to the year end. Provided that Kostner can sell the product and it is attractive to the members, this may prove to be a profitable decision.
- Kostner have increased their cash using an issue of share capital $1,500,000 and increasing their gearing further by taking out a further loan of $1,100,000. Although this will have helped the liquidity of the company, there will be additional costs (and therefore reduced profitability) in interest charges.
- The provision in the accounts in respect of the legal claim against Kostner will have affected the profitability of the company in terms of the legal costs and any compensation which may be due to be paid out. Management should review their safety guidelines and ensure that such accidents are unlikely to be the cause of negligence on the part of Kostner. Management should also investigate whether the manufacturer of the equipment was negligent and whether a claim may be made regarding the fault.
- The operating profit of the business has significantly decreased from 35% in 20X7 to 17% in 20X8, with the biggest increase in operating costs (60% increase year on year). The information provided does not split down the costs, but as the cost of personal trainers is likely to be deemed a cost of sales, and other salaries in administration costs, it is expected that rental costs may be an issue here. They have sold property and are likely to be leasing gyms and properties, which may go some way to explaining the increase in rental costs. A service industry such as gyms, will have the bulk of their costs in premises and staff. Other costs, which may fall into this category include insurances, utilities and legal and professional costs. The impact of the legal claim may be greater than just the provision of $50,000 in the financial statements, but profitability may be affected by a subsequent increase in insurance and legal costs as a result. Management should review the operating costs and ensure that the costs are relevant to the income streams.

Liquidity

- Net increase in cash over the year of $5,918,000 is explained by:
  - Cash outflow from operating activities of $3,382,000
  - Cash inflow from investing activities of $9,140,000
  - Cash inflow from financing activities of $160,000

ANSWERS

- Accounts receivable balance has increased by $722,000 year on year, this can be partly explained by two new revenue streams for the business, both of which are paid for in arrears by the consumers (the Fitness Festival receivable of $325,000 and the $300,000 from the studio hire). The remaining increase of $97,000 ($722,000 – $325,000 – $300,000) relates to the only remaining revenue invoiced with credit terms, that of the TotemPow licence. The absence of the credit controller has clearly had an impact on the recoverability of these debts, and management should address a temporary replacement to cover the collection of debts in her absence.
- By purchasing the ProBizz drinks in a high volume, and so close to the year-end, means that cash is tied up in the inventory and cannot be used to pay suppliers (which has seen an increase at year end).
- It looks like they are taking out long term finance to fund the short-term operations of the business. Normally long-term finance would be taken out to fund long term purchases of property, plant and equipment but there has been minimal purchase in the year (per the cash flow). Therefore, this seems a bit of a strange strategy and it is likely that the financing arrangement has been put in place to fund day to day operational costs rather than investing in future business.

Overall points to make

- The trade receivables, inventories and cash balances are all increased year on year, but this may be a timing issue due to when suppliers may be paid. It may also be a deliberate decision made by management to show a strong asset base at year end.
- Although the cash position at year end is positive and shows a significant increase from an overdraft to a positive balance, the operating cash flow should be compared with the operating profit. Comparing the operating profit of $550,000 to the net operating cash outflow of $3,382,000 highlights a significant issue whereby the organisation cannot seem to cover its day to day costs. The further that the operating cash flow is from the operating profit, the greater the potential issue.
- The reasons for Kostner having an overall cash inflow are ones which are tricky to repeat on an ongoing basis, namely the issue of share capital ($1,500,000), the increase in the 10% loan ($1,100,000) and the sale of a significant non-current asset with proceeds of $9,900,000. Management need to address the issue of a negative operating cash flow position as a matter of urgency rather than relying on increasing their gearing (by increasing loans) and issuing new share capital to fund the shortfall.
- The issue of shares may be contentious with the shareholders as their previous holdings may have become diluted, and together with the fall in profits (and lack of dividends paid during the year) may potentially cause investors to sell their holdings, making the business an attractive one for a takeover by a competitor.
- Given the issues stated above, there may be a significant issue regarding the going concern of Kostner and management should take urgent action to address this.

(b)

- Liquidity and profitability can sometimes be at odds with each other. For example, profitability is increased by buying the ProBizz drink in bulk, however, the cash to purchase this will be tied up for longer (it cannot be used for other purposes within the business until the drinks are sold).
- The profit and loss statement may show no significant issues regarding the going concern of a company, however, a cash flow statement can show in more detail where the cash has been spent. An organisation should have an operating cash inflow of a similar size to the operating profit in order to prove that the business can cover its day to day expenses simply by operating in a normal manner. Kostner has seen a net cash inflow, but this is mainly because of non-trading conditions (share issue, loan increase, sale of a significant asset).
- Delays in paying suppliers may result in losing out on settlement discounts, therefore impacting profitability.

- Cash flows can also highlight where the cash is coming from, so if the trade payables are increasing year on year, with a operating cash outflow, it is a possible sign that the business is withholding payments in order to fund other areas of its business (payroll, taxes etc).

Section A

Consolidated statement of financial position

253 $ 195,000

	$
Fair value at acquisition (200,000 × 30% × $1.75)	105,000
Share of post-acquisition retained earnings ((750 – 450) × 30%)	90,000
	195,000

254 The correct answer is: $689,370

Consideration transferred

	$
Cash	250,000
Deferred consideration (400,000/1.08)	370,370
Shares (30,000 × $2.30)	69,000
	689,370

255 $ 40,000 increase

($1.2 million/8 × 4/12) × 80% = $40,000

The adjustment will reduce depreciation over the next eight years, so it will increase retained earnings.

256 The correct answer is: $105 million

	$'000
Shares (18m × 2/3 × $5.75)	69,000
Deferred consideration (18m × $2.42 × 1/1.1^2)	36,000
	105,000

257 The correct answers are:

Account	
Current liabilities	Debit
Retained earnings	Credit

This adjustment reduces (debits) the liability and the credit is to retained earnings. The re-measurement relates to the post-acquisition period, so goodwill is not affected.

258

Fair value	Share of net assets
$260,000	$192,000

		Fair value		*Share of net assets*
	$	$	$	$
Consideration transferred		800,000		800,000
Non-controlling interest at fair value		220,000		
Non-controlling interest at share of net assets				152,000
		1,020,000		952,000
Fair value of net assets:				
Shares	100,000		100,000	
Retained earnings	570,000		570,000	
FV adjustment – customer list	90,000		90,000	
		(760,000)		(760,000)
		260,000		192,000

259 The correct answer is: Record the net assets at the carrying amounts shown above and credit profit or loss with $1.2 million

This combination results in a bargain purchase of $1.2 million which should be credited to profit or loss.

260 The correct answer is: $15,800

	Total $	Group share
Additional depreciation charged as a result of the fair value adjustment on acquisition of Sam Co ($5,000/5 =$1,000) × 80% group share	1,000	800
Impairment of goodwill in Tait Co (50,000 × 40%) × 75% group share	20,000	15,000
	21,000	15,800

261 The correct answer is: Current assets $1.195 million and current liabilities $0.5 million

	$
Current assets (700,000 + 500,000)	1,200,000
Current assets	
Less: Unrealised profit on inventory ($100,000 × ¼) × 20%	(5,000)
Cash in transit	
No effect as asset in the subsidiary is exchanged for asset in the parent	
	1,195,000
Current liabilities (300,000 + 200,000)	500,000

262 The correct answer is:

ANSWERS

		$	$
Debit	Retained earnings	25,200	
Debit	Non-controlling interest	16,800	
Debit	Property, plant and equipment	28,000	
Credit	Goodwill		70,000

The increase due to the use of fair value is $70,000 ($160,000-$90,000) which should be adjusted by a credit to goodwill in its entirety.

		$	$
Debit	Property, plant and equipment	70,000	
Credit	Goodwill		70,000

An additional depreciation charge is required for 3 years (31 Dec 20X4, 20X5 and 20X6), therefore

$70,000/5 years × 3 years = $42,000. Therefore property, plant and equipment is increased by $28,000 ($70,000-42,000).

As the non-controlling interest is valued at fair value, the adjustment for the depreciation needs to be split between the group earnings ($42,000 × 60% = $25,200) and the NCI ($42,000 × 40% = $16,800). As Boat Co has acquired 60% of Anchor Co, the NCI share of this adjustment to earnings is 40% of the additional depreciation charge.

		$	$
Debit	Retained earnings	25,200	
Debit	NCI	16,800	
Credit	Property, plant and equipment		42,000

Therefore, to summarise

		$	$
Debit	Retained earnings	25,200	
Debit	NCI	16,800	
Debit	Property, plant and equipment	28,000	
Credit	Goodwill		70,000

263 The correct answer is: $15,000

	$
Subsidiary profits ($200,000 × 6/12)	100,000
Write off goodwill (per question, this is fully impaired)	(10,000)
Additional depreciation ($300,000/10 × 6/12)	(15,000)
	75,000
NCI at 20%	15,000

Remember to apportion the profits of the subsidiary as acquired part way through the accounting period.

Depreciation to be calculated on the fair value of the asset belonging to Sat Co. Time apportioned for the six months of investment by Pull Co in Sat Co.

264 The correct answers are:

- It will be included at its fair value on acquisition plus share of post-acquisition earnings of Penguin Co.
- It will be included as a separate component of equity.
- 25% of the impairment in the goodwill arising on acquisition will be debited to it.

If the proportionate method was used, non-controlling interest on acquisition would have been lower at $692,500 (25% × ($1,000,000 + $1,770,000)). Non-controlling interest is included in the equity of the Zebra group, not non-current liabilities.

265 $ 18,000

	$'000	$'000
Fair value of consideration transferred		
Cash consideration		β
Contingent consideration		250
Plus: Fair value of NCI at acquisition		100
Less: fair value of net assets acquired		
Shares	500	
Retained losses at acquisition (W)	(270)	
		230
Goodwill		300

Working

Retained losses at acquisition

	$'000
Retained losses at 1 January 20X0	(300)
Profit to the date of acquisition (120 × 3/12 months)	30
Retained losses at the date of acquisition	(270)

266 The correct answers are:

Where a parent company is satisfied that there has been a gain on a bargain purchase (negative goodwill), it should be recognised in the consolidated statement of profit or loss immediately	**TRUE**	
If the liabilities of the acquired entity are overstated, then goodwill will also be overstated	**TRUE**	

A gain on bargain purchase will be credited to the consolidated statement of profit or loss immediately. It is not recognised in the consolidated statement of financial position.

If liabilities are overstated, then the net assets would be understated. This would cause any goodwill recognised to be overstated.

ANSWERS

Consolidated statement of profit or loss and other comprehensive income

267 The correct answer is: $144,000

Consolidated cost of sales

	$
Paprika	60,000
Salt	100,000
Additional depreciation for year (200,000 – 120,000)/8	10,000
Unrealised profit in inventory (32,000 × 25%) = $8,000 × 3/4	6,000
Less: Intragroup sales sold by Salt Co to Paprika Co	(32,000)
	144,000

$132,000 option deducts the unrealised profit instead of adding it on.

$176,000 omits to cancel the intragroup sales of $32,000.

$140,000 calculates the unrealised profit assuming ¾ of goods are sold to third parties, instead of ¾ goods remaining in inventory at year end.

268 The correct answer is: Decrease by $11.5 million

	$m
Decrease	12.0
Increase ($2m × 25% (profit margin))	0.5
Net decrease	11.5

269 The correct answer is: Group retained earnings will be reduced by $160,000

	$'000
Loss of investment income (Spider) (10m × 8% × 6/12)	(400)
Saving of interest payable (Fly) group share (400 × 60%)	240
Therefore the net impact is to reduce retained earnings by	160

270 The correct answer is: $50,000

	$
Profit to 30 June 20X8 (1.6m × 6/12)	800,000
Additional depreciation on FVA ((2m/20) × 6/12)	(50,000)
Goodwill impairment	(500,000)
	250,000
NCI share 20%	50,000

271 $ 717,463

	$
Basil Co	547,700
Parsley Co (206,900 × 10/12)	172,417
PURP ((46,000 × 30/130) × 25%)	(2,654)
	717,463

272 $ 80,000

$2m × 25/ 125 × 20% = $80,000

273 $ 510 ,000

	$'000
Dorset Co profit for the year	1,300
Intragroup interest (5m × 8%)	(400)
NCI in Dorset Co ((1,300 – 400) × 30%)	270
York Co post-acquisition profit (2.4m × 6/12)	1,200
NCI in York Co (1,200 × 20%)	240
Total NCI (270 + 240)	510

274 The correct answers are:

Revenue must be reduced by a total of $120,000	**TRUE**	
Cost of sales must be reduced by a total of $110,000	**TRUE**	
Non-controlling interest must be reduced by $2,000	**TRUE**	

A mark-up of 20% means that the selling price will be 20% higher than the cost of the goods being sold. This means that cost of sales can be calculated as $100,000 ($120,000 × 100/120) and gross profit can be calculated as $20,000 ($120,000 × 20/120 or $120,000 – $100,000).

Whenever there is intragroup trading of goods, there will always need to be an adjustment to revenue and cost of sales to remove the effects of the sale. In this case, Silver Co has recorded a sale of $120,000 and Pearl Co will have recorded a purchase (ie cost of sales) of $120,000, which will need to be eliminated:

Dr Revenue $120,000

Cr Cost of sales $120,000

Similarly, since Pearl Co has only sold half of these goods to a third party by the year end, it means that half of the inventory remains in the group financial statements. The carrying amount of these unsold goods will be inflated from a group perspective because it includes the unrealised intragroup profit. Therefore $10,000 ($20,000 gross profit × 50%) of unrealised profit should be eliminated through an adjustment to the carrying amount of inventories and, consequently, an increase in cost of sales:

Dr Cost of sales $10,000

Cr Inventories $10,000

This means that, in total, revenue has been reduced (debited) by $120,000 and cost of sales has been reduced (credited) by $110,000 ($120,000 – $10,000). As the sale was made by the subsidiary, it means that the unrealised profit on the inventories relates partly to the group and partly to the non-controlling interest. Therefore, the non-controlling interest in the subsidiary will be reduced by its percentage ownership of the subsidiary. In this case, the non-controlling interest would be reduced by $2,000 ($10,000 unrealised profit × 20%). Note that if the subsidiary was wholly owned or it was the parent who made the intragroup sale, this final adjustment to the non-controlling interest would not be required.

Disposals of subsidiaries

275 $145,000

	$	$
Sales proceeds		450,000
Share capital	100,000	
Retained earnings	185,000	
Goodwill	20,000	
		(305,000)
		145,000

276 $ 280,000

(680,000 – 400,000)

277 $245,000 profit

	$
Disposal proceeds	950,000
Goodwill on disposal (600,000 – (700,000 × 70%))	(110,000)
Share of net assets at disposal (850,000 × 70%)	(595,000)
	245,000

278 $ 80,000

	$'000
Consideration	580
Non-controlling interest at 20% share of net assets (640 × 25%)	160
Fair value of net assets	(640)
Goodwill at acquisition	100
Impairment at 20%	(20)
Carrying amount	80

Only the goodwill on the acquisition of Habanero Co will be included in the consolidated statement of financial position as Bonnet Co has been disposed of during the year.

279 $ 8m profit

	$m
Proceeds	50
Less: net assets at disposal	(39)
Less: carrying amount of goodwill (W)	3
Profit on disposal	8

Working

Goodwill at acquisition

	$m
Consideration	28

	$m
Less: net assets at acquisition	(22)
Goodwill at acquisition	6
Impairment	(3)
Carrying amount of goodwill at the date of disposal	3

Accounting for associates

280 The correct answer is: $144 million

	$m
Cost (75m × $1.60)	120
Share of post-acquisition retained earnings (100 – 20) × 30%	24
	144

281 The correct answer is: Credit group inventory $48,000

The sale is an upstream transaction from the associate to the parent. The associate is the seller and therefore the unrealised profit of $48,000 ($2m × 25/125 × 40% × 30%) must be deducted from the share of profit of the associate. The parent is the buyer and will therefore hold the inventory at year end. The adjustment is therefore:

DEBIT Share of profit of associate

CREDIT Group inventory

282 The correct answer is: $5,230,000

	$'000
Cost of investment	5,000
Share of post-acquisition profit (8,500 – 7,400) × 25%	275
PURP (600 × 30% × 25%)	(45)
	5,230

283 $ 10,200,000

	$'000
Cost of investment	10,000
Share of post-acquisition profit (6,000 × 8/12) – 1,000) × 30%	900
Impairment	(700)
	10,200

284 $ 591,000

Share of profit of associate ($1,980,000 × 30%) = $594,000

Unrealised profit ($160,000/4) × 25% × 30% = $3,000

Amount recognised as share of profit of associate $591,000 ($594 – 3)

285 The correct answers are:

ANSWERS

Cost of sales	DR
Investment in associate	CR

This is a downstream transaction as the parent sold goods to the associate. The parent was the seller and therefore earned the unrealised profit. An adjustment to cost of sales is needed to eliminate the unrealised profit. The associate holds the goods in inventories at year end. However, as the financial statements of the associate are not consolidated on a line by line basis, the unrealised profit is instead eliminated from the Investment in associate.

286

Associate 1	Associate 2
Acquisition of 50% of Castur Co. Zuckal Co has appointed two of the five board members.	Acquisition of 15% of Furnitt Co. Zuckal Co can appoint one of Furnitt Co's five board members. No party can appoint more than two.

The 50% owned in Castur Co will give significant influence as Zuckai Co will not have the power to direct operating decisions but will be able to participate in the financial and operating decisions.

The 15% owned in Fumitt Co will also give significant influence as no individual party will have control or the ability to appoint two board members. It is important that candidates understand the 20% holding is a rebuttable presumption and candidates need to read all of the information provided and not merely concentrate on the % holdings given.

287 $ 127,760

The profit attributable to the equity shareholders of Alpha Co will include:

- 100% of Alpha Co's profit for the year of $80,200, less the provision for unrealised profit of $1,000 ($2,000 × 50%), which would be adjusted for the intra group sale.
- 80% of Bravo Co's post acquisition profits for the year, which is $13,840 ($51,900 × 4/12 months × 80%)
- 40% of Charlie Co's profit for the year, being Alpha Co's share of the associate's profit, which is $34,720 ($86,800 × 40%

Only 80% of Bravo Co's post acquisition profits are included because 20% will be attributable to the non-controlling interests in Bravo Co. The question is specifically asking for the amounts attributable to the equity shareholders of Alpha Co, not the consolidated profit for the year of the Alpha Group

	Profit attributable to equity shareholders of Alpha Co ($)
Alpha Co ($80,200 - $1,000)	79,200
Bravo Co ($51,900 × 4/12 months × 80%)	13,840
Charlie Co ($86,800 × 40%)	34,720
Total	127,760

Presentation of published financial statements

288 The correct answer is: The liability has arisen during the current accounting period

The fact that a liability has arisen during the current accounting period does not make it a current liability. The other options would all lead to classification as a current liability.

289 The correct answer is: A revaluation surplus of a factory building

The revaluation surplus on the factory will be presented under 'other comprehensive income'. Increases in the valuation of investment properties and profit on disposal of an investment go through profit or loss. The treatment of a government grant depends on the purpose of the grant, but ultimately it is included in profit or loss.

290 Government grants

Inventories, provisions and intangible assets are shown separately. There is no such requirement for government grants.

291 The correct answer is: The time between acquisition of assets for processing and receipt of cash from customers

292 The correct answer is: As a deduction from retained earnings in the statement of changes in equity

Statement of cash flows

293 $160 million

	$m
Issue of shares	
Share capital and premium b/f (500 + 100)	600
Bonus issue (500/0.50 × 1/10)	100
Cash received (β)	400
Share capital and premium c/f (750 + 350)	1,100
Dividends paid	
Retained earnings b/f	1,740
Profit for the year	480
Dividend paid (β)	(240)
Retained earnings c/f	1,980
Cash inflow from financing activities (400 – 240)	160

294 The correct answer is: $1,440,000

	$'000
Balance b/f	1,860
Revaluation	100
Disposal	(240)
Depreciation	(280)
	1,440
Additions (β)	1,440

	$'000
Balance c/f	2,880

295 The correct answer is: $8.5 million

	$'000
Carrying amount 20X3	14,400
Depreciation	(2,500)
Sale of plant	(3,000)
Revaluation	2,000
Environmental provision	4,000
	14,900
Purchases (β)	8,500
	23,400

296 $ 293 million

	$m
B/f	410
Depreciation	(115)
Revaluation	80
Acquired under lease agreements (12 + 5 + 1)	18
Purchases (β)	287
C/f	680

In addition to the cash purchase of PPE of $287m, cash expenditure was also incurred on the direct costs of arranging the lease of $1m and the deposit paid of $6m therefore the total is $293m.

297 $ 2,100,000

	$'000
B/f (2,000 + 800)	2,800
Additions (6,500 – 2,500 – 50* + 1,800)	5,750
Payments made (β)	(2,050)
C/f (4,800 + 1,700)	6,500

*The direct costs of $50,000 incurred on arranging new lease contracts would be included in the initial measurement of the right-of-use asset but would **not** be included as part of the lease liability. An adjustment is therefore needed to remove the effect of the direct costs when calculating the lease payments made.

Section B

Root Co and Branch Co case

298 $ 268 million

	$m
Cash	210
Shares (116m × 100/200)	58
	268

299 The correct answer is: $5.6 million

	Acquisition	Movement (2 years)
	$m	$m
Property	20	(2)
Brand	25	(5)
		(7)

$7 million × 80% = $5.6 million

300 $ 16 million

$56m × 40/140

301 The correct answers are:

Accounts	
Cost of sales	Debit
Inventories	Credit

The unrealised profit is added to cost of sales and removed from inventories.

302 The correct answer is: Control of the subsidiary has been lost

Exclusion from consolidation is only allowed when control has been lost.

Port Co and Alfred Co case

303

Share capital	Share premium
$	$
235,000	1,115,000

Issue of shares

	Draft	*New issue*	*Revised*
	$'000	$'000	$'000
Share capital	200	35	235

ANSWERS

	Draft	New issue	Revised
	$'000	$'000	$'000
Share premium	500	615	1,115
Fair value of proceeds		650	

304 $ 500,000

	$'000
Net assets at date of acquisition	
Share capital	100
Share premium	85
Retained earnings 331 – (96 × 2/12)	315
	500

305 The correct answers are:

- The non-controlling interest share of profit is part of the consolidated statement of profit or loss
- If a subsidiary is acquired during the year, its results are apportioned over the year of acquisition

The statement of financial position shows all non-current assets. Goodwill is not amortised, it is subject to an annual impairment review.

306 $ 404,000

Port Co $364,000 and Alfred Co ($240,000 × 2/12) = $404,000

307 The correct answer is: $2,912,000

	Port Co	Alfred Co
	$'000	$'000
Port retained earnings	2,900	
Alfred post-acquisition (96,000 × 2/12)		16
Share of Alfred Co: (16 × 75%)	12	
	2,912	

Polestar Co case

308 $ 22.3 million

	$'000
Share capital	6,000
Retained earnings at 30.9.X3	14,300
Fair value adjustment on property	2,000
	22,300

309 The correct answer is: $130 million

(110m + (66m × 6/12) – 13m intragroup)

310 The correct answers are:

Account	
Liability	Debit
Profit or loss	Credit

IFRS 3 *Business Combinations* states that changes to the contingent consideration should result in a remeasurement to fair value with any gain or loss taken to the profit or loss. The effect would adjust the goodwill figure if there arose new information regarding the position at acquisition date. However, if the contingent consideration, being cash in this instance which is dependent on a certain level of profit being achieved, then the adjustment is made to the statement of profit or loss. (IFRS 3: para. 58)

311 $ 150,000

Unrealised profit = 9m – 5.4m = 3.6m

Still in inventory = 3.6m × 1.5/9 = 600,000 × 25% = 150,000

312 The correct answer is: The non-controlling interest will be allocated its share of any goodwill impairment

The other options are incorrect.

Plateau Co case

313 The correct answer is: $12,750,000

((3m/2 × $6) + (3m × $1.25))

314 The correct answer is: Should be recognised at $1 million and not amortised

The contract is estimated to have an indefinite life.

315 The correct answer is: $3,900,000

	$'000
NCI at acquisition (1m shares @ $3.25)	3,250
NCI share of post-acquisition retained earnings ((W) 2,600 × 25%)	650
	3,900

Working

	$'000
Retained earnings per draft	2,900
Less unrealised profit ($2.7m × 50/150 × 1/3)	(300)
	2,600

316 $ 10,500,000

	$'000
Cost (4m × 30% × $7.50)	9,000
Share of post-acquisition retained earnings (5,000 × 30%)	1,500

	$'000
	10,500

317 The correct answers are:

Account	
Cost of sales	Debit
Investment in associate	Credit

Plateau Co is the seller and therefore this is a downstream transaction. The unrealised profit is eliminated by decreasing cost of sales. The unrealised profit is within the inventory of the associate which is not presented in the consolidated statement of financial position and therefore an adjustment is made to the investment in associate.

Pinto Co case

318 The correct answer is: $10,000 received

	$
B/f current (asset)	–
B/f deferred tax	30,000
Charge for the year	160,000
Received (balance)	10,000
C/f (current + deferred)	200,000

319 $ 1,130,000

	$'000
Proceeds from sale of plant (240 – 90)	150
Purchase of plant (W)	(1,440)
Proceeds from sale of investment property	160
	1,130

Working

	$'000
B/f	1,860
Revaluation gain	100
Disposal	(240)
Depreciation	(280)
Purchases (β)	1,440
	2,880

320 The correct answer is: $150,000

	$'000
Opening retained earnings	860
Add: profit for the year	280
Less: Dividend paid	β
Closing retained earning	990

321 The correct answers are:

- Financing activities
- Operating activities

Dividends paid can be presented under operating activities or financing activities.

322 The correct answer is: The proceeds from sale of plant

It is the profit on disposal of the plant that will be adjusted against profit before tax, not the proceeds of disposal.

Woolf Co case

323 $1,100,000

	$'000
Bfwd (1,700 + 800)	2,500
Right-of-use asset acquired (1,540 – 40)	1,500
Cash movement (balancing figure)	(1,100)
Cfwd (2,000 + 900)	2,900

Option $400,000 is the movement between the two years ignoring the effect of the new lease. Option $1,500,000 is the actual lease amount rather than the cash movement. Option $1,900,000 uses the correct figures, but subtracts the new lease during the year which makes the cash movement now $1,900,000.

324 The correct answer is: Cash inflow of $1,860,000

	$'000
Profit before taxation	50
Adjustments for	
Depreciation (per the question)	2,200
Interest received (per the question)	(40)
Release of grant (working)	(250)
Working capital movement (per the question)	(100)
Cash inflow from operations	1,860

Working

Government grant

	$'000
Bfwd (400 + 900)	1,300
Grant received in the year	950

ANSWERS

	$'000
Cash movement (balancing figure)	(250)
Cfwd (600 + 1,400)	2,000

Option B of $2,110,000 ignores the cash movement of the grant ($250,000). Option C adds on the cash movement of the grant instead of subtracting it. Option D of $3,060,000 adds on the value of the government grant received ($950,000) instead of recognising the net movement in grants.

325 The correct answer is: Option (3) only

Both of options (1) and (2) will decrease the balances of working capital assets (trade receivables and inventory). This will result in a working capital inflow in both cases. Only option (3) will result in an overall working capital outflow.

326 The correct answer is: Cash proceeds from the sale of a factory

This would be included within the movements of cash from investing activities. Investing activities represents payments made to invest in assets used by the company to generate profits and the proceeds from the sale of those assets, such as payments to acquire non-current assets, payments to acquire shares in other companies and the proceeds from the sale of non-current assets.

327 The correct answer is: Options (1) and (2)

Presenting the whole grant as a separate item in the statement of profit or loss is acceptable for grants received relating to income for which the expenditure has already been incurred, but not for assets as the grant income should be recognised over the useful life of the asset purchased.

Section C

328 Pedantic Co

Text references

Chapters 8 and 9.

Top Tips

The first point to note here is that the subsidiary was acquired mid-year. Remember this when it comes to working out the depreciation on the fair value adjustment. This question had lots to do but no really technical areas. In the exam, you should set up your proforma in the spreadsheet response option, transfer the numbers as they are provided in the question, then start working through the adjustments. Transfer the total per your working to the proforma when you have completed each working.

Easy marks

There were lots of easy marks here. There were lots of marks available in the statement of financial position even if you did not get the goodwill quite right. Correctly calculating the figures from the share exchange would have gained you marks on goodwill, share capital and share premium.

Marking guide		Marks
(a) Statement of financial position:		
Property, plant and equipment	2	
Goodwill	5	
Current assets	1.5	
Equity shares	1	
Share premium	1	
Retained earnings	2	
Non-controlling interest	2	
10% loan notes	0.5	
Current liabilities	1	
		16
(b) 1 mark per valid point to maximum	4	
		4
Total		20

(a) **Pedantic Co – consolidated statement of financial position at 30 September 20X8**

	$'000
Non-current assets	
Property, plant and equipment (40,600 + 12,600 + 1,800 (W6))	55,000
Goodwill (W2)	4,500

	$'000
	59,500
Current assets (16,000 + 6,600 – 800 – 600 + 200) (or see (W9))	21,400
Total assets	80,900
Equity attributable to owners of the parent	
Share capital (10,000 + 1,600 (W5))	11,600
Share premium (W5)	8,000
Retained earnings (W3)	35,700
	55,300
Non-controlling interests (W4)	6,100
	61,400
Non-current liabilities	
10% loan notes (3,000 + 4,000)	7,000
Current liabilities (8,200 + 4,700 – 400 (W9))	12,500
	80,900

(b) Pedantic Co cannot take assurance from the Tradhat group financial statements that Trilby Co would be able to meet its liability in respect of the goods. The group financial statements will have aggregated the assets and liabilities of all the group companies and it will not be possible to use them to calculate liquidity ratios for any one company.

This is important, because Pedantic Co's contract would not be with the Tradhat group, it would be with Trilby Co. If Trilby Co defaulted on its obligations, the Tradhat group would be under no legal obligation to step in, so that the fact that the group has a strong financial position is not really relevant. It would only become relevant if Tradhat group were willing to offer a parent company guarantee.

In the absence of a parent company guarantee, Pedantic Co must base its decision on the financial position of Trilby Co as shown in its individual company financial statements. It should also obtain references from other suppliers of Trilby Co, specifically those who supply it with large orders on 90-day credit terms

Workings

1 ***Group structure***

Pedantic Co

1.4.X8 ↓ 60% Mid-year acquisition, six months before year end

Sophistic Co

2 ***Goodwill***

	$'000	$'000
Consideration transferred (W5)		9,600
Fair value of non-controlling interests		5,900
Less: Fair value of net assets at acquisition:		
Share capital	4,000	

BPP

	$'000	$'000
Retained earnings	5,000	
Fair value adjustment (W6)	2,000	
		(11,000)
Goodwill		4,500

3 ***Retained earnings***

	Pedantic Co	Sophistic Co
	$'000	$'000
Per question	35,400	6,500
Movement on FV adjustment (W6)		(200)
PUP (W7)		(800)
Pre-acquisition		(5,000)
		500
Group share (500 × 60%)	300	
	35,700	

4 ***Non-controlling interests***

	$'000
NCI at acquisition	5,900
NCI share of post-acquisition retained earnings ((W3) 500 × 40%)	200
	6,100

5 ***Share exchange***

	Debit	Credit
	$'000	$'000
Consideration transferred (4,000 × 60% × 2/3 = 1,600 × $6)	9,600	
Share capital of Pedantic Co (1,600 × $1)		1,600
Share premium of Pedantic Co (1,600 × $5)		8,000

6 ***Fair value adjustments***

	Acq'n	Mov't	Year end
	$'000	$'000	$'000
	1.4.X8	6/12	30.9.X8
Plant (*$2m/5 × 6/12)	2,000	(200)*	1,800

7 ***Intragroup trading***

	$'000	$'000
Eliminate unrealised profit		
Cost of sales/retained earnings ((8,000 – 5,200) ×	800	

ANSWERS

	$'000	$'000
40/140)		
Inventories (SOFP)		800

8 ***Current assets (supplementary Working)***

	$'000
Pedantic Co	16,000
Sophistic Co	6,600
Unrealised profit in inventory (W7)	(800)
Intercompany receivables (per question)	(600)
Cash in transit (W9)	200
	21,400

9 ***Cash in transit***

	Debit	Credit
Receivables		600
Payables	400	
Cash	200	

329 Gold Co

Text reference

Chapters 9 and 10.

Top Tips

Make sure that you read the requirement carefully before doing anything. You are asked to prepare the goodwill calculation and the consolidated statement of profit or loss. No other statement of financial position balances are required.

Easy marks

There are some standard adjustments for transactions such as dividends paid and intragroup trading that shouldn't cause you too many problems.

Examining Team's comments

This was a fairly straightforward consolidated financial statements question. The examining team reminded candidates of the importance of providing workings to support their calculations. Ensure you present workings or use formula in the spreadsheet response area.

Marking guide	Marks	
(a) Goodwill	6	
		6
(b) Revenue/cost of sales	5.5	
Other, incl. NCI	8.5	
		14
Total		20

(a) **Goodwill**

	$'000	$'000
Consideration transferred		
Deferred cash (90% × 16,000 × $2.42 × 0.9091)		31,680
Shares (90% × 16,000 × 3/5 × $8.40)		69,120
		100,800
Non-controlling interest (NCI) (10% × 16,000 × $3.50)		5,600
		106,400
Fair value of net assets at acquisition:		
Carrying amount of net assets at 1.4.20X4:		
Equity shares	16,000	
Retained earnings: at 1 Oct 20X1	56,000	
1 October 20X1–1 January 20X2 (9,920 × 3/12)	2,480	
Fair value adjustments: Plant	2,600	
Contingent liability	(850)	
		(76,230)
Carrying amount at 31 March 20X5		30,170

(b) **Consolidated statement of profit or loss for the year ended 30 September 20X2**

		$'000
Revenue	(103,360 + (60,800 × 9/12) – 5,400 (W1))	143,560
Cost of sales	(81,920 + (41,600 × 9/12) – 5,400 (W1) + 240 (W1) + 650 (W2))	(108,610)
Gross profit		34,950
Distribution costs	(2,560 + (2,980 × 9/12))	(4,795)
Administrative expenses	(6,080 + (3,740 × 9/12))	(8,885)
Share of profit of associate	(3,000 × 40%)	1,200
Finance costs	(672 + 136 (W3) + 2,376 (W4))	(3,184)
Profit before tax		19,286
Income tax expense	(4,480 + (2,560 × 9/12))	(6,400)
Profit for the year		12,886
Profit attributable to:		
Owners of the parent		12,207
Non-controlling interests (W5)		679
		12,886

Workings

1 ***Intercompany and PUP***

Post-acquisition sales = ($600 × 9) = $5,400; PUP = (1,200 × 25/125) = $240

2 ***FV depreciation on plant***

($2,600/3 × 9/12) = $650

3 ***Convertible loan***

Calculate liability component

		$'000	DF @ 8%	$'000
Interest	(10,000 × 6%)	600	3.993	2,396
Principal		10,000	0.681	6,810
Liability				9,206
Interest charge to profit or loss:		9,206 × 8%		736
Already charged				(600)
				136

4 ***Deferred cash consideration***

Unwinding of discount on deferred consideration (see goodwill calculation) = $31,680 × 10% × 9/12 = $2,376

5 ***NCI***

		$'000
Silver's profit for the year	($9,920 × 9/12)	7,440
FV Depreciation (W2)		(650)
		6,790
NCI @ 10%		679

330 Paradigm Co

Text reference

Chapter 9.

Top Tips

There are two important issues in this question – Strata Co showed a pre-acquisition loss and had a negative fair value adjustment. The question was otherwise straightforward.

Easy marks

Five marks are allocated for the goodwill calculation and plenty of marks are available for standard consolidation issues.

Examining Team's comments

The question included a fair value adjustment for plant which was below its carrying amount – which many candidates treated as a surplus. Most candidates correctly calculated and accounted for the value of the share exchange and the NCI but there were some errors in calculating the number of loan notes issued. Some candidates incorrectly calculated post-acquisition profit as $6 million.

Marking guide		Marks
Statement of financial position		
Property, plant and equipment	1.5	
Goodwill	5	
Equity investments	1	
Inventories	1	
Trade receivables	1.5	
Cash and cash equivalents	1	
Equity shares	1.5	
Share premium	0.5	
Retained earnings	3	
Non-controlling interest	1.5	
10% loan notes	1	
Trade payables	1	
Bank overdraft	0.5	
		20
Total		20

Consolidated statement of financial position as at 31 March 20X3

	$'000	$'000
ASSETS		
Non-current assets		
Property, plant and equipment (47,400 + 25,500 – 2,500 (W6))		70,400
Goodwill (W1)		8,500
Financial asset: equity investments (7,100 + 3,900)		11,000
		89,900
Current assets		
Inventories (17,400 + 8,400 – 600 (W2))	25,200	
Trade receivables (14,800 + 9,000 – 900 (W3) – 2,800 interco)	20,100	
Cash and cash equivalents (5,100 + 900 (W3))	6,000	
		51,300
Total assets		141,200
EQUITY AND LIABILITIES		
Equity attributable to owners of Paradigm Co		
Share capital (40,000 + 6,000 (W1))		46,000
Share premium (W1)		6,000
Retained earnings (W4)		34,000
		86,000

ANSWERS

	$'000	$'000
Non-controlling interest (W5)		8,800
		94,800
Non-current liabilities		
10% loan notes (8,000 + 1,500 (W1))		9,500
Current liabilities		
Trade payables (17,600 + 13,000 – 2,800 intercompany)	27,800	
Overdraft	9,100	
		36,900
Total equity and liabilities		141,200

Workings

1 ***Goodwill***

	$'000	$'000
Consideration transferred:		
Shares (20m × 2/5 × 75% × $2)		12,000
Loan notes (15m × 100/1,000)		1,500
		13,500
Non-controlling interest (5m × $1.2)		6,000
		19,500
Net assets at acquisition;		
Share capital	20,000	
Retained earnings ((4,000) + (2,000))	(6,000)	
Fair value adjustment (W5)	(3,000)	
		(11,000)
Goodwill		8,500

2 ***PURP***

Intercompany sales in inventory $4.6m

PURP = $4.6m × 15/115 = $600,000

3 ***Intercompany cash in transit***

	$'000	$'000
Debit Cash	900	
Credit Receivables		900

4 ***Retained earnings***

	Paradigm Co	Strata Co
	$'000	$'000
Per draft	26,600	4,000

	Paradigm Co	Strata Co
	$'000	$'000
Add back pre-acquisition loss		6,000
		10,000
PURP (W2)	(600)	
Gain (loss) on equity investments*	(400)	700
Movement on fair value adjustment (W6)		500
		11,200
Group share of Strata Co – 75% × 11,200	8,400	
Group retained earnings	34,000	

*Loss on equity investments in Paradigm Co: (7,500 – 7,100)

5 ***Non-controlling interest***

	$'000
Fair value at acquisition (W1)	6,000
Share of post-acquisition retained earnings (11,200 (W4) × 25%)	2,800
	8,800

6 ***PPE carrying amount***

	$'000
FVA on plant (W1)	3,000
Depreciation (3,000/3 yrs × 6/12)	(500)
Carrying amount	2,500

331 Viagem Co

Text reference

Chapter 9.

Top Tips

The goodwill impairment must be deducted from the consolidated profit or loss. The subsidiary has been owned for nine months so revenue and expenses must be time-apportioned. You have not been told that the parent has accounted for the unwinding of the discount on the deferred consideration, so you should assume that (as is normal for this exam) you have to make this adjustment.

Easy marks

There were plenty of marks available here for standard workings.

Marking guide	Marks	
(a) Goodwill	6	
		6
(b) Consolidated statement of profit or loss:		

ANSWERS

Revenue	2	
Cost of sales	2	
Distribution costs	1	
Administrative expenses	2	
Share of profit of associate	1.5	
Finance costs	2	
Income tax	1	
Profit for year – attributable to parent	0.5	
– attributable to NCI	2	
		14
Total		20

(a) **Consolidated goodwill at acquisition**

	$'000	$'000
Consideration transferred:		
Shares (9m × 2/3 × $6.50)		39,000
Deferred consideration ((9m × $1.76)/1.1)		14,400
		53,400
Non-controlling interest ((10m × $2.50) × 10%)		2,500
		55,900
Fair value of net assets:		
Share capital	10,000	
Retained earnings: b/f	35,000	
three months to 1 Jan 20X2 (6,200 × 3/12)	1,550	
FVA on plant	1,800	
Contingent liability	(450)	
		(47,900)
Goodwill		8,000

(b) **Consolidated statement of profit or loss for the year ended 30 September 20X2**

	$'000
Revenue (64,600 + (38,000 × 9/12) – 7,200 (W2))	85,900
Cost of sales (51,200 + (26,000 × 9/12) – 7,200 + 300 (W2) + 450 (W3))	(64,250)
Gross profit	21,650
Distribution costs (1,600 + (1,800 × 9/12))	(2,950)
Administrative expenses (3,800 + (2,400 × 9/12) + 2,000 (goodwill impairment))	(7,600)
Finance costs (W4)	(1,500)
Share of profit of associate (2,000 × 40%)	800
Profit before tax	10,400

	$'000
Income tax expense (2,800 + (1,600 × 9/12))	(4,000)
Profit for the year	6,400

	$'000
Profit attributable to	
Owners of the parent (ß)	6,180
Non-controlling interest (W5)	220
	6,400

Workings

1 ***Group structure***

Viagem Co

1 Jan 20X2 ↓ 90% Mid-year acquisition, nine months before year end

Greca Co

2 ***Intragroup trading***

		$'000	$'000
Intragroup trading (800 × 9 months)			
Debit	Revenue	7,200	
Credit	Cost of sales		7,200
PURP (1,500 × 25/125)			
Debit	Cost of sales	300	
Credit	Group inventory (SFP)		300

3 ***Fair value adjustment***

	Acquisition	Movement	Year end
	$'000	$'000	$'000
Plant	1,800	(450)*	1,350

*(1,800/3) × 9/12

4 ***Finance costs***

	$'000
Viagem Co per statement of profit or loss	420
Unwinding of discount on deferred consideration:	
((14,400 × 10%) × 9/12)	1,080
	1,500

5 ***Non-controlling interest***

	$'000
Profit for the year (6,200 × 9/12)	4,650

	$'000
Depreciation on fair value adjustment (W3)	(450)
Goodwill impairment	(2,000)
	2,200
Non-controlling share 10%	220

332 McIlroy Co

(a) Clarke Co is considered as a discontinued operation as it has been disposed of in the year and it appears to satisfy the criteria of:

- Representing a separate major line of business; and
- Being part of a single coordinated plan to dispose of a separate line of business.

As Clarke Co is a discontinued operation, it's results for the period and any gain or loss on disposal will be presented on the face of the consolidated statement of profit or loss as a separate line item.

(b) **Consolidated statement of profit or loss for the year ended 30 September 20X8**

	$
Continuing operations	
Revenue (W1)	4,237,760
Cost of sales (W1)	(1,912,490)
Gross profit	2,325,270
Administrative expenses (W1)	(630,280)
Operating profit (W1)	1,694,990
Investment income (W1)	78,000
Profit before tax	1,772,990
Income tax expense (W1)	(376,700)
Profit for the year from continuing operations	1,396,290
Discontinued operations	
Profit for the year from discontinued operations (437,200 – 17,980 (W4))	419,420
Profit for the year	1,815,710
Profit attributable to	
Owners of McIlroy Co	1,616,236
Non-controlling interest (W2)	199,474

(c) **Retained earnings as at 30 September 20X8**

	McIlroy Co	Spieth Co
	$	$
Retained earnings at 30 September 20X8	3,419,310	581,580

	McIlroy Co	Spieth Co
	$	$
Less: Pre-acquisition retained earnings		(180,600)
Less: Excess depreciation relating to fair value adjustment		(40,000)
Less: PURP adjustment (W5)		(5,400)
		355,580
Group percentage of Spieth Co's post acquisition retained earnings (80% × $355,580)	284,464	
Add: McIlroy Co profit on disposal of Clarke Co ($582,000 - $268,000)	314,000	
Less: Goodwill impairment	(30,000)	
	3,987,774	

Note. Because the only accounting that has taken place in respect of the disposal of Clarke Co is to record the disposal proceeds in the suspense account, the gain on disposal in the individual financial statements of McIlroy Co needs to be recorded in McIlroy Co's retained earnings.

Workings

1 ***Consolidation schedule***

	McIlroy Co	Spieth Co	Adj	Consol
	$	$	$	$
Revenue	3,463,760	828,000	(54,000)	4,237,760
Cost of sales – per Q	(1,558,690)	(402,400)	54,000	(1,912,490)
– PURP (W5)		(5,400)		
Admin expenses – per Q	(486,700)	(103,580)		(630,280)
– FV depreciation (80,000/8yrs)		(10,000)		
– Impairment of goodwill	(30,000)			
Investment income	318,000		(240,000)	78,000
Income tax expense	(302,000)	(74,700)		(376,700)
	1,404,370	231,920		

2 ***Non-controlling interest in year***

	$
Spieth Co (20% × 231,920 (W1))	46,384

		$
Clarke Co (35% × 437,400)		153,090
		199,474

3 ***Goodwill – Clarke Co***

	$	$
Consideration transferred		268,000
Non-controlling interest at acquisition (274,200 × 35%)		95,970
		363,970
Less Net assets at acquisition		
Share capital	100,000	
Retained earnings	174,200	
		(274,200)
Goodwill		89,770
Impairment loss		(25,000)
Goodwill at date of disposal		64,770

4 ***Group profit/loss on disposal of Clarke Co***

	$	$
Sale proceeds		582,000
Less carrying amount of goodwill at disposal (W3)		(64,770)
Less carrying amount of net assets at disposal		
Share capital	100,000	
Retained earnings (286,000 + 437,400)	723,400	
		(823,400)
Add back attributable to non-controlling interest (823,400 × 35%)		288,190
Loss on disposal		(17,980)

5 ***PURP***

	%	$
Selling price	100	54,000
Cost	(80)	(43,200)
Gross profit	20	10,800
× 1/2 in inventory		5,400

333 Plastik Co

Text references

Chapters 3, 4 and 15.

Top Tips

This is quite a time-pressured question so you need to work logically and be prepared to move on if you find individual workings tricky. Create the proforma in the spreadsheet response for the consolidated statement of profit or loss. Go methodically through the workings, showing your calculations or formula clearly.

Easy marks

There are some marks available for figures that can be lifted straight from the question and good, clear workings will help you to fill in several gaps.

Marking guide	Marks	
(a) Goodwill	4	
		4
(b) Group retained earnings	4	
Non-controlling interest	2	
		6
(c) Consolidated statement of profit or loss and other comprehensive income		
Revenue	1.5	
Cost of sales	2.5	
Distribution costs	0.5	
Administrative expenses (including goodwill impairment)	1	
Finance costs	1	
Income tax expense	0.5	
Gain on revaluation of properties	1	
Non-controlling interest:		
• profit for the year	1	
• total comprehensive income	1	
		10
Total		20

(a) **Goodwill**

	$'000	$'000
Consideration transferred – 4.8m shares @ $3		14,400
Deferred consideration (7.2m × $0.275 × 1/1.1)		1,800
		16,200
Fair value of NCI (1.8m shares @ $2.50)		4,500
		20,700
Fair value of net assets:		
Shares	9,000	

ANSWERS

	$'000	$'000
Retained earnings (3,500 – (2,000 × 9/12))	2,000	
Fair value adjustment – property	4,000	
		(15,000)
Goodwill at acquisition		5,700

(b) (i) **Retained earnings**

	Plastik Co	Subtrak Co
	$'000	$'000
Per question	6,300	3,500
Less pre-acquisition (1,500 + (2,000 × 3/12))		(2,000)
Goodwill impairment		(500)
Unwinding of discount on deferred consideration (1,800 (a) × 10% × 9/12)	(135)	
Depreciation on FVA		(100)
PURP (600,000 × 25/125)	(120)	
	6,045	900
Share of Subtrak Co (900 × 80%)	720	
	6,765	

(ii) **Non-controlling interest**

	$'000
NCI at acquisition (see goodwill)	4,500
Share of post-acquisition retained earnings (900 × 20%)	180
Share of property revaluation gain (600 × 20%)	120
	4,800

(c) **Consolidated statement of profit or loss and other comprehensive income for the year ended 30 September 20X4**

	$'000
Revenue (62,600 + (30,000 × 9/12) – 2,700 (W2))	82,400
Cost of sales (45,800 + (24,000 × 9/12) – 2,580 (W2) + 100 (b))	61,320
Gross profit	21,080
Distribution costs (2,000 + (1,200 × 9/12))	(2,900)
Administrative expenses (3,500 + (1,800 × 9/12) + 500 (goodwill))	(5,350)
Finance costs (200 + 135 (see retained earnings))	(335)
Profit before tax	12,495
Income tax (3,100 + (1,000 × 9/12))	(3,850)
	8,645
Other comprehensive income	

	$'000
Gain on revaluation of property (1,500 + 600)	2,100
Total comprehensive income	10,745
Profit for the year attributable to:	
Owners of the parent (β)	8,465
Non-controlling interest (W1)	180
	8,645
Total comprehensive income attributable to:	
Owners of the parent (β)	10,445
Non-controlling interest (W1)	300
	10,745

Workings

1 ***Non-controlling interests***

	Profit for year	Total comprehensive income
	$'000	$'000
Per (b) above	900	900
Gain on property revaluation		600
	900	1,500
NCI 20%	180	300

2 ***Intragroup trading***

	$'000	$'000
(1) *Cancel intragroup sales/purchases*		
Debit Group revenue (300,000 × 9)	2,700	
Credit Group cost of sales		2,700
(2) *Eliminate unrealised profit*		
Debit Cost of sales (600,000 × 25/125)	120	
Credit Group inventories		120

334 Laurel Co

Statement of financial position as at 31 December 20X9

	$m
Non-current assets	
Property, plant and equipment (220 + 160 + 140 + (W7) 3)	523.0
Goodwill (W2)	36.0
Investment in associate (W3)	96.8

ANSWERS

	$m
	655.8
Current assets	
Inventories (384 + 234 + 58 – (W6) 10)	666.0
Trade receivables (275 + 166 + 124)	565.0
Cash and cash equivalents (42 + 10 + 28)	80.0
	1,311.0
	1,966.8
Equity attributable to owners of the parent	
Share capital – $1 ordinary shares	500.0
Share premium	46.0
Retained earnings (W4)	357.3
Non-controlling interests (W5)	89.5
	992.8
Current liabilities	
Trade payables (457 + 343 +174)	974.0
	1,966.8

Workings

1 ***Group structure***

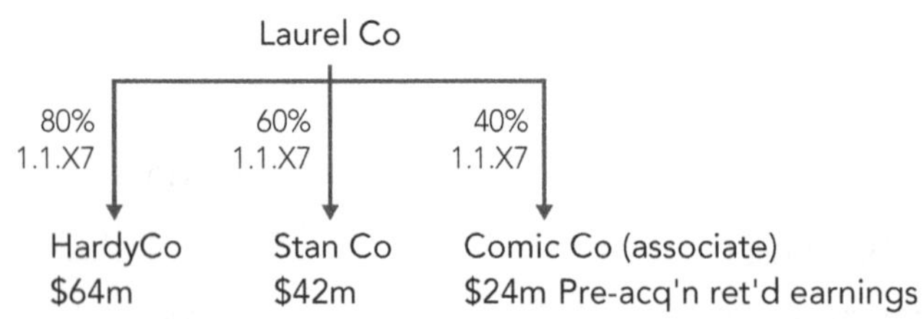

2 ***Goodwill***

	Hardy	Stan
	$m	$m
Consideration transferred	160	140
Non-controlling interests (at fair value)	39	35
	199	175
Fair value of net assets at acq'n:		
Share capital	96	100
Share premium	3	0
Retained earnings	64	42
Fair value adjustment (W7)	0	12
	(163)	(154)
	36	21

BPP

	Hardy	Stan
	$m	$m
Impairment losses	(15)	(6)
Carrying amount of goodwill	21	15

3 ***Investment in associate***

	$m
Cost of associate	70
Share of post-acquisition retained reserves (W4)	29.2
Unrealised profit (W6)	(2.4)
	96.8

4 ***Consolidated retained earnings***

	Laurel	Hardy	Stan	Comic
	$m	$m	$m	$m
Per question	288	128	76	97
Less: PUP re Hardy Co (W6)	(10)			
PUP re Comic Co (W6)	(2.4)			
Fair value adjustment movement (W7)			(9)	
Less pre-acquisition retained earnings		(64)	(42)	(24)
		64	25	73
Group share of post-acquisition retained earnings:				
Hardy Co (64 × 80%)	51.2			
Stan Co (25 × 70%)	17.5			
Comic Co (73 × 40%)	29.2			
Less group share of impairment losses Hardy Co (15 × 80%)	(12.0)			
Less group share of impairment losses Stan Co (6 × 70%)	(4.2)			
	357.3			

5 ***Non-controlling interests***

	Laurel	Stan
	$m	$m
Non-controlling interests at acquisition (W2)	39	35
NCI share of post-acquisition retained earnings:		
Hardy Co (64 × 20%)	12.8	
Stan Co (25 × 30%)		7.5
Less NCI share of impairment losses in Hardy Co (15 × 20%)	(3)	
Less NCI share of impairment losses in Stan Co (6 × 30%)		(1.8)

ANSWERS

	Laurel	Stan
	$m	$m
	48.8	40.7

6 ***Unrealised profit***

Laurel Co's sales to Hardy Co: $32m – $22m = $10m

DR Retained earnings (Laurel Co)	$10m	
CR Group inventories		$10m

Laurel Co's sales to Comic Co (associate) ($22m – $10m) ½ × 40% share = $2.4m

DR Retained earnings (Laurel Co)	$2.4m	
CR Investment in associate		$2.4m

7 ***Fair value adjustments***

	At acquisition date	Movement	At year end
	$m	$m	$m
PPE (57 – 45)	+12	(9)*	+3
Presented in	Goodwill	Ret'd earnings	PPE

*Extra depreciation $12m × ¾

335 Paladin Co

Text references

Chapters 4 and 8.

Top Tips

This is a pretty straightforward consolidated statement of financial position. Set out the proformas and then work methodically through the numbers. There are quite a few adjustments to retained earnings, so make sure your retained earnings working is very clear.

Easy marks

There are a lot of easy marks in this question. The complications are dealing with the deferred payment and the unwinding of the discount, capitalising and amortising the intangible asset and remembering to deduct the intercompany balance from receivables and payables. Most of the rest of it is quite easy, the PURP is only in the parent and two marks are available for investment in associate, which is not a complicated working. Part (b) is easy marks for correctly assessing the situation.

Examining Team's comments

The parts of this question that related to basic consolidation adjustments were well dealt with by most candidates. Errors occurred in the more complex aspects. Some candidates failed to discount the deferred consideration and some did not treat the customer relationship as an intangible asset. Others deducted the post-acquisition additional depreciation from the goodwill. Some students only deducted 25% of the impairment loss on the investment in associate, when the loss applied to the whole of the investment. A common error was to offset the subsidiary's overdraft against the parent's bank balance. No such right of offset exists.

Marking guide		Marks
Consolidated statement of financial position		
Property, plant and equipment	2	
Goodwill	4	
Other intangibles	2	
Investment in associate	2	
Inventories	1	
Trade receivables	1	
Cash and cash equivalents	0.5	
Equity shares	0.5	
Retained earnings	4	
Non-controlling interest	2	
Deferred tax	0.5	
Bank overdraft	0.5	
Deferred consideration	1	
Trade payables	1	
Marks Available	22	
		20
Total		20

Consolidated statement of financial position as at 30 September 20X1

	$'000
ASSETS	
Non-current assets	
Property, plant and equipment (40,000 + 31,000 + 3,000 (W6))	74,000
Goodwill (W2)	15,000
Intangible assets (7,500 + 2,500 (W6))	10,000
Investment in associate (W3)	7,700
	106,700
Current assets	
Inventories (11,200 + 8,400 – 600 (W7))	19,000
Trade receivables (7,400 + 5,300 – 1,300 (W7))	11,400
Cash and cash equivalents	3,400
	33,800
Total assets	140,500
EQUITY AND LIABILITIES	
Equity attributable to owners of Paladin	
Share capital	50,000
Retained earnings (W4)	35,200
	85,200

	$'000
Non-controlling interests (W5)	7,900
	93,100
Non-current liabilities	
Deferred tax (15,000 + 8,000)	23,000
Current liabilities	
Overdraft	2,500
Trade payables (11,600 + 6,200 – 1,300 (W7))	16,500
Deferred consideration (5,000 + 400 (W2))	5,400
	24,400
Total equity and liabilities	140,500

Workings

1 ***Group structure***

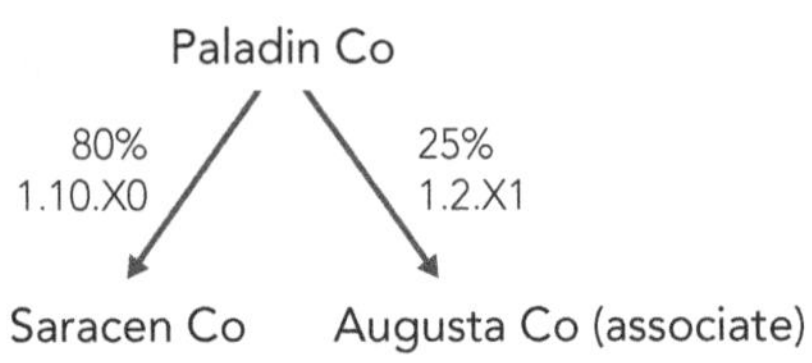

2 ***Goodwill***

	$'000	$'000
Consideration transferred:		
Cash		32,000
Deferred consideration		5,000
		37,000
Non-controlling interest		7,000
		44,000
Fair value of net assets:		
Share capital	10,000	
Retained earnings	12,000	
Fair value adjustment on plant	4,000	
Intangible asset	3,000	
		(29,000)
Goodwill		15,000

3 ***Investment in associate***

	$'000
Cost of investment	10,000
Share of post-acquisition retained earnings (800 (W4) × 25%)	200
Impairment	

	$'000
	(2,500)
	7,700

4 ***Retained earnings***

	Paladin Co	Saracen Co	Augusta Co
	$'000	$'000	$'000
Per question – 1.10.20X0	25,700	12,000	31,800
– year to 30.9.20X1	9,200	6,000	1,200
		18,000	33,000
PURP (W7)	(600)		
Depreciation on fair value adjustments (W6)		(1,500)	
Unwinding of discount (5,400 – 5,000 (W2))	(400)		
Less pre-acquisition retained earnings to 1.10.20X0		(12,000)	(31,800)
Less pre-acquisition to 1.2.X1 (1,200 × 4/12)		–	(400)
		4,500	800
Saracen Co (4,500 × 80%)	3,600		
Augusta Co (800 × 25%)	200		
Impairment of investment in associate (W3)	(2,500)		
	35,200		

5 ***Non-controlling interests***

	$'000
NCI at acquisition (W2)	7,000
Share of post-acquisition retained earnings (4,500 (W4) × 20%)	900
	7,900

6 ***Fair value adjustments***

	Acquisition		Movement	Year end
	$'000		$'000	$'000
Plant	4,000	1/4	(1,000)	3,000
Intangible asset (customer relationships)	3,000	1/6	(500)	2,500
	7,000		(1,500)	5,500

7 ***Intragroup trading***

Unrealised profit:

		$'000	$'000
Debit	Cost of sales/retained earnings (2,600 × 30/130)	600	
Credit	Inventories		600

ANSWERS

Current account:

		$'000	$'000
Debit	Group trade payables	1,300	
Credit	Group trade receivables		1,300

at the year end, so this is the only option which would require adjustment. The others have all taken place after the year end.

336 Dargent Co

Text references

Chapters 7, 8 and 11.

Top Tips

This question required good knowledge of accounting for groups including correctly accounting for intragroup trading, dividends and accounting for new acquisitions (including goodwill).

Easy marks

Calculating the plant and machinery and goodwill (including consideration) carried the most marks in this question. Lay out the consolidation workings clearly, ensuring accurate time apportionment of earnings, goods in transit, intra-group balances and dealing with the investment in the associate. Don't forget the easy marks regarding the loan and the interest. Trickier points were the calculation of the fair value adjustment for the decommissioning of the mine. Remember to only time apportion SPL and not SOFP balances!

Examining Team's comments

Most candidates prepared good consolidation workings, including the time-apportioned retained earnings at the date of acquisition, and few made any errors with the calculation of the purchase consideration of the acquisition of the subsidiary. The intra-group balances, goods in transit and the principles behind the investment in the associate were generally dealt with to allow candidates to earn high or maximum marks.

Marking guide	Marks	
Property, plant and equipment	2	
Goodwill: consideration	2.5	
Goodwill: fair value net assets	2	
Investments in associate	1	
Inventory	1.5	
Receivables	1	
Bank	0.5	
Equity shares and share premium	1	
Retained earnings: post-acquisition sub	2	
Retained earnings: other	2	
Non-controlling interests	1.5	
8% loan notes	0.5	
Environmental provision	1.5	
Current liabilities	1	
		20

Marking guide	Marks
Total	20

Dargent Co – consolidated statement of financial position as at 31 March 20X6

	$'000	$'000
ASSETS		
Non-current assets		
Property, plant and equipment (75,200 + 31,500 + 4,000 re mine – 200 depreciation)		110,500
Goodwill (W1))		11,000
Investment in associate (4,500 + 1,200 (W3)		5,700
		127,200
Current assets		
Inventories (19,400 + 18,800 + 700 GIT – 800 URP (W2)	38,100	
Trade receivables (14,700 + 12,500 – 3,000)	24,200	
Cash and cash equivalents (1,200 + 600)	1,800	
		64,100
Total assets		191,300
EQUITY AND LIABILITIES		
Equity attributable to owners of the parent		
Equity shares of $1 each (50,000 + 10,000 (W1))		60,000
Other equity reserves (share premium) (W1)	22,000	
Retained earnings (W3)	37,390	59,390
		119,390
Non-controlling interest (W4)		9,430
Total equity		128,820
Non-current liabilities		
8% loan notes (5,000 + 15,000 consideration)	20,000	
Accrued loan interest (W3)	300	
Environmental provision (4,000 + 80 interest (W3))	4,080	24,380
Current liabilities (24,000 + 16,400 – (3,000 –700 GIT) intra-group W2))		38,100
Total equity and liabilities		191,300

Workings (figures in brackets are in $'000)

ANSWERS

Workings

1 ***Goodwill in Latree Co***

	$'000	$'000
Controlling interest		
Share exchange (20,000 × 75% × 2/3 = 10,000 × $3.20)		32,000
8% loan notes (20,000 × 75% × $1,000/1,000)		15,000
Non-controlling interest (20,000 × 25% × $1.80)		9,000
		56,000
Equity shares	20,000	
Retained earnings at 1 April 20X5	19,000	
Earnings 1 April 20X5 to acquisition (8,000 × 9/12)	6,000	
Fair value adjustments – asset re mine	4,000	
– Provision re mine	(4,000)	(45,000)
Goodwill arising on acquisition		11,000

The share exchange of $32 million would be recorded as share capital of $10 million (10,000 × $1) and share premium of $22 million (10,000 × ($3.20 – $1.00)).

Applying the group policy to the environmental provision would mean adding $4 million to the carrying amount of the mine and the amount recorded as a provision at the date of acquisition. This has no overall effect on goodwill, but it does affect the consolidated statement of financial position and post-acquisition profit.

2 ***Inventory***

The inventory of Latree Co includes unrealised profit (URP) of $600,000 (2,100 × 40/140). Similarly, the goods in transit sale of $700,000 includes URP of $200,000 (700 × 40/140).

3 ***Consolidated retained earnings***

	$'000
Dargent Co's retained earnings	36,000
Latree Co's post-acquisition profit (1,720 × 75% see below)	1,290
Unrecorded share of Amery's retained profit ((6,000 – 2,000) × 30%)	1,200
Outstanding loan interest at 31 March 20X6 (15,000 × 8% × 3/12)	(300)
URP in inventory (W2)	(800)
	37,390
The adjusted post-acquisition profits of Latree Co are:	
As reported and time apportioned (8,000 × 3/12)	2,000
Interest on environmental provision (4,000 × 8% × 3/12)	(80)
Additional depreciation re: mine (4,000/5 years × 3/12)	(200)
	1,720

4 ***Non-controlling interest***

	$'000
Fair value on acquisition (W1)	9,000

	$'000
Post-acquisition profit (1,720 × 25% (W4)	430
	9,430

337 Party Co

Text reference

Chapter 8.

Top Tips

This question required good knowledge of accounting for groups including correctly accounting for intragroup trading (and unrealised profit), deferred consideration (and use of discounting) and accounting for disposals of a subsidiary (including treatment of goodwill). In part B, the analysis of the group should ensure references to the scenario, taking figures from the financial statements and explaining the usefulness of consolidated accounts.

Easy marks

It is important to show your workings clearly, as marks can be gained by showing where you have obtained the numbers in your consolidated statement of financial position.

Examining Team's comments

Candidates struggled with the deferred consideration calculation, and mark up and margin continue to cause confusion. The goodwill calculation was generally done well, but ensure practice of how to treat fair value adjustments. Part B of the question neglected to mention the related parties impact of consolidated financial statements (ie the intragroup trading being removed from the calculations), and many candidates failed to mention the possible favourable trading conditions that group companies benefit from.

Marking guide		Marks	
(a)	Property plant and equipment	0.5	
	Goodwill	4	
	Current assets	2.5	
	Share capital	0.5	
	Retained earnings	3.5	
	Revaluation surplus	0.5	
	NCI	1.5	
	Deferred consideration	1.5	
	Current liabilities	0.5	
			15
(b)	Limitations of interpretation using consolidated financial statements	5	
			5
Total			20

(a) **Consolidated statement of financial position of the Party group as at 30 September 20X5**

	$'000
ASSETS	

ANSWERS

	$'000
Non-current assets	
Property, plant and equipment (392,000 + 84,000)	476,000
Investments (120,000 – 92,000 – 28,000)	0
Goodwill (W3)	32,396
	508,396
Current assets (94,700 + 44,650 + 60 FV – 250 URP)	139,160
Total assets	647,556
EQUITY AND LIABILITIES	
Equity	
Share capital	190,000
Retained earnings (W5)	209,398
Revaluation surplus	41,400
	440,798
Non-controlling interest (W4)	15,392
Total equity	456,190
Non-current liabilities	
Deferred consideration (23,996 + 1,920)	25,916
Current liabilities (137,300 + 28,150)	165,450
Total equity and liabilities	647,556

Workings

1 ***Group structure***

Party Co owns 80% of Streamer Co.

Party Co has owned Streamer Co for one year.

2 **Net assets**

	Acquisition	SOFP date	Post acq
	$'000	$'000	$'000
Share capital	60,000	60,000	0
Retained earnings	34,000	36,500	2,500
Revaluation surplus	4,000	4,000	0
Fair value adj inventory	600	60	(540)
	98,600	100,560	1,960

3 ***Goodwill***

	$'000
Cash	92,000
Deferred cash (28m × 0.857)	23,996

	$'000
NCI at acquisition	15,000
Less: Net assets at acquisition	(98,600)
Goodwill at acquisition	32,396

4 ***Non-controlling interest***

	$'000
NCI at acquisition	15,000
NCI % of Streamer post acquisition (1,960 × 20%)	392
	15,392

5 ***Retained earnings***

	$'000
Party Co	210,000
P's % of Streamer post acquisition RE (1,960 × 80%)	1,568
Unwinding discount on deferred consideration (23,996 × 8%)	(1,920)
Unrealised profit (1,000 × 25%)	(250)
	209,398

(b) The consolidated financial statements of the Party Group are of little value when trying to assess the performance and financial position of its subsidiary, Streamer Co. Therefore the main source of information on which to base any investment decision would be Streamer Co's individual financial statements. However, where a company is part of a group, there is the potential for the financial statements (of a subsidiary) to have been subject to the influence of related party transactions. In the case of Streamer Co, there has been a considerable amount of post-acquisition trading with Party Co and, because of the related party relationship, there is the possibility that this trading is not at arm's length (ie not at commercial rates). Indeed, from the information in the question, Party Co sells goods to Streamer Co at a much lower margin than it does to other third parties. This gives Streamer Co a benefit which is likely to lead to higher profits (compared to what they would have been if it had paid the market value for the goods purchased from Party Co). Had the sales of $8m been priced at Party Co's normal prices, they would have been sold to Streamer Co for $10.9 million (at a margin of 25% these goods cost $6m; if sold at a normal margin of 45% they would have been sold at $6m/55% × 100). This gives Streamer Co a trading 'advantage' of $4.9 million ($10.9 million – $6 million).

There may also be other aspects of the relationship where Party Co gives Streamer Co a benefit which may not have happened had Streamer Co not been part of the group, eg access to technology/research, cheap finance, etc.

The main concern is that any information about the 'benefits' Party Co may have passed on to Streamer Co through related party transactions is difficult to obtain from published sources. It may be that Party Co has deliberately 'flattered' Streamer Co's financial statements specifically in order to obtain a high sale price and a prospective purchaser would not necessarily be able to determine that this had happened from either the consolidated or entity financial statements.

PART D: PREPARATION OF FINANCIAL STATEMENTS (III)

338 Fresco Co

Text references

Chapters 4 and 17.

Top Tips

There was a lot to get through in this question. Create the proforma financial statements in the spreadsheet response option and then go through the question and transfer any figures that can go straight from the trial balance to the financial statements. You need to do workings for PPE and for the right-of-use asset but these were not complicated. Remember to transfer the totals per your workings to the financial statements.

Easy marks

The statement of changes in equity was all straightforward. If you had remembered the transfer to retained earnings it was possible to score full marks on this. The PPE working made it possible to score marks on both the statement of profit or loss and other comprehensive income and the statement of financial position, so it was worth spending a bit of time on this. The lease working, on the other hand, carried very few marks.

Examining Team's comments

Most candidates showed a sound knowledge of preparing financial statements.

Some candidates deducted the loss on the fraud from revenue for the year rather adding it to expenses and treating it as a prior year adjustment, with the other entry being a deduction from receivables.

There were some difficulties with the lease, mainly involving the timing of the lease payments and the initial deposit. Many candidates were confused with the tax, especially failing to realise that the tax for the year was a refund.

Marking guide	Marks	
(a) Statement of profit or loss and other comprehensive income:		
Revenue	0.5	
Cost of sales	3	
Distribution costs	0.5	
Administrative expenses	0.5	
Finance costs	1.5	
Income tax	1	
Other comprehensive income	1	
		8
(b) Statement of financial position:		
Property, plant and equipment	2.5	
Inventory	0.5	
Trade receivables	0.5	
Share capital	1	
Share premium	1	
Revaluation surplus	1	

Marking guide		Marks
Retained earnings	2	
Current tax	0.5	
Non-current lease obligation	0.5	
Deferred tax	1	
Trade payables	0.5	
Current lease obligation	0.5	
Bank overdraft	0.5	
		12
Total		20

(a)

Statement of profit or loss and other comprehensive income for the year ended 31 March 20X2

	$'000
Revenue	350,000
Cost of sales (W1)	(311,000)
Gross profit	39,000
Distribution costs (W1)	(16,100)
Administrative expenses (W1)	(29,900)
Finance costs (300 + 2,300 (W3))	(2,600)
Loss before tax	(9,600)
Income tax (W5)	1,800
Loss for the year	(7,800)
Other comprehensive income:	
Gain on revaluation of property (W2)	4,000
Total comprehensive loss for the year	(3,800)

(b)

Statement of financial position as at 31 March 20X2

	$'000
ASSETS	
Non-current assets	
Property, plant and equipment (W2)	62,700
Current assets	
Inventories	25,200
Trade receivables (28,500 – 4,000 (W4))	24,500
Tax asset (W5)	2,400
Total assets	114,800

ANSWERS

	$'000
EQUITY AND LIABILITIES	
Equity	
Share capital 50c shares (45,000 + 9,000 (W6))	54,000
Share premium (5,000 + 4,500 (W6))	9,500
Revaluation surplus (4,000 – 500 (W2))	3,500
Retained earnings (5,100 – 1,000 (W4) – 7,800 + 500 (W2))	(3,200)
	63,800
Non-current liabilities	
Deferred tax (W5)	3,000
Lease liability (W3)	15,230
Current liabilities	
Trade and other payables	27,300
Lease liability (19,300 – 15,230 (W3))	4,070
Bank overdraft	1,400
Total equity and liabilities	114,800

Workings

1 ***Expenses***

	Cost of sales	Distribution costs	Administrative expenses
	$'000	$'000	$'000
Per trial balance	298,700	16,100	26,900
Depreciation (W2)	7,800	–	–
Amortisation (W2)	4,500	–	–
Fraud – current year cost (W4)	–	–	3,000
	311,000	16,100	29,900

2 ***Property, plant and equipment***

	Freehold property	Plant and equipment	Right of use plant	Total
	$'000	$'000	$'000	$'000
Cost	48,000	47,500		
Acc. amortisation/depreciation	(16,000)	(33,500)		
Balance 1 April 20X1 (FVFLP $23,000 + deposit $2,000)	32,000	14,000	25,000	
Revaluation surplus*	4,000			
Revised carrying amount	36,000			

	Freehold property	Plant and equipment	Right of use plant	Total
	$'000	$'000	$'000	$'000
Depreciation:				
36,000/8	(4,500)			
14,000 × 20%		(2,800)		
25,000/5 (lease term is equal to useful life)	–	–	(5,000)	
	31,500	11,200	20,000	62,700

The transfer to retained earnings = 4,000/8 = 500

3 ***Lease liability***

	$'000
Present value of future lease payments	23,000
Interest 10%	2,300
Instalment 31.3.X2	(6,000)
Balance 31.3.X2	19,300
Interest 10%	1,930
Instalment 31.3.X3	(6,000)
Balance 31.3.X3	15,230

4 ***Fraud***

	Debit	Credit
	$'000	$'000
Retained earnings – prior year	1,000	
Current year profit	3,000	
Receivables		4,000

5 ***Tax credit***

	$'000
Underprovided in prior year	800
Tax refund due (asset in SFP)	(2,400)
Reduction in deferred tax provision (3,200 – (12,000 × 25%))	(200)
Current tax (credit to profit or loss)	(1,800)

6 ***Share issue***

Shares issued = 13.5m/0.75 = 18m

		$'000
Share capital	18m × 50c	9,000
Share premium	18m × 25c	4,500
		13,500

339 Loudon Co

Text references

Chapters 3, 12, 14 and 16.

Top Tips

There is no set format for the schedule of adjustments, however, it is advised to start by setting out the proforma statement of financial position and a separate working which starts with the retained earnings per the trial balance. Then, work methodically through the information, performing relevant calculations and working out which parts of calculations result in an adjustment to profit, which in turn will impact on retained earnings, and which adjustments impact on the statement of financial position. Transfer the totals per your workings to the statement of financial position or as an adjustment to retained earnings as you go along.

Easy marks

Non-current assets is generally a well-liked topic and you should have been able to score well in that section.

Examining Team's comments

This is a typical example of a published financial statements exam question. Candidates do not need to deal with the adjustments in order and may be advised to address the areas they feel most comfortable with first. Read the requirements carefully before starting.

Marking guide	Marks	
(a) Adjust profit	8	
		8
(b) SFP	12	
		12
Total		20

(a)

Schedule of adjusted retained earnings of Loudon as at 30 September 20X8

	$'000
Retained earnings per trial balance	4,122
Adjustments:	
Add back issue costs of loan	125
Loan finance costs (W1)	(390)
Building depreciation (W2)	(900)
Impairment (W2)	(3,600)
Factory depreciation (W2)	(3,885)
Disposal gain on factory (W2)	500
Unwinding of discount on environmental provision ($1,228 × 5%)	(61)
Deferred tax adjustment (W3)	(203)
Adjusted retained earnings	(4,292)

(b)

Statement of financial position as at 30 September 20X8

	$'000
Assets	
Non-current assets	
Property, plant and equipment ($11,500 + $22,015) (W2)	33,515
Current assets (per TB)	14,700
Total assets	48,215
Equity and liabilities	
Equity	
Equity shares $1 each (per TB)	10,000
Retained earnings (part (a))	(4,292)
	5,708
Non-current liabilities	
5% loan note (W1)	5,015
Environmental provision ($1,228 + $61 (part(a))	1,289
Deferred Taxation (W3)	1,703
	8,007
Current liabilities (per TB)	34,500
Total equity and liabilities	48,215

Workings

1 ***Loan note***

The issue costs should be deducted from the proceeds of the loan note and not charged as an expense. This gives the loan note an opening carrying amount of $4,875,000 ($5,000,000 - $125,000). The finance cost of the loan note, at the effective interest rate of 8% applied to the carrying amount of the loan is $390,000. The actual interest paid is $250,000 (see TB) which leaves a closing carrying amount of $5,015,000 for inclusion as a non-current liability in the statement of financial position.

Opening balance 1 October 20X7	Finance costs 8% × opening balance	Interest paid 5% × principal	Closing balance 30 September 20X8
$'000	$'000	$'000	$'000
4,875	390	(250)	5,015

2 ***Non-current assets***

	$'000
Office Building	
Carrying amount at 1 September 20X7 ($20,000 – $4,000)	16,000

ANSWERS

	$'000
Depreciation to 1 April 20X8 ($20,000/25 years × 6/12 months)	(400)
Carrying amount at 1 April 20X8	15,600
Impairment	(3,600)
Fair value at 1 April 20X8	12,000
Depreciation to 30 September 20X8 ($12,000/12 years × 6/12 months)	(500)
	11,500

Factories

Carrying amount at 1 September 20X7 ($40,000 – $11,100)	28,900
Disposal at carrying amount	(3,000)
Carrying amount at 1 September 20X8	25,900
Depreciation for the year to 30 September 20X8 ($25,900 × 15%)	(3,885)
	22,015

Disposal of factory

Proceeds	3,500
Carrying amount	(3,000)
Gain in disposal	500

3 ***Deferred tax***

	$'000
Tax written down value of PPE at 30 September 20X8	25,000
Carrying amount of PPE at 30 September 20X8 per SOFP	(33,515)
	8,515
Deferred tax provision required at 30 September 20X8 ($8,515 × 20%)	1,703
Deferred tax provision at 30 September 20X7 (per TB)	(1,500)
Deferred tax charge for year ended 30 September 20X8	203

340 Print Co

Text references

Chapters 3, 6, 12, 15 and 17.

Top Tips

Create the proforma financial statements in the spreadsheet response option. Work through each of the notes, producing the relevant workings. Remember to show your calculations or formulae and to include the totals per your workings in the proforma you have created.

Easy marks

Inventories, depreciation and the tax refund are fairly straightforward adjustments.

You must ensure that all trial balance items are included either in the relevant working or within the financial statements themselves. It is often noted by the marking team that some balances are not transferred from the trial balance into the answer and, therefore, what are considered to be easy marks are lost.

Examiner's comments

Overall, the preparation of financial statements is an integral part of the FR syllabus and is something that should be practised. Please ensure that you attempt to use the relevant practice workspace available on the ACCA website so that you get used to completing your answer in the CBE environment. It is vital that you show all workings.

Where you are provided with a spreadsheet response option, if you use the functionality of the spreadsheet, markers will be able to view your workings within the cell. If you do not use the spreadsheet to calculate your figures, you must ensure that you set out all workings and calculations so that the marker is able to follow through what you have done and award marks accordingly.

On a final note, when practicing Print Co, do not forget to make sure that all trial balance items have been used or transferred into the relevant statements/workings and, when completing the statement of financial position, transfer your own profit for the year from the statement of profit or loss into retained earnings within equity

Marking guide	Marks	
(a) Statement of profit or loss	8	
		8
(b) Assets	6	
Equity and liabilities	6	
		12
Total		20

(a)

Statement of profit or loss for the year ended 30 June 20X2

	$'000
Revenue	97,400
Cost of sales (W1)	(63,910)
Gross profit	**33,490**
Distribution costs	(7,200)
Administrative expenses (29,570 + 3,375 (W5))	(32,945)
Profit from operations	**(6,655)**
Finance costs (750 +350 (W4))	(400)
Loss before tax	**(7,055)**
Income tax refund	2,530
Net loss for the period	**(4,525)**

(b)

Statement of financial position as at 30 June 20X2

	$'000	$'000
Assets		

ANSWERS

	$'000	$'000
Non-current assets		
Property, plant and equipment		50,340
Current assets		
Inventories	5,560	
Trade and other receivables	25,010	
Taxation	2,530	
Bank	4,700	
	37,800	
Non-current assets held for sale	1,100	
		38,900
Total assets		**89,240**
Equity and liabilities		
Equity		
Ordinary share capital (29,600 + 7,000 (W7))	36,600	
Other components of equity (15,500 + 7,000 (W7))	22,500	
Retained earnings (11,470 - 4,525)	6,945	
		66,045
Non-current liabilities		
Bank loan (30,000 - 14,000 (W7))	16,000	
Provisions (W5)	2,250	
		18,250
Current liabilities		
Trade and other payables (4,170 - 350)	3,920	
Provisions (W5)	1,125	
		4,945
Total equity and liabilities		**89,240**

Workings

1 ***Cost of sales***

	$'000
Opening inventory	6,850
Production costs	60,150
Less closing inventory (W6)	(5,560)
Depreciation charge (W2)	2,070
Held for sale asset (HFS asset) impairment (W3)	400
	63,910

2 ***Property, plant and equipment***

	Land	Plant and machinery	Total
	$'000	$'000	$'000
Cost			
Brought forward	45,000	16,200	61,200
HFS asset	-	(2,400)	(2,400)
	45,000	13,800	58,800
Accumulated depreciation			
Brought forward	-	(7,290)	(7,290)
Charge for the year (13,800 × 15%)	-	(2,070)	(2,070)
HFS asset accumulated depreciation (2,400 - 1,500)	-	900	900
	-	(8,460)	(8,460)

3 ***Held for sale asset***

	$'000
Carrying amount at 1 July 20X1	1,500
Fair value less costs to sell at 30 June 20X2	(1,100)
Impairment loss to be recognised in the year ended 30 June 20X2	400

Tutorial note. A non-current asset classified as held for sale (ie, a held for sale asset) should be measured at the lower of its carrying amount and fair value less costs to sell. The fair value less costs to sell at 30 June 20X2 will be the same as the net sales proceeds received on 1 July 20X2. The above working simplifies this to a single adjustment since no accounting has been done to date, but it could also be shown as:

	$'000	$'000
Carrying amount at 1 July 20X1	1,500	
Fair value less costs to sell at 1 July 20X1	1,140	
Impairment		360
Fair value less costs to sell at 30 June 20X2 (using net proceeds received on 1 July 20X2)	1,100	
Further impairment required		40
Total impairment for year ended 30 June 20X2		400

4 ***Finance costs***

	$'000
Included in TB (30,000 × 5% × 6/12)	750

	$'000
Correction of error (14,000 × 5% × 6/12)	(350)
	400

5 ***Onerous contract***

	$'000
Price per unit	450
Cost of conversion	600
	1,050
Net realisable value	900
Loss per unit	(150)

	$'000
Loss on fulfilling contract ($150 × 22,500 units)	3,375

	$'000
Loss expected in the next 12 months (current) (3,375 × 1/3 years)	1,125
Loss expected beyond 12 months (non-current) (3,375 - 1,125)	2,250
	3,375

> **Tutorial note.** As the loss on fulfilling the contract ($3.375m) is lower than the cost of cancelling the contract ($4m), a loss of $3.375m should be provided for.

6 ***Inventory***

	$'000
Cost of units requiring modification ($1,400 × 700 units)	980
Net realisable value of units requiring additional modification (($1,600 - $400) × 700 units)	(840)
Inventory write down required	140

	$'000
Closing inventory (Note (2))	5,700
Inventory write down	(140)
Adjusted closing inventory	5,560

7 ***Correction of share issue and bank loan***

	$'000
Share capital (7,000 share × $1)	7,000
Share premium (other components of equity) (14,000 proceeds - 7,000 share capital)	7,000
Proceeds received and incorrectly included as part of the bank loan	14,000

341 Xtol Co

Text references

Chapters 17, 18 and 19.

Top Tips

You have two financial statements to produce here, so be very organised. Create the proforma for both financial statements before you start to work through the notes. Note that you will have to work out the effects of the rights issue to get the dividend payments.

Examining Team's comments

This question was generally well answered. Most of the errors that occurred involved the agency sale, the rights issue (such as failing to notice that the shares were 25c, not $1), the convertible loan note and the tax.

Marking guide	Marks	
(a) Statement of profit or loss		
Revenue	1	
Cost of sales	2	
Distribution costs	0.5	
Administrative expenses	0.5	
Agency sales	1	
Finance costs	1.5	
Income tax	1.5	
		8
(b) Statement of financial position		
Property, plant and equipment	1.5	
Inventory	0.5	
Trade receivables	0.5	
Share capital	0.5	
Share premium	0.5	
Equity option	1	
Retained earnings	2	
Deferred tax	1	
Loan note	1.5	
Trade payables	1.5	
Bank overdraft	0.5	
Current tax payable	1	
		12
Total		20

(a)

Statement of profit or loss for the year ended 31 March 20X4

	$'000
Revenue (490,000 – 20,000 (W3))	470,000

	$'000
Cost of sales (W1)	(294,600)
Gross profit	175,400
Distribution costs (W1)	(33,500)
Administrative expenses (W1)	(36,800)
Other operating income – agency sales (W3)	2,000
Finance costs (13,380 + 900 + 1,176 (W4) – 10,880 (W5))	(4,576)
Profit before tax	102,524
Income tax expense (28,000 + 3,200 + 3,700 (W6))	(34,900)
Profit for the year	67,624

(b)

Statement of financial position as at 31 March 20X4

	$'000	$'000
ASSETS		
Non-current assets		
Property, plant and equipment (W2)		168,000
Current assets		
Inventories	61,000	
Trade receivables	63,000	
		124,000
Total assets		292,000
EQUITY AND LIABILITIES		
Equity		
Equity shares 25c		56,000
Share premium		25,000
Other component of equity – equity option (W4)		4,050
Retained earnings (26,080 – 10,880 (W5) + 67,624)		82,824
		167,874
Non-current liabilities		
Deferred tax (4,600 + 3,700 (W6))	8,300	
5% convertible loan note (50,000 – 4,050 (W4) + 1,176)	47,126	
		55,426
Current liabilities		
Trade payables (32,200 + 3,000 (W3))	35,200	
Bank overdraft	5,500	
Current tax payable	28,000	

	$'000	$'000
		68,700
Total equity and liabilities		292,000

Workings

1 ***Expenses***

	Cost of sales	Distribution costs	Administrative expenses
	$'000	$'000	$'000
Per question	290,600	33,500	36,800
Agent not principal	(15,000)		
Depreciation – property (W2)	5,000		
Depreciation – plant and equipment (W2)	14,000		
	294,600	33,500	36,800

2 ***Property, plant and equipment***

	Property	Plant and equipment	Total
	$'000	$'000	$'000
Cost per TB	100,000	155,500	255,500
Acc depreciation b/d per TB	(25,000)	(43,500)	(68,500)
	75,000	112,000	187,000
Depreciation property (100,000/20 years)	(5,000)		(5,000)
Depreciation P&E (112,000 × 12.5%)	–	(14,000)	(14,000)
	70,000	98,000	168,000

3 ***Agency transaction***

Should have been:		Did:		Correction:	
	$'000		$'000		$'000
DR Cash	20,000	DR Cash	20,000	DR Revenue	20,000
CR Other income (10%)	2,000	CR Revenue	20,000	CR Cost of sales	15,000
CR Trade payables	18,000	DR Cost of sales	15,000	CR Other income	2,000
		CR Cash	15,000	CR Trade payables	3,000
DR Trade payables	15,000				
CR Cash	15,000				

4 ***Loan notes***

		$'000	$'000
PV of principal	(50,000 × 0.79)		39,500
PV interest flows:			
20X4	50,000 × 5% = 2,500 × 0.93 =	2,325	
20X5	50,000 × 5% = 2,500 × 0.86 =	2,150	
20X6	50,000 × 5% = 2,500 × 0.79 =	1,975	
			6,450
Debt component			45,950
Equity component (β)			4,050
Cash received			50,000
Liability component b/d	1.4.20X3	45,950	
Effective interest	(45,950 × 8%)	3,676	
Cash coupon paid		(2,500)	
Liability component c/d	31.3.20X4	47,126	

Adjustment required:		
DR Loan notes	4,050	
CR Other components of equity		4,050
DR Finance costs (3,676 – 2,500)	1,176	
CR Loan notes		1,176

5 ***Dividend paid***

	$'000	$'000
Before rights issue (56,000 × $1/25c × 5/7 = 160m × 4c)		6,400
After rights issue (56,000 × $1/25c × 2c)		4,480
		10,880
DR Retained earnings	10,880	
CR Loan note interest and dividends paid		10,880

6 ***Tax***

		$'000	$'000
Current tax:	DR Income tax (P/L)	28,000	
	CR Current tax payable		28,000
Deferred tax:			
B/d (per TB)			4,600
To P/L			3,700

	$'000	$'000
C/d		8,300

342 Mims Co

Workbook references

Chapter 22

Top Tips

From an exam technique perspective, it is advised that you set up the answer/layout for the requirements first. For example, for Mims Co, lay out the working for the statement of profit or loss, the statement of changes in equity and the statement of cash flow extracts within the spreadsheet. Leave a couple of rows between each statement so that it is easy for the marker to distinguish between where one statement ends and another begins.

Easy marks

In this question, revenue, distribution costs and finance costs did not require adjustment as a result of the additional information and could be transferred directly to the statement of profit or loss. Including these balances in this statement attracted marks from the marking scheme. Similarly, the share capital and retained earnings in the trial balance at 1 January 20X5 could have been included in the opening balances on the statement of changes in equity.

Examiner comments

You should refer to the Examiners' report for the Sep/Dec 2021 exam which can be found at www.accaglobal.com

Overall, the preparation of financial statements is an integral part of the FR syllabus and is something that should be practiced. Please ensure that you attempt to use the relevant practice workspace available on the ACCA website so that you get used to competing your answer on a spreadsheet.

It is vital that you show all workings. If you use the functionality of the spreadsheet, markers will be able to view your workings within the cell. If you do not use the spreadsheet to calculate your figures, you must ensure that you set out all workings and calculations so that the marker is able to follow through what you have done and award marks accordingly.

When completing this question, don't forget to make sure that all trial balance items have been used or transferred into the relevant statements, and when asked to prepare a statement of changes in equity, ensure that you transfer the profit for the year into retained earnings.

Marking guide	Marks	
(a) Statement of profit or loss	12	
		12
(b) Statement of changes in equity	5	
		5
(c) Extracts from statement of cash flows	3	
		3
Total		20

(a)

Statement of profit or loss for the year ended 31 December 20X5

	$'000
Revenue	24,300
Cost of sales (11,600 – 700 inventory)	(10,900)
Gross profit	**13,400**
Administrative expenses (10,900 + 1,400 provision + 1,300 promoting brand + 100 amortisation – 1,000 investment property depreciation – 3,000 dividend)	(9,700)
Distribution costs	(7,300)
Loss from operations	**(3,600)**
Finance costs	(1,400)
Investment income (500 + 2,000 investment property gain)	2,500
Loss before taxation	**(2,500)**
Taxation (140 – 1,200 current + 500 movement in deferred tax)	560
Loss for the year	**1,940**

(b)

Statement of changes in equity for the year ended 31 December 20X5

	Share capital	Share premium	Retained earnings
	$'000	$'000	$'000
Balance at 1 January 20X5	60,000	–	43,200
Prior period error	–	–	(700)
Restated balance 1 January 20X5	60,000		42,500
Share issue	15,000	37,500	–
Profit of the year	–	–	(1,940)
Dividends paid (75,000 × $0.04)	–	–	(3,000)
Balance 31 December 20X5	75,000	37,500	37,560

(c)

Extracts from statement of cash flows for the year ended 31 December 20X5

	$'000
Cash flows from investing activities	
Purchase of brand	(2,000)
Purchase of investment property	(20,000)
Net cash used investing activities	(22,000)
Cash flows from financing activities	
Proceeds from issue of share capital	52,500
Dividends paid	(3,000)
Net cash from financing activities	

	$'000
	49,500

343 Atlas Co

Text references

Chapters 3, 4, 16 and 18.

Top Tips

This is a standard question – preparation of financial statements from a trial balance.

Easy marks

While there were a few difficult bits, some marks were available for items which just needed to be brought across from the trial balance and dealing correctly with PPE and tax would have brought in five marks.

Marking guide

		Marks	
(a)	Statement of profit or loss and OCI		
	Revenue	1	
	Cost of sales	2	
	Distribution costs	0.5	
	Administrative expenses	0.5	
	Finance costs	0.5	
	Income tax	2.5	
	Other comprehensive income	1	
			8
(b)	Statement of financial position		
	Property, plant and equipment	3.5	
	Inventory	0.5	
	Trade receivables	0.5	
	Retained earnings	2.5	
	Deferred tax	1.5	
	Trade payables	0.5	
	Current tax	0.5	
	Bank overdraft	0.5	
			10
(c)	Earnings per share	2	
			2
Total			20

(a)

Statement of profit or loss and other comprehensive income for the year ended 31 March 20X3

	$'000
Revenue	550,000
Cost of sales (W1)	(428,000)
Gross profit	122,000
Distribution costs	(21,500)
Administrative expenses	(30,900)
Finance costs	(700)
Profit before tax	68,900
Income tax expense ((27,200 – 1,200) + (9,400 – 6,200))	(29,200)
Profit for the year	39,700
Other comprehensive income:	
Gain on revaluation of property (W2)	7,000
Total comprehensive income for the year	46,700

(b)

Statement of financial position as at 31 March 20X3

	$'000	$'000
ASSETS		
Non-current assets		
Property, plant and equipment (W2)		100,500
Current assets		
Inventories	43,700	
Trade receivables	42,200	
		85,900
Total assets		186,400
EQUITY AND LIABILITIES		
Equity		
Share capital		50,000
Share premium		20,000
Revaluation surplus		7,000
Retained earnings (11,200 + 39,700 – dividend 20,000)		30,900
		107,900
Non-current liabilities		
Deferred tax		9,400

	$'000	$'000
Current liabilities		
Trade and other payables	35,100	
Tax payable	27,200	
Overdraft	6,800	
		69,100
		186,400

Workings

1 ***Expenses***

	Cost of sales	Distribution costs	Administrative expenses
	$'000	$'000	$'000
Per TB	411,500	21,500	30,900
Depreciation (W2)	16,500	–	–
	428,000	21,500	30,900

2 ***Property, plant and equipment***

	Land	Buildings	Plant	Total
	$'000	$'000	$'000	$'000
Cost	10,000	50,000	94,500	
Accumulated depreciation	–	(20,000)	(24,500)	
Balance 1 April 20X3	10,000	30,000	70,000	110,000
Revaluation surplus	2,000	5,000		7,000
Revalued amount	12,000	35,000		
Depreciation (35/14) (70 × 20%)	–	(2,500)	(14,000)	(16,500)
	12,000	32,500	56,000	100,500

(c) EPS = 39,700/100,000 = $0.40

344 Moby Co

Top Tips

The issues to deal with here were the contract with performance obligations satisfied over time, the revaluation and the deferred tax. None of these were complicated, but make sure you know how to calculate contract assets/liabilities and how to deal with deferred tax on a revaluation.

Easy marks

There were quite a few marks for items which only had to be lifted from the trial balance, so it was important to get workings down and collect those marks. The lease and the loan note were both simple and worth several marks.

ANSWERS

Marking guide		Marks
(a) Statement of profit or loss and other comprehensive income		
Revenue	2	
Cost of sales	3.5	
Distribution costs	0.5	
Administrative expenses	1	
Finance costs	2	
Income tax expense	2	
Gain on revaluation	1	
Deferred tax on gain	1	
		13
(b) Statement of changes in equity		
Opening balances	1	
Share issue	2	
Dividend	1	
Total comprehensive income	2	
Closing balances	1	
		7
Total		20

(a)

Statement of profit or loss and other comprehensive income for the year ended 30 September 20X3

	$'000
Revenue (227,800 + 10,000 (W3))	237,800
Cost of sales (W1)	(187,900)
Gross profit	49,900
Distribution costs	(13,500)
Administrative expenses (W1)	(16,350)
Finance costs (900 + 4,000 (W5) + 2,930 (W6))	(7,830)
Profit before tax	12,220
Income tax expense (W4)	(350)
Profit for the year	11,870
Other comprehensive income:	
Gain on revaluation of land and buildings (W2)	4,400
Deferred tax on gain (W4)	(1,100)
Total other comprehensive income	3,300
Total comprehensive income for the year	15,170

(b)

Statement of changes in equity for the year ended 30 September 20X3

	Share capital	Share premium	Retained earnings	Revaluation surplus	Total
	$'000	$'000	$'000	$'000	$'000
Balance at 1 October 20X2	45,000	–	19,800	–	64,800
Share issue	800	3,200			4,000
Dividend paid			(2,000)		(2,000)
Total comprehensive income	–	–	11,870	3,300	15,170
Balance at 30 September 20X3	45,800	3,200	29,670	3,300	81,970

Workings

1 ***Expenses***

	Cost of sales	Distribution costs	Administrative expenses
	$'000	$'000	$'000
Per question	164,500	13,500	16,500
Contract (W3)	8,000		
Depreciation (W2) – building	2,400		
– owned plant	6,000		
– leased plant	7,000		
Insurance provision reversal	–	–	(150)
	187,900	13,500	16,350

2 ***Property, plant and equipment***

	Land	Building	Plant	Leased plant
	$'000	$'000	$'000	$'000
Cost 1.10.X2	12,000	48,000	65,700	35,000
Depreciation b/f	–	(10,000)	(17,700)	(7,000)
	12,000	38,000	48,000	28,000
Revaluation	4,000	400	–	–
	16,000	38,400	48,000	28,000
Depreciation:				
Building (38,400/16)		(2,400)		
Plant (48,000 × 12.5%)			(6,000)	
Leased (35,000/5) (shorter of lease term and useful life)				(7,000)

ANSWERS

3 ***Contract with performance obligations satisfied over time***

	$'000
Revenue (work certified)	10,000
Costs incurred	(8,000)
Profit to date	2,000
Contract asset	
Revenue recognised	10,000
Amounts invoiced	(4,000)
Contract asset	6,000
Trade receivables	
Amounts invoiced	4,000
Amounts received from customers	Nil
Trade receivable	4,000

4 ***Income tax***

	$'000
Deferred tax balance:	
On taxable temporary difference ($24m × 25%)	6,000
On revaluation (4,400 × 25%)	1,100
Liability at 30 September 20X3	7,100
Balance b/f at 1 October 20X2	8,000
Reduce balance by	900
Income tax charge:	
Provision for year	3,400
Prior year over-provision	(1,050)
Reduction in deferred tax balance	(900)
Deferred tax on revaluation debited to revaluation surplus	(1,100)
Charge for year	350

5 ***Loan note***

	$'000
Proceeds	40,000
Interest 10%	4,000
Balance	44,000

6 ***Leased plant***

	$'000
Present value of future lease payments	35,000
Interest 10%	3,500
Instalment paid	(9,200)
Balance 30.9.X2	29,300
Interest 10% 20X3	2,930

345 Haverford Co

Text reference

Chapters 5, 6, 12 & 16.

Top Tips

Where adjustments to profit are requested, ensure that these are clearly stated, especially if the question asks for a schedule of adjustments, or wants a clear explanation of what the adjustments are made up of. Show your workings, the Examining Team frequently states that these are not clearly given (if at all) and this is vital for gaining maximum marks. You do not need to prepare a full statement or profit or loss.

Easy marks

Statement of changes in equity, using the already given details in the question regarding the dividend paid and the transfer of profit figures. Ensure the workings are shown clearly as marks are gained for showing method as well as a correct figure (credit is given where the final answer may be wrong but the method itself is correct).

Examining Team's comments

Candidates struggled with the treatment of a bonus issue of shares and that any impairment should not reduce a revaluation surplus to a negative reserve figure.

Marking guide	Marks	
(a) Convertible loan notes	1	
Contract	2	
Depreciation/impairment	2	
Inventory	1	
		6
(b) Opening balances	1	
Convertible loan notes	1	
Bonus issue	2	
Profit/Dividend/revaluation	2	
		6
(c) PPE	1	
Contract	2	
Other current assets	2	
Equity	0.5	
Convertible loan notes	2	

ANSWERS

Marking guide	Marks	
Current liabilities	0.5	
		8
Total		20

(a)

Adjustments to Haverford Co's profit for the year ended 31 December 20X7

	$'000
Draft profit	2,250
Convertible loan notes (W1)	(135)
Contract revenue (W2)	5,600
Contract cost of sales (W2)	(1,900)
Depreciation (W4)	(720)
Property impairment (W4)	(480)
Closing inventories	390
Revised profit	5,005

(b)

Statement of changes in equity for the year ended 31 December 20X7

	Share capital	OCE	Retained earnings	Revaluation surplus	Option
	$'000	$'000	$'000	$'000	$'000
Balance as at 1 January 20X7	20,000	3,000	6,270	800	–
Profit – from (a)	–	–	5,005	–	–
Revaluation loss (W4)	–	–	–	(800)	–
Bonus issue (W3)	4,000	(3,000)	(1,000)	–	–
Convertible loan notes issued (W1)	–	–	–	–	424
Dividend paid	–	–	(3,620)	–	–
Balance as at 31 December 20X7	24,000	–	6,655	–	424

(c)

Statement of financial position for Haverford Co as at 31 December 20X7

	$'000
ASSETS	
Non-current assets	
Property (W3)	16,000
Current assets	
Inventory (W5)	4,700
Trade receivables	5,510

	$'000
Contract asset (W2)	4,200
Cash	10,320
Total assets	40,730
EQUITY AND LIABILITIES	
Equity	
Share capital	24,000
Retained earnings	6,655
Convertible option	424
Total equity	31,079
Non-current liabilities	
Convertible loan notes (W1)	7,711
Current liabilities	1,940
Total equity and liabilities	40,730

Workings

1 ***Convertible loan notes***

	Payment	Discount rate	Present value
	$'000	$'000	$'000
20X7	320	0.943	302
20X8	320	0.890	285
20X9	8,320	0.840	6,989
			7,576

As the full amount of $8m has been taken to liabilities, adjustment required is:

Debit Liability	$424k	
Credit Equity		$424k

The liability should then be held at amortised cost, using the effective interest rate.

Balance b/f	Interest 6%	Payment	Balance c/f
$'000	$'000	$'000	$'000
7,576	455	(320)	7,711

As only $320k has been recorded in finance costs:

Debit	Finance costs	$135k	
Credit	Liability		$135k

2 ***Contract with customer***

	$'000
Revenue recognised (14,000 × 40%)	5,600

ANSWERS

	$'000
Costs to date	(1,900)
Profit recognised to date	3,700

Statement of financial position

	$'000
Revenue recognised ($14,000 × 40%)	5,600
Less: amounts invoices	(1,400)
Contract asset	4,200
Amounts invoiced to date	1,400
Amounts received from customers	(1,400)
Adjustment to trade receivables	Nil

$5.6m should be recorded in revenue, and $1.9m in cost of sales, giving an overall increase to the draft profit of $3.7m. $4.2m should then be recorded in the statement of financial position as a current asset.

3 ***Bonus issue***

The 1 for 5 bonus issue will lead to an increase in share capital of $4m ($20m × 1/5). Of this, $3m will be debited to other components of equity to take it to zero. The remaining $1m will be deducted from retained earnings.

Adjustment

Debit Share premium	$3m	
Debit Retained earnings	$1m	
Credit Share capital		$4m

4 ***Property***

The asset should first be depreciated. $18m/25 = $720k. This should be deducted from the draft profit and the asset, giving a carrying amount of $17,280k.

Debit Draft profit	$720k	
Credit Property		$720k

Then the asset should be revalued from $17,280k to $16,000k, giving a revaluation loss of $1,280k. As the revaluation surplus is only $800k, only $800k can be debited to this, with the remaining $480k being debited from the draft profit for the year.

Debit Revaluation surplus	$800k	
Debit Draft profit	$480k	
Credit Property		$1,280k

5 ***Inventories***

Closing inventories should be adjusted from $4,310k to $4,700k.

Debit Inventories	$390k	

Credit Draft profit	$390k

346 Flamingo Co

(a) **Flamingo Co**

Extract from draft statement of cash flows for the year ended 31 December 2012

	$	$
Net cash from operating activities (W1)		1,919,785
Cash flows from investing activities		
Purchase of property, plant and equipment (W1)	(2,992,700)	
Proceeds from sales of property, plant and equipment	825,000	
Payments to acquire right of use assets	(20,000)	
Net cash used in investing activities		(2,187,700)
Cash flows from financing activities		
Proceeds from issue of ordinary share capital (W3)	600,000	
Lease obligations paid (W4)	(5,000)	
Dividends paid (W5)	(93,000)	
Net cash from financing activities		502,000
Net increase in cash and cash equivalents		234,085
Cash and cash equivalents at beginning of period		112,800
Cash and cash equivalents at end of period		346,885

Workings

1 ***Net cash from operating activities***

	$
Per question	1,697,785
Add: PPE depreciation	260,000
Add: RoU asset depreciation	5,000
Less: gain on sale of PPE (825,000 – 782,000)	(43,000)
Revised net cash from operating activities	1,919,785

2 ***Purchase of PPE***

	$
Opening balance	5,828,400
Add: revaluation surplus	200,000
Less: depreciation	(260,000)
Less: disposal of PPE	(782,000)
Cash purchase (β)	2,992,700

ANSWERS

	$
Closing balance	7,979,100

3 ***Share issue***

	$
Opening balance share capital	2,400,000
Opening balance share premium	200,000
1 for 6 bonus issue (2,400,000 × 1/6)	400,000
Issue for cash (β)	600,000
Closing balance share capital	3,000,000
Closing balance share premium	600,000

4 ***Payment of lease obligations***

	$
Initial measurement of RoU asset	540,000
Less: direct costs	(20,000)
Initial measurement of lease liability	520,000
Repayments for cash (β)	5,000
Closing balance of lease liability	515,000

5 ***Dividends paid***

	$
Retained earnings	1,917,560
Add: profit	912,345
Less: bonus issue	(400,000)
Dividends paid (β)	(93,000)
Closing balance	2,522,905

(b) It is argued that the statement of cash flows contains information that is more useful to the users of financial statements than the statements of profit or loss and statements of financial position as the users are more likely to understand what a cash flow represents. Cash flows are not affected by, for example, accounting policy choices and accounting estimates and therefore a user would not require such a full understanding of accounting in order to understand the statement of cash flows compared with the other primary statements.

The focus on 'profit' can be misleading as it does not always give a useful or meaningful picture of a company's operations and the users may be unclear as to what a profit means for the business. Many users would see a company making a profit of, for example, $100,000 and assume that it could afford to pay its employees more or to make a dividend payment of the same amount, but they would need to look at the profit in conjunction with the cash flows to determine if it was affordable to the company.

It is often said that 'cash is king' and companies which use cash faster than they generate it will find it difficult to continue as a going concern. It is important to look not just at the total cash and cash equivalents, but at the movements in the period and the reasons for those movements in order to understand the true cash position of the company. A company may have an overall net increase in cash and equivalents, but if it has funded that by selling its assets and borrowings it will be looked on less favourably by users than a company that generates positive cash from its operations.

The statement of cash flows should be used in conjunction with the other primary financial statements in order to fully understand the performance and position of a company.

347 Dickson Co

(a)

Statement of cash flows for year ended 31 March 20X8

	\$'000	\$'000
Cash flows from investing activities		
Development expenditure (W1)	(190)	
Purchase of property, plant & equipment (W1)	(192)	
Proceeds from sale of property, plant & equipment	110	
Net cash used in investing activities		(272)
Cash flows from financing activities		
Proceeds from rights issue (W2)	300	
Proceeds from issue of debentures (W3)	50	
Payment of lease liabilities (W3)	(31)	
Dividends paid (W2)	(156)	
Net cash from financing activities		163

Workings

1 ***Assets***

	Property, plant and equipment	Development expenditure	Right-of-use asset
	\$'000	\$'000	\$'000
B/d	657	160	80
Disposals	(103)		
P/L	(47)		(10)
OCI	100		
Additions (β)		190	
Amortisation		(60)	
New right-of-use asset			56
Cash additions (β)	192	–	–
C/d	799	290	126

ANSWERS

2 ***Equity***

	Share capital and premium	Revaluation surplus	Retained earnings
	$'000	$'000	$'000
B/d	500	60	255
P/L			180
OCI		100	
Bonus issue (400/8)	50		(50)
Rights issue (β)	300		
Dividend paid (β)	–	–	(156)
C/d	850	160	229

3 ***Liabilities***

	Debentures	Leases
	$'000	$'000
B/d	100	92*
SPLOCI		
New lease		56
Cash received (paid) (β)	50	(31)
C/d	150	117

*Non-current + current

(b) The statement of cash flows is one of the primary financial statements and should be used in conjunction with the other primary financial statements to help the users of financial statements to better understand how the activities of the company have generated or used cash in the period.

Users can gain further appreciation of the change in net assets, of the entity's financial position (liquidity and solvency) and the entity's ability to adapt to changing circumstances by affecting the amount and timing of cash flows. A statement of cash flows enhances comparability as cash flows are not affected by differing accounting policies used for the same type of transactions or events.

Cash flow information of a historical nature can be used as an indicator of the amount, timing and certainty of future cash flows. Past forecast cash flow information can be checked for accuracy as actual figures emerge. The relationship between profit and cash flows can be analysed as can changes in prices over time.

(c) Dickson Co has reported a profit for the year of $180,000 and has made a cash inflow from operations of $40,000. This a positive factor which shows that the normal business of the company is generating sufficient cash for it to support itself. However, there are some issues to highlight:

- The operating profit for the year ended 31 March 20X8 was $357,000 (see appendix for calculation) which is significantly higher than the cash flow from operations ($40,000). This suggests that there may be issues over the working capital cycle (the time it takes to recover the money from operations).
- In particular, inventories have increased from $227,000 to $360,000 year on year (a 59% increase), with a notable decrease in trade receivables (a drop of 15%). We are not given the revenue figures for the prior year, but this information suggests that sales may be on the decline as more inventory is held and both cash and trade receivables have declined.

- With the increase in inventory, Dickson Co should review whether there is any risk of obsolescence. There is the potential that inventory is overstated at 31 March 20X8 which is over-inflating the gross profit.
- Investments have been classified as cash equivalents, however, it should be something to review as investments should only be classified as such if they are readily convertible to known amounts of cash.

  Development expenditure of $190,000 was capitalised during the year. It is important that these expenses are genuine development expenditure (as opposed to research costs which must be expensed) and that future income will be generated from these projects. There is a risk that costs will not have been correctly capitalised in line with IAS 38 *Intangible Assets*, leading to understated expenses in the statement of profit and loss, and an overstated profit for the year ended 31 March 20X8.
- The new rights share issue has raised $300,000 and the debenture issue a further $50,000. Such financing of a company should be restricted to funding capital investments, and Dickson Co has spent $192,000 on new property, plant and equipment and a further $190,000 on development expenditure. However, this is partially offset by the proceeds of sale on property, plant and equipment of $110,000. This leaves a net outflow of $272,000 spent on capital purchases to support the future business of Dickson Co. This leaves $78,000 from the financing activities of 20X8 which Dickson Co has used to support the general funding of the business. This is not a sustainable option, especially as this financing has contributed to the large dividend payment of $156,000 during the year. The justification for this dividend is questionable given the cash position of the company.

Conclusion

The Board should carefully review the current inventory holding and the working capital cycle. Any future capital financing should be for specific long-term objectives. Also, all capitalised costs must meet the IAS 38 criteria and be amortised accordingly. It is recommended that the Board does not issue a sizeable dividend next year in order to support the working capital of the business.

Appendix

	$'000
Profit before tax	342
Add: finance costs	15
Operating profit	357

ANSWERS

Mock Exams

ACCA

Financial Reporting (FR)

Mock Exam 1

ACCA CBE Practice Exam 1

Questions	
Time allowed	3 hours
This mock exam is divided into three sections: Section A: ALL 15 questions are compulsory and MUST be attempted Section B: ALL 15 questions are compulsory and MUST be attempted Section C: BOTH questions are compulsory and MUST be attempted	

DO NOT OPEN THIS EXAM UNTIL YOU ARE READY TO START UNDER EXAMINATION CONDITIONS

Section A

ALL 15 questions are compulsory and MUST be attempted

1 Identify, by selecting the relevant box in the table below, whether the following statements are true or false regarding the duties of the IFRS Interpretations Committee.

To interpret the application of IFRS Accounting Standards	**TRUE**	**FALSE**
To work directly with national standard setters to bring about convergence with IFRS Accounting Standards	**TRUE**	**FALSE**
To provide guidance on financial reporting issues not specifically addressed in IFRS Accounting Standards	**TRUE**	**FALSE**
To publish draft interpretations for public comment	**TRUE**	**FALSE**

(2 marks)

2 For each of the following, identify whether the acquisition would or would not be treated as a subsidiary of Poulgo Co as at 31 December 20X7?

The acquisition of 60% of Zakron Co's equity share capital on 1 March 20X7. Zakron Co's activities are significantly different from the rest of the Poulgo group of companies.	**SUBSIDIARY**	**NOT A SUBSIDIARY**
The offer to acquire 70% of Unto Co's equity share capital on 1 November 20X7. The negotiations were finally signed off during January 20X8.	**SUBSIDIARY**	**NOT A SUBSIDIARY**
The acquisition of 45% of Speeth Co's equity share capital on 31 December 20X7. Poulgo Co is able to appoint three of the ten members of Speeth Co's board.	**SUBSIDIARY**	**NOT A SUBSIDIARY**

(2 marks)

3 On 1 January 20X6, Gardenbugs Co received a $30,000 government grant relating to equipment which cost $90,000 and had a useful life of six years. The grant was netted off against the cost of the equipment. On 1 January 20X7, when the equipment had a carrying amount of $50,000, its use was changed so that it was no longer being used in accordance with the grant. This meant that the grant needed to be repaid in full but by 31 December 20X7, this had not yet been done.

Using the drag and drop options in the table below, create the journal entry required to reflect the correct accounting treatment of the government grant and the equipment in the financial statements of Gardenbugs Co for the year ended 31 December 20X7?

	Debit	Credit
Depreciation expense	▼	
Liability		▼
Property, plant and equipment	▼	

Pull down list

- $10,000
- $15,000
- $20,000

- $30,000

(2 marks)

4 The following two issues relate to Spiko Co's mining activities:

- Issue 1: Spiko Co began operating a new mine in January 20X3 under a five-year government licence which required Spiko Co to landscape the area after mining ceased at an estimated cost of $100,000.
- Issue 2: During 20X4, Spiko Co's mining activities caused environmental pollution on an adjoining piece of government land. There is no legislation which requires Spiko Co to rectify this damage, however, Spiko Co does have a published environmental policy which includes assurances that it will do so. The estimated cost of the rectification is $1,000,000.

In accordance with IAS 37 *Provisions, Contingent Liabilities and Contingent Assets*, which of the following statements is correct in respect of Spiko Co's financial statements for the year ended 31 December 20X4?

O A provision is required for the cost of both issues 1 and 2

O Both issues 1 and 2 require disclosure only

O A provision is required for the cost of issue 1 but issue 2 requires disclosure only

O Issue 1 requires disclosure only and issue 2 should be ignored **(2 marks)**

5 Parket Co acquired 60% of Suket Co on 1 January 20X7. The following extract has been taken from the individual statements of profit or loss for the year ended 31 March 20X7:

	Parket Co	Suket Co
	$'000	$'000
Cost of sales	710	480

Parket Co consistently made sales of $20,000 per month to Suket Co throughout the year. At the year end, Suket Co held $20,000 of this in inventory. Parket Co made a mark-up on cost of 25% on all sales to Suket Co.

What is Parket Co's consolidated cost of sales for the year ended 31 March 20X7?

$ [ ] **(2 marks)**

6 Quilo Co has decided to change its depreciation method to better reflect the pattern of use of its equipment.

Which of the following correctly reflects what this change represents and how it should be applied?

O It is a change of accounting policy and must be applied prospectively

O It is a change of accounting policy and must be applied retrospectively

O It is a change of accounting estimate and must be applied retrospectively

O It is a change of accounting estimate and must be applied prospectively **(2 marks)**

7 Included within the financial assets of Zinet Co at 31 March 20X9 are the following two recently purchased investments in publicly traded equity shares:

- Investment 1 – 10% of the issued share capital of Haruka Co. This shareholding was acquired as a long-term investment as Zinet Co wishes to participate as an active shareholder of Haruka Co.
- Investment 2 – 10% of the issued share capital of Lukas Co. This shareholding was acquired for speculative purposes and Zinet Co expects to sell these shares in the near future.

Neither of these shareholdings gives Zinet Co significant influence over the investee companies.

Wherever possible, the directors of Zinet Co wish to avoid taking any fair value movements to profit or loss, so as to minimise volatility in reported earnings.

How should the fair value movements in these investments be reported in Zinet Co's financial statements for the year ended 31 March 20X9?

- O In profit or loss for both investments
- O In other comprehensive income for both investments
- O In profit or loss for investment 1 and in other comprehensive income for investment 2
- O In other comprehensive income for investment 1 and in profit or loss for investment 2 **(2 marks)**

8 Shiba Co entered into lease for a right of use asset on 1 January 20X7. The lease contract is for four years and the useful life of the asset is six years. Information relating to the lease is as follows:

Initial lease liability	$48,000
Deposit paid on 1 January 20X7	$2,000
Direct costs incurred by Shiba Co	$5,000
Maintenance costs of $2,000 per annum	$8,000

What will be the carrying amount of the right of use asset at 31 December 20X8?

- O $41,250
- O $31,500
- O $27,500
- O $36,667

(2 marks)

9 Trasten Co operates in an emerging market with a fast-growing economy where prices increase frequently.

Which **TWO** of the following statements are true when using historical cost accounting compared to current value accounting in this type of market?

- ☐ Capital employed which is calculated using historical costs is understated compared to current value capital employed
- ☐ Historical cost profits are overstated in comparison to current value profits
- ☐ Capital employed which is calculated using historical costs is overstated compared to current value capital employed
- ☐ Historical cost profits are understated in comparison to current value profits **(2 marks)**

10 Patula Co acquired 80% of Sanka Co on 1 October 20X5. At this date, some of Sanka Co's inventory had a carrying amount of $600,000 but a fair value of $800,000. By 31 December 20X5, 70% of this inventory had been sold by Sanka Co.

The individual statements of financial position at 31 December 20X5 for both companies show the following:

	Patula Co	Sanka Co
	$'000	$'000
Inventories	3,250	1,940

What will be the total inventories figure in the consolidated statement of financial position of Patula Co as at 31 December 20X5?

- O $5,250,000

- O $5,330,000
- O $5,130,000
- O $5,238,000

(2 marks)

11 Top Trades Co has been trading for a number of years and is currently going through a period of expansion.

An extract from the statement of cash flows for the year ended 31 December 20X7 for Top Trades Co is presented as follows:

	$'000
Net cash from operating activities	995
Net cash used in investing activities	(540)
Net cash used in financing activities	(200)
Net increase in cash and cash equivalents	255
Cash and cash equivalents at the beginning of the period	200
Cash and cash equivalents at the end of the period	455

Which of the following statements is correct according to the extract of Top Trades Co's statement of cash flows?

- O The company has good working capital management
- O Net cash generated from financing activities has been used to fund the additions to non-current assets
- O Net cash generated from operating activities has been used to fund the additions to non-current assets
- O Existing non-current assets have been sold to cover the cost of the additions to non-current assets

(2 marks)

12 Rooney Co acquired 70% of the equity share capital of Marek Co, its only subsidiary, on 1 January 20X6. The fair value of the non-controlling interest in Marek Co at acquisition was $1.1 million. At that date the fair values of Marek Co's net assets were equal to their carrying amounts, except for a building which had a fair value of $1.5 million above its carrying amount and 30 years remaining useful life.

During the year to 31 December 20X6, Marek Co sold goods to Rooney Co, giving rise to an unrealised profit in inventory of $550,000 at the year end. Marek Co's profit after tax for the year ended 31 December 20X6 was $3.2 million.

What amount will be presented as the non-controlling interest in the consolidated statement of financial position of Rooney Co as at 31 December 20X6?

$ [ ]

(2 marks)

13 When a gain on a bargain purchase (negative goodwill) arises, IFRS 3 *Business Combinations* requires an entity to first of all review the measurement of the assets, liabilities and consideration transferred in respect of the combination.

When a bargain purchase is confirmed it should be [(1) ▼] to [(2) ▼].

Pull down list 1

- Credited
- Debited

Pull down list 2

- Positive goodwill
- Profit or loss
- Retained earnings

(2 marks)

14 On 1 October 20X5, Anita Co purchased 75,000 of Binita Co's 100,000 equity shares when Binita Co's retained earnings amounted to $90,000.

On 30 September 20X7, extracts from the statements of financial position of the two companies were:

	Anita Co	Binita Co
	$'000	$'000
Equity shares of $1 each	125	100
Retained earnings	300	150
Total	425	250

What is the total equity which should appear in Anita Co's consolidated statement of financial position as at 30 September 20X7?

- O $125,000
- O $470,000
- O $345,000
- O $537,500

(2 marks)

15 On 1 October 20X1, Bash Co borrowed $6 million for a term of one year, exclusively to finance the construction of a new piece of production equipment. The interest rate on the loan is 6% and is payable on maturity of the loan. The construction commenced on 1 November 20X1 but no construction took place between 1 December 20X1 and 31 January 20X2 due to employees taking industrial action. The asset was available for use on 30 September 20X2 having a construction cost of $6 million.

What is the carrying amount of the production equipment in Bash Co's statement of financial position as at 30 September 20X2?

$ [ ]

(2 marks)

Section B

ALL 15 questions are compulsory and MUST be attempted

Aphrodite Co

Each question is worth 2 marks.

The following scenario relates to questions 16–20.

Aphrodite Co has a year end of 31 December and operates a factory which makes computer chips for mobile phones. It purchased a machine on 1 July 20X3 for $80,000 which had a useful life of ten years and is depreciated on the straight-line basis, time apportioned in the years of acquisition and disposal. The machine was revalued to $81,000 on 1 July 20X4. There was no change to its useful life at that date.

A fire at the factory on 1 October 20X6 damaged the machine leaving it with a lower operating capacity. The accountant considers that Aphrodite Co will need to recognise an impairment loss in relation to this damage. The accountant has ascertained the following information at 1 October 20X6:

(1) The carrying amount of the machine is $60,750.

(2) An equivalent new machine would cost $90,000.

(3) The machine could be sold in its current condition for a gross amount of $45,000. Dismantling costs would amount to $2,000.

(4) In its current condition, the machine could operate for three more years which gives it a value in use figure of $38,685.

16 In accordance with IAS 16 *Property, Plant and Equipment*, what is the depreciation charged to Aphrodite Co's profit or loss in respect of the machine for the year ended 31 December 20X4?

- O $9,000
- O $8,000
- O $8,263
- O $8,500

(2 marks)

---

17 IAS 36 *Impairment of Assets* contains a number of examples of internal and external events which may indicate the impairment of an asset.

In accordance with IAS 36, which of the following would definitely **NOT** be an indicator of the potential impairment of an asset (or group of assets)?

- O An unexpected fall in the market value of one or more assets
- O Adverse changes in the economic performance of one or more assets
- O A significant change in the technological environment in which an asset is employed making its software effectively obsolete
- O The carrying amount of an entity's net assets being below the entity's market capitalisation

(2 marks)

---

18 What is the total impairment loss associated with Aphrodite Co's machine at 1 October 20X6?

- O $nil
- O $17,750
- O $22,065
- O $15,750

(2 marks)

19 The accountant has decided that it is too difficult to reliably attribute cash flows to the damaged machine and that it would be more accurate to calculate the impairment on the basis of the factory as a cash generating unit.

In accordance with IAS 36, which of the following is **TRUE** regarding cash generating units?

- O A cash-generating unit to which goodwill has been allocated should be tested for impairment every five years
- O A cash-generating unit must be a subsidiary of the parent
- O There is no need to consistently identify cash-generating units based on the same types of asset from period to period
- O A cash-generating unit is the smallest identifiable group of assets for which independent cash flows can be identified **(2 marks)**

---

20 On 1 July 20X7, it is discovered that the damage to the machine is worse than originally thought. The machine is now considered to be worthless and the recoverable amount of the factory as a cash generating unit is estimated to be $950,000.

At 1 July 20X7, the cash generating unit comprises the following assets:

	$'000
Building	500
Plant and equipment (including the damaged machine at a carrying amount of $35,000)	335
Goodwill	85
Net current assets (at recoverable amount)	250
	1,170

In accordance with IAS 36, what will be the carrying amount of Aphrodite Co's plant and equipment when the impairment loss has been allocated to the cash generating unit?

- O $262,500
- O $300,000
- O $237,288
- O $280,838 **(2 marks)**

(Total = 10 marks)

Blocks Co

The following scenario relates to questions 21–25.

On 1 January 20X5, Blocks Co entered into new agreements as follows:

- Agreement one: This agreement meets the definition of a lease under IFRS 16 *Leases* and grants Blocks Co the right to use a piece of machinery. Under the terms of the agreement, Blocks Co must pay a deposit of $20,000 on inception of the lease on 1 January 20X5 followed by five equal annual instalments of $55,000, starting on 31 December 20X5. The present value of the future lease payments on 1 January 20X5 is $200,000. The interest rate implicit in the lease is 11.65%.
- Agreement two: This agreement meets the definition of a lease under IFRS 16 *Leases* and grants Blocks Co the right to use a van for nine months. The fair value of the van is $120,000

and it has an estimated useful life of five years. The agreement requires Blocks Co to make no payment in month one and $4,800 per month in months 2–9. Blocks Co wishes to take advantage of any optional recognition exemptions available under IFRS 16.

- Agreement three: This is a sale and leaseback relating to a cutting machine purchased by Blocks Co on 1 January 20X4 for $300,000. The carrying amount of the machine as at 31 December 20X4 was $250,000. On 1 January 20X5, it was sold to Cogs Co for $370,000 (being its fair value) and Blocks Co will lease the machine back for five years, the remainder of its useful life, at $80,000 per annum. The present value of the annual payments is $350,000 and the transaction satisfies the IFRS 15 criteria to be recognised as a sale.

21 According to IFRS 16 *Leases*, which of the following gives the measurement of a right of use asset at the commencement of a lease?

- O Sum of all rental payments to be paid to the lessor **less** any initial direct costs and dismantling costs
- O The amount of the initial measurement of the lease liability **plus** any initial direct costs and dismantling costs
- O The amount of the initial measurement of the lease liability **less** any initial direct costs and dismantling costs
- O Sum of all rental payments to be paid to the lessor **plus** any initial direct costs and dismantling costs **(2 marks)**

---

22 For agreement two, what amount of asset should be initially recognised on commencement of the lease?

- O $5,500
- O $10,000
- O $0
- O $11,000 **(2 marks)**

---

23 The following calculations have been prepared for agreement one:

Year	Interest	Annual payment	Balance
	$	$	$
31 December 20X7	15,484	(55,000)	93,391
31 December 20X8	10,880	(55,000)	49,271
31 December 20X9	5,729	(55,000)	0

In respect of the lease obligation, match the values attributable to the non-current liability and current liability to in the statement of financial position as at 31 December 20X7?

Value		Statement of financial position
$44,120		Non-current liability
$49,271		Current liability
$93,391		
$Nil		

(2 marks)

24 For agreement one, what is the finance cost charged to profit or loss for the year ended 31 December 20X6?

$ ______ **(2 marks)**

25 For agreement three, what profit should be recognised for the year ended 31 December 20X5 as a result of the sale and leaseback (to the nearest whole $)?

$ ______ **(2 marks)**

(Total = 10 marks)

Mighty IT Co

The following scenario relates to questions 26–30.

Mighty IT Co provides hardware, software and IT services to small business customers.

Mighty IT Co has developed an accounting software package. The company offers a supply and installation service for $1,000 and a separate two-year technical support service for $500. Alternatively, it also offers a combined goods and services contract which includes both of these elements for $1,200. Payment for the combined contract is due one month after the date of installation.

In December 20X5, Mighty IT Co revalued its corporate headquarters. Prior to the revaluation, the carrying amount of the building was $2 million and it was revalued to $2.5 million.

Mighty IT Co also revalued a sales office on the same date. The office had been purchased for $500,000 earlier in the year, but subsequent discovery of defects reduced its value to $400,000. No depreciation had been charged on the sales office and any impairment loss is allowable for tax purposes.

Mighty IT Co's income tax rate is 30%.

26 In accordance with IFRS 15 *Revenue from Contracts with Customers*, when should Mighty IT Co recognise revenue from the combined goods and services contract?

- ○ Supply and install: on installation; Technical support: over two years

- O Supply and install: when payment is made; Technical support: over two years
- O Supply and install: on installation; Technical support: on installation
- O Supply and install: when payment is made; Technical support: when payment is made **(2 marks)**

---

27 For each combined contract sold, what is the amount of revenue which Mighty IT Co should recognise in respect of the supply and installation service in accordance with IFRS 15?

- O $700
- O $800
- O $1,000
- O $1,200 **(2 marks)**

---

28 Mighty IT Co sells a combined contract on 1 January 20X6, the first day of its financial year. Mighty IT Co financial statements are prepared in accordance with IFRS 15.

What is the total amount for deferred income which will be reported in Mighty IT Co's statement of financial position as at 31 December 20X6?

$ [ ] **(2 marks)**

---

29 In accordance with IAS 12 *Income Taxes*, what is the impact of the property revaluations on the income tax expense of Mighty IT Co for the year ended 31 December 20X5?

- O Income tax expense increases by $180,000
- O Income tax expense increases by $120,000
- O Income tax expense decreases by $30,000
- O No impact on income tax expense **(2 marks)**

---

30 In January 20X6, the accountant at Mighty IT Co produced the company's draft financial statements for the year ended 31 December 20X5. He then realised that he had omitted to consider deferred tax on development costs. In 20X5, development costs of $200,000 had been incurred and capitalised. Development costs are deductible in full for tax purposes in the year they are incurred. The development is still in process at 31 December 20X5.

What adjustment is required to the income tax expense in Mighty IT Co's statement of profit or loss for the year ended 31 December 20X5 to account for deferred tax on the development costs?

- O Increase of $200,000
- O Increase of $60,000
- O Decrease of $60,000
- O Decrease of $200,000 **(2 marks)**

(Total = 10 marks)

Section C

BOTH questions are compulsory and MUST be attempted

31 Triage Co

After preparing a draft statement of profit or loss (before interest and tax) for the year ended 31 March 20X6 (before any adjustments which may be required by Notes (1) to (4) below), the summarised trial balance of Triage Co as at 31 March 20X6 is:

	$'000	$'000
Equity shares of $1 each		50,000
Retained earnings as at 1 April 20X5		3,500
Draft profit before interest and tax for year ended 31 March 20X6		30,000
6% convertible loan notes (Note (1))		40,000
Freehold property (original life 25 years) – at cost (Note (2))	75,000	
Plant and equipment – at cost (Note (2))	72,100	
Accumulated depreciation at 1 April 20X5: property		15,000
plant and equipment		28,100
Trade receivables (Note (3))	28,000	
Other current assets	9,300	
Current liabilities		17,700
Deferred tax (Note (4))		3,200
Interest payment (Note (1))	2,400	
Current tax (Note (4))	700	0
	187,500	187,500

The following notes are relevant:

(1) Triage Co issued 400,000 $100 6% convertible loan notes on 1 April 20X5. Interest is payable annually in arrears on 31 March each year. The loans can be converted to equity shares on the basis of 20 shares for each $100 loan note on 31 March 20X8 or redeemed at par for cash on the same date. An equivalent loan without the conversion rights would have required an interest rate of 8%.

The present value of $1 receivable at the end of each year, based on discount rates of 6% and 8%, are:

		6%	8%
End of year:	1	0.94	0.93
	2	0.89	0.86
	3	0.84	0.79

(2) Non-current assets:

The directors decided to revalue the freehold property at $66.3 million on 1 October 20X5. Triage Co does not make an annual transfer from the revaluation surplus to retained earnings to reflect the realisation of the revaluation gain; however, the revaluation will give rise to a deferred tax liability at the company's tax rate of 20%.

The freehold property is depreciated on a straight-line basis and plant and equipment at 15% per annum using the reducing balance method.

No depreciation has yet been charged on any non-current assets for the year ended 31 March 20X6.

(3) In September 20X5, the directors of Triage Co discovered a fraud. In total, $700,000 which had been included as receivables in the above trial balance had been stolen by an employee. $450,000 of this related to the year ended 31 March 20X5, the rest to the current year. The directors are hopeful that 50% of the losses can be recovered from the company's insurers.

(4) A provision of $2.7 million is required for current income tax on the profit of the year to 31 March 20X6. The balance on current tax in the trial balance is the under/over provision of tax for the previous year. In addition to the temporary differences relating to the information in note (ii), at 31 March 20X6, the carrying amounts of Triage Co's net assets are $12 million more than their tax base.

Required

(a) Prepare a schedule of adjustments required to the draft profit before interest and tax (in the above trial balance) to give the profit or loss of Triage Co for the year ended 31 March 20X6 as a result of the information in Notes (1) to (4) above. **(5 marks)**

(b) Prepare the statement of financial position of Triage Co as at 31 March 20X6. **(12 marks)**

(c) The issue of convertible loan notes can potentially dilute the basic earnings per share (EPS).

Calculate the diluted earnings per share for Triage Co for the year ended 31 March 20X6 (there is no need to calculate the basic EPS). **(3 marks)**

Note. A statement of changes in equity and the notes to the statement of financial position are not required.

(Total = 20 marks)

32 Gregory Co

Gregory Co is a listed company and, until 1 October 20X5, it had no subsidiaries. On that date, it acquired 75% of Tamsin Co's equity shares by means of a share exchange of two new shares in Gregory Co for every five acquired shares in Tamsin Co. These shares were recorded at the market price on the day of the acquisition and were the only shares issued by Gregory Co during the year ended 31 March 20X6.

The summarised financial statements of Gregory Co as a single entity at 31 March 20X5 and as a group at 31 March 20X6 are:

Statements of profit or loss for the year ended

	31 March 20X6	31 March 20X5
	Gregory group	Gregory Co single entity
	$'000	$'000
Revenue	46,500	28,000
Cost of sales	(37,200)	(20,800)
Gross profit	9,300	7,200
Operating expenses	(1,800)	(1,200)
Profit before tax (operating profit)	7,500	6,000
Income tax expense	(1,500)	(1,000)
Profit for the year	6,000	5,000
Profit for year attributable to:		

	31 March 20X6	31 March 20X5
	Gregory group	Gregory Co single entity
	$'000	$'000
Equity holders of the parent	5,700	
Non-controlling interest	300	
	6,000	

Statements of financial position as at

	31 March 20X6	31 March 20X5
	$'000	$'000
Assets		
Non-current assets		
Property, plant and equipment	54,600	41,500
Goodwill	3,000	–
	57,600	41,500
Current assets	44,000	36,000
Total assets	101,600	77,500
Equity and liabilities		
Equity		
Equity shares of $1 each	46,000	40,000
Other component of equity (share premium)	6,000	–
Retained earnings	18,700	13,000
Equity attributable to owners of the parent	70,700	53,000
Non-controlling interest	3,600	–
	74,300	53,000
Current liabilities	27,300	24,500
Total equity and liabilities	101,600	77,500

Other information:

(1) Each month since the acquisition, Gregory Co's sales to Tamsin Co were consistently $2 million. Gregory Co had chosen to only make a gross profit margin of 10% on these sales as Tamsin Co is part of the group.

6 months

(2) The values of property, plant and equipment held by both companies have been rising for several years.

(3) On reviewing the above financial statements, Gregory Co's chief executive officer (CEO) made the following observations:

(i) I see the profit for the year has increased by $1 million which is up 20% on last year, but I thought it would be more as Tamsin Co was supposed to be a very profitable company.

(ii) I have calculated the earnings per share (EPS) for 20X6 at 13 cents (6,000/46,000 × 100) and for 20X5 at 12.5 cents (5,000/40,000 × 100) and, although the profit has increased 20%, our EPS has barely changed.

(iii) I am worried that the low price at which we are selling goods to Tamsin Co is undermining our group's overall profitability.

(iv) I note that our share price is now $2.30, how does this compare with our share price immediately before we bought Tamsin Co?

Required

(a) Reply to the four observations of the CEO. **(8 marks)**

(b) Using the above financial statements, calculate the following ratios for Gregory Co for the years ended 31 March 20X6 and 20X5 and comment on the comparative performance:

(1) Return on capital employed (ROCE)

(2) Net asset turnover

(3) Gross profit margin

(4) Operating profit margin

Four marks are available for the ratio calculations. **(12 marks)**

Note. Your answers to (a) and (b) should reflect the impact of the consolidation of Tamsin Co during the year ended 31 March 20X6.

(Total = 20 marks)

Answers

DO NOT TURN THIS PAGE UNTIL YOU HAVE COMPLETED THE MOCK EXAM

A plan of attack

Managing your nerves

As you start this mock exam a number of thoughts are likely to cross your mind. Developing an awareness of what is going on emotionally within you may help you manage your nerves. Remember, you are unlikely to banish the flow of adrenaline, but the key is to harness it to help you work steadily and quickly through your answers.

Working through this mock exam will help you develop the exam stamina you will need to keep going for three hours.

Managing your time

Planning and time management are two of the key skills which complement the technical knowledge you need to succeed. To keep yourself on time, do not be afraid to note your target completion times for each question in Section A, for each case and in total for Section B and for each question and in total for Section C. . As all the questions are compulsory, you do not have to spend time wondering which question to answer. If you can't answer an OT question in Section A or B, flag it or make a note in your scratch pad to remind yourself to go back to it later.

Doing the exam

Actually doing the exam is a personal experience. There is not a single right way. As long as you submit complete answers to all questions after the three hours are up, then your approach obviously works.

Looking through the exam

Section A has 15 OTQs. This is the section of the exam where the examining team can test knowledge across the breadth of the syllabus. Make sure you read these questions carefully. The distractors are designed to present plausible, but incorrect, answers. Don't let them mislead you. Remember there is no negative marking, so you should always have an educated guess at the OT questions and should never leave a question unanswered.

Section B has 15 OTQs in total – questions 16–30. These are arranged as three scenarios with five questions each.

Scenario 1 is on impairment of assets.

Scenario 2 is on leasing.

Scenario 3 is on revenue recognition.

Section C has two 20-mark questions.

Question 31 is on accounting adjustments and the preparation of a statement of financial position.

Question 32 is on interpretation of financial statements.

Section A

ALL 15 questions are compulsory and MUST be attempted

1 The correct answers are:

To interpret the application of IFRS Accounting Standards	**TRUE**	
To work directly with national standard setters to bring about convergence with IFRS Accounting Standards		**FALSE**
To provide guidance on financial reporting issues not specifically addressed in IFRS Accounting Standards	**TRUE**	
To publish draft interpretations for public comment	**TRUE**	

ANSWERS

2 The correct answers are:

The acquisition of 60% of Zakron Co's equity share capital on 1 March 20X7. Zakron Co's activities are significantly different from the rest of the Poulgo group of companies.	**SUBSIDIARY**	
The offer to acquire 70% of Unto Co's equity share capital on 1 November 20X7. The negotiations were finally signed off during January 20X8.		**NOT A SUBSIDIARY**
The acquisition of 45% of Speeth Co's equity share capital on 31 December 20X7. Poulgo Co is able to appoint three of the ten members of Speeth Co's board.		**NOT A SUBSIDIARY**

3

	Debit	Credit
Depreciation expense	\$20,000	
Liability		\$30,000
Property, plant and equipment	\$10,000	

The repayment of the grant must be treated as a change in accounting estimate. The carrying amount of the asset must be increased as the netting off method has been used. The resulting extra depreciation must be charged immediately to profit or loss.

	Original	As if no grant	Adjustment
	\$	\$	\$
Cost	90,000	90,000	
Grant	(30,000)		
	60,000		
Depreciation	(10,000) [1 yr]	(30,000) [2 yr]	Debit Dep'n exp 20,000
Carrying amount	50,000 [1/1/X7]	60,000 [31/12/X7]	Debit PPE 10,000
			Credit Liability 30,000

4 The correct answer is: A provision is required for the cost of both issues 1 and 2

5 \$ 774,000

710,000 + (480,000 × 3/12) – (20,000 × 3) + (20,000 × 25/125) = \$774,000

6 The correct answer is: It is a change of accounting estimate and must be applied prospectively

7 The correct answer is: In other comprehensive income for investment 1 and in profit or loss for investment 2

Note. Investment 2 is held for trading.

8 The correct answer is: \$27,500

The asset would be initially measured as $55,000 ($48,000 + $2,000 + $5,000). It is then depreciated over four years (the shorter of the lease term and its useful life) for two years from 1 January 20X7 to 31 December 20X8.

	$
Initial measurement	55,000
Depreciation ($55,000/4 × 2)	(27,500)
Carrying amount at 31 December 20X8	27,500

The maintenance costs are expensed over the length of the contract.

9 The correct answers are:

- Capital employed which is calculated using historical costs is understated compared to current value capital employed
- Historical cost profits are overstated in comparison to current value profits

This is the case in a period of increasing prices.

10 The correct answer is: $5,250,000

3,250 + 1,940 + (800 – 600 × 30%) = 5,250,000

11 The correct answer is: Net cash generated from operating activities has been used to fund the additions to non-current assets

12 $ 1,880,000

	$'000	$'000
FV of NCI at acquisition		1,100
Profit for year × 30%	3,200	
Dep'n on FVA (1.5m/30)	(50)	
Unrealised profit	(550)	
	2,600 × 30%	780
		1,880

13 When a bargain purchase is confirmed it should be credited to profit or loss .

14 The correct answer is: $470,000

Retained earnings = 300 + ((150 – 90) × 75%) = 345

Total equity = 125 + 345 = 470

15 $ 6,270,000

	$'000
Production cost of PPE	6,000
Capitalisation of borrowing costs:	
$6m × 6% × 9/12 =	270

	$'000
Total cost capitalised (and carrying amount) at 30 September 20X2	6,270

Section B

ALL 15 questions are compulsory and MUST be attempted

Aphrodite Co

16 The correct answer is: $8,500

Depreciation 1 January to 30 June 20X4 (80,000/10 × 6/12) = 4,000

Depreciation 1 July to 31 December 20X4 (81,000/9 × 6/12) = 4,500

Total depreciation = 8,500

17 The correct answer is: The carrying amount of an entity's net assets being below the entity's market capitalisation

This means that the share price is high, so the market has positive expectations of the entity.

18 The correct answer is: $17,750

VIU is lower than FV (less costs to sell), so impairment is 60,750 – 43,000 = $17,750

19 The correct answer is: A cash-generating unit is the smallest identifiable group of assets for which independent cash flows can be identified

20 The correct answer is: $262,500

The impairment loss of $220m (1,170 – 950) is allocated: $35m to damaged plant and $85m to goodwill, the remaining $100m allocated proportionally to the building and the undamaged plant. The carrying amount of the plant will then be $262,500.

Blocks Co

21 The correct answer is: The amount of the initial measurement of the lease liability **plus** any initial direct costs and dismantling costs

22 The correct answer is: $0

As the assets are of low value (less than $5,000) the rentals will be expensed to profit or loss on a straight-line basis over the period of the lease; no asset is recognised in the statement of financial position.

23 The correct answers are:

Value	Statement of financial position
$49,271	Non-current liability
$44,120	Current liability

24 $ 19,607

Year 1 200,000 × 11.65% = 23,300

Year 2 (200,000 + 23,300 – 55,000) × 11.65% = $19,607

25 $ 6,486

Profit on sale = 120,000

Amount relating to rights retained = 120,000 × 350,000/370,000 = 113,514

Amount relating to rights transferred = 120,000 – 113,514 = 6,486

ANSWERS

Mighty IT Co

26 The correct answer is: Supply and install: on installation; Technical support: over two years

The performance obligation for the goods is satisfied when the package is supplied. The technical support obligation is satisfied over time.

27 The correct answer is: $800

1,000/1,500 × 1,200 = $800

28 $ [200]

500/1,500 × 1,200 = 400/2 = $200

29 The correct answer is: Income tax expense decreases by $30,000

$30,000 (400 – 500 × 30%).

Revaluation and deferred tax of headquarters goes through OCI.

30 The correct answer is: Increase of $60,000

$60,000 (200 × 30%)

Debit Income tax expense Credit Deferred tax liability

Section C

BOTH questions are compulsory and MUST be attempted

31 Triage Co

Text references

Chapter 16.

Top Tips

Make sure you are clear how to set out a schedule of adjustments. You must show the effect on profit or loss in order to get the marks.

Easy marks

This was quite a demanding question and none of the marks were very easy, but if you dealt with it methodically and remembered to look at the impact of the adjustments on the statement of financial position, there were plenty of marks available.

Examining Team's comments

Some candidates prepared a series of workings but did not attempt to summarise them or state their effect on profit or loss. Some candidates did not attempt to calculate the debt component of the convertible loan note or did not correctly split the depreciation of the leased property into the periods before and after the revaluation.

Marking guide

	Marks	
(a) Schedule of adjustments		
Profit before interest and tax	0.5	
Loan finance costs	1	
Depreciation charges	1.5	
Fraud loss	0.5	
Income tax	1.5	
		5
(b) Statement of financial position		
Property, plant and equipment	2.5	
Trade receivables	1	
Other current assets	0.5	
Equity shares	0.5	
Equity option	1	
Revaluation surplus	1	
Retained earnings	1.5	
Deferred tax	1	
Loan note	1.5	
Current liabilities	0.5	
Current tax payable	1	
		12
(c) Diluted EPS	3	
		3
Total		

ANSWERS

Marking guide	**Marks**
20

(a) This question should be answered using the spreadsheet response option in the ACCA exam software. An example of how this would be laid out when using the software and the formula that could be applied is shown below:

Spreadsheet

Edit Format

100%

11

B $'00 06	=SUM(B1:B5)	
	A	B
		$'000
1	Draft profit before interest and tax per trial balance	30,000
2	Adjustment re: Note 1 Convertible loan note finance costs (W1)	(3,023)
3	Note 2 Depreciation of freehold property (1,500 + 1,700 (W2)) Depreciation of plant and equipment (W2)	(3,200) (6,600)
4	Note 3 Current year loss on fraud (700 – 450 see below)	(250)
5	Note 4 Income tax expense (2,700 + 700 – 800 (W3))	(2,600)
6	Profit for the year	14,327

Triage Co – Schedule of adjustments to profit for the year ended 31 March 20X6

	$'000
Draft profit before interest and tax per trial balance	30,000
Adjustments re:	
Note (1)	
Convertible loan note finance costs (W1)	(3,023)

BPP

	$'000
Note (2)	
Depreciation of freehold property (1,500 + 1,700 (W2))	(3,200)
Depreciation of plant and equipment (W2)	(6,600)
Note (3)	
Current year loss on fraud (700 – 450 see below)	(250)
Note (4)	
Income tax expense (2,700 + 700 – 800 (W3))	(2,600)
Profit for the year	14,327

The $450,000 fraud loss in the previous year is a prior period adjustment (reported in the statement of changes in equity).

The possible insurance claim is a contingent asset and should not be recognised.

(b)

Triage Co – Statement of financial position as at 31 March 20X6

	$'000	$'000
Assets		
Non-current assets		
Property, plant and equipment (64,600 + 37,400 (W2)		102,000
Current assets		
Trade receivables (28,000 – 700 fraud)	27,300	
Other current assets per trial balance	9,300	36,600
Total assets		138,600
Equity and liabilities		
Equity		
Equity shares of $1 each		50,000
Other component of equity (W1)	2,208	
Revaluation surplus (7,800 – 1,560 (W2))	6,240	
Retained earnings (W4)	17,377	25,825
		75,825
Non-current liabilities		
Deferred tax (W3)	3,960	
6% convertible loan notes (W1)	38,415	42,375
Current liabilities		
Per trial balance	17,700	
Current tax payable	2,700	20,400
Total equity and liabilities		138,600

ANSWERS

(c) Diluted earnings per share (W5): 29 cents

In Workings below, all monetary figures in brackets are in $'000.

Workings

1 ***6% convertible loan notes***

The convertible loan notes are a compound financial instrument having a debt and an equity component which must both be quantified and accounted for separately:

Year ended 31 March	Outflow	8%	Present value
	$'000		$'000
20X6	2,400	0.93	2,232
20X7	2,400	0.6	2,064
20X8	42,400	0.79	33,496
Debt component			37,792
Equity component (= balance)			2,208
Proceeds of issue			40,000

The finance cost will be $3,023,000 (37,792 × 8%) and the carrying amount of the loan notes at 31 March 20X6 will be $38,415,000 (37,792 + (3,023 – 2,400)).

2 ***Non-current assets***

Freehold property

The gain on revaluation and carrying amount of the freehold property is:

	$'000
Carrying amount at 1 April 20X5 (75,000 – 15,000)	60,000
Depreciation to date of revaluation (1 October 20X5) (75,000/25 × 6/12)	(1,500)
Carrying amount at revaluation	58,500
Gain on revaluation = balance	7,800
Revaluation at 1 October 20X5	66,300
Depreciation to year ended 31 March 20X6 (66,300/19.5 years × 6/12)	(1,700)
Carrying amount at 31 March 20X6	64,600

Annual depreciation is $3m (75,000/25 years); therefore the accumulated depreciation at 1 April 20X5 of $15m represents five years' depreciation. At the date of revaluation (1 October 20X5), there will be a remaining life of 19.5 years.

Of the revaluation gain, $6.24m (80%) is credited to the revaluation surplus and $1.56m (20%) is credited to deferred tax.

Plant and equipment

	$'000
Carrying amount at 1 April 20X5 (72,100 – 28,100)	44,000
Depreciation for year ended 31 March 20X6 (15% reducing balance)	(6,600)
Carrying amount at 31 March 20X6	37,400

3 ***Deferred tax***

	$'000
Provision required at 31 March 20X6:	
Revalued property and other assets (7,800 + 12,000) × 20%	3,960
Provision at 1 April 20X5	(3,200)
Increase in provision	760
Revaluation of land and buildings (7,800 × 20%)	(1,560)
Balance credited to profit or loss	(800)

4 ***Retained earnings***

	$'000
Balance at 1 April 20X5	3,500
Prior period adjustment (fraud)	(450)
Adjusted profit for year (from (a))	14,327
Balance at 31 March 20X6	17,377

5 ***Diluted EPS***

The maximum additional shares on conversion is 8 million (40,000 × 20/100), giving total shares of 58 million.

The loan interest 'saved' is $2.418m (3,023 (from (W1) above × 80% (ie after tax)), giving adjusted earnings of $16.745m (14,327 + 2,418)).

Therefore diluted EPS is $\frac{\$16{,}745{,}00 \times 100}{58 \text{ million shares}} = 29 \text{ cents}$

32 Gregory Co

Chapter references

Chapters 20 and 21.

Top Tips

It's not all about the ratios. You have to look at the financial statements combined with the information in the question and work out what is going on with the company. In this case it's important to consider the group aspects.

Easy marks

The ratios were easy marks and if they were considered in the light of the rest of the information it should have been possible to get good marks for the comments.

Examining Team's comments

This question combined interpretation with an element of consolidation and candidates found it challenging. In part (a) most candidates launched into irrelevant detail regarding ratio movements without stopping to consider the reason for the difference between the two years' financial statements. The ratio calculations in part (b) were generally well done. The comments on comparative performance were generally inadequate – to say that a ratio has gone up or down and that this is good or bad is not enough.

Marking guide	Marks	
(a) 2 marks for each reply to the CEO's observations	8	
		8
(b) 1 mark for each pair of ratios	4	
1 mark per relevant comment up to	8	
		12
Total		20

(a) **Note.** References to 20X6 and 20X5 are to the years ending 31 March 20X6 and 20X5 respectively.

Comment (1)

I see the profit for the year has increased by $1m which is up 20% on last year, but I thought it would be more as Tamsin Co was supposed to be a very profitable company.

There are two issues with this statement. First, last year's profit is not comparable with the current year's profit because in 20X5 Gregory Co was a single entity and in 20X6 it is now a group with a subsidiary. A second issue is that the consolidated statement of profit or loss for the year ended 31 March 20X6 only includes six months of the results of Tamsin Co, and, assuming Tamsin Co is profitable, future results will include a full year's profit. This latter point may, at least in part, mitigate the CEO's disappointment.

Comment (2)

I have calculated the EPS for 20X6 at 13 cents (6,000/46,000 × 100 shares) and at 12.5 cents for 20X5 (5,000/40,000 × 100) and, although the profit has increased 20%, our EPS has barely changed.

The stated EPS calculation for 20X6 is incorrect for two reasons. First, it is the profit attributable to only the equity shareholders of the parent which should be used and, second, the 6 million new shares were only in issue for six months and should be pro-rated by 6/12 months. Thus, the correct EPS for 20X6 is 13.3 cents (5,700/43,000 × 100). This gives an increase of 6% (13.3 – 12.5)/12.5) on 20X5 EPS which is still less than the increase in profit. The reason why the EPS may not have increased in line with reported profit is that the acquisition was financed by a share exchange which increased the number of shares in issue. Thus, the EPS takes account of the additional consideration used to generate profit, whereas the trend of absolute profit does not take additional consideration into account. This is why the EPS is often said to be a more accurate reflection of company performance than the trend of profits.

Comment (3)

I am worried that the low price at which we are selling goods to Tamsin Co is undermining our group's overall profitability.

Assuming the consolidated financial statements have been correctly prepared, all intragroup trading has been eliminated, thus the pricing policy will have had no effect on these financial statements. The comment is incorrect and reflects a misunderstanding of the consolidation process.

Comment (4)

I note that our share price is now $2.30, how does this compare with our share price immediately before we bought Tamsin Co?

The increase in share capital is 6 million shares, the increase in the share premium is $6m, thus the total proceeds for the 6 million shares was $12m giving a share price of $2.00 at the date of acquisition of Tamsin Co. The current price of $2.30 presumably reflects the market's favourable view of Gregory Co's current and future performance.

(b)

	20X6	20X5
Return on capital employed (ROCE) (7,500/74,300 × 100)	10.1%	11.3%
Net asset turnover (46,500/74,300)	0.63 times	0.53 times
Gross profit margin (9,300/46,500 × 100)	20.0%	25.7%
Operating profit margin (7,500/46,500 × 100)	16.1%	21.4%

Looking at the above ratios, it appears that the overall performance of Gregory Co has declined marginally; the ROCE has fallen from 11.3% to 10.1%. This has been caused by a substantial fall in the gross profit margin (down from 25.7% in 20X5 to 20% in 20X6); this is over a 22% (5.7%/25.7%) decrease. The group/company have relatively low operating expenses (at around 4% of revenue), so the poor gross profit margin feeds through to the operating profit margin. The overall decline in the ROCE, due to the weaker profit margins, has been mitigated by an improvement in net asset turnover, increasing from 0.53 times to 0.63 times. Despite the improvement in net asset turnover, it is still very low with only 63 cents of sales generated from every $1 invested in the business, although this will depend on the type of business Gregory Co and Tamsin Co are engaged in.

On this analysis, the effect of the acquisition of Tamsin Co seems to have had a detrimental effect on overall performance, but this may not necessarily be the case; there could be some distorting factors in the analysis. As mentioned above, the 20X6 results include only six months of Tamsin Co's results, but the statement of financial position includes the full amount of the consideration for Tamsin Co. (The consideration has been calculated (see comment (4) above) as $12m for the parent's 75% share plus $3.3m (3,600 – 300 share of post-acquisition profit] for the non-controlling interest's 25%, giving total consideration of $15.3m). The above factors disproportionately increase the denominator of ROCE which has the effect of worsening the calculated ROCE. This distortion should be corrected in 20X7 when a full year's results for Tamsin Co will be included in group profit. Another factor is that it could take time to fully integrate the activities of the two companies and more savings and other synergies may be forthcoming such as bulk buying discounts.

The non-controlling interest share in the profit for the year in 20X6 of $300,000 allows a rough calculation of the full year's profit of Tamsin Co at $2.4m (300,000/25% × 12/6, ie the $300,000 represents 25% of 6/12 of the annual profit). This figure is subject to some uncertainty such as the effect of probable increased post-acquisition depreciation charges. However, a profit of $2.4m on the investment of $15.3m represents a return of 16% (and would be higher if the profit was adjusted to a pre-tax figure) which is much higher than the current year ROCE (at 10.1%) of the group. This implies that the performance of Tamsin Co is much better than that of Gregory Co (as a separate entity) and that Gregory Co's performance in 20X6 must have deteriorated considerably from that in 20X5 and this is the real cause of the deteriorating performance of the group.

Another issue potentially affecting the ROCE is that, as a result of the consolidation process, Tamsin Co's net assets, including goodwill, are included in the statement of financial position at fair value, whereas Gregory Co's net assets appear to be based on historical cost (as there is no revaluation surplus). As the values of property, plant and equipment have been rising, this in effect favourably flatters the 20X5 ratios. This is because the statement of financial position of 20X5 only contains Gregory Co's assets which, at historical cost, may considerably understate their fair value and, on a comparative basis, overstate 20X5 ROCE.

In summary, although on first impression the acquisition of Tamsin Co appears to have caused a marginal worsening of the group's performance, the distorting factors and imputation of the non-controlling interest's profit in 20X6 indicate the underlying performance may be better than the ratios portray and the contribution from Tamsin Co is a very significant positive. Future performance may be even better.

Without information on the separate financial statements of Tamsin Co, it is difficult to form a more definite view.

This type of question would be answered using the word processing response option in the ACCA CBE exam software. Some interpretation questions will include pre-formatted tables for the ratio calculations. If you are provided with a pre-formatted table, you must use it. If not, create your own table in the software.

The below shows how this answer could be presented in the word processing software.

Ratio	Working	20X6	20X5
Return on capital employed (ROCE)	(7,500/74,300 × 100)	10.1%	11.3%
Net asset turnover	(46,500/74,300)	0.63 times	0.53 times
Gross profit margin	(9,300/46,500 × 100)	20.0%	25.7%
Operating profit margin	(7,500/46,500 × 100)	16.1%	21.4%

Gross profit, operating profit and net asset turnover

Looking at the above ratios, it appears that the overall performance of Gregory Co has declined marginally; the ROCE has fallen from 11.3% to 10.1%. This has been caused by a substantial fall in the gross profit margin (down from 25.7% in 20X5 to 20% in 20X6); this is over a 22% (5.7%/25.7%) decrease. The group/company have relatively low operating expenses (at around 4% of revenue), so the poor gross profit margin feeds through to the operating profit margin. The overall decline in the ROCE, due to the weaker profit margins, has been mitigated by an improvement in net asset turnover, increasing from 0.53 times to 0.63 times. Despite the improvement in net asset turnover, it is still very low with only 63 cents of sales generated from every $1 invested in the business, although this will depend on the type of business Gregory Co and Tamsin Co are engaged in.

Effect of acquisition

On this analysis, the effect of the acquisition of Tamsin Co seems to have had a detrimental effect on overall performance, but this may not necessarily be the case: there could be some distorting factors in the analysis. As mentioned above, the 20X6 results include only six months of Tamsin Co's results, but the statement of financial position includes the full amount of the consideration for Tamsin Co. (The consideration has been calculated (see comment (4) above) as $12m for the parent's 75% share plus $3.3m [3,600 – 300 share of post-acquisition profit] for the non-controlling interest's 25%, giving total consideration of $15.3m). The above factors disproportionately increase the denominator of ROCE, which has the effect of worsening the calculated ROCE. This distortion should be corrected in 20X7 when a full year's results for Tamsin Co will be included in group profit. Another factor is that it could take time to fully integrate the activities of the two companies and more savings and other synergies may be forthcoming such as bulk buying discounts.

The non-controlling interest share in the profit for the year in 20X6 of $300,000 allows a rough calculation of the full year's profit of Tamsin Co at $2.4m (300,000/25% × 12/6, ie the $300,000 represents 25% of 6/12 of the annual profit). This figure is subject to some uncertainty such as the effect of probable increased post-acquisition depreciation charges. However, a profit of $2.4m on the investment of $15.3m represents a return of 16%

(and would be higher if the profit was adjusted to a pre-tax figure), which is much higher than the current year ROCE (at 10.1%) of the group. This implies that the performance of Tamsin Co is much better than that of Gregory Co (as a separate entity) and that Gregory Co's performance in 20X6 must have deteriorated considerably from that in 20X5 and this is the real cause of the deteriorating performance of the group.

Another issue potentially affecting the ROCE is that, as a result of the consolidation process, Tamsin Co's net assets, including goodwill, are included in the statement of financial position at fair value, whereas Gregory Co's net assets appear to be based on historical cost (as there is no revaluation surplus). As the values of property, plant and equipment have been rising, this in effect favourably flatters the 20X5 ratios. This is because the statement of financial position of 20X5 only contains Gregory Co's assets, which, at historical cost, may considerably understate their fair value and, on a comparative basis, overstate 20X5 ROCE.

Conclusion

In summary, although on first impression the acquisition of Tamsin Co appears to have caused a marginal worsening of the group's performance, the distorting factors and imputation of the non-controlling interest's profit in 20X6 indicate the underlying performance may be better than the ratios portray and the contribution from Tamsin Co is a very significant positive. Future performance may be even better.

Without information on the separate financial statements of Tamsin Co, it is difficult to form a more definite view.

ACCA

Financial Reporting (FR)

Mock Exam 2

ACCA Specimen CBE

Questions	
Time allowed	3 hours
This mock exam is divided into three sections: Section A: ALL 15 questions are compulsory and MUST be attempted Section B: ALL 15 questions are compulsory and MUST be attempted Section C: BOTH questions are compulsory and MUST be attempted	

DO NOT OPEN THIS EXAM UNTIL YOU ARE READY TO START UNDER EXAMINATION CONDITIONS

Section A

ALL 15 questions are compulsory and MUST be attempted

1 Consolidated financial statements are presented on the basis that the companies within the group are treated as if they are a single economic entity.

Which **TWO** of the following are requirements of preparing consolidated financial statements?

☐ All subsidiaries must adopt the accounting policies of the parent in their individual financial statements

☐ Subsidiaries with activities which are substantially different to the activities of other members of the group should not be consolidated

☐ All entity financial statements within a group should normally be prepared to the same accounting year end prior to consolidation

☐ Unrealised profits within the group must be eliminated from the consolidated financial statements **(2 marks)**

2 On 1 October 20X4, Flash Co acquired an item of plant under a five-year lease agreement. Under the terms of the agreement, an immediate deposit of $2 million is payable on inception of the lease and the present value of future lease payments at that date have been calculated as $22,745,000. Annual rentals of $6 million are payable on 30 September each year for five years. The agreement had an implicit rate of interest of 10% per annum.

What is the current liability for the leased plant in Flash Co's statement of financial position as at 30 September 20X5?

$ ☐ **(2 marks)**

3 Quartile Co is in the jewellery retail business which can be assumed to be highly seasonal. For the year ended 30 September 20X5, Quartile Co assessed its operating performance by comparing selected accounting ratios with those of its business sector average as provided by an agency. Assume that the business sector used by the agency is a meaningful representation of Quartile Co's business.

Which **TWO** of the following circumstances may invalidate the comparison of Quartile Co's ratios with those of the sector average?

☐ In the current year, Quartile Co has experienced significant rising costs for its purchases

☐ The sector average figures are compiled from companies whose year ends are between 1 July 20X5 and 30 September 20X5

☐ Quartile Co does not revalue its properties, but is aware that other entities in this sector do

☐ During the year, Quartile Co discovered an error relating to the inventory count at 30 September 20X4. This error was correctly accounted for in the financial statements for the current year ended 30 September 20X5 **(2 marks)**

4 Financial statements represent transactions in words and numbers. To be useful, financial information must represent faithfully these transactions in terms of how they are reported.

Identify, by selecting the relevant box in the table below, whether the statement regarding faithful representation is true or false.

Charging the rental payments for an item of plant to the statement of profit or loss where the rental agreement meets the criteria for a lease and no recognition exemptions are available	**TRUE**	**FALSE**
Including a convertible loan note in equity on the basis that the holders are likely to choose the equity option on conversion	**TRUE**	**FALSE**
Treating redeemable preference shares as part of equity in the statement of financial position	**TRUE**	**FALSE**
Derecognising factored trade receivables sold without recourse to the seller	**TRUE**	**FALSE**

(2 marks)

5 A parent sells goods to its 80% owned subsidiary during the financial year, some of which remains in inventory at the year end.

Using the drag and drop options below, select the correct adjustment required in the consolidated statement of financial position to eliminate any unrealised profit in inventory?

Group retained earnings		Credit
Inventory		Debit
Non-controlling interest		

(2 marks)

6 Which of the following criticisms does **NOT** apply to historical cost financial statements during a period of rising prices?

- O They are difficult to verify because transactions could have happened many years ago
- O They contain mixed values; some items are at current values and some are at out of date values
- O They understate assets and overstate profit
- O They overstate gearing in the statement of financial position **(2 marks)**

7 On 1 October 20X4, Kalatra Co commenced drilling for oil from an undersea oilfield. Kalatra Co is required to dismantle the drilling equipment at the end of its five-year licence. This has an estimated cost of $30m on 30 September 20X9. Kalatra Co's cost of capital is 8% per annum and $1 in five years' time has a present value of 68 cents.

What is the provision which Kalatra Co would report in its statement of financial position as at 30 September 20X5 in respect of its oil operations?

- O $32,400,000
- O $22,032,000
- O $20,400,000
- O $1,632,000 **(2 marks)**

8 When a parent is evaluating the assets of a potential subsidiary, certain intangible assets can be recognised separately from goodwill, even though they have not been recognised in the subsidiary's own statement of financial position.

Which of the following is an example of an intangible asset of the subsidiary which may be recognised separately from goodwill when preparing consolidated financial statements?

- O A new research project which the subsidiary has correctly expensed to profit or loss but the directors of the parent have reliably assessed to have a substantial fair value
- O A global advertising campaign which was concluded in the previous financial year and from which benefits are expected to flow in the future
- O A contingent asset of the subsidiary from which the parent believes a flow of future economic benefits is possible
- O A customer list which the directors are unable to value reliably **(2 marks)**

9 On 1 October 20X4, Pyramid Co acquired 80% of Square Co's 9 million equity shares. At the date of acquisition, Square Co had an item of plant which had a fair value of \$3 million in excess of its carrying amount. At the date of acquisition it had a useful life of five years. Pyramid Co's policy is to value non-controlling interests at fair value at the date of acquisition. For this purpose, Square Co's shares had a value of \$3.50 each at that date. In the year ended 30 September 20X5, Square Co reported a profit of \$8 million.

Using the pull-down list provided, identify the amount at which the non-controlling interests in Square Co should be valued in the consolidated statement of financial position of the Pyramid group as at 30 September 20X5?

[▼]

Pull down list

- \$12,220,000
- \$26,680,000
- \$7,780,000
- \$7,900,000

(2 marks)

10 Caddy Co acquired 240,000 of Ambel Co's 800,000 equity shares for \$6 per share on 1 October 20X4. Ambel Co's profit for the year ended 30 September 20X5 was \$400,000 and it paid an equity dividend on 20 September 20X5 of \$150,000.

On the assumption that Ambel Co is an associate of Caddy Co, what would be the carrying amount of the investment in Ambel Co in the consolidated statement of financial position of Caddy Co as at 30 September 20X5?

- O \$1,560,000
- O \$1,395,000
- O \$1,515,000
- O \$1,690,000 **(2 marks)**

11 Identify whether the following costs should or should not be capitalised in the initial carrying amount of an item of plant.

Cost of a three-year plant maintenance agreement		The initial carrying amount of plant should include (1)
Cost of installing a new power supply required to operate the plant		The initial carrying amount of plant should include (2)
Cost of transporting the plant to the factory		The initial carrying amount of plant should NOT include (1)
Cost of a three-week training course for staff to operate the plant		The initial carrying amount of plant should NOT include (2)

(2 marks)

12 When a single entity makes purchases or sales in a foreign currency, it will be necessary to translate the transactions into its functional currency before the transactions can be included in its financial records.

In accordance with IAS 21 *The Effect of Changes in Foreign Currency Exchange Rates*, which **TWO** of the following foreign currency exchange rates may be used to translate the foreign currency purchases and sales?

☐ The rate that existed on the day that the purchase or sale took place

☐ The rate that existed at the beginning of the accounting period

☐ An average rate for the year, provided there have been no significant fluctuations throughout the year

☐ The rate that existed at the end of the accounting period **(2 marks)**

13 Fork Co owns an 80% investment in Spoon Co which it purchased several years ago. The goodwill on acquisition was valued at $1,674,000 and there has been no impairment of that goodwill since the date of acquisition.

On 30 September 20X4, Fork Co disposed of its entire investment in Spoon Co, details of which are as follows:

	$'000
Sales proceeds of Fork Co's entire investment in Spoon Co	5,580
Cost of Fork Co's entire investment in Spoon Co	3,720

Immediately before the disposal, the consolidated financial statements of Fork Co included the following amounts in respect of Spoon Co:

	$'000
Carrying amount of the net assets (excluding goodwill)	4,464
Carrying amount of the non-controlling interests	900

What is the profit on disposal (before tax) which will be recorded in Fork Co's CONSOLIDATED statement of profit or loss for the year ended 30 September 20X4 (in whole $)?

$ [ ] **(2 marks)**

14 On 1 October 20X4, Hoy Co had $2.5 million of equity share capital (shares of 50 cents each) in issue.

No new shares were issued during the year ended 30 September 20X5, but on that date there were outstanding share options which had a dilutive effect equivalent to issuing 1.2 million shares for no consideration.

Hoy's profit after tax for the year ended 30 September 20X5 was $1,550,000.

In accordance with IAS 33 *Earnings per Share*, what is Hoy's diluted earnings per share for the year ended 30 September 20X5?

- O $0.25
- O $0.41
- O $0.31
- O $0.42

(2 marks)

15 The following information has been taken or calculated from Fowler Co's financial statements for the year ended 30 September 20X5:

Cash cycle at 30 September 20X5	70 days
Inventory turnover	six times
Year-end trade payables at 30 September 20X5	$230,000
Credit purchases for the year ended 30 September 20X5	$2,000,000
Cost of sales for the year ended 30 September 20X5	$1,800,000

Complete the following table, using the tokens provided, in order to reflect Fowler Co's cash cycle at 30 September 20X5.

Add / subtract		Days
▼	Inventory turnover days	▼
▼	Receivables collection period	▼
	Trade payables period	▼
	Fowler Co's cash cycle at 30 September 20X5	= 70 days

Pull down list

- 42 days
- 51 days
- 61 days
- 89 days
- Add
- Subtract

(2 marks)

Section B

ALL 15 questions are compulsory and MUST be attempted

Telepath Co

The following scenario relates to questions 16–20.

Telepath Co has a year end of 30 September and owns an item of plant which it uses to produce and package pharmaceuticals. The plant cost $750,000 on 1 October 20X0, and at that date, had an estimated useful life of five years. A review of the plant on 1 April 20X3 concluded that the plant would last for a further three and a half years and that its fair value was $560,000.

Telepath Co adopts the policy of revaluing its non-current assets to their fair value but does not make an annual transfer from the revaluation surplus to retained earnings to represent the additional depreciation charged due to the revaluation.

On 30 September 20X3, Telepath Co was informed by a major customer that it would no longer be placing orders with Telepath Co. As a result, Telepath revised its estimates that net cash inflows earned from the plant for the next three years would be:

Year ended 30 September	$
20X4	220,000
20X5	180,000
20X6	200,000

Telepath Co's cost of capital is 10% which results in the following discount factors:

Value of $1 at 30 September	$
20X4	0.91
20X5	0.83
20X6	0.75

Telepath Co also owns Rilda Co, a 100% subsidiary, which is treated as a cash-generating unit. On 30 September 20X3, there was an impairment to Rilda's assets of $3,500,000. The carrying amount of the assets of Rilda Co immediately before the impairment were:

	$
Goodwill	2,000,000
Factory building	4,000,000
Plant	3,500,000
Receivables and cash (at recoverable amount)	2,500,000
	12,000,000

16 Use the options below to complete the following definition in accordance with IAS 36 *Impairment of Assets*.

An asset is impaired when its [▼] is [▼] than its recoverable amount. The recoverable amount of an asset is defined as the higher of its fair value less costs of disposal and its [▼].

BPP

Pull down list

- Carrying amount
- Greater
- Historical cost
- Less
- Replacement cost
- Value in use

(2 marks)

---

17 Prior to considering any impairment, what is the carrying amount of Telepath Co's plant and the balance on the revaluation surplus at 30 September 20X3?

	Plant carrying amount	Revaluation surplus
	$'000	**$'000**
O	480	Nil
O	300	185
O	480	185
O	300	Nil

(2 marks)

---

18 Calculate the value in use of Telepath Co's plant as at 30 September 20X3 (in whole $).

$ [ ] **(2 marks)**

---

19 Which of the following are **TRUE** in accordance with IAS 36 *Impairment of Assets*?

(1) A cash-generating unit is the smallest identifiable group of assets for which individual cash flows can be identified and measured

(2) When considering the impairment of a cash-generating unit, the calculation of the carrying amount and the recoverable amount does not need to be based on exactly the same group of net assets

(3) When it is not possible to calculate the recoverable amount of a single asset, then that of its cash-generating unit should be measured instead

O (1) only

O (2) and (3)

O (3) only

O (1) and (3) **(2 marks)**

---

20 Calculate the carrying amount of Rilda Co's plant at 30 September 20X3 after the impairment loss has been correctly allocated to its assets (in whole $).

$ [ ] **(2 marks)**

(Total = 10 marks)

Neutron Co

The following scenario relates to questions 21–25.

At a board meeting in June 20X3, Neutron Co's directors made the decision to close down one of its factories by 30 September 20X3 and market both the building and the plant for sale. The decision had been made public, was communicated to all affected parties and was fully implemented by 30 September 20X3.

The directors of Neutron Co have provided the following information relating to the closure:

(1) Of the factory's 250 employees, 50 will be retrained and deployed to other subsidiaries within the Neutron group during the year ended 30 September 20X4 at a cost of $125,000. The remainder accepted redundancy at an average cost of $5,000 each.

(2) The factory's plant had a carrying amount of $2.2 million, but is only expected to sell for $500,000, incurring $50,000 of selling costs. The factory itself is expected to sell for a profit of $1.2 million.

(3) The company also rented a number of machines in the factory under short-term leases which have an average of three months to run after 30 September 20X3. The present value of these future lease payments at 30 September 20X3 was $1 million, however, the lessor has stated that they will accept $850,000 if paid on 30 October 20X3 as a full settlement.

(4) Penalty payments, due to the non-completion of supply contracts, are estimated to be $200,000, 50% of which is expected to be recovered from Neutron Co's insurers.

21 Which **TWO** of the following are required if an operation is to be classified as a discontinued operation in accordance with IFRS 5 *Non-current Assets Held for Sale and Discontinued Operations*?

- ☐ The operation represents a separate major line of business or geographical area
- ☐ The operation is a subsidiary
- ☐ The operation has been sold or is held for sale
- ☐ The operation is considered not to be capable of making a future profit following a period of losses **(2 marks)**

---

22 IFRS 5 *Non-current Assets Held for Sale and Discontinued Operations* prescribes the recognition criteria for non-current assets held for sale. For an asset or a disposal group to be classified as held for sale, the sale must be highly probable.

Which **TWO** of the following must apply for the sale to be considered highly probable?

- ☐ A buyer must have been located
- ☐ The asset must be marketed at a reasonable price
- ☐ Management must be committed to a plan to sell the asset
- ☐ The sale must be expected to take place within the next six months **(2 marks)**

---

23 Calculate the employee cost associated with the closure and sale of Neutron Co's factory which should be charged to profit or loss for the year ended 30 September 20X3 (in whole $).

$ ☐ **(2 marks)**

---

24 What is the profit or loss on discontinued operations relating to property, plant and equipment for the year ended 30 September 20X3?

- O $1.75 million loss

- O $1.75 million profit
- O $550,000 loss
- O $550,000 profit **(2 marks)**

---

25 In respect of the leases and penalty payments, what provision is required in the statement of financial position of Neutron Co as at 30 September 20X3?

- O $950,000
- O $1,200,000
- O $1,050,000
- O $1,100,000 **(2 marks)**

(Total = 10 marks)

Speculate Co

The following scenario relates to questions 26–30.

Speculate Co is preparing its financial statements for the year ended 30 September 20X3. The following issues are relevant:

(1) Financial assets

Shareholding A – a long-term investment in 10,000 of the equity shares of another company. These shares were acquired on 1 October 20X2 at a cost of $3.50 each. Transaction costs of 1% of the purchase price were incurred. On 30 September 20X3 the fair value of these shares is $4.50 each.

Shareholding B – a short-term speculative investment in 2,000 of the equity shares of another company. These shares were acquired on 1 December 20X2 at a cost of $2.50 each. Transaction costs of 1% of the purchase price were incurred. On 30 September 20X3 the fair value of these shares is $3.00 each.

Where possible, Speculate Co makes an irrevocable election for the fair value movements on financial assets to be reported in other comprehensive income.

(2) Taxation

The existing debit balance on the current tax account of $2.4 million represents the over/under provision of the tax liability for the year ended 30 September 20X2. A provision of $28 million is required for income tax for the year ended 30 September 20X3. The existing credit balance on the deferred tax account is $2.5 million and the provision required at 30 September 20X3 is $4.4 million.

(3) Revenue

On 1 October 20X2, Speculate Co sold one of its products for $10 million. As part of the sale agreement, Speculate Co is committed to the ongoing servicing of the product until 30 September 20X5 (ie three years after the sale). The sale value of this service has been included in the selling price of $10 million. The estimated cost to Speculate Co of the servicing is $600,000 per annum and Speculate Co's gross profit margin on this type of servicing is 25%. Ignore discounting.

26 Match the financial instrument to its appropriate classification in accordance with IFRS 9 *Financial Instruments*.

Financial instrument		Classification
A contract to exchange financial instruments with another entity under conditions that are potentially unfavourable		A financial liability
Cash		An equity instrument
An equity instrument of another entity		A financial asset
A contract that evidences the residual interest in the assets of an entity after deducting all of its liabilities		A financial asset

(2 marks)

---

27 In respect of the financial assets of Speculate Co, what amount will be included in other comprehensive income for the year ended 30 September 20X3.

- O Nil
- O $9,650
- O $10,000
- O $10,650

(2 marks)

---

28 Calculate the total amount which will be charged to the statement of profit or loss for the year ended 30 September 20X3 in respect of taxation.

$ [ ]

(2 marks)

---

29 What is the amount of deferred income which Speculate Co should recognise in its statement of financial position as at 30 September 20X3 relating to the contract for the supply and servicing of products?

- O $1.2 million
- O $1.6 million
- O $600,000
- O $1.5 million

(2 marks)

30 Which **TWO** of the following are **TRUE** in respect of the income which Speculate Co has deferred at 30 September 20X3?

- ☐ The deferred income will be split evenly between the current and non-current liabilities in Speculate Co's statement of financial position as at 30 September 20X3
- ☐ The costs associated with the deferred income of Speculate Co should be recognised in the statement of profit or loss at the same time as the revenue is recognised
- ☐ The deferred income can only be recognised as revenue by Speculate Co when there is a signed written contract of service with its customer
- ☐ When recognising the revenue associated with the service contract of Speculate Co, the stage of its completion is irrelevant **(2 marks)**

(Total = 10 marks)

Section C

Both questions are compulsory and MUST be attempted

31 Kandy Co

After preparing a draft statement of profit or loss for the year ended 30 September 20X5 and adding the current year's draft profit (before any adjustments required by Notes (1) to (3) below) to retained earnings, the summarised trial balance of Kandy Co as at 30 September 20X5 is:

	$'000	$'000
Equity shares of $1 each		20,000
Retained earnings as at 30 September 20X5		15,500
Proceeds of 6% loan note (Note (1))		30,000
Investment properties at fair value (Note (2))	20,000	
Land ($5 million) and buildings – at cost (Note (2))	35,000	
Plant and equipment – at cost (Note (2))	58,500	
Accumulated depreciation at 1 October 20X4: buildings		20,000
plant and equipment		34,500
Current assets	68,700	
Current liabilities		43,400
Deferred tax (Notes (2) and (3))		2,500
Interest paid (Note (1))	1,800	
Current tax (Note (3))		1,100
Suspense account (Note (2))	–	17,000
	184,000	184,000

The following notes are relevant:

(1) The loan note was issued on 1 October 20X4 and incurred issue costs of $1 million which were charged to profit or loss. Interest of $1.8 million ($30 million at 6%) was paid on 30 September 20X5. The loan is redeemable on 30 September 20X9 at a substantial premium which gives an effective interest rate of 9% per annum. No other repayments are due until 30 September 20X9.

(2) Non-current assets:

On 1 October 20X4, Kandy owned two investment properties. The first property had a carrying amount of $15 million and was sold on 1 December 20X4 for $17 million. The disposal proceeds have been credited to a suspense account in the trial balance above. On 31 December 20X4, the second property became owner occupied and so was transferred to land and buildings at its fair value of $6 million. Its remaining useful life on 31 December 20X4 was considered to be 20 years. Ignore any deferred tax implications of this fair value.

The price of property has increased significantly in recent years and so the directors decided to revalue the land and buildings. The directors accepted the report of an independent surveyor who, on 1 October 20X4, valued the land at $8 million and the buildings at $39 million on that date. This revaluation specifically excludes the transferred investment property described above. The remaining life of these buildings at 1 October 20X4 was 15 years. Kandy does not make an annual transfer to retained profits to reflect the realisation of the revaluation gain; however, the revaluation will give rise to a deferred tax liability. The income tax rate applicable to Kandy is 20%.

Plant and equipment is depreciated at 12.5% per annum using the reducing balance method.

No depreciation has yet been charged on any non-current asset for the year ended 30 September 20X5.

(3) A provision of $2.4 million is required for income tax on the profit for the year to 30 September 20X5. The balance on current tax in the trial balance is the under/over provision of tax for the previous year. In addition to the temporary differences relating to the information in note (ii), Kandy has further taxable temporary differences of $10 million as at 30 September 20X5.

Required

(a) Prepare a schedule of adjustments required to the retained earnings of Kandy Co as at 30 September 20X5 as a result of the information in Notes (1) to (3) above. **(8 marks)**

(b) Prepare the statement of financial position of Kandy Co as at 30 September 20X5.

Note. The notes to the statement of financial position are not required. **(9 marks)**

(c) Prepare the extracts from Kandy Co's statement of cash flows for operating and investing activities for the year ended 30 September 20X5 which relate to property, plant and equipment. **(3 marks)**

(Total = 20 marks)

32 Tangier group

The summarised consolidated financial statements for the year ended 30 September 20X5 (and the comparative figures) for the Tangier group are shown below.

Consolidated statements of profit or loss for the year ended 30 September

	20X5	20X4
	$m	$m
Revenue	2,700	1,820
Cost of sales	(1,890)	(1,092)
Gross profit	810	728
Administrative expense	(345)	(200)
Distribution costs	(230)	(130)
Finance costs	(40)	(5)
Profit before taxation	195	393
Income tax expense	(60)	(113)
Profit for the year	135	280

Consolidated statements of financial position as at 30 September

	20X5	20X5	20X4	20X4
	$m	$m	$m	$m
Non-current assets				
Property, plant and equipment		680		310
Intangible asset: manufacturing licences		300		100
Goodwill		230		200
		1,210		610

	20X5	20X5	20X4	20X4
	$m	$m	$m	$m
Current assets				
Inventory	200		110	
Trade receivables	195		75	
Bank	–	395	120	305
Total assets		1,605		915
Equity shares of $1 each		330		250
Other components of equity		100		–
Retained earnings		375		295
		805		545
Non-current liabilities				
5% secured loan notes	100		100	
10% secured loan notes	300	400	–	100
Current liabilities				
Bank overdraft	110		–	
Trade payables	210		160	
Current tax payable	80	400	110	270
Total equity and liabilities		1,605		915

At 1 October 20X4, the Tangier group consisted of the parent, Tangier Co, and two wholly owned subsidiaries which had been owned for many years. On 1 January 20X5, Tangier Co purchased a third 100% owned investment in a subsidiary called Raremetal Co. The consideration paid for Raremetal Co was a combination of cash and shares. The cash payment was partly funded by the issue of 10% loan notes. On 1 January 20X5, Tangier Co also won a tender for a new contract to supply aircraft engines which Tangier Co manufactures under a recently acquired long-term licence. Raremetal Co was purchased with a view to securing the supply of specialised materials used in the manufacture of these engines. The bidding process had been very competitive and Tangier Co had to increase its manufacturing capacity to fulfil the contract.

Required

(a) Comment on how the new contract and the purchase of Raremetal Co may have affected the comparability of the consolidated financial statements of Tangier Co for the years ended 30 September 20X4 and 20X5. **(5 marks)**

(b) Calculate appropriate ratios and comment on Tangier Co's profitability and gearing. Your analysis should identify instances where the new contract and the purchase of Raremetal Co have limited the usefulness of the ratios and your analysis.

Note. Your ratios should be based on the consolidated financial statements provided and you should not attempt to adjust for the effects of the new contract or the consolidation. Working capital and liquidity ratios are not required. There are up to 5 marks available for the ratio calculations. **(12 marks)**

(c) Explain what further information you might require to make your analysis more meaningful. **(3 marks)**

(Total = 20 marks)

Answers

DO NOT TURN THIS PAGE UNTIL YOU HAVE COMPLETED THE MOCK EXAM

A plan of attack

It is important to have a plan for how you will tackle the exam so you can go into the exam feeling confident that you know what you are doing and how you are going to apply your exam technique.

First things first

You have three hours for this exam. This exam is the examining team's specimen exam, so it is a good indication of what you will see in your exam. Read it carefully.

The Financial Reporting exam has 15 2-mark questions in Section A, 15 2-mark questions in Section B and two long-form questions in Section C. All questions are compulsory. Therefore, you do not have to spend time working out which questions to answer.

It's a good idea to just start with the Section A questions. Once you have them done, you will feel more relaxed. Leave any that you are unsure of and come back to them later but don't leave any unanswered.

Section B: Questions 16–20 are on non-current assets. Questions 21–25 are on discontinued operations. Questions 26–30 cover three issues – financial assets, taxation and revenue. For each of these Section B questions, make sure you read the scenario carefully.

Question 31 requires you to adjust retained earnings and prepare a statement of financial position and some cash flow extracts. In the exam, you would answer this requirement in the spreadsheet response option. Make sure you access the ACCA CBE practice platform in advance of the exam to ensure you understand how to use the software. You should practice some questions using the software in order to establish your exam technique. There is nothing difficult in Question 31, but you need to work methodically.

Question 32 is an interpretation question. Remember that you do not get marks for simply saying that a ratio has improved or deteriorated, nor for explaining what a ratio shows. You must explain the movements using the information provided in the scenario. In the exam, you would answer this requirement using the word processing response option. Ensure you know how to enter a table into the word processing response option (for ratios) and how to do basic formatting of the text.

You've got spare time at the end of the exam...?

If you have allocated your time properly, then you shouldn't have time on your hands at the end of the exam and you should start by checking the Section A questions to make sure you have left none unanswered as there is no negative marking and therefore nothing to lose from taking an educated guess. But if you find yourself with five or ten minutes to spare, check over your work to make sure that there are no silly arithmetical errors.

Forget about it!

And don't worry if you found the exam difficult. More than likely, other candidates will too. If this were the real thing, you would need to forget the exam the minute you leave the exam hall and think about the next one. Or, if it's the last one, celebrate!

Section A

ALL 15 questions are compulsory and MUST be attempted

1 The correct answers are:

- All entity financial statements within a group should normally be prepared to the same accounting year end prior to consolidation
- Unrealised profits within the group must be eliminated from the consolidated financial statements

Adjustments will be made on consolidation for different accounting policies. Subsidiaries with dissimilar activities are still consolidated.

2 $ 4,098,050

Year	Opening	Interest @ 10%	Payment	Closing
	$	$	$	$
30 Sept X5	22,745,000	2,274,500	(6,000,000)	19,019,500
30 Sept X6	19,019,500	1,901,950	(6,000,000)	14,921,450
			Current	4,098,050

3 The correct answers are:

- The sector average figures are compiled from companies whose year ends are between 1 July 20X5 and 30 September 20X5
- Quartile Co does not revalue its properties, but is aware that other entities in this sector do

Rising costs will have affected all of the business sector and the inventory adjustment will have been corrected in the prior year, so no actual effect in 20X5.

4 The correct answers are:

Charging the rental payments for an item of plant to the statement of profit or loss where the rental agreement meets the criteria for a lease and no recognition exemptions are available		**FALSE**
Including a convertible loan note in equity on the basis that the holders are likely to choose the equity option on conversion		**FALSE**
Treating redeemable preference shares as part of equity in the statement of financial position		**FALSE**
Derecognising factored trade receivables sold without recourse to the seller	**TRUE**	

Trade receivables factored without recourse are no longer an asset of the seller and therefore the statement is true. The other statements are all false.

5 The correct answers are:

Inventory	Credit
Group retained earnings	Debit

As the sale is made by the parent, there is no charge against non-controlling interest.

6 The correct answer is: They are difficult to verify because transactions could have happened many years ago

Historical cost transactions are easy to verify because there will be a record of the transaction.

7 The correct answer is: $22,032,000

Dismantling provision at 1 October 20X4 is $20.4 million (30,000 × 0.68) discounted

This will increase by an 8% finance cost by 30 September 20X5 = $22,032,000

8 The correct answer is: A new research project which the subsidiary has correctly expensed to profit or loss but the directors of the parent have reliably assessed to have a substantial fair value

The research project only as the customer list cannot be reliably valued. The advertising campaign cannot be capitalised and contingent assets are not recognised.

9 $7,780,000

	$'000
FV NCI at 1 October 14 (9000 × 20% × $3.50)	6,300
Post-acquisition profit (8000 – (3000/5)) = 7,400 at 20%	1,480
	7,780

10 The correct answer is: $1,515,000

	$'000
Cost (240,000 × $6)	1,440
Share of associate's profit (400 × 240/800)	120
Less dividend received (150 × 240/800)	(45)
	1,515

11 The correct answers are:

Cost of installing a new power supply required to operate the plant	The initial carrying amount of plant should include (1)
Cost of transporting the plant to the factory	The initial carrying amount of plant should include (2)
Cost of a three-year plant maintenance agreement	The initial carrying amount of plant should NOT include (1)
Cost of a three-week training course for staff to operate the plant	The initial carrying amount of plant should NOT include (2)

12 The correct answers are:

- The rate that existed on the day that the purchase or sale took place
- The rate that existed at the end of the accounting period

13 $ 342,000

	$'000	$'000
Sales proceeds		5,580
Net assets at disposal	4,464	

	$'000	$'000
Goodwill at disposal	1,674	
Less: carrying amount of NCI	(900)	(5,238)
		342

14 The correct answer is: $0.25

(1,550/(2,500 × 2 + 1,200)) = $0.25

15

Add / subtract		Days
Add	Inventory turnover days	61 days
Subtract	Receivables collection period	51 days
	Trade payables period	42 days
	Fowler Co's cash cycle at 30 September 20X5	= 70 days

Inventory turnover is 61 days (365/6)

Trade payables period is 42 days (230,000 × 365/2)

Therefore, receivables collection period is 51 days (70 – 61 + 42)

Section B

ALL 15 questions are compulsory and MUST be attempted

Telepath Co

16 An asset is impaired when its [carrying amount] is [greater] than its recoverable amount. The recoverable amount of an asset is defined as the higher of its fair value less costs of disposal and its [value in use].

17 The correct answer is:

Plant carrying amount	Revaluation surplus
$'000	$'000
480	185

Annual depreciation prior to the revaluation is $150,000 (750/5). At the date of revaluation (1 April 20X3), the carrying amount is $375,000 (750 – (150 × 2.5 yrs)). Revalued to $560,000 with a remaining life of 3.5 years results in a depreciation charge of $160,000 per annum which means $80,000 for six months. The carrying amount at 30 September 20X3 is therefore $480,000 (560 – 80).

Alternative calculation: $560,000 – ($560,000/3.5 × 6/12) = $480,000.

The revaluation surplus has a balance of $185,000 (560,000 – 375,000).

18 $ [499,600]

	Cash flow	Discount factor at 10%	Present value
	$'000		$'000
Year ended: 30 September 20X4	220	0.91	200.2
30 September 20X5	180	0.83	149.4
30 September 20X6	200	0.75	150.0
			499.6

19 The correct answer is: (1) and (3)

The assets of the CGU must remain the same when calculating impairment.

20 $ [2,800,000]

	Carrying amount before	Impairment loss	Carrying amount after
	$'000	$'000	$'000
Goodwill	2,000	2,000	–
Property	4,000	800	3,200
Plant	3,500	700	2,800
Cash and receivables	2,500	–	2,500
	12,000	3,500	8,500

Neutron Co

21 The correct answers are:

- The operation represents a separate major line of business or geographical area
- The operation has been sold or is held for sale

The operation does not have to be a subsidiary. Future profit forecasts are not relevant.

22 The correct answers are:

- The asset must be marketed at a reasonable price
- Management must be committed to a plan to sell the asset

A buyer does not need to have been specifically located

The sale must be expected to take place within the next 12 months.

23 $ 1,000,000

200 employees at $5,000 = $1,000,000 redundancy costs. The retraining costs are a future cost.

24 The correct answer is: $1.75 million loss

Impairment loss on plant is $1,750,000 (2,200,000 – (500,000 – 50,000)).

25 The correct answer is: $1,050,000

Onerous contract $850,000 + penalty payments $200,000 = $1,050,000.

The possible insurance receipt should be ignored as there is no certainty that it would be received and it would not be netted off against the provision anyway.

Speculate Co

26 The correct answers are:

Financial instrument	Classification
A contract to exchange financial instruments with another entity under conditions that are potentially unfavourable	A financial liability
A contract that evidences the residual interest in the assets of an entity after deducting all of its liabilities	An equity instrument
Cash	A financial asset
An equity instrument of another entity	A financial asset

27 The correct answer is: $9,650

Shareholding A is not held for trading as an election made – FVTOCI.

Shareholding B is held for trading and so FVTPL (transaction costs are not included in carrying amount).

Cost of shareholding A is 10,000 × $3.50 × 1.01 = $35,350.

FV at 30 September 20X3 10,000 × $4.50 = $45,000.

Gain = 45,000 – 35,350 = $9,650.

28 $ 32,300

	$'000
DT provision required at 30 September 20X3	4,400
DT Provision at 1 October 20X2	(2,500)
	1,900
Write off of the under provision for the year ended 30 September 20X2	2,400
Income tax for the year ended 30 September 20X3	28,000
Charge for the year ended 30 September 20X3	32,300

29 The correct answer is: $1.6 million

At 30 September 20X3, there are two more years of servicing work, thus $1.6 million ((600,000 × 2) × 100/75) must be treated as deferred income.

30 The correct answers are:

- The deferred income will be split evenly between the current and non-current liabilities in Speculate Co's statement of financial position as at 30 September 20X3
- The costs associated with the deferred income of Speculate Co should be recognised in the statement of profit or loss at the same time as the revenue is recognised

A written service contract is not needed, but the stage of completion is important in recognising revenue.

Section C

Both questions are compulsory and MUST be attempted

31 Kandy Co

Marking guide	Marks	
(a) Schedule of retained earnings as at 30 September 20X4		
Retained earnings per trial balance	0.5	
Issue costs	1	
Loan finance costs	1	
Gains on investment properties	1	
Depreciation charges	3	
Income tax expense	1.5	
		8
(b) Statement of financial position		
Property, plant and equipment	2	
Current assets	0.5	
Equity shares	0.5	
Revaluation surplus	2	
Deferred tax	1	
6% loan note	1.5	
Current liabilities (per trial balance)	0.5	
Current tax payable	1	
		9
(c) Extracts from the statement of cash flows		
Cash flows from operating activities:		
Add back depreciation	1	
Less gain on revaluation of investment property	0.5	
Less gain on disposal of investment property	0.5	
Cash flows from investing activities:		
Investment property disposal proceeds	1	
		3
Total		20

(a)

Schedule of retained earnings of Kandy as at 30 September 20X5

	$'000
Retained earnings per trial balance	15,500
Adjustments re:	
Note (1)	
Add back issue costs of loan note (W1)	1,000
Loan finance costs (29,000 × 9%) (W1)	(2,610)

	$'000
Note (2)	
Gain on disposal of investment property (17,000 – 15,000)	2,000
Gain on revaluation of investment property prior to transfer (6,000 – 5,000)	1,000
Depreciation of buildings (W2)	(2,825)
Depreciation of plant and equipment (W2)	(3,000)
Note (3)	
Income tax expense (W3)	(800)
Adjusted retained earnings	10,265

You would use the spreadsheet response option to answer this question in the CBE exam. When using the spreadsheet software, it is essential that you show your workings. You can do so by either using formula within the cells or by setting out your workings on the face of your answer. Below is an extract from the spreadsheet software showing how your answer may be presented:

Spreadsheet

Edit Format

100% | 11

C6 =-29000*0.09

	A	B	C	D	E	F	G	H
1	(a) Adjustment to retained earnings					W1 Building depreciation		
2			$0			Depreciation on buildings		2600
3	RE per TB		15500			Depreciation on IP transferred		225
4	Adjustments:							2825
5	Add issue costs of loan		1000					
6	Less Finance costs		-2610			P&E depreciation		
7	Add Gain on disposal		2000			CA per TB		24000
8	Add Gain on FV adjustment		1000			Depreciation RB basis		3000
9	Less Building depreciation (W1)		-2825					
10	Less P&E depreciation		-3000			Income tax		

C6	=-29000*0.09							
	A	B	C	D	E	F	G	H
	(W2)							
11	Less Income tax (W)		-800			Provision for current yr		2400
12			10265			Less overprovision		-1100
13						DT		-500
14								800

You should note the following:

- The answer is set out clearly with brief descriptions given to explain the adjustments made
- Simple calculations such as that shown in the highlighted cell C6 can be performed using formula within the cell.
- More complex workings such as the depreciation and income tax calculations should be set out separate workings with the total included in the main answer by entering the formula =H14 in cell C11
- Subtotals and totals should be included using the sum function, for example in cell C12, the formula =SUM(C3:C11) should be used

(b)

Statement of financial position as at 30 September 20X5

	$'000	$'000
Assets		
Non-current assets		
Property, plant and equipment (50,175 + 21,000 (W2))		71,175
Current assets (per trial balance)		68,700
Total assets		139,875
Equity and liabilities		
Equity		
Equity shares of $1 each		20,000
Revaluation surplus (32,000 – 6,400 (W2) and (W3))	25,600	
Retained earnings (from (a))	10,265	35,865
		55,865
Non-current liabilities		
Deferred tax (W3)	8,400	
6% loan note (W1)	29,810	38,210
Current liabilities		
Per trial balance	43,400	
Current tax payable	2,400	45,800

	$'000	$'000
Total equity and liabilities		139,875

In the Workings below, monetary figures in brackets are in $'000.

Workings

1 ***Loan notes***

The issue costs should be deducted from the proceeds of the loan note and not charged as an expense. The finance cost of the loan note, at the effective rate of 9% applied to the carrying amount of the loan note of $29 million (30,000 – 1,000), is $2,610,000. The interest actually paid is $1.8 million. The difference between these amounts of $810,000 (2,610 – 1,800) is added to the carrying amount of the loan note to give $29,810,000 (29,000 + 810) for inclusion as a non-current liability in the statement of financial position.

2 ***Non-current assets***

Land and buildings

The gain on revaluation and carrying amount of the land and buildings will be:

	$'000
Carrying amount at 1 October 20X4 (35,000 – 20,000)	15,000
Revaluation at that date (8,000 + 39,000)	47,000
Gain on revaluation	32,000
Buildings depreciation for the year ended 30 September 20X5:	
Land and buildings existing at 1 October 20X4 (39,000/15 years)	2,600
Transferred investment property (6,000/20 × 9/12)	225
	2,825
Carrying amount at 30 September 20X5 (47,000 + 6,000 – 2,825)	50,175
Plant and equipment	
Carrying amount at 1 October 20X4 (58,500 – 34,500)	24,000
Depreciation for year ended 30 September 20X5 (12.5% reducing balance)	(3,000)
Carrying amount at 30 September 20X5	21,000

3 ***Taxation***

	$'000
Income tax expense	
Provision for year ended 30 September 20X5	2,400
Less over provision in previous year	(1,100)
Deferred tax (see below)	(500)
	800

	$'000
Deferred tax	
Provision required at 30 September 20X5 ((10,000 + 32,000) × 20%)	8,400
Provision at 1 October 20X4	(2,500)

	$'000
Movement in provision	5,900
Charge to revaluation of land and buildings (32,000 × 20%)	(6,400)
Balance – credit to profit or loss	(500)

You would also use the spreadsheet response area to prepare the statement of financial position. The recommended way to do this is to create a proforma statement of financial position, such as that shown below, and then to enter your figures in the relevant cells as you complete your workings.

Spreadsheet

Edit Format

100%

	A	B	C	D	E	F	G	H
24	Kandy Co							
25	Statement of financial position as at 30 September 20X5							
26								
27	Non-current assets							
28	Land and buildings							
29	Plant and equipment							
30	Investment property							
31								
32	Current assets							
33								
34	Equity							
35	Equity shares							
36	Retained earnings							

Remember that you can cross reference to any relevant workings undertaken to arrive at the answers for requirement (a) and do not need to recreate them for inclusion in the statement of financial position. For example, when calculating the carrying amount of plant and equipment, the depreciation for the year has already been calculated and therefore the depreciation can be included in the calculation by referring to the cell in which the depreciation calculation was presented. This can be seen in highlighted cell H30 which refers to another cell containing the calculation.

Highlighted cell C29 cross references to cell H31 which is the total of the plant and equipment working. Cell H31 itself uses the sum formula to arrive at the total.

Spreadsheet

Edit Format

100% ▾

11 ▾

H30	=-H8							
	A	B	C	D	E	F	G	H
24	Kandy Co							
25	Statement of financial position as at 30 September 20X5							
26								
27	Non-current assets						Plant and equipment carrying amount	
28	Land and buildings						Cost per TB	58500
29	Plant and equipment		21000				Acc dep per TB	- 34500
30	Investment property						Depreciation	-3000
31							Carrying amount	21000
32	Current assets							
33								
34	Equity							
35	Equity shares							

(c)

	$'000
Cash flows from operating activities:	
Add back depreciation	5,825
Deduct gain on revaluation of investment property	(1,000)
Deduct gain on disposal of investment property	(2,000)
Cash flows from investing activities:	
Investment property disposal proceeds	17,000

32 Tangier group

Marking guide	Marks
(a) Analysis of results	

A like for like comparison taking account of the consolidation and the contract	5	
		5
(b) Up to 5 marks for ratio calculations	5	
Profitability	4.5	
Gearing and interest cover	2.5	
		12
(c) Additional information		
Any three of the six suggestions provided	3	
		3
Total		20

(a) **Note.** References to '20X5' are in respect of the year ended 30 September 20X5 and '20X4' refers to the year ended 30 September 20X4.

The key matter to note is that the ratios for 20X4 and 20X5 will not be directly comparable because two significant events, the acquisition of Raremetal Co and securing the new contract, have occurred between these dates. This means that the underlying financial statements are not directly comparable. For example, the 20X4 statement of profit or loss (SOPL) will not include the results of Raremetal Co or the effect of the new contract. However, the 20X5 SOPL will contain nine months of the results of Raremetal Co (although intragroup transactions will have been eliminated) and nine months of the effects of the new contract (which may have resulted in either a net profit or loss). Likewise, the 20X4 statement of financial position does not contain any of Raremetal Co's assets and liabilities, whereas that of 20X5 contains all of the net assets of Raremetal Co and the cost of the new licence. This does not mean that comparisons between the two years are not worthwhile, just that they need to be treated with caution. For some ratios, it may be necessary to exclude all of the subsidiaries from the analysis and use the single entity financial statements of Tangier Co as a basis for comparison with the performance of previous years. Similarly, it may still be possible to compare some of the ratios of the Tangier group with those of other groups in the same sector although not all groups will have experienced similar acquisitions.

Assuming there has been no impairment of goodwill, the investment in Raremetal Co has resulted in additional goodwill of $30 million which means that the investment has cost more than the carrying amount of Raremetal Co's net assets. Although there is no indication of the precise cost, it is known to have been achieved by a combination of a share exchange (hence the $180 million new issue of shares) and a cash element (funded from the proceeds of the loan issue and the decrease in the bank balance). Any intragroup sales have been eliminated on consolidation and it is not possible to determine in which individual company any profit on these intragroup sales will be reported; it is therefore difficult to measure any benefits of the investment. Indeed, the benefit of the investment might not be a financial one but merely to secure the supply of raw materials. It would be useful to establish the cost of the investment and the profit (if any) contributed by Raremetal Co so that an assessment of the benefit of the investment might be made.

You would answer Requirement (a) using the word processing response area. You should arrange your answer in paragraphs and could consider using the bullet point list option if you consider it a better way to lay out your answer. Taking the first part of the full answer as an example, you could set out your answer in the word processing response area as follows:

Word Processor

The ratios for 20X4 and 20X5 will not be directly comparable because two significant events: the acquisition of Raremetal Co and securing the new contract. This means that the underlying financial statements are not directly comparable.

For example:

- the 20X4 statement of profit or loss (SOPL) will not include the results of Raremetal Co or the effect of the new contract
- the 20X5 SOPL will contain nine months of the results of Raremetal Co (although intragroup transactions will have been eliminated) and nine months of the effects of the new contract (which may have resulted in either a net profit or loss)
- the 20X4 statement of financial position (SOFP) does not contain any of Raremetal Co's assets and liabilities
- the 20X5 SOFP contains all of the net assets of Raremetal Co and the cost of the new licence.

(b) Relevant ratios

	20X5	20X4
Gross profit margin % (810/2,700 × 100)	30.0%	40.0%
Operating profit margin (235/2,700 × 100)	8.7%	21.9%
ROCE (235/(805 + 400))	19.5%	61.7%
Non-current asset turnover (2,700/1,210)	2.23 times	2.98 times
Debt/equity (400/805)	49.7%	18.3%
Interest cover (235/40)	5.9 times	79.6 times

Although the calculation of ratios is numerical, it is likely that the word processing response area will be provided in the exam to answer the interpretations question. You may be presented with a pre-formatted response area (a blank table), in which case you should use that to structure your answer. If you are not provided with a pre-formatted response area, you can use the table within the word processing response area to set out your calculations. An example is shown below. In the exam, this would be extended to include a row for each ratio.

Word Processor

Ratio	Working	20X5	Working	20X4
Gross profit margin	810/2700 × 100	30%	728/1820 x 100	40%

All of the issues identified in part (a) make a comparison of ratios difficult and, if more information was available, then some adjustments may be required. For example, if it is established that the investment is not generating any benefits, then it might be argued that the inclusion of the goodwill in the ROCE and non-current asset turnover is unjustified (it may be impaired and should be written off). Goodwill has not been excluded from any of the following ratios.

The increase in revenues of 48.4% (880/1,820 × 100) in 20X5 will be partly due to the consolidation of Raremetal Co and the revenues associated with the new contract. Yet, despite these increased revenues, the company has suffered a dramatic fall in its profitability. This has been caused by a combination of a falling gross profit margin (from 40% in 20X4 to only 30% in 20X5) and markedly higher operating overheads (operating profit margin has fallen from 21.9% in 20X4 to 8.7% in 20X5). Again, it is important to note that some of these costs will be attributable to the consolidation of Raremetal Co and some to the new contract. It could be speculated that the 73% increase in administrative expenses may be due to one-off costs associated with the tendering process (consultancy fees, etc) and the acquisition of Raremetal Co and the 77% increase in higher distribution costs could be due to additional freight, packing and insurance cost of the engines, delivery distances may also be longer – even to foreign countries (although some of the increase in distribution costs may also be due to consolidation).

This is all reflected in the ROCE falling from an impressive 61.7% in 20X4 to only 19.5% in 20X5 (though even this figure is respectable). The fall in the ROCE is attributable to a dramatic fall in profit margin at operating level (from 21.9% in 20X4 to only 8.7% in 20X5) which has been compounded by a reduction in the non-current asset turnover, with only $2·23 being generated from every $1 invested in non-current assets in 20X5 (from $2.98 in 20X4).

The information in the question points strongly to the possibility (even probability) that the new contract may be responsible for much of the deterioration in Tangier Co's operating performance. For example, it is likely that the new contract may account for some of the increased revenue; however, the bidding process was 'very competitive' which may imply that Tangier Co had to cut its prices (and therefore its profit margin) in order to win the contract.

The costs of fulfilling the contract have also been heavy: investment in property, plant and equipment has increased by $370 million (at carrying amount), representing an increase of 61% (no doubt some of this increase will be due to the acquisition of Raremetal Co). The increase in licence costs to manufacture the new engines has cost $200 million plus any amortisation and there is also the additional goodwill of $30 million.

An eight-fold increase in finance cost caused by the increased borrowing at double the interest rate of the borrowing in 20X4 and (presumably) some overdraft interest has led to the dramatic fall in the company's interest cover (from 79.6 in 20X4 to only 5.9 in 20X5). The finance cost of the new $300 million 10% loan notes to partly fund the investment in Raremetal Co and other non-current assets has also increased debt/equity (one form of gearing measure) from 18.3% in 20X4 to 49.7% in 20X5 despite also issuing $180 million in new equity shares. At this level, particularly in view of its large increase from 20X4, it may give debt holders (and others) cause for concern as there is increased risk for all Tangier Co's lenders. If it could be demonstrated that the overdraft could not be cleared for some time, this would be an argument for including it in the calculation of debt/equity, making the 20X5 gearing level even worse. It is also apparent from the movement in the retained earnings that Tangier Co paid a dividend during 20X5 of $55 million (295,000 + 135,000 – 375,000) which may be a questionable policy when the company is raising additional finance through borrowings and contributes substantially to Tangier Co's overdraft.

Overall, the acquisition of Raremetal Co to secure supplies appears to have been an expensive strategy, perhaps a less expensive one might have been to enter into a long-term supply contract with Raremetal Co.

(c) Further information which would be useful to obtain would therefore include:

(1) The cost of the investment in Raremetal Co, the carrying amount of the assets acquired and whether Tangier Co has carried out a goodwill impairment test as required under IFRS Accounting Standards.

(2) The benefits generated from the investment; for example, Raremetal Co's individual financial statements and details of sales to external customers (not all of these benefits will be measurable in financial terms).

(3) The above two pieces of information would demonstrate whether the investment in Raremetal Co had been worthwhile.

(4) The amount of intragroup sales made during the year and those expected to be made in the short to medium term.

(5) The pricing strategy agreed with Raremetal Co so that the effects on the profits reported in the individual financial statements of Raremetal Co and Tangier Co can be more readily determined.

(6) More information is needed to establish if the new contract has been detrimental to Tangier Co's performance. The contract was won sometime between 1 October 20X4 and 1 January 20X5 and there is no information of when production and sales started, but clearly there has not been a full year's revenue from the contract. Also there is no information on the length or total value of the contract.

Again, you would answer Requirement (b) using the word processing response area. You consider using the bullet point list option or the numbered list option to set out your answer. You can use bold or underline to add emphasis to any key points.

- The **cost** of the investment in Raremetal Co, the **carrying amount** of the assets acquired and whether Tangier Co has carried out a goodwill **impairment** test as required under IFRS Standards.
- The **benefits generated** from the investment; for example, Raremetal Co's individual financial statements and details of sales to external customers (not all of these benefits will be measurable in financial terms).
- The above two pieces of information would demonstrate whether the investment in Raremetal Co had been worthwhile.
- The amount of **intragroup sales** made during the year and those expected to be made in the short to medium term.
- The pricing strategy agreed with Raremetal Co so that the **effects on the profits** reported in the individual financial statements of Raremetal Co and Tangier Co can be more readily determined.
- More information is needed to establish if the new contract has been detrimental to Tangier Co's performance. The contract was won sometime between 1 October 20X4 and 1 January 20X5 and there is no information of when production and sales started, but clearly there has not been a full year's revenue from the contract. Also, there is no information on the length or total value of the contract.

ACCA

Financial Reporting (FR)

Mock Exam 3

ACCA CBE Practice Exam 2

Questions	
Time allowed	3 hours
This mock exam is divided into three sections: Section A: ALL 15 questions are compulsory and MUST be attempted Section B: ALL 15 questions are compulsory and MUST be attempted Section C: BOTH questions are compulsory and MUST be attempted	

DO NOT OPEN THIS EXAM UNTIL YOU ARE READY TO START UNDER EXAMINATION CONDITIONS

Section A

ALL 15 questions are compulsory and MUST be attempted

1 Which of the following is a possible advantage of a rules-based system of financial reporting?

- O It encourages the exercise of professional judgement
- O It prevents a fire-fighting approach to the formulation of standards
- O It offers accountants more protection in the event of litigation
- O It ensures that no standards conflict with each other **(2 marks)**

2 IFRS 10 *Consolidated Financial Statements* states that 'A parent shall prepare consolidated financial statements using uniform accounting policies for like transactions and other events in similar circumstances'.

Which of the following situations requires an adjustment because of this constraint?

- O A subsidiary has been acquired and its land is to be included in the consolidated financial statements at fair value
- O A subsidiary carries its assets at historical cost, but the parent's assets are carried at revalued amounts
- O There have been intragroup transactions during the year which have resulted in unrealised profit in inventory at the year end
- O There has been intragroup trading which has resulted in intragroup balances for receivables and payables at the year end **(2 marks)**

3 The following trial balance extract relates to Topsy Co as at 30 April 20X6:

	$'000	$'000
Land at cost	800	
Building:		
Valuation at 1 May 20X2	1,500	
Accumulated depreciation at 30 April 20X5		90
Revaluation surplus at 30 April 20X5		705

On 1 May 20X2, when the carrying amount of the building was $750,000, it was revalued for the first time to $1.5m and its remaining useful life at that date was estimated to be 50 years. Topsy Co has correctly accounted for this revaluation in the above trial balance. However, Topsy Co has not yet charged depreciation for the year ended 30 April 20X6 or transferred the excess depreciation from the revaluation surplus to retained earnings at 30 April 20X6.

In February 20X6, the land, but not the building, was independently valued at $950,000. This adjustment has yet to be made for the year ended 30 April 20X6.

What is the balance on the revaluation surplus of Topsy Co as at 30 April 20X6 after the required adjustments have been made?

- O $555,000
- O $690,000
- O $840,000
- O $870,000 **(2 marks)**

4 Plow Co purchased 3,500 of the 10,000 $1 equity shares of Styre Co on 1 August 20X4 for $6.50 per share.

Styre Co's profit for the year ended 31 July 20X5 was $7,500. Styre Co paid a dividend of $0.50 per share on 31 December 20X4.

Calculate the carrying amount of the investment in Styre Co in the consolidated statement of financial position of Plow Co as at 31 July 20X5 (to the nearest whole $).

$ [ ] **(2 marks)**

5 Identify, by selecting the relevant box in the table below, whether the following statements are correct or incorrect when calculating the impairment loss of an asset.

Assets should be carried at the lower of their carrying amount and recoverable amount	CORRECT	INCORRECT
The recoverable amount of an asset is the higher of value in use and fair value less costs of disposal	CORRECT	INCORRECT

(2 marks)

6 Which of the following statements is **NOT** true?

- O In some countries, accounting standards can be a detailed set of rules which companies must follow
- O Local accounting standards can be influenced by the tax regime within a country
- O Accounting standards on their own provide a complete system of regulation
- O Accounting standards are particularly important where a company's shares are publicly traded **(2 marks)**

7 A company had issued share capital on 1 January 20X9 of 2,000,000 equity $1 shares. On 1 October 20X9, a rights issue was made on a one for four basis which was fully taken up.

On 30 September 20X9, each share had a market value of $3.25, giving a theoretical ex-rights value of $2.84 per share.

In accordance with IAS 33 *Earnings per Share*, what is the weighted average number of shares in issue for the year ended 31 December 20X9?

- O 2,341,549 shares
- O 1,935,769 shares
- O 2,125,000 shares
- O 2,431,778 shares **(2 marks)**

8 Which **TWO** of the following would result in a credit to the deferred tax account?

- ☐ Interest receivable, which will be taxed when the interest is received
- ☐ A loan, the repayment of which will have no tax consequences
- ☐ Interest payable, which will be allowable for tax when paid
- ☐ Prepaid expenses, which have been deducted to calculate the taxable profits of the previous year **(2 marks)**

9 IFRS 15 *Revenue from Contracts with Customers* states that, where performance obligations are satisfied over time, entities should apply an appropriate method of measuring progress.

Which **TWO** of the following are appropriate **OUTPUT** methods of measuring progress?

- ☐ Total costs to date of the contract as a percentage of total contract revenue
- ☐ Physical milestones reached as a percentage of physical completion

☐ Surveys of performance completed to date as a percentage of total contract revenue

☐ Labour hours expended as a percentage of total expected labour hours **(2 marks)**

10 Fifer Co has a current ratio of 1.2:1 which is below the industry average. Fifer Co wants to increase its current ratio by the year end.

Which of the following actions, taken before the year end, would lead to an increase in the current ratio?

- O Return some inventory which had been purchased for cash and obtain a full refund on the cost
- O Make a bulk purchase of inventory for cash to obtain a large discount
- O Make an early payment to suppliers, even though the amount is not due
- O Offer early payment discounts in order to collect receivables more quickly **(2 marks)**

11 On 1 October 20X8, Picture Co acquired 60% shares in Frame Co. At 1 April 20X8, the credit balances on the revaluation surpluses relating to Picture Co and Frame Co's equity financial asset investments stood at $6,400 and $4,400 respectively.

The following extract was taken from the financial statements for the year ended 31 March 20X9:

	Picture Co	Frame Co
	$	$
Other comprehensive income: loss on fair value of equity financial asset investments	(1,400)	(800)

Assume the losses accrued evenly throughout the year.

What is the amount of the revaluation surplus in the consolidated statement of financial position of Picture Co as at 31 March 20X9?

- O $4,520
- O $4,760
- O $5,240
- O $9,160 **(2 marks)**

12 A local authority department is responsible for waste collections. They have an annual budget to provide a regular collection service from households in the local area. The budget was increased to enable the department to increase the percentage of waste disposed of in an environmentally friendly manner.

Which of the following is the best measurement to justify the increase in the budget?

- O An increase in the number of collections made during the period
- O The percentage of waste recycled rather than being placed in landfill sites
- O The fair value of the machinery used in making the collections
- O A breakdown of expenditure between the cost of making collections and the cost of processing waste **(2 marks)**

13 Panther Co owns 80% of Tiger Co. An extract from the companies' individual statements of financial position as at 30 June 20X8 shows the following:

	Panther Co	Tiger Co
	$'000	$'000
Property, plant and equipment (carrying amount)	370	285

On 1 July 20X7, Panther Co sold a piece of equipment which had a carrying amount of $70,000 to Tiger Co for $150,000. The equipment had an estimated remaining life of five years when sold.

What is the carrying amount of property, plant and equipment in the consolidated statement of financial position of Panther Co as at 30 June 20X8?

$ [ ]

(2 marks)

14 On 1 July 20X7, Lime Co acquired 90% of Soda Co's equity share capital. On this date, Soda Co had an internally generated customer list which was valued at $35m by an independent team of experts. At 1 July 20X7, Soda Co was also in negotiations with a potential new major customer. If the negotiations are successful, the new customer will sign the contract on 15 July 20X7 and the value of the total customer base would then be worth $45m.

What amount would be recognised for the customer list in the consolidated statement of financial position of Lime Co as at 1 July 20X7?

- O $0
- O $10m
- O $35m
- O $45m

(2 marks)

15 Identify whether the following statements relating to goodwill are correct or incorrect?

Goodwill is amortised over its useful life with the charge expensed to profit or loss	CORRECT	INCORRECT
On the investment in an associate, any related goodwill should be separately identified in the consolidated financial statements	CORRECT	INCORRECT
The testing of goodwill for impairment is only required when circumstances exist which indicate potential impairment	CORRECT	INCORRECT
If the fair value of a subsidiary's contingent liabilities can be reliably measured at the date of acquisition, they should be included in consolidated net assets and will increase goodwill	CORRECT	INCORRECT

(2 marks)

Section B

ALL 15 questions are compulsory and MUST be attempted

Artem Co

Each question is worth 2 marks.

The following scenario relates to questions 16–20.

Artem Co prepares financial statements to 30 June each year.

During the year to 30 June 20X5, the company spent $550,000 on new plant as follows:

	$'000
Plant cost	525
Delivery to site	3
Building alterations to accommodate the plant	12
Costs of initial testing of the new plant	2
Plant operator training costs	8

Artem Co's fixtures and fittings were purchased on 1 July 20X2 at a cost of $50,000. The directors have depreciated them on a straight-line basis over an estimated useful life of eight years assuming a $5,000 residual value. At 1 July 20X4, the directors realise that the remaining useful life of the fixtures is five years. There is no change to the estimated residual value.

Artem Co began a research project in October 20X3 with the aim of developing a new type of machine. If successful, Artem Co will manufacture the machines and sell them to customers as well as using them in their own production processes. During the year ended 30 June 20X4, costs of $25,000 were incurred on conducting feasibility studies and some market research. During the year ended 30 June 20X5, a further $80,000 was incurred on constructing and testing a prototype of the machine.

16 In accordance with IAS 16 *Property, Plant and Equipment*, what is the value of additions to plant for Artem Co for the year ended 30 June 20X5?

$ [ ] **(2 marks)**

---

17 Which of the following is **TRUE** in relation to the change in the remaining useful life of the fixtures and fittings?

- O It is a change of accounting policy which should be retrospectively applied
- O It is a change of accounting policy which should be disclosed in the notes to the financial statements
- O It is a change of accounting estimate which should be retrospectively applied
- O It is a change of accounting estimate which should be prospectively applied **(2 marks)**

---

18 In accordance with IAS 16 *Property, Plant and Equipment*, what is the depreciation charge for the fixtures and fittings for Artem Co for the year ended 30 June 20X5?

- O $7,500
- O $9,000
- O $7,750
- O $6,750

(2 marks)

19 Identify the correct accounting treatment for the $25,000 costs incurred on the research project during the year ended 30 June 20X4 and select the reason why it is correct in accordance with IAS 38 *Intangible Assets*.

In accordance with IAS 38 *Intangible Assets*, the $25,000 costs incurred on the research project during the year ended 30 June 20X4 should be:

Accounting treatment	Reason
(1) ▼	(2) ▼

Pull down list 1

- Capitalise as research
- Capitalised as PPE
- Provide for
- Written off to profit or loss

Pull down list 2

- As future economic benefits are expected from the use and sale of machinery
- As machinery will be put into use once completed
- They are research costs at 30 June 20X4

(2 marks)

---

20 In accordance with IAS 38, which of the following is true when Artem Co moves to the production and testing stage of the prototype during the year ended 30 June 20X5?

○ The project has moved to the development stage. If the IAS 38 development expenditure criteria are met, Artem Co can choose whether or not to recognise the $80,000 costs as an intangible non-current asset

○ The project is still in its research stage and the $80,000 costs incurred by Artem Co cannot be recognised as an intangible non-current asset until a product is ready for sale

○ The project has moved to the development stage. If the IAS 38 development expenditure criteria are met, Artem Co must recognise the $80,000 costs as an intangible non-current asset

○ The project is still in its research stage and so Artem Co must expense the $80,000 costs to profit or loss **(2 marks)**

(Total = 10 marks)

Maykorn Co

The following scenario relates to questions 21–25.

Maykorn Co prepares its financial statements to 30 September each year. Maykorn Co's draft financial statements were finalised on 20 October 20X3. They were authorised for issue on 15 December 20X3 and the annual general meeting of shareholders took place on 23 December 20X3.

On 30 September 20X3, Maykorn Co moved out of one of its properties and put it up for sale. The property met the criteria as held for sale on 30 September 20X3. On 1 October 20X2, the property had a carrying amount of $2.6m and a remaining life of 20 years. The property is held under the revaluation model. The property was expected to sell for a gross amount of $2.5m with selling costs estimated at $50,000.

Maykorn Co decided to sell an item of plant during the year ended 30 September 20X3. On 1 October 20X2, the plant had a carrying amount of $490,000 and a remaining useful life of seven years. The plant met the held for sale criteria on 1 April 20X3. At 1 April 20X3, the plant had a fair value less costs to sell of $470,000, which had fallen to $465,000 at 30 September 20X3.

21 Identify, by selecting the relevant box in the table below, whether the following statements are true and in accordance with IAS 10 *Events After the Reporting Period*, for Maykorn Co?

All events which occur between 30 September 20X3 and 15 December 20X3 should be considered as events occurring after the reporting period	**TRUE**	**FALSE**
An event which occurs between 30 September 20X3 and 15 December 20X3 and which provides evidence of a condition which existed at 30 September 20X3 should be considered as an adjusting event	**TRUE**	**FALSE**

(2 marks)

---

22 In accordance with IAS 10, identify whether the following events would be classed as adjusting or non-adjusting events in Maykorn Co's financial statements for the year ended 30 September 20X3?

During October 20X3, there was evidence of a permanent diminution in the carrying amount of a property held at 30 September 20X3	**ADJUSTING**	**NON-ADJUSTING**
On 1 December 20X3, the acquisition of a subsidiary was completed, following lengthy negotiations which began in September 20X3	**ADJUSTING**	**NON-ADJUSTING**
The sale of inventory during October 20X3 at a value less than its cost. This inventory was included in the financial statements at cost on 30 September 20X3	**ADJUSTING**	**NON-ADJUSTING**
The insolvency of a major customer during October 20X3, whose balance was included within receivables at 30 September 20X3	**ADJUSTING**	**NON-ADJUSTING**

(2 marks)

---

23 What is the total amount charged to Maykorn Co's profit or loss in respect of the property for the year ended 30 September 20X3?

- O $130,000
- O $180,000
- O $150,000
- O $100,000

(2 marks)

---

24 In accordance with IFRS 5 *Non-current Assets Held for Sale and Discontinued Operations*, what is the carrying amount of the plant in Maykorn Co's statement of financial position as at 30 September 20X3?

- O $420,000
- O $470,000
- O $455,000

O $465,000 **(2 marks)**

---

25 Which of the following items should be classed as an asset held for sale under IFRS 5?

- O Maykorn Co's head office building is to be demolished, at which point the land will be put up for sale. A number of prospective bidders have declared an interest and the land is expected to sell within a few months of the demolition
- O An item of plant was put up for sale at the start of the year for $500,000. Six parties have made a bid to Maykorn Co for the plant but none of these bids have been above $200,000
- O A chain of retail outlets are currently advertised for sale. Maykorn Co has provisionally accepted a bid, subject to surveys being completed. The surveys are not expected to highlight any problems. The outlets are currently empty
- O A brand name which Maykorn Co purchased in 20X2 is associated with the sale of potentially harmful products. Maykorn Co has decided to stop producing products under this brand, which is currently held within intangible assets **(2 marks)**

(Total = 10 marks)

Vitrion Co

The following scenario relates to questions 26–30.

Vitrion Co issued $2m 6% convertible loan notes on 1 April 20X2. The convertible loan notes are redeemable on 31 March 20X5 at par for cash or can be exchanged for equity shares in Vitrion Co on that date. Similar loan notes without the conversion option carry an interest rate of 9%.

The following table provides information about discount rates:

	6%	9%
Year 1	0.943	0.917
Year 2	0.890	0.842
Year 3	0.840	0.772

On 1 April 20X3, Vitrion Co purchased 50,000 $1 equity shares in Gowhizzo Co at $4 per share, incurring transaction costs of $4,000. The intention is to hold the shares for trading. By 31 March 20X4 the shares are trading at $7 per share. In addition to the gain on investment, Vitrion Co also received a dividend from Gowhizzo Co during the year to 31 March 20X4.

26 In accordance with IAS 32 *Financial Instruments: Presentation*, which of the following describes an equity instrument?

- O A contractual obligation to deliver cash or another financial asset to another entity
- O A contract which is evidence of a residual interest in the assets of an entity after deducting all of its liabilities
- O A contractual right to exchange financial instruments with another entity under potentially favourable conditions
- O A contract which gives rise to both a financial asset of one entity and a financial liability of another **(2 marks)**

---

27 In accordance with IAS 32, how should the issue of the convertible loan notes be recognised in Vitrion Co's financial statements?

BPP

- O As debt. Interest should be charged at 6% because it cannot be assumed that loan note holders will choose the equity option
- O As equity because the loan notes are convertible to equity shares
- O As debt and equity because the convertible loan notes contain elements of both
- O As debt. Interest should be charged at 9% to allow for the conversion of the loan notes **(2 marks)**

---

28 What amount in respect of the loan notes will be shown under non-current liabilities in Vitrion Co's statement of financial position as at 1 April 20X2 (to the nearest $'000)?

- O $2,000,000
- O $1,848,000
- O $1,544,000
- O $2,701,000 **(2 marks)**

---

29 In accordance with IFRS 9 *Financial Instruments*, at what amount will the Gowhizzo Co shares be shown under investments in equity instruments in Vitrion Co's statement of financial position as at 31 March 20X4?

- O $204,000
- O $354,000
- O $346,000
- O $350,000 **(2 marks)**

---

30 Where should the gain on the investment in Gowhizzo Co and its dividend be recognised in Vitrion Co's financial statements for the year ended 31 March 20X4?

- O Both in profit or loss
- O Gain on investment in other comprehensive income and the dividend in profit or loss
- O Gain on investment in profit or loss and the dividend in other comprehensive income
- O Both in other comprehensive income **(2 marks)**

(Total = 10 marks)

Section C

BOTH questions are compulsory and MUST be attempted

31 Laurel Co

On 1 January 20X6, Laurel Co acquired 60% of the equity share capital of Rakewood Co in a share exchange in which Laurel Co issued three new shares for every five shares it acquired in Rakewood Co. The share issue has not yet been recorded by Laurel Co. Additionally, on 31 December 20X6, Laurel Co will pay to the shareholders of Rakewood Co $1.62 per share acquired. Laurel Co's cost of capital is 8% per annum.

At the date of acquisition, shares in Laurel Co and Rakewood Co had a market value of $7.00 and $2.00 each respectively.

Statements of profit or loss for the year ended 30 September 20X6

	Laurel Co	Rakewood Co
	$'000	$'000
Revenue	84,500	52,000
Cost of sales	(58,200)	(34,000)
Gross profit	26,300	18,000
Distribution costs	(2,000)	(1,600)
Administrative expenses	(4,100)	(2,800)
Investment income (Note (4))	500	400
Finance costs	(300)	–
Profit before tax	20,400	14,000
Income tax expense	(4,800)	(3,600)
Profit for the year	15,600	10,400

Equity as at 1 October 20X5

	$'000	$'000
Equity shares of $1 each	20,000	15,000
Retained earnings	72,000	25,000

The following information is relevant:

(1) At the date of acquisition, Laurel Co conducted a fair value exercise on Rakewood Co's net assets which were equal to their carrying amounts with the following exceptions:

- An item of plant had a fair value of $4m above its carrying amount. At the date of acquisition it had a remaining life of two years.
- Inventory of $800,000 had a fair value of $1m. All of this inventory had been sold by 30 September 20X6.

(2) Laurel Co's policy is to value the non-controlling interest at fair value at the date of acquisition. For this purpose Rakewood Co's share price at 1 January 20X6 can be deemed to be representative of the fair value of the shares held by the non-controlling interest.

(3) Laurel Co had traded with Rakewood Co for many years before the acquisition. Sales from Rakewood Co to Laurel Co throughout the year ended 30 September 20X6 were consistently $1.2m per month. Rakewood Co made a mark-up on cost of 20% on these sales. Laurel Co had $1.8m of these goods in inventory as at 30 September 20X6.

(4) Laurel Co's investment income consists of:

- Its share of a dividend of $500,000 paid by Rakewood Co in August 20X6.
- A dividend of $200,000 received from Artic Co, a 25% owned associate which it has held for several years. The profit after tax of Artic Co for the year ended 30 September 20X6 was $2.4 million.

(5) Assume, except where indicated otherwise, that all items of income and expense accrue evenly throughout the year.

(6) There were no impairment losses within the group during the year ended 30 September 20X6.

Required

(a) Calculate the consolidated goodwill at the date of acquisition of Rakewood Co. **(7 marks)**

(b) Prepare the consolidated statement of profit or loss for Laurel Co for the year ended 30 September 20X6. **(13 marks)**

(Total = 20 marks)

32 Archway Co

Landing Co is considering the acquisition of Archway Co, a retail company. The summarised financial statements of Archway Co for the year ended 30 September 20X6 are:

Statement of profit or loss

	$'000
Revenue	94,000
Cost of sales	(73,000)
Gross profit	21,000
Distribution costs	(4,000)
Administrative expenses	(6,000)
Finance costs	(400)
Profit before tax	10,600
Income tax expense (at 20%)	(2,120)
Profit for the year	8,480

Statement of financial position

	$'000	$'000
ASSETS		
Non-current assets		
Property, plant and equipment		29,400

	$'000	$'000
Current assets		
Inventory	10,500	
Bank	100	10,600
Total assets		40,000
EQUITY AND LIABILITIES		
Equity		
Equity shares of $1 each		10,000
Retained earnings		8,800
		18,800
Current liabilities		
4% loan notes (redeemable 1 November 20X6)	10,000	
Trade payables	9,200	
Current tax payable	2,000	21,200
Total equity and liabilities		40,000

From enquiries made, Landing Co has obtained the following information:

(1) Archway Co pays an annual licence fee of $1m to Cardol Co (included in cost of sales) for the right to package and sell some goods under a well-known brand name owned by Cardol Co. If Archway Co is acquired, this arrangement would be discontinued. Landing Co estimates that this would not affect Archway Co's volume of sales, but without the use of the brand name packaging, overall sales revenue would be 5% lower than currently.

(2) Archway Co buys 50% of its purchases for resale from Cardol Co, one of Landing Co's rivals, and receives a bulk buying discount of 10% off normal prices (this discount does not apply to the annual licence fee referred to in Note (1) above). This discount would not be available if Archway Co is acquired by Landing Co.

(3) The 4% loan notes have been classified as a current liability due to their imminent redemption. As such, they should not be treated as long-term funding. However, they will be replaced immediately after redemption by 8% loan notes with the same nominal value, repayable in ten years' time.

(4) Landing Co has obtained some of Archway Co's retail sector average ratios for the year ended 30 September 20X6. It has then calculated the equivalent ratios for Archway Co as shown below:

	Sector average	Archway Co
Annual sales per square metre of floor space	$8,000	$7,833
Return on capital employed (ROCE)	18.0%	58.5%
Net asset (total assets less current liabilities) turnover	2.7 times	5.0 times
Gross profit margin	22.0%	22.3%
Operating profit (profit before interest and tax) margin	6.7%	11.7%
Gearing (debt/equity)	30.0%	Nil

A note accompanying the sector average ratios explains that it is the practice of the sector to carry retail property at market value. The market value of Archway Co's retail property is $3m more than its carrying amount (ignore the effect of any consequent additional depreciation) and gives 12,000 square metres of floor space.

Required

(a) After making adjustments to the financial statements of Archway Co which you think may be appropriate for comparability purposes, restate:

   (1) Revenue;

   (2) Cost of sales;

   (3) Finance costs;

   (4) Equity (assume that your adjustments to profit or loss result in retained earnings of $2.3 million at 30 September 20X6); and

   (5) Non-current liabilities.

(5 marks)

(b) Recalculate comparable sector average ratios for Archway Co based on your restated figures in (a) above. **(6 marks)**

(c) Comment on the performance and gearing of Archway Co compared to the retail sector average as a basis for advising Landing Co regarding the possible acquisition of Archway Co. **(9 marks)**

(Total = 20 marks)

Answers

DO NOT TURN THIS PAGE UNTIL YOU HAVE COMPLETED THE MOCK EXAM

A plan of attack

If this were the real Financial Reporting exam and you had been told to begin, what would be going through your mind?

You should be reminding yourself of all of the areas of the course you know about and are comfortable with. Hopefully you have practised enough OT questions to have a good attempt at any topics that comes up. There are three questions in Section B – at least one of them is likely to be on an area you are happy with, so do that question first to gain some confidence then tackle the others. In some ways, Section C should be the least daunting as you know that the questions will require accounts preparation and interpretation and you should be prepared to answer those. So stay calm and focus on the positives!

Deciding where to start

Most candidates will start on Section A as there will be some questions in that section that you may find easy and some more difficult. Don't spend a lot of time on anything you really don't know. You are not penalised for wrong answers, so you should answer all of them. If all else fails – guess!

Section B has 15 2-mark questions in total arranged around three scenarios. In this mock exam, they cover:

- Scenario 1 is on non-current assets.
- Scenario 2 is on events after the reporting date and assets held for sale and discontinued operations.
- Scenario 3 deals with financial instruments.

If you are good at financial instruments and less so on assets held for sale and discontinued operations, it might be a good idea to start with the questions in scenario 3 first, then scenario 1 before finishing with scenario 2. As these are OT questions, make sure you provide an answer to every question, even if it is an educated guess.

Section C has two 20-mark questions.

Question 31 is a consolidated financial statements preparation question.

Question 32 deals with accounting adjustments and interpretation of financial statements.

You will get better at Section C questions the more you practise. Make sure some of that practice time is spent using the ACCA CBE software so you are familiar with it on exam day.

All of these questions are compulsory.

This means that you do not have to waste time wondering which questions to answer.

Allocating your time

BPP's advice is always allocate your time **according to the marks for the question** in total and for the parts of the question. But **use common sense.**If you're confronted by a Section A question on a topic of which you know nothing, pick an answer and move on. Use the time to pick up marks elsewhere.

After the exam...forget about it!

And don't worry if you found the exam difficult. More than likely other candidates will too. If this were the real thing you would need to **forget** the exam the minute you left the exam hall and **think about the next one**. Or, if it's the last one, **celebrate**!

Section A

ALL 15 questions are compulsory and MUST be attempted

1 The correct answer is: It offers accountants more protection in the event of litigation

The other options are advantages of a principles-based system.

2 The correct answer is: A subsidiary carries its assets at historical cost, but the parent's assets are carried at revalued amounts

This situation involves different accounting policies.

3 The correct answer is: $840,000

	$	$
At 30 April 20X5		705,000
Increase in value of land in the year ($900,000 – $750,000)		150,000
		855,000
Annual transfer to retained earnings		
Depreciation based on revalued amount ($1,500,000/50 years)	30,000	
Depreciation based on historic cost ($750,000/50 years)	(15,000)	
		(15,000)
At 30 April 20X6		840,000

4 $ 23,625

		$
Cost of investment	3,500 × 6.50	22,750
Share of post-acq profit	35% × 7,000	2,625
Less dividend received	3,500 × $0.50	(1,750)
		23,625

5 The correct answers are:

Assets should be carried at the lower of their carrying amount and recoverable amount	**CORRECT**	
The recoverable amount of an asset is the higher of value in use and fair value less costs of disposal	**CORRECT**	

6 The correct answer is: Accounting standards on their own provide a complete system of regulation

A system of regulation will also include tax rules and company legislation.

7 The correct answer is: 2,341,549 shares

1 January X9–30 September X9	2,000,000 × 3.25/2.84 × 9/12	1,716,549
1 October X9–31 December X9	2,500,000 × 3/12	625,000
		2,341,549

8 The correct answers are:

- Interest receivable, which will be taxed when the interest is received
- Prepaid expenses, which have been deducted to calculate the taxable profits of the previous year

9 The correct answers are:

- Physical milestones reached as a percentage of physical completion
- Surveys of performance completed to date as a percentage of total contract revenue

The other options are input methods of measurement.

10 The correct answer is: Make an early payment to suppliers, even though the amount is not due

This will reduce assets and liabilities by the same amount and so increase the ratio.

11 The correct answer is: $4,760

(6,400 – 1,400 loss – (800 loss × 60% × 6/12)) = 4,760

12 The correct answer is: The percentage of waste recycled rather than being placed in landfill sites

This measurement relates to the environmental impact.

13 $ 591,000

Carrying amount 370,000 + 285,000 – 64,000 (see below) = 591,000

The unrealised profit on the sale is 80,000 (150,000 – 70,000) of which 64,000 (80,000 × 4 years/5 years) is still unrealised at 30 June 20X8.

14 The correct answer is: $35m

This is the valuation at acquisition.

15 The correct answers are:

Goodwill is amortised over its useful life with the charge expensed to profit or loss		**INCORRECT**
On the investment in an associate, any related goodwill should be separately identified in the consolidated financial statements		**INCORRECT**
The testing of goodwill for impairment is only required when circumstances exist which indicate potential impairment		**INCORRECT**
If the fair value of a subsidiary's contingent liabilities can be reliably measured at the date of acquisition, they should be included in consolidated net assets and will increase goodwill	**CORRECT**	

Section B

ALL 15 questions are compulsory and MUST be attempted

Artem Co

16 $ 542,000

	$'000
Plant cost	525
Delivery to site	3
Building alterations to accommodate the plant	12
Costs of initial testing of the new plant	2
	542

Training costs are not included within the capitalised amount of new plant.

17 The correct answer is: It is a change of accounting estimate which should be prospectively applied

18 The correct answer is: $6,750

Carrying amount at date of revised remaining life is (50,000 – (50,000 – 5,000)/8 years × 2 years) = 38,750

Depreciation year ended 30 June 20X5 is therefore 38,750 – 5,000/5 years = 6,750 pa

19

Accounting treatment	Reason
Written off to profit or loss	They are research costs at 30 June 20X4

In accordance with IAS 38 *Intangible Assets*, the $25,000 costs incurred on the research project during the year ended 30 June 20X4 should be as above.

20 The correct answer is: The project has moved to the development stage. If the IAS 38 development expenditure criteria are met, Artem Co must recognise the $80,000 costs as an intangible non-current asset

IAS 38 does not allow a choice regarding whether or not to capitalise development costs.

Maykorn Co

21 The correct answers are:

All events which occur between 30 September 20X3 and 15 December 20X3 should be considered as events occurring after the reporting period	**TRUE**	
An event which occurs between 30 September 20X3 and 15 December 20X3 and which provides evidence of a condition which existed at 30 September 20X3 should be considered as an adjusting event	**TRUE**	

22 The correct answers are:

During October 20X3, there was evidence of a permanent diminution in the carrying amount of a property held at 30 September 20X3	**ADJUSTING**	

On 1 December 20X3, the acquisition of a subsidiary was completed, following lengthy negotiations which began in September 20X3		**NON-ADJUSTING**
The sale of inventory during October 20X3 at a value less than its cost. This inventory was included in the financial statements at cost on 30 September 20X3	**ADJUSTING**	
The insolvency of a major customer during October 20X3, whose balance was included within receivables at 30 September 20X3	**ADJUSTING**	

23 The correct answer is: $180,000

Property is depreciated by $130,000 ($2,600,000/20) giving a carrying amount of $2,470,000. When classed as held for sale, property is revalued to its fair value of $2,500,000 (as it is carried under the revaluation model, $30,000 would go to revaluation surplus). Held for sale assets are measured at the lower of carrying amount (now $2,500,000) and fair value less costs to sell ($2,500,000 – $50,000 = $2,450,000), giving an impairment of $50,000. Total charge to profit or loss is $130,000 + $50,000 = $180,000.

24 The correct answer is: $455,000

Carrying amount at 1 April is $455,000 (490 – (490/7 × 6/12)).

25 The correct answer is: A chain of retail outlets are currently advertised for sale. Maykorn Co has provisionally accepted a bid, subject to surveys being completed. The surveys are not expected to highlight any problems. The outlets are currently empty

This is the only option where there is evidence of a 'highly probable' sale.

Vitrion Co

26 The correct answer is: A contract which is evidence of a residual interest in the assets of an entity after deducting all of its liabilities

27 The correct answer is: As debt and equity because the convertible loan notes contain elements of both

28 The correct answer is: $1,848,000

120,000 × 0.917	110,040	
120,000 × 0.842	101,040	
2,120,000 × 0.772	1,636,640	
	1,847,720	rounded to 1,848,000

29 The correct answer is: $350,000

50,000 shares at $7 each

30 The correct answer is: Both in profit or loss

The Gowhizzo shares are held for trading rather than long term investment purposes.

ANSWERS

Section C

BOTH questions are compulsory and MUST be attempted

31 Laurel Co

Text reference

Chapter 9.

Top Tips

This question requires calculation of goodwill on acquisition and the preparation of a consolidated statement of profit or loss. Take care in calculating retained earnings at acquisition, which must include the first three months of the current year. Whenever you see Note (5) realise that you are dealing with a mid-year acquisition. This means that the income and expenses of the subsidiary must be multiplied by 9/12 throughout. Note that all of Laurel's investment income (per Note (4)) will be disregarded.

Easy marks

The goodwill calculation is straightforward as long as you take care in calculating the retained earnings.

Marking guide			Marks	
(a) Goodwill				
	Share exchange		1	
	Deferred consideration		1	
	NCI		1	
	Net assets:	Equity shares	0.5	
		Retained earnings	1.5	
		Fair value adjustments	2	
				7
(b) Statement of profit or loss				
	Revenue		1.5	
	Cost of sales		4.5	
	Distribution costs		0.5	
	Administrative expenses		0.5	
	Investment income		1.5	
	Finance costs		1.5	
	Income tax		1	
	NCI		2	
				13
Total				20

(a) **Laurel Co: Consolidated goodwill on acquisition of Rakewood Co**

Investment at cost

	$'000	$'000
Shares (15,000 × 60% × 3/5 × $7.00)		37,800

	$'000	$'000
Deferred consideration (9,000 × $1.62/1.08)		13,500
Non-controlling interest (15,000 × 40% × $2.00)		12,000
		63,300
Net assets (based on equity) of Rakewood Co as at 1 January 20X6		
Equity shares	15,000	
Retained earnings at 1 October 20X5	25,000	
Earnings 1 October 20X5 to acquisition (10,400 × 3/12)	2,600	
Fair value adjustments:		
plant	4,000	
inventory	200	
Net assets at date of acquisition		(46,800)
Consolidated goodwill		16,500

In the FR exam, you would answer this requirement using the spreadsheet response option. A good approach is to set up the proforma working for goodwill, showing consideration, non-controlling interest, share capital, retained earnings and fair value adjustments. When creating proforma workings, it is important to leave some blank rows so that you can insert additional components into the working that are unique to that question. For example, deferred consideration isn't in every question, so you might not include that in a proforma but will add it when you read through the information. The standard proforma goodwill calculation is:

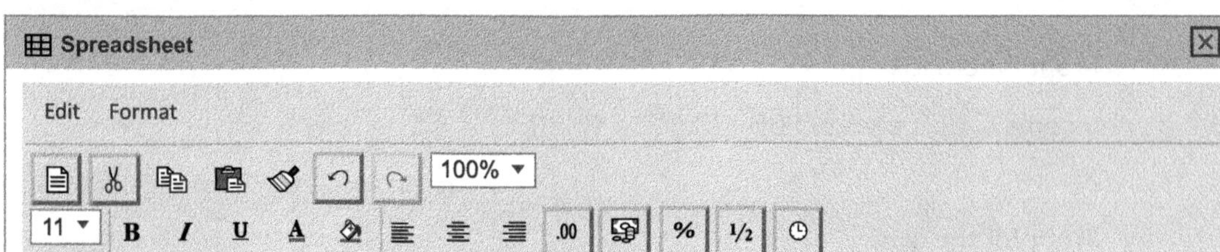

8 12	=B6-B11		
	A	B	C
1	Consideration:		
2	Cash		
3	Shares		
4			
5	Non-controlling interest		
6			
7	FV of assets and liabilities acquired:		
8	Share capital		

8 12	=B6-B11		
	A	B	C
9	Retained earnings		
10	Fair value adjustments		
11			
12	Goodwill		

(b)

Laurel Co: Consolidated statement of profit or loss for the year ended 30 September 20X6

	$'000
Revenue (84,500 + (52,000 × 9/12) – (1,200 × 9 months) intragroup sales)	112,700
Cost of sales (working)	(74,900)
Gross profit	37,800
Distribution costs (2,000 + (1,600 × 9/12))	(3,200)
Administrative expenses (4,100 + (2,800 × 9/12))	(6,200)
Investment income (400 × 9/12)	300
Income from associate (2,400 × 25% based on underlying earnings)	600
Finance costs (300 + (13,500 × 8% × 9/12 re deferred consideration))	(1,110)
Profit before tax	28,190
Income tax expense (4,800 + (3,600 × 9/12))	(7,500)
Profit for the year	20,690
Profit for year attributable to:	
Owners of the parent	18,370
Non-controlling interest	
((10,400 × 9/12) – 200 re inventory – (1,500 depreciation – 300 URP) × 40%)	2,320
	20,690

Working

Cost of sales

	$'000
Laurel Co	58,200
Rakewood Co (34,000 × 9/12)	25,500
Intragroup purchases (1,200 × 9 months)	(10,800)

	$'000
Fair value inventory adjustment	200
URP in inventory at 30 September 20X6 (1,800 × 20/120)	300
Additional depreciation (4,000/2 years × 9/12)	1,500
	74,900

In the FR exam, you would show your workings in the spreadsheet response option. The examiners' reports frequently state that candidates lose marks in accounts preparation questions such as this one because they do not show their workings clearly. You can set out your workings either by writing the calculation, as is shown in cell A3 and A5 or by using the formula available within the spreadsheet as is shown in cell B2. You can also use the SUM function for totals, as is shown in cell B7.

Spreadsheet

Edit Format

100% | 11

=34000*9/12

	A	B	C
1	Laurel Co per question	58200	
2	Rakewood Co (34,000 × 9/12)	25,500	
3	Intragroup purchases (1,200 × 9 months)	-10800	
4	Fair value inventory adjustment	200	
5	URP in inventory at 30 September 20X6 (1,800 × 20/120)	300	
6	Additional depreciation (4,000/2 years × 9/12)	1,500	
7		=SUM(B1:B6)	

32 Archway Co

Text reference

Chapter 19.

Top tips

This is an interpretation question taking account of a prospective acquisition. As always with interpretation questions, most of the marks are not for ratios. You must take account of all the information and consider the group aspects. How would Archway's results look following its acquisition by Landing?

Easy marks

The ratios based on the amended figures are an easy five marks – but don't spend too long on them.

Marking guide		Marks
(a) Revenue	0.5	
Cost of sales	2	
Loan interest	0.5	
Equity	1.5	
Non-current liabilities	0.5	
		5
(b) 1 mark per ratio	6	
		6
(c) 1 mark per relevant comment	9	
		9
Total		20

(a) **Archway Co's restated figures**

On the assumption that Landing Co purchases Archway Co, the following adjustments relate to the effects of Notes (1) to (3) in the question and the property revaluation:

	$'000
Revenue (94,000 × 95%)	89,300
Cost of sales (see below)	76,000
Loan interest (10,000 × 8%)	800
Equity (10,000 + 2,300 RE + 3,000 revaluation)	15,300
Non-current liabilities: 8% loan notes	10,000

The cost of sales should be first adjusted for the annual licence fee of $1m, reducing this to $72m. Half of these, $36m, are net of a discount of 10% which equates to $4m (36,000/90% – 36,000). Adjusted cost of sales is $76m (73,000 – 1,000 + 4,000).

(b) These figures would give the following ratios:

Annual sales per square metre of floor space	(89,300/12,000)	$7,442
ROCE	(13,300 – 10,000)/(15,300 + 10,000) × 100	13%
Net asset turnover	(89,300/(15,300 + 10,000))	3.5 times
Gross profit margin	((89,300 – 76,000)/89,300 × 100)	15%
Operating profit margin	((13,300 – 10,000)/89,300 × 100)	3.7%

Gearing (debt/equity)	(10,000/15,300)	65.4%

Despite being calculations, the ratio calculations are normally completed in the word processor response option. You may be provided with a pre-formatted response option table for ratios. If not, you can easily create one using within the word processor.

Word Processor

Ratio	Working	Restated
Annual sales per square metre of floor space	(89,300/12,000)	$7,442
ROCE	(13,300 – 10,000)/(15,300 + 10,000) × 100	13%
Net asset turnover	(89,300/(15,300 + 10,000))	3.5 times
Gross profit margin	((89,300 – 76,000)/89,300 × 100)	15%
Operating profit margin	((13,300 – 10,000)/89,300 × 100)	3.7%
Gearing (debt/equity)	(10,000/15,300)	65.4%

(c) **Performance**

	Archway Co as reported	Archway Co as adjusted	Sector average
Annual sales per square metre of floor space	$7,833	$7,442	$8,000
ROCE	58.5%	13%	18.0%
Net asset turnover	5.0 times	3.5 times	2.7 times
Gross profit margin	22.3%	15%	22.0%
Operating profit margin	11.7%	3.7%	6.7%
Gearing (debt/equity)	nil	65.4%	30.0%

A comparison of Archway Co's ratios based upon the reported results compares very favourably to the sector average ratios in almost every instance. ROCE is particularly impressive at 58.5% compared to a sector average of 18%; this represents a return of more than three times the sector average. The superior secondary ratios of profit margin and asset utilisation (net asset turnover) appear to confirm Archway Co's above average performance. It is only sales per square metre of floor space which is below the sector average. The unadjusted figure is very close to the sector average, as too is the gross profit margin, implying a comparable sales volume performance. However, the reduction in selling prices caused by the removal of the brand premium causes sales per square metre to fall marginally.

As indicated in the question, should Archway Co be acquired by Landing Co, many figures particularly related to the statement of profit or loss would be unfavourably impacted as shown above in the workings for Archway Co's adjusted ratios. When these effects are taken into account and the ratios are recalculated, a very different picture emerges. All the performance ratios, with the exception of net asset turnover, are significantly reduced due to the assumed cessation of the favourable trading arrangements. The most dramatic effect is on the ROCE, which, having been more than three times the sector average, would be 27.8% (18.0 – 13.0)/18.0 × 100) below the sector average (at 13.0% compared to 18.0%). Analysing the component parts of the ROCE (net asset turnover and profit margins), both aspects are lower when the reported figures are adjusted.

The net asset turnover (although adjusted to a lower multiple) is still considerably higher than the sector average. The fall in this ratio is due to a combination of lower revenues (caused by the loss of the branding) and the increase in capital employed (equal to net assets) due to classifying the loan notes as debt (non-current). Gross margin deteriorates from 22.3% to only 15.0% caused by a combination of lower revenues (referred to above) and the loss of the discount on purchases. The distribution costs and administrative expenses for Archway Co are less than those of its retail sector in terms of the percentage of sales revenue (at 11.3% compared to 15.3%), which mitigates (slightly) the dramatic reduction in the profit before interest and tax. The reduction in sales per square metre of floor space is caused only by the reduced (5%) volume from the removal of the branded sales.

Gearing

The gearing ratio of nil based on the unadjusted figures is not meaningful due to previous debt being classified as a current liability because of its imminent redemption. When this debt is replaced by the 8% loan notes and (more realistically) classified as a non-current liability, Archway Co's gearing is much higher than the sector average. There is no information as to how the increased interest payable at 8% (double the previous 4%) compares to the sector's average finance cost. If such a figure were available, it may give an indication of Archway Co's credit status although the doubling of the rate does imply a greater degree of risk in Archway Co seen by the lender.

Summary and advice

Based upon Archway Co's reported figures, its purchase by Landing Co would appear to be a good investment. However, when Archway Co's performance is assessed based on the results and financial position which might be expected under Landing Co's ownership, the recalculated ratios are generally inferior to Archway Co's retail sector averages. In an investment decision such as this, an important projected ratio would be the return on the investment (ROI) which Landing Co might expect. The expected net profit after tax can be calculated as \$2m ((3,300 before interest and tax – 800 interest) × 80% post-tax), however, there is no information in the question as to what the purchase consideration of Archway Co would be. That said, at a (probable) minimum purchase price based on Archway Co's net asset value (with no goodwill premium), the ROI would only be 7.9% (2,000/25,300 × 100) which is very modest and should be compared to Landing Co's existing ROI. A purchase price exceeding \$25.3m would obviously result in an even lower expected ROI. It is possible that under Landing Co's management, Archway Co's profit margins could be improved, perhaps coming to a similar arrangement regarding access to branded sales (or franchising) as currently exists with Cardol Co, but with a different company. If so, the purchase of Archway Co may still be a reasonable acquisition.

You will use the word processor response option when answering the interpretation question. You should make your answer as clear as possible for the marker by providing headings and inserting space between sections. Using extended bullet points and adding emphasis with bold text or underlines can also help to make your answer clearer. You could lay out your answer as follows:

Word Processor

Paragraph

Ratio comparison

	Archway Co as reported	Archway Co as adjusted	Sector average
Annual sales per square metre of floor space	$7,833	$7,442	$8,000
ROCE	58.5%	13%	18.0%
Net asset turnover	5.0 times	3.5 times	2.7 times
Gross profit margin	22.3%	15%	22.0%
Operating profit margin	11.7%	3.7%	6.7%
Gearing (debt/equity)	nil	65.4%	30.0%

A comparison of Archway Co's ratios based upon the reported results **compares very favourably** to the sector average ratios in almost every instance.

Archway Co as reported

- ROCE is particularly impressive at 58.5% compared to a sector average of 18%; this represents a return of more than three times the sector average.
- The superior secondary ratios of profit margin and asset utilisation (net asset turnover) appear to confirm Archway Co's above average performance.
- It is only sales per square metre of floor space that is below the sector average. The unadjusted figure is very close to the sector average, as too is the gross profit margin, implying a comparable sales volume performance. However, the reduction in selling prices caused by the removal of the brand premium causes sales per square metre to fall marginally.

Archway Co adjusted

- Many figures particularly related to the statement of profit or loss would be **unfavourably impacted** as shown above in the workings for Archway Co's adjusted ratios.
- All the performance ratios, with the exception of net asset turnover, are significantly reduced due to the assumed cessation of the favourable trading arrangements.
- The most dramatic effect is on the ROCE, which, having been more than three times the sector average, would be 27.8% (18.0 – 13.0)/18.0 × 100) below the sector average (at 13.0% compared to 18.0%). Analysing the component parts of the ROCE (net asset turnover and profit margins), both aspects are lower when the reported figures are adjusted.
- The net asset turnover (although adjusted to a lower multiple) is still considerably higher than the sector average. The fall in this ratio is due to a combination of lower revenues (caused by the loss of the branding) and the increase in capital employed (equal to net assets) due to classifying the loan notes as debt (non-current).
- Gross margin deteriorates from 22.3% to only 15.0% caused by a combination of lower revenues (referred to above) and the loss of the discount on purchases. The distribution costs and administrative expenses for Archway Co are less than those of its retail sector in terms of the percentage of sales revenue (at 11.3% compared to 15.3%), which

ANSWERS

mitigates (slightly) the dramatic reduction in the profit before interest and tax. The reduction in sales per square metre of floor space is caused only by the reduced (5%) volume from the removal of the branded sales.

Gearing

The gearing ratio of nil based on the unadjusted figures is not meaningful due to previous debt being classified as a current liability because of its imminent redemption. When this debt is replaced by the 8% loan notes and (more realistically) classified as a non-current liability, Archway Co's gearing is much higher than the sector average. There is no information as to how the increased interest payable at 8% (double the previous 4%) compares to the sector's average finance cost. If such a figure were available, it may give an indication of Archway Co's credit status, although the doubling of the rate does imply a greater degree of risk in Archway Co seen by the lender.

Summary and conclusion

- Based upon Archway Co's reported figures, its purchase by Landing Co would appear to be a good investment.
- However, when Archway Co's performance is assessed based on the results and financial position which might be expected under Landing Co's ownership, the recalculated ratios are generally inferior to Archway Co's retail sector averages. In an investment decision such as this, an important projected ratio would be the return on the investment (ROI) which Landing Co might expect.
- The expected net profit after tax can be calculated as $2m ((3,300 before interest and tax – 800 interest) × 80% post-tax), however, there is no information in the question as to what the purchase consideration of Archway Co would be.
- That said, at a (probable) minimum purchase price based on Archway Co's net asset value (with no goodwill premium), the ROI would only be 7.9% (2,000/25,300 × 100), which is very modest and should be compared to Landing Co's existing ROI.
- A purchase price exceeding $25.3m would obviously result in an even lower expected ROI.
- It is possible that under Landing Co's management, Archway Co's profit margins could be improved, perhaps coming to a similar arrangement regarding access to branded sales (or franchising) as currently exists with Cardol Co, but with a different company. If so, the purchase of Archway Co may still be a reasonable acquisition.

ACCA

Financial Reporting (FR)

Mock Exam 4

Section C is the ACCA Sept/Dec 21 exam

Questions	
Time allowed	3 hours
This mock exam is divided into three sections: Section A: ALL 15 questions are compulsory and MUST be attempted Section B: ALL 15 questions are compulsory and MUST be attempted Section C: BOTH questions are compulsory and MUST be attempted	

DO NOT OPEN THIS EXAM UNTIL YOU ARE READY TO START UNDER EXAMINATION CONDITIONS

Section A

ALL 15 questions are compulsory and MUST be attempted

1 According to the *Conceptual Framework for Financial Reporting* of the International Accounting Standards Board (IASB), verifiability means that "different knowledgeable and independent observers could reach a consensus of faithful representation".

Which of the following procedures directly verifies that the relevant balances are faithfully represented? ***(ACCA Examiner's report September 2019)***

- O Confirming the cash balance by conducting a physical count of cash
- O Confirming the inventory by reviewing the year-end list of inventory
- O Confirming a revaluation of land by agreeing the revaluation surplus to a minute of the board meeting where the directors agreed its estimate
- O Confirming the carrying amount of receivables by reviewing the year-end statements issued to customers at that date **(2 marks)**

2 Cyanide Co had the following bank loans outstanding during the whole of 20X7 which form the company's general borrowings for the year:

	$m
9% loan repayable 20X9	30
11% loan repayable 20Y2	48

Cyanide Co began construction of a qualifying asset on 1 April 20X7 and $12 million of the loan funding was transferred to the construction project on that date to fund construction. On 1 August 20X7, an additional $4 million was transferred for the same purpose.

Calculate the borrowing costs which can be capitalised in respect of this project for the year ended 31 December 20X7. Round the capitalisation rate to one decimal place to calculate your answer.

- O $1,098,667
- O $823,998
- O $1,500,000
- O $700,000

(2 marks)

3 Extracts from the statements of financial position of Polonium Co are as follows:

Statements of financial position as at 30 September

	20X5	*20X4*
	$m	$m
Ordinary shares of $1 each	750	500
Share premium	350	100

On 1 October 20X4, a bonus issue of one new share for every ten held was made, financed from share premium. This was followed by a further issue for cash.

Using the pull-down list, what amount will appear under 'cash flows from financing activities' in the statement of cash flows of Polonium Co for the year ended 30 September 20X5 in respect of share issues?

[▼]

Pull down list

- $250 million
- $450 million
- $500 million
- $550 million

(2 marks)

4 Radium Co purchased a machine on 1 October 20X7 for $1,500,000. The machine has a useful life of 10 years with an estimated residual value of $75,000. It is Radium Co's policy to depreciate over the useful lives of non-current assets on a straight-line basis.

On 1 January 20X8, Radium Co purchased an upgraded motherboard to improve the capacity of the machine. This cost $30,000 and has a useful life of five years (no residual value).

Using the click and drag options below, select the correct depreciation expense for the year to 31 March 20X8.

$71,250		Depreciation expense for the original machine
$72,250		
$75,000		Depreciation expense for the motherboard
$750		
$1,500		
$6,000		

5 Muchmoo Co has a dairy farm with a herd of 100 cattle. Muchmoo Co produces milk and dairy produce, including butter and a specialist blue vein cheese for sale to the public and local farm shops. Once the dairy cows have ceased to produce milk, they are looked after by the farmer's daughter who runs an animal sanctuary, where they live out their days grazing on the fields in Snowdonia.

The financial accountant of Muchmoo Co is unsure of how to account for the different products and the herd of cattle.

Using the options provided, select the correct accounting standard to value the various assets of Muchmoo Co. Note that each option may be used more than once or not at all.

Inventories (IAS 2)		Dairy cows
Property, Plant and Equipment (IAS 16)		Pasteurised milk, cheese, butter
Agriculture (IAS 41)		Raw milk from the cows
Intangible Assets (IAS 38)		

(2 marks)

6 During the year ended 31 December 20X4, Bloop Co incurred expenditure on two projects:

- Project 1 costs relate to the evaluation of alternatives for improved production systems to be implemented during 20X5 and 20X6. The company spent $1m on related salaries and materials and $2m on design equipment (which had an expected life of four years).
- Project 2 involves the testing of a new product which will be introduced to the market in 20X5 and is expected to generate profits over a four-year period. The company spent $4m on salaries and materials. The policy is to charge a full year's depreciation on assets.

What is the **TOTAL** charge to profit or loss for the year ended 31 December 20X4?
(ACCA Examiner's report December 2019)

O $5.5 million

O $3 million

O $1.5 million

O $1 million

(2 marks)

7 Pootle Co received a government grant on 1 September 20X4. The conditions of the grant state that Pootle Co must employ a local worker on a full-time contract over a five-year period. Pootle Co expects to meet the conditions of the grant.

The full amount of the grant received has been recorded as 'Other income' for the year ended 31 December 20X4.

What is the adjustment required to correctly account for the grant as at 31 December 20X4?
(ACCA Examiner's report March/June 2021)

Account name		
Accrued income		Debit
Deferred income		Credit
Other income		
Bank		

(2 marks)

8 Which of the following meet(s) the recognition criteria for an asset and/or a liability?

(1) Green Co spent $100,000 providing health and safety training to its staff

(2) Green Co has been told by a brand consultancy that the value of its internally created brands is $2,000,000

(3) Green Co is suing a supplier for $450,000 for losses that it suffered due to faulty goods. Green Co is likely, though not certain, to win the court case

(4) Green Co has sold goods subject to a five-year warranty on which it expects some claims will be made

(ACCA Examiner's report September 2018)

- O 1 and 2
- O 3 and 4
- O 2 only
- O 4 only

(2 marks)

9 Which of the following events taking place after the year end but before the financial statements were authorised for issue would require adjustment in accordance with IAS 10 *Events After the Reporting Period*?

- O Three lines of inventory held at the year-end were destroyed by flooding in the warehouse
- O The directors announced a major restructuring
- O Two lines of inventory held at the year-end were discovered to have faults rendering them unsaleable
- O The value of the company's investments fell sharply

(2 marks)

10 Root Co acquired 30% of the 100,000 equity shares in Branch Co for $7.50 per share on 1 January 20X7, when Branch Co had retained earnings of $460,000 and a balance on the revaluation surplus of $50,000. At the year-end date of 31 December 20X7, Branch Co had retained earnings of $370,000 and a balance of $70,000 on the revaluation surplus. Root Co considered that its investment in Branch Co had suffered an impairment loss of $40,000.

Calculate the carrying amount of Root's investment in Branch.
(ACCA Examiner's report March 2020)

$ [   ]

(2 marks)

11 Tonton Co acquired 9,000 shares in Pogo Co on 1 August 20X3 at a cost of $6.40 per share. Tonton Co incurred transaction costs of $9,000 for this transaction. Tonton Co elected to hold these shares at fair value through other comprehensive income.

At 31 December 20X3, the fair value of the Pogo Co shares was $7.25 per share and selling costs were expected to be 4%.

What is the value of the Pogo Co shares in Tonton Co's individual financial statements at 31 December 20X3? ***(ACCA Examiner's report March 2019)***

- O $65,250
- O $74,250
- O $62,640
- O $66,600

(2 marks)

12 Which of the following ratios are likely to DECREASE due to a significant revaluation gain on a depreciating asset at the start of the year?

(1) Return on capital employed (ROCE)

(2) Gearing (debt/equity)

(3) Operating profit margin

(4) Net asset turnover

(ACCA Examiner's report September/December 2020)

- O 1, 2, 3 and 4
- O 1, 2 and 3 only
- O 2, 3 and 4 only
- O 1 and 4 only

(2 marks)

13 Using the drag and drop options below, complete the statement to show how IAS 8 *Accounting policies, Changes in Accounting Estimates and Errors* require accounting policies to be adopted in the financial statements.

Each statement may be used more than once or not at all.

Prospectively		A company decides to change the accounting policy of the valuation of non-current assets. This change must be applied
Retrospectively		A company discovers a fundamental error in the valuation of inventories. The correction should be made

(2 marks)

14 A company's statement of financial position at 31 December 20X4 included land at a cost of \$200,000 and a deferred tax liability of \$60,000. On 1 March 20X5, the land was professionally valued at \$250,000. This valuation was incorporated into the financial statements for the year to 31 December 20X5. No other non-current assets have been revalued. Other taxable temporary differences increased during the year to 31 December 20X5 by \$40,000. The relevant rate of tax is 20%.

What are the balances at 31 December 20X5 on the revaluation surplus and the deferred tax liability? ***(ACCA Examiner's report December 2019)***

- O Revaluation surplus of \$50,000 and deferred tax liability of \$68,000
- O Revaluation surplus of \$50,000 and deferred tax liability of \$78,000
- O Revaluation surplus of \$40,000 and deferred tax liability of \$78,000
- O Revaluation surplus of \$40,000 and deferred tax liability of \$62,000

(2 marks)

15 A 60% owned subsidiary sold goods to its parent for \$150,000 at a mark-up of 25% on cost during the year ended 30 June 20X5. One fifth of these goods remained unsold as at 30 June 20X5.

What is the debit adjustment to be made to group retained earnings to reflect the unrealised profit in inventory at 30 June 20X5?

(ACCA Examiner's report September 2018)

- O $6,000
- O $3,600
- O $2,400
- O $4,500

(2 marks)

BPP

Section B

ALL 15 questions are compulsory and MUST be attempted

Chestnut Co

The following scenario relates to questions 16–20.

The following issues relating to Chestnut Co's non-current assets are outstanding for the year ended 31 December 20X7:

(1) Factory: At 1 January 20X7, Chestnut Co's factory had a carrying amount of $5m. It has a remaining useful life of ten years at that date. On 31 December 20X7, there was an impairment review of the factory and the recoverable amount was deemed to be $2.5m. Chestnut Co's factory had previously been revalued upwards and the revaluation surplus has a credit balance of $1m relating to this factory.

(2) Head Office: Chestnut Co's head office cost $12m on 1 January 20X1 and is being depreciated over a 40-year life. On 31 December 20X4, there was an impairment review of the head office and the recoverable amount was deemed to be $9m. A more recent valuation, at 31 December 20X7, has estimated that the recoverable amount of the head office is $11m.

(3) Machinery: On 1 April 20X7, Chestnut Co received a grant of $2.6m towards new production machinery. The machinery cost $4m and is expected to have a useful life of five years. Depreciation is charged on a straight-line proportionate basis. Chestnut Co uses the cost model when accounting for its head office, and the deferred income method in relation to government grants

16 Which of the following assets belonging to Chestnut Co require an annual impairment review? ***(Sep/Dec 2021)***

- O The head office only
- O The machinery only
- O Both the head office and the machinery
- O Neither the head office nor the machinery **(2 marks)**

---

17 In accordance with IAS 36 Impairment of Assets, what is the correct journal entry to reflect the depreciation and the impairment of Chestnut Co's factory for the year ended 31 December 20X7? ***(Sep/Dec 2021)***

- O Dr Statement of profit or loss $1.5m, Dr Revaluation surplus $1m, Cr Non-current assets $2.5m
- O Dr Statement of profit or loss $2.5m, Cr Non-current assets $2.5m
- O Dr Non-current assets $2.5m, Cr Statement of profit or loss $1.5m, Cr Non-current assets $1m
- O Dr Non-current assets $2.5m, Cr Statement of profit or loss $2.5m **(2 marks)**

---

18 What is the carrying amount of Chestnut Co's head office in the statement of financial position as at 31 December 20X7? ***(Sep/Dec 2021)***

- O $8.25m
- O $9.9m
- O $10.8m
- O $11m **(2 marks)**

---

19 Which of the following statements relating to government grants is correct? ***(Sep/Dec 2021)***

- O The deferred income method should always be used for grants related to assets
- O Grants related to income must be disclosed separately in the statement of profit or loss as other income
- O The deferred income method should only be used if the grant is repayable
- O Grants related to assets can be accounted for using either the deferred income method or by deducting from the asset's carrying amount **(2 marks)**

---

20 What is the carrying amount of the non-current liability in respect of the government grant in Chestnut Co's statement of financial position as at 31 December 20X7? ***(Sep/Dec 2021)***

- O $2.08m
- O $1.69m
- O $2.21m
- O $1.56m **(2 marks)**

(Total = 10 marks)

Diaz Co

The following scenario relates to questions 21–25.

The following is an extract from Diaz Co's trial balance as at 31 December 20X8:

	Debit	*Credit*
	$m	$m
Inventory at 31 December 20X8	8.6	
Trade receivables	6.2	
5% loan notes		9.0

The inventory count was completed on 31 December 20X8, but two issues have been noted. First, products with a sales value of $0.6m had been incorrectly excluded from the count. Second, items costing $0.2m which had been included in the count were damaged and could only be sold for 50% of the normal selling price. Diaz Co makes a mark-up of 50% on both of these items.

Diaz Co entered into a factoring agreement with Finaid Co on 31 December 20X8. In accordance with the agreement, Diaz Co sold trade receivables with a carrying amount of $6.2m to Finaid Co for $6m. Under the terms of the factoring agreement, after six months Finaid Co will return any unpaid receivables to Diaz Co for collection. Finaid Co will also charge Diaz Co a fee of 5% of any uncollected balances at the end of each month.

The 5% loan notes were issued for $9m on 1 July 20X8. Diaz Co incurred issue costs of $0.5m associated with this, which have been expensed within finance costs. The loan note interest is payable each 30 June and the loan note is repayable at a premium, giving them an effective interest rate of 8%.

21 In accordance with IAS 32 *Financial Instruments: Presentation*, which of the items in the trial balance would be classified as financial instruments?

- O Closing inventory and trade receivables only
- O 5% loan notes only
- O Trade receivables and 5% loan notes only
- O Closing inventory, trade receivables and 5% loan notes **(2 marks)**

22 What is the correct carrying amount of inventory to be recognised in Diaz Co's financial statements as at 31 December 20X8?

- O $8.95m
- O $9.0m
- O $8.9m
- O $9.15m **(2 marks)**

---

23 In an attempt to improve reported profit, the directors of Diaz Co want to change the valuation method of inventory from first in first out (FIFO) to an average cost method.

Which, if any, of the following statements regarding the potential change in inventory valuation is/are correct?

(1) The change will represent a change in accounting estimate

(2) The financial statements will be adjusted prospectively

- O 1 only
- O 2 only
- O Both 1 and 2
- O Neither 1 nor 2 **(2 marks)**

---

24 Which of the following statements regarding the factoring arrangement is **NOT** true?

- O $6m received should be recorded in the liabilities of Diaz Co at 31 December 20X8
- O $0.2m should be expensed in Diaz Co's statement of profit or loss for the year ended 31 December 20X8
- O A total of the 5% monthly fee should be expensed in Diaz Co's statement of profit or loss for the year ended 31 December 20X9
- O The receivables will remain as an asset in the financial statements of Diaz Co at 31 December 20X8 **(2 marks)**

---

25 In respect of the 5% loan notes, how much should be expensed within Diaz Co's statement of profit or loss for the year ended 31 December 20X8?
(ACCA Examiner's report Mar/Jun 2019)

- O $0.68m
- O $0.45m
- O $0.72m
- O $0.34m **(2 marks)**

(Total = 10 marks)

Bargi Co

26 Bargi Co is in the process of preparing its financial statements for the year ended 31 December 20X6. There are three transactions which have not yet been accounted for:

1 October 20X6	A sale was made for a large piece of technical equipment which included a three-year service plan. The total sales price was $1.8m, which was paid on 1

	October 20X6 and the technical equipment was delivered on that date. On its own, the technical equipment would normally be sold for $1,750,000 and a three-year service plan would normally be sold for $165,000.
18 November 20X6	Machinery sold by Bargi Co in January 20X6 was found to be faulty and various parts were replaced by Bargi Co under warranty. Bargi Co would normally sell the replacement parts for $80,000. The total cost to Bargi Co of these replacement parts was $60,000.
1 December 20X6	Bargi Co entered into a contract for the sale of goods for $200,000. Bargi Co received $200,000 on 1 December 20X6. Bargi Co has the right to repurchase these goods on 1 April 20X7 for $240,000.

Required

Which **TWO** of the following criteria are required before an entity should account for a contract in accordance with IFRS 15 Revenue from Contracts with Customers?
(Mar/Jun 2022)

- ☐ All parties to the contract have approved the contract
- ☐ The contract must be in writing
- ☐ The contract must have commercial substance
- ☐ It is possible that the consideration will be collected from the customer **(2 marks)**

---

27 IFRS 15 Revenue from Contracts with Customers requires the transaction price to be allocated to the performance obligations in the contract.

Required

Where each performance obligation is satisfied at a point in time, how should the allocation of the transaction price be made? ***(Mar/Jun 2022)***

- O The transaction price should be spread equally over the period from when the contract is first agreed to when it is completed
- O The transaction price should be allocated relative to the stand-alone selling price of the component parts at the date of the contract inception
- O An agreed percentage of the transaction price should be allocated to the stand-alone selling price of any goods sold with the balance spread equally over the term of the contract
- O The transaction price should be allocated based on the cost of the component parts at the date on which the contract is first agreed **(2 marks)**

---

28 In relation to the sale made on 1 October 20X6, what is the amount that will be reported as the contract liability for the service plan at 31 December 20X6 (to the nearest $'000)?
(Mar/Jun 2022)

$ [ ] ,000 **(2 marks)**

29 Which of the following statements is correct in relation to the warranty work undertaken on 18 November 20X6? ***(Mar/Jun 2022)***

- O Revenue should include $80,000 to reflect the selling value of the goods provided in repairing the machine to avoid affecting the gross profit margin of Bargi Co
- O Cost of sales will include $60,000 for the cost of the goods used, assuming no provision has previously been made by Bargi Co for a warranty liability
- O Revenue should include $60,000 to match the actual costs incurred by Bargi Co and net off to give nil effect on profit
- O Cost of sales will be reduced by $60,000 for the cost of the goods used, assuming no provision has previously been made by Bargi Co for a warranty liability **(2 marks)**

---

30 Match the relevant amounts to show how Bargi Co should account for the contract on 1 December 20X6 in its financial statements for the year ended 31 December 20X6.
(Mar/Jun 2022)

Amount		
		Statement of profit or loss
$0		Revenue
$10,000		Interest expense
$30,000		**Statement of financial position**
$200,000		Cash
		Liability

(2 marks)

(Total = 10 marks)

Section C

BOTH questions are compulsory and MUST be attempted

31 Treats Co

This scenario relates to two requirements.

Treats Co manufactures confectionery. The following sector average ratios have been obtained for the year ended 30 September 20X6:

Ratio	**Sector average**
Return on year-end capital employed (ROCE)	28.8%
Net asset turnover	2.4 times
Gross profit margin	55%
Operating profit margin	12%
Current ratio	1.8:1
Inventory turnover period	25 days
Gearing (debt/equity)	43%
Receivables collection period	15 days

Extracts from the financial statements of Treats Co for the year ended 30 September 20X6 are as follows:

	$'000
Revenue	214,553
Cost of sales	(108,009)
Gross profit	**106,544**
Operating expenses	(99,078)
Profit from operations	**7,466**
Finance costs	(1,329)
Profit before taxation	**6,137**
Taxation	(1,783)
Profit for the year	**4,354**

Statement of Financial Position:

	$'000
ASSETS	
Non-current assets:	
Property, plant and equipment (note (1))	**61,984**
Current assets:	
Inventories	30,393
Trade and other receivables	17,603
	47,996

	$'000
Total Assets	**109,980**
EQUITY and LIABILITIES	
Equity:	
Ordinary shares	7,000
Other components of equity (Share premium)	13,605
Retained earnings	5,363
Total equity (note (2))	**25,968**
Non-current liabilities:	
Borrowings	**33,621**
Current liabilities:	
Trade and other payables	25,390
Overdraft (note (3))	24,090
Current tax liabilities	911
	50,391
Total Equity and Liabilities	**109,980**

The following information is also relevant:

(1) The property, plant and equipment relates to retail stores operated by Treats Co and the manufacturing plant, all of which are depreciated on a straight line basis over 20 years. The original cost of these assets was $637.84m and the directors are now considering replacing and updating much of the plant and equipment.

(2) Treats Co paid a dividend of $7.14m during the year despite the concern raised by some directors over the existing overdraft.

(3) The overdraft is used for working capital management purposes and does not form part of the long-term financing of Treats Co.

(4) Treats Co sells its products through supermarket chains in addition to its owned retail stores. Most companies in the sector exclusively sell through their own retail stores.

Note. The following preformatted table relates to part (a) of the question and has been replicated in the response area.

Ratio	**Workings**	**Treats Co**	**Sector average per question**
Return on year-end capital employed (ROCE)		to be calculated	28.8%
Net asset turnover		to be calculated	2.4 times
Gross profit margin		to be calculated	55%
Operating profit margin		to be calculated	12%
Current ratio		to be calculated	1.8:1

Ratio	Workings	Treats Co	Sector average per question
Inventory turnover period		to be calculated	25 days
Gearing (debt/equity)		to be calculated	43%
Receivables collection period		to be calculated	15 days

Required

(a) Calculate for Treats Co the equivalent ratios to those provided for the confectionery manufacturing sector.

Note. The preformatted table relating to part (a) (see below) has also been replicated in the question scenario for your information. **(5 marks)**

Ratio	Working	Treats Co	Sector
Return on year-end capital employed (ROCE)		12.5%	28.8%
Net asset turnover		3.6 times	2.4 times
Gross profit margin		49.7%	55%
Operating profit margin		3.5%	12%
Current ratio		0.95:1	1.8:1
Inventory turnover period		103 days	25 days
Gearing (debt/equity)		129%	43%
Receivables collection period		30 days	15 days

(b) Analyse the performance and financial position of Treats Co in comparison to its sector averages. **(15 marks)**

(Total = 20 marks)

32 Perd Co

This scenario relates to two requirements.

Perd Co acquired 80% of Sebastian Co on 1 April 20X6. Non-controlling interest is valued at fair value.

Extracts from the draft financial statements of both entities are shown below:

Statement of profit or loss for the year ended 31 March 20X8

	Perd Co	Sebastian Co
	$'000	$'000
Revenue	58,200	34,300
Cost of sales	(34,340)	(20,400)
Gross profit	**23,860**	**13,900**
Operating expenses	(18,040)	(7,130)
Profit from operations	**5,820**	**6,770**
Investment income	3,000	-

	Perd Co	Sebastian Co
	$'000	$'000
Finance costs	(3,240)	(1,600)
Profit before tax	**5,580**	**5,170**
Tax	(1,560)	(1,480)
Profit for the year	**4,020**	**3,690**

Statement of financial position as at 31 March 20X8:

	Perd Co	Sebastian Co
	$'000	$'000
Total assets	**297,310**	**110,540**

The following information is relevant:

(1) The cost of Perd Co's investment in Sebastian Co has been excluded from the total assets listed above. As part of the consideration for Sebastian Co, $8m is due to be paid on 1 April 20X8. Perd Co recorded a liability of $7.547m in its individual statement of financial position at 31 March 20X7 which correctly represents the liability at that date. No other accounting entries have been made in relation to this consideration for the year ended 31 March 20X8. Perd Co has a cost of capital of 6%.

(2) On acquisition of Sebastian Co, the goodwill was correctly calculated at $3.2m. In the year to 31 March 20X7, goodwill was deemed to have been impaired by $400,000. A further impairment of $300,000 is to be recognised for the year ended 31 March 20X8. Impairment losses are charged to operating expenses.

(3) At 1 April 20X6, Sebastian Co's property had a carrying amount of $11m but a fair value of $14m. At this date, the property had a remaining life of 15 years. Sebastian Co sold the property for $15m on 30 September 20X7. For the year ended 31 March 20X8, Sebastian Co has recorded the historic cost depreciation and the historic cost profit on disposal of the property in operating expenses. Depreciation is charged on a pro-rata basis.

(4) Perd Co made sales of $9m to Sebastian Co during the year ended 31 March 20X8. Sebastian Co had only paid for $2m of these goods at 31 March 20X8. These sales were made at a mark-up on cost of 25%, and Sebastian Co holds one third of these goods at 31 March 20X8.

(5) At 31 March 20X8, the Perd group decided to revalue its non-current assets for the first time. Perd Co's assets were deemed to have increased by $4.1m and Sebastian Co's assets by $0.7m. Neither company has recorded the revaluation in its individual financial statements. Ignore deferred tax.

(6) Sebastian Co paid a dividend of $1m in the year, which has been correctly recorded by both companies.

Required

(a) Prepare the consolidated statement of profit or loss and other comprehensive income for the Perd group for the year ended 31 March 20X8. **(15 marks)**

(b) Calculate the total assets that would be recognised in the consolidated statement of financial position for the Perd group as at 31 March 20X8. **(5 marks)**

(Total = 20 marks)

Answers

DO NOT TURN THIS PAGE UNTIL YOU HAVE COMPLETED THE MOCK EXAM

A plan of attack

Managing your nerves

As you start this mock exam a number of thoughts are likely to cross your mind. Developing an awareness of what is going on emotionally within you may help you manage your nerves. Remember, you are unlikely to banish the flow of adrenaline, but the key is to harness it to help you work steadily and quickly through your answers.

Working through this mock exam will help you develop the exam stamina you will need to keep going for three hours.

Managing your time

Planning and time management are two of the key skills which complement the technical knowledge you need to succeed. To keep yourself on time, note your target completion times for Section A, for each case and in total for Section B and for each question and in total for Section C. As all the questions are **compulsory**, you do not have to spend time wondering which question to answer. If you can't answer an OT question in Section A or B, flag it or make a note in your scratch pad to remind yourself to go back to it later.

Doing the exam

Actually doing the exam is a personal experience. There is not a single **right way**. As long as you submit complete answers to all questions after the three hours are up, then your approach obviously works.

Looking through the exam

Section A has 15 OTQs. This is the section of the exam where the examining team can test knowledge across the breadth of the syllabus. Make sure you read these questions carefully. The distractors are designed to present plausible, but incorrect, answers. Don't let them mislead you. Remember there is no negative marking, so you should always have an educated guess at the OT questions and should never leave a question unanswered.

Section B has 15 OTQs in total – questions 16–30. These are arranged as three scenarios with five questions each.

Scenario 1 is on revenue

Scenario 2 is on financial instruments and inventory

Scenario 3 is on impairment of assets and government grants

Section C has two 20-mark questions.

Question 31 requires

Question 32 requires the

Section A

ALL 15 questions are compulsory and MUST be attempted

1 The correct answer is: Confirming the cash balance by conducting a physical count of cash

This is the only option that objectively verifies the existence of cash.

All other options verify the asset against an internal document: ie a 'list of inventory', a 'board minute' and a 'receivable statement'.

2 The correct answer is: $1,098,667

Weighted average capitalisation rate =

(9% × 30/78) + (11% × 48/78) = 3.5% + 6.8% = 10.3%

ANSWERS

		$
Borrowing costs =	\$12m × 10.3% × 9/12	927,000
+	\$4m × 10.3% × 5/12	171,667
		1,098,667

3 \$500 million

	\$m
B/f (500 + 100)	600
Cash received (β)	500
C/f (750 + 350)	1,100

The bonus issue is irrelevant as no cash is received.

4 The correct answers are:

\$71,250	Depreciation expense for the original machine
\$1,500	Depreciation expense for the motherboard

	\$'000
Machine ((1,500,000 – 75,000)/10 × 6/12	71,250
Motherboard ((30,000/5) × 3/12)	1,500
	72,750

5 The correct answers are:

Agriculture (IAS 41)	Dairy cows
Inventories (IAS 2)	Pasteurised milk, cheese, butter
Agriculture (IAS 41)	Raw milk from the cows

Dairy cows are classified as biological assets and therefore accounted for under IAS 41 as they are a living animal.

Raw milk from the cows is classified as agricultural produce at the point of harvest under IAS 41 as this is effectively the 'harvest' from the biological assets (the cows). It is not sold in this condition and must go through a process prior to being held as inventory (IAS 2) as pasteurised milk, butter or cheese.

6 The correct answer is: \$1.5 million

Project 1 expenditure on the "evaluation of alternatives" could never be classified as an asset. Therefore the full $1m relating to salaries and materials should be charged to profit or loss. Also, the depreciation for the design equipment should be expensed ($2m/4); $1.5m in total. The project 2 costs associated with the testing of a new product which will be introduced to the market in 20X5 should be capitalised in 20X4 and written off from 20X5 for the next four years. Consequently, there will be no project 2 costs charged to profit or loss during 20X4.

The first option charges $1.5m for project 1 and $4m for project 2.

The second option writes off all costs associated with project 1 (including the design equipment).

The fourth option charges the $1m for project 1 salaries and materials only.

	$
Fair value less costs of disposal (6.3m – 150,000)	6,150,000
Value in use	5,800,000
Recoverable amount is therefore:	6,150,000
Impairment loss (β)	850,000
Carrying amount	7,000,000

7 The correct answers are:

Account name	
Other income	Debit
Deferred income	Credit

DEBIT Other income	$56,000	
CREDIT Deferred income		$56,000

$60,000 / (5 years × 12 months) = $1,000 per month

So, Pootle Co should have only recognised $4,000 ($1,000 × 4 months) of income in the statement of profit or loss for the year ended 31 December 20X4, with the remaining $56,000 recognised as deferred income in the statement of financial position.

8 The correct answer is: 4 only

Green Co has sold goods subject to a five-year warranty on which it expects some claims will be made.

This is because a legal obligation (the warranty) has been created as a result of the sales contract.

The $100,000 expenditure on the health and safety training does not meet the definition of an asset because Green Co does not control their staff (ie they could leave their jobs at any time) and it is not certain that the health and safety training will produce economic benefits.

As the brand has been internally generated, it cannot be reliably measured and so it does not meet the definition of an asset.

The court case against the supplier cannot be recognised as an asset because the economic benefits are not sufficiently certain. It may, however, be a contingent asset and disclosed in the notes to the financial statements.

9 The correct answer is: Two lines of inventory held at the year-end were discovered to have faults rendering them unsaleable

We can assume that these faults also existed at the year end, so this is the only option which would require adjustment. The others have all taken place after the year end.

10 $ 164,000

	$
Cost of investment (30,000 × $7.50)	225,000
Post-acquisition loss in retained earnings (($370,000 – $460,000) × 30%)	(27,000)
Post-acquisition increase in revaluation surplus (($70,000-$50,000) × 30%)	6,000
Impairment	(40,000)
	164,000

11 The correct answer is: $65,250

9,000 shares × $7.25 = $65,250

Question is testing the knowledge of IFRS 13 which states that 'the fair value of an asset shall not be adjusted for transaction costs'.

12 The correct answer is: 1, 2, 3 and 4

The revaluation is at the beginning of the year and will affect the depreciation for the year and therefore operating profit:

ROCE – increased depreciation will reduce profit and capital employed will increase due to the revaluation surplus but the denominator (including the revaluation surplus) will increase more.

Gearing – increase in equity due to the revaluation surplus will decrease the ratio as debt will not be affected.

Operating profit margin – reduction in profit due to increased depreciation.

Asset turnover – increase in assets (PPE) due to revaluation even if the asset has one year's worth of depreciation.

13 The correct answers are:

Retrospectively	A company decides to change the accounting policy of the valuation of non-current assets. This change must be applied
Retrospectively	A company discovers a fundamental error in the valuation of inventories. The correction should be made

14 The correct answer is: Revaluation surplus of $40,000 and deferred tax liability of $78,000

The gain on the land revaluation is $50,000 and the associated deferred tax is $10,000 (20%). The journal entries for the land revaluation and its associated deferred tax are:

Debit	Land	$50,000	
Debit	Revaluation surplus	$10,000	
Credit	Revaluation surplus		$50,000
Credit	Deferred tax		$10,000

The closing balance on the revaluation surplus should then be $40,000 The opening balance on deferred tax is $60,000 which will be increased by the adjustment of $10,000 (above) for the land revaluation and $8,000 for the increase in taxable temporary differences ($40,000 × 20% per question). The closing balance on deferred tax should then be $78,000.

The first and second options do not take account of the deferred tax on the land revaluation.

The fourth option deducts the deferred tax on the taxable temporary differences instead of adding it on.

15 The correct answer is: $3,600

$150,000 × 25/125 × 1/5 × 60% = $3,600

The first option calculates the adjustment as if the sale was made by the parent

$150,000 × 25/125 × 1/5 = $6,000

The third option calculates using the NCI percentage as opposed to the group share

$150,000 × 25/125 × 1/5 × 40%= $2,400

The fourth option calculates using a margin as opposed to a mark-up

$150,000 × 25% × 1/5 × 60% = $4,500

Section B

ALL 15 questions are compulsory and MUST be attempted

Chestnut Co

16 The correct answer is: Neither the head office nor the machinery

The head office and machinery only need an impairment review where there are any indications that these assets might be impaired. The fact that they have been impaired before does not mean that an annual impairment review is required regardless of whether there are any indicators of impairment.

17 The correct answer is: Dr Statement of profit or loss $1.5m, Dr Revaluation surplus $1m, Cr Non-current assets $2.5m

At 1 January 20X7, Chestnut Co's factory had a carrying amount of $5m and a useful life of ten years. Therefore, the annual depreciation charge required would be $0.5m ($5m / 10 years) and the carrying amount at 31 December 20X7 would be $4.5m ($5m - $0.5m).

The recoverable amount of the factory was deemed to be $2.5m, which means that an impairment loss of $2m is required ($4.5m - $2.5m). As there is an existing revaluation surplus of $1m relating to this factory, the impairment loss is treated as a revaluation decrease and the impairment loss should first be debited to the revaluation surplus before any remaining loss is debited to the statement of profit or loss.

Therefore, the carrying amount of the factory within non-current assets will reduce by $2.5m in total and the split of the impairment loss will be $1m to the revaluation surplus and $1.5m to the statement of profit or loss.

18 The correct answer is: $9.9m

On 31 December 20X4, the carrying amount of the head office would have been $10.8m ($12m x 36/40 years) before the impairment review on that date. Following the impairment review, the head office would have been impaired to its recoverable amount of $9m with an impairment loss of $1.8m ($10.8m - $9m) being charged to the statement of profit or loss.

The valuation of $11m on 31 December 20X7 means that there is a reversal of this original impairment loss. In accordance with IAS 36, an increase to the carrying amount of the head office attributable to the reversal of an impairment loss must not exceed the carrying amount that would have been determined had no impairment loss been recognised for the asset in prior years.

As the head office is accounted for under the cost model (rather than the revaluation model), the impairment loss can only be reversed to the extent that the asset is carried at the amount that it would have been had no impairment taken place.

This would be $9.9m, being $12m less seven years' depreciation (1 January 20X1 to 31 December 20X7) at $0.3m per year ($12m / 40 years).

19 The correct answer is: Grants related to assets can be accounted for using either the deferred income method or by deducting from the asset's carrying amount

IAS 20 states that government grants related to assets, including non-monetary grants at fair value, shall be presented in the statement of financial position either by setting up the grant as deferred income or by deducting the grant in arriving at the carrying amount of the asset

20 The correct answer is: $1.69m

The $2.6m grant should be released over the five-year useful life of the asset, beginning on 1 April 20X7. Therefore, nine months should be released in 20X7, giving $0.39m ($2.6m / 5 years x 9/12 months). This leaves $2.21m ($2.6m - $0.39m) total deferred income at 31 December 20X7.

As $0.52m ($2.6m / 5 years) will be released to the statement of profit or loss over the next 12 months, this means that $0.52m of deferred income will be a current liability and $1.69m ($2.21m - $0.52m) will be a non-current liability.

Diaz Co

21 The correct answer is: Trade receivables and 5% loan notes only

Trade receivables have been factored, but Diaz Co still retains the risks and rewards of the receivables (as Finaid Co can seek redress from Diaz Co on the unpaid balances). Therefore, a financial liability under IFRS 9 should be recognised.

The loan notes are an obligation to transfer economic benefit on the part of Diaz Co. This is a debenture loan, which is a financial instrument under IAS 32.

Closing inventory is classified as an asset of Diaz Co and IAS 32 does not recognise physical assets as financial instruments.

22 The correct answer is: $8.95m

This is the $8.6m plus the $0.4m missing items ($0.6m × 100/150) less the write down of $0.05m ($200,000 – $150,000 NRV. The items would normally be sold for $300,000 but actually being sold at $150,000).

23 The correct answer is: Neither 1 nor 2

Change in the basis of valuation of inventory is a change of accounting policy (not accounting estimate). The financial statements will be adjusted retrospectively.

24 The correct answer is: $0.2m should be expensed in Diaz Co's statement of profit or loss for the year ended 31 December 20X8

As Diaz Co still retains the risks and rewards of the receivables, this is an example of factoring with recourse. The receivables are still an asset of the company (so the fourth statement is correct that the receivables remain as an asset in the financial statements). Diaz Co is required to pay amounts received from the factor in respect of any losses (the first statement showing the liability of $6m remaining outstanding). The finance cost of the factoring (the monthly charge) is to be expensed as incurred (the third statement).

The $6m received from Finaid is in effect a loan, and will be recorded as such. The receivable is not derecognised and so there is no 'loss on derecognition' expense to be recorded in the statement of profit or loss (second statement).

25 The correct answer is: $0.34m

The loan notes should initially be recorded at the net proceeds of $8.5m. The effective interest rate of 8% would then be expensed in relation to this, being $0.68m. As the loan notes were only issued on 1 July 20X8, the expense for the year would be $0.34m ($0.68m × 6/12).

Bargi Co

26 The correct answers are:

- All parties to the contract have approved the contract
- The contract must have commercial substance

Although all parties to the contract must approve it, the contract itself does not need to be in writing. Although it may be in writing, and there are often good legal or commercial reasons for doing this, a contract could also be oral or in accordance with other customary business practices.

When it comes to the consideration that will be collected from the customer, it is not sufficient for it simply to be 'possible' that consideration will be collected. Instead, it must be 'probable' that the consideration will be collected. In evaluating whether the collectability of an amount of consideration is probable, an entity must consider only the customer's ability and intention to pay that amount of consideration when it is due.

27 The correct answer is: The transaction price should be allocated relative to the stand-alone selling price of the component parts at the date of the contract inception

In accordance with IFRS 15, an entity must allocate the transaction price of a contract to each performance obligation identified on a relative stand-alone selling price basis. To do this, the entity must determine the stand-alone selling price of the distinct good or service underlying each performance obligation in the contract and allocate the transaction price in proportion to those stand-alone selling prices.

28 $ [142] ,000

A contract liability represents the entity's obligation to transfer goods or services to a customer for which the entity has received consideration (or the amount is due) from the customer.

In this case, Bargi Co has received $1.8m on 1 October 20X6, but part of that consideration relates to a three-year (ie 36 month) service plan. Therefore, by the year end of 31 December 20X6, there will still be 33 months (36 months - 3 months), over which Bargi Co will need to perform its obligation to the customer relating to the service plan.

As the total stand-alone selling price of each performance obligation is greater than the total contract price of $1.8m, then the discount needs to be allocated to each performance obligation:

	$'000
Technical equipment – stand-alone selling price	1,750
Service plan – stand-alone selling price	165
Total of stand-alone selling prices	1,915
Total contract price	1,800
Discount on contract	115
Revenue to be recognised for the service plan:	
Total revenue ($1,800,000 x ($165,000/$1,915,000))	155
Deferred revenue ($155,000 x 33/36 months)	142
Revenue recognised in the year ended 31 December 20X6	13

29 The correct answer is: Cost of sales will include $60,000 for the cost of the goods used, assuming no provision has previously been made by Bargi Co for a warranty liability

Two out of the four options include references to revenue, but no additional revenue should be recognised in these circumstances. Those candidates who realised that repairs made under warranty would not result in additional revenue could then work out that neither of these options could be the correct answer.

Using replacement parts would result in a reduction in Bargi Co's inventory and so would reduce inventories and increase cost of sales.

30 The correct answers are:

Amount	**Statement of profit or loss**
$0	Revenue

Amount	Statement of profit or loss
$10,000	Interest expense

Amount	Statement of financial position
$200,000	Cash
$210,000	Liability

The transaction on 1 December 20X6 represents a repurchase agreement where Bargi Co has the right to repurchase the goods sold in four months' time. This is referred to as a 'call option'. Where an entity has the right (or obligation) to repurchase an asset, the customer does not obtain control of that asset. This is because the customer is limited in their ability to direct the use of, and obtain substantially all of the remaining benefits from, the asset even though the customer may have physical possession of that asset.

Depending on the circumstances, this can result in various different outcomes. For Bargi Co, as they can repurchase the goods for an amount that is equal to or more than the original selling price of the asset, this should be treated as a financing arrangement and no revenue should be recognised.

Instead, Bargi Co would recognise the cash received as a financial liability in accordance with IFRS 9 Financial Instruments. Between 1 December 20X6 and 1 April 20X7, Bargi Co would also recognise $40,000 of interest expense for the difference between the exercise price ($240,000) and the cash received ($200,000). Since the transaction took place on 1 December 20X6, this means that there should be $10,000 ($40,000 x 1/4 months) of interest expense recognised in the year ended 31 December 20X6.

Section C

BOTH questions are compulsory and MUST be attempted

31 Treats Co

Marking guide		Marks	
(a)	Ratio analysis	5	
	Maximum		5
(b)	Performance	6	
	Position/conclusion	9	
		15	
	Maximum		15
Total			20

(a)

Ratio	Working	Treats Co	Sector
Return on year-end capital employed (ROCE)	7,466/(25,968 + 33,621)	12.5%	28.8%
Net asset turnover	214,553/(25,968 + 33,621)	3.6 times	2.4 times
Gross profit margin	106,544/214,553	49.7%	55%
Operating profit margin	7,466/214,553	3.5%	12%
Current ratio	47,996/50,391	0.95:1	1.8:1
Inventory turnover period	(30,393/108,009) x 365	103 days	25 days
Gearing (debt/equity)	33,621/25,968	129%	43%
Receivables collection period	17,603/214,553	30 days	15 days

(b)

Word Processor

Performance

Treats Co's gross profit margin is slightly below the market average. This is not surprising as Treats Co sells goods to supermarkets which are likely at lower margins than goods sold directly to the public.

However, Treats Co's operating profit margin is *significantly* below the industry average. It is unclear what the cause of this is but it does suggest cost control issues as this is much worse than the sector average, compared to the difference in gross profit margin.

The fact that the assets held by the company are old and may need replacing may mean there have been large repairs and maintenance expenses in the year or have had impairment charges applied to them.

ROCE is much lower than the industry average. This is as a direct result of the low operating profit margin as the net asset turnover is above the sector average.

The fact that the ROCE is low in comparison to the industry average is concerning as this figure would drop further following an investment in property, plant and equipment (PPE). Currently Treats Co does not have the cash to acquire assets, so replacements are likely to lead to an increase in debt (whether due to loans or leasing assets), which would further reduce the ROCE.

The net asset turnover is higher than the industry average. Again, it must be noted that once the PPE is replaced, this figure will be significantly reduced.

Position

The current ratio is significantly lower than the industry average. This is likely to be due to the significant overdraft which Treats Co uses for working capital management.

It appears that a lot of cash is tied up in inventories. This could be due to the need to hold large volumes of goods to meet the supermarket contracts but could also signify issues over demand for Treats Co's products.

The inventory holding period is more than four times longer than the industry average. Considering that Treats Co sells perishable food products, this is of concern as items may require to be written down/off.

Treats Co's receivables collection period is not particularly high at 30 days but is still twice that of the industry average. This is likely to be due to the supermarket contract which will demand much longer payment terms.

Most of the sector sells goods solely through their own stores and so these are likely to be cash sales. As a result, the receivables days ratio is not comparable with many companies in the sector.

The gearing ratio is significantly higher than the industry average, which is a significant concern, particularly in the light of Treats Co's cash position. Treats Co is likely to need investment in non-current assets; it is doubtful whether it will be possible to raise debt finance to do this.

The large dividend payment is questionable as $7.14m has been paid despite the entity being overdrawn and in need of investment.

Conclusion

Overall, the results are mixed and further information is required to fully investigate the performance and financial position of Treats Co. Further investigation is required of the composition of operating expenses. Neither the inventory nor the cash position looks very strong in comparison to the industry averages; however, the receivables is reasonable – further aged analysis of inventory and the classification of receivables would also be useful to explain these positions. Finally, gearing is high and so more information relating to the terms of borrowings would also be useful.

Other points which could be made:

- Gross margin – Treats Co still makes a 50% margin. This may be because Treats Co is a larger company (as shown in the supermarket contract) and can exercise economies of scale in managing costs or negotiating purchase discounts.
- Gross margin – It is unclear what proportion of goods are sold to the supermarkets versus direct to the public. More information on this would help to further understand Treats Co's margin compared to the sector average.
- Operating margin – This may get worse if assets are replaced or if impairments are needed. New assets are likely to have higher depreciation, which will further reduce the margin (as will impairment charges).

32 Perd Co

Marking guide		Marks	
(a)	Revenue/COS	3.5	
	Other income and expenses	8	
	Profit/OCI appropriation	3.5	
		15	
	Maximum		15
(b)	Total assets	5	
	Maximum		5
Total			20

(a)

Consolidated statement of profit or loss and other comprehensive income for Perd Co for the year ended 31 March 20X8

Spreadsheet

Edit Format

100% 11

	A	B	C	D	E
1					$'000
2	Revenue		(58,200 + 34,300 – 9,000 intra-group)		83,500
3	Cost of sales		(34,340 + 20,400 – 9,000 + 600 unrealised profit)		(46,340)
4	Gross profit				37,160
5	Operating expenses		(W1)		(28,270)
6	Profit from operations				8,890
7	Investment income		(3,000 – 800 dividend from S [$1m x 80%])		2,200
8	Finance costs		(3,240 + 1,600 + 453 unwinding (W2))		(5,293)
9	Profit before tax				5,797
10	Tax		(1,560 + 1,480)		(3,040)
11	**Profit for the year**				**2,757**
12	**Other comprehensive**				

	A	B	C	D	E
	income				
13	Gain on revaluation		(4,100 + 700)		4,800
14	**Total comprehensive income**				**7,557**
15	Profit attributable to: Shareholders of Perd Co				2,639
16	Non-controlling interests		(W3)		118
17					**2,757**
18	**Total comprehensive income attributable to:** Shareholders of Perd Co				7,299
19	Non-controlling interests		(W3)		258
20					**7,557**

(b)

Total assets:

Spreadsheet

Edit Format

	A	B	C
1			$'000
2	Perd Co		297,310
3	Sebastian Co		110,540
4	Goodwill		3,200
5	Impairment (400 + 300)		(700)
6	Unrealised profit		(600)
7	Intra-group balance		(7,000)
8	Revaluation gain		4,800
9			**407,550**

ANSWERS

Workings

1 ***Operating expenses***

	A	B	C
10			$'000
11	Perd Co		18,040
12	Sebastian Co		7,130
13	Impairment		300
14	Fair value depreciation ($3m/15 years x 6/12)		100
15	Removal of Sebastian profit on disposal (see below)		5,100
16	Group profit on disposal (see below)		(2,400)
17			28,270

Sebastian Co would have recorded a profit on disposal based on historical cost. At 30 September 20X7, the property would have had a carrying amount of $9,900, being $11m less 1.5 years' depreciation ($11m/15 x 1.5 = $1.1m). Therefore, the profit on disposal would have been $5.1m, being $15m less $9.9m.

The group profit on disposal would be based on the carrying amount to the group. The carrying amount of the property in the consolidated financial statements at 30 September 20X7 would have been $12.6m ($14m less 1.5 years' depreciation). Therefore, the profit on disposal will be $2.4m ($15m less $12.6m).

2 ***Unwinding discount***

	A	B	C
18			$'000
19	$7.547m x 6% = $0.453m		453

3 ***Non-controlling interest***

	A	B	C
20			$'000
21	Profit for the year		3,690
22	Adjusted profit on disposal ($5.1m - $2.4m)		(2,700)
23	Fair value depreciation		(100)
24	Goodwill impairment		(300)
25	**NCI share of profit at 20%**		**118**
26	Total comprehensive income		
27	Profit (from above)		118
28	20% × 700 revaluation gain		140
49	**Total comprehensive income**		**258**

ANSWERS

Tell us what you think

Got comments or feedback on this book? Let us know.
Use your QR code reader:

Or, visit:
https://bppgroup.fra1.qualtrics.com/jfe/form/SV_9TrxTtw8jSvO7Pv

Need to get in touch with customer service?

www.bpp.com/request-support

Spotted an error?

www.bpp.com/learningmedia/Errata